BOHEMIAN PARIS

Acknowledgments

I am grateful to the National Endowment for the Humanities for a generous grant, which made possible my research in Paris during 1979–80. I also thank the Institute for Advanced Study for appointing me a Visitor in 1983–84, providing facilities and an atmosphere that were ideal for getting finished.

Of the numerous friends, colleagues, and students whose comments, suggestions, or criticisms I appreciated and valued, I especially need to thank the following. I hope each of them will find evidence that I listened seriously to what he or she told me, even if I have not been able to take full advantage of the advice or help: Maurice Agulhon, Michael Fried, Daniel P. Rodgers, James Henry Rubin, Carl E. Schorske, Debora Silverman, Anthony Vidler. Isobel Abelson was a concerned and patient typist. Elisabeth Sifton provided a warm welcome at Viking, and her many acute suggestions added clarity and readability to every page. My wife, Jayn, both improved my prose and made it possible to keep my work in balance with my life.

Princeton
March 1985   *J.S.*

TO MY CHILDREN, MICOL AND JESSICA
Bohemians or Not

JERROLD SEIGEL

BOHEMIAN PARIS

Culture, Politics, and the Boundaries
of Bourgeois Life,
1830–1930

Elisabeth Sifton Books
VIKING

ELISABETH SIFTON BOOKS · VIKING
Viking Penguin Inc., 40 West 23rd Street,
New York, New York 10010, U.S.A.
Penguin Books Ltd, Harmondsworth,
Middlesex, England
Penguin Books Australia Ltd, Ringwood,
Victoria, Australia
Penguin Books Canada Limited, 2801 John Street,
Markham, Ontario, Canada L3R 1B4
Penguin Books (N.Z.) Ltd, 182–190 Wairau Road,
Auckland 10, New Zealand

First published in 1986 by Viking Penguin Inc.
Published simultaneously in Canada

LIBRARY OF CONGRESS CATALOGING IN PUBLICATION DATA
Seigel, Jerrold.
Bohemian Paris: culture, politics, and the
boundaries of bourgeois life, 1830–1930.
"Elisabeth Sifton Books."
Bibliography: p.
Includes index.
1. Paris (France)—Popular culture—History—19th
century.   2. Bohemianism—France—Paris—History—19th
century.   I. Title.
DC715.S42   1986   944'.36   85-40559
ISBN 0-670-80723-0

Printed in the United States of America by
R. R. Donnelley & Sons, Harrisonburg, Virginia
Set in Bodoni Book

CONTENTS

LIST OF ILLUSTRATIONS

ix

PART I

BOHEMIANS AND BOURGEOIS

CHAPTER 1

The Boundaries
of Bohemia

Bohemia, bordered on the North by hope, work and gaiety, on the
South by necessity and courage; on the West and East by slander
and the hospital.

HENRY MURGER,
Bohemian Life, 1849

The land of Bohemia is a sad country, bounded on the North by
need, on the South by poverty, on the East by illusion, and on the
West by the hospital. It is irrigated by two inexhaustible streams:
impudence and shame.

ALPHONSE DE CALONNE,
Voyage au pays de Bohème, 1852

ITS BORDERS WERE POVERTY AND HOPE, art and illusion, love and
shame, work, gaiety, courage, slander, necessity, and the hospital.
For its nineteenth-century discoverers and explorers, Bohemia was
an identifiable country with visible inhabitants, but one not marked
on any map. To trace its frontiers was to cross constantly back and
forth between reality and fantasy. We shall have to make that
crossing many times in our attempt to follow Bohemia through a
century of its history.

Explorers recognized Bohemia by signs: art, youth, the underworld, the gypsy life-style. To Henry Murger, the most influential
mapper, Bohemia was the realm of young artists struggling to sur-
mount the barriers poverty erected against their vocations, "all
those who, driven by an unstinting sense of calling, enter into art

with no other means of existence than art itself." They lived in Bohemia because they could not—or not yet—establish their citizenship anywhere else. Ambitious, dedicated, but without means and unrecognized, they had to turn life itself into an art: "Their everyday existence is a work of genius."[1]

Yet even Murger admitted that not all Bohemians were future artists. Other reporters did not think even the majority were. To that sharp-eyed social anatomist Honoré de Balzac, Bohemia was more simply the country of youth. All the most talented and promising young people lived in it, those in their twenties who had not yet made their names but who were destined eventually to lead their nation as "diplomats . . . writers, administrators, soldiers, journalists, artists! In fact all kinds of ability, of talent, are represented there. It is a microcosm. If the emperor of Russia bought up Bohemia for twenty million—assuming it were willing to take leave of the boulevard pavements—and transferred it to Odessa, in a year Odessa would be Paris." In their genius for life, Balzac's Bohemians resembled Murger's. "Bohemia has nothing and lives from what it has. Hope is its religion, faith in itself its code, charity is all it has for a budget."[2]

Artists and the young were not alone in their ability to make more of life than objective conditions seemed to permit. Some who were called Bohemians did so in more murky and mysterious ways, in the darker corners of society. "By Bohemians," a stage figure of the 1840s declared, "I understand that class of individuals whose existence is a problem, social condition a myth, fortune an enigma, who have no stable residence, no recognized retreat, who are located nowhere and whom one encounters everywhere! who have no single occupation and who exercise fifty professions; of whom most get up in the morning without knowing where they will dine in the evening; rich today, famished tomorrow, ready to live honestly if they can and some other way if they can't." The nature of these Bohemians was less easy to specify than either Murger's or Balzac's. They might be unrecognized geniuses or confidence men. The designation "Bohemian" located them in a twilight zone between ingenuity and criminality.[3]

These alternative images of Bohemia are ones we still recognize when we use the term: more recent incarnations like the Beat Generation of the 1950s or the hippiedom of the 1960s contained these real or potential elements, too. Artistic, youthful, unattached, inventive, or suspect, Bohemian styles are recurring features of modern life. Have they not always existed? In a way, yes: ancient Cynics, wandering medieval poets, eighteenth-century literary hacks—all exhibit features of Bohemia. But written references to Bohemia as a special, identifiable kind of life appear only in the nineteenth century. It was in the 1830s and 1840s, to begin with in France, that the terms "Bohemia," *"la Bohème,"* and "Bohemian" first appeared in this sense. The new vocabulary played on the common French word for gypsy—*bohémien*—which erroneously identified the province of Bohemia, which is now part of modern Czechoslovakia, as the gypsies' place of origin. There are universal and timeless elements in Bohemianism, but as a defined and recognized social phenomenon it belongs to the modern era: the world shaped by the French Revolution and the growth of modern industry. What new needs did Bohemia meet?

From the start, Bohemianism took shape by contrast with the image with which it was commonly paired: bourgeois life. The opposition is so well established and comes so easily to mind that it may mislead us, for it implies a form of separation and an intensity of hostility often belied by experience. Bohemia has always exercised a powerful attraction on many solid bourgeois, matched by the deeply bourgeois instincts and aspirations of numerous Bohemians. This mysterious convergence sometimes leads to accusations of insincerity, even dishonesty: "Scratch a Bohemian, find a bourgeois." But the quality revealed by scraping away that false appearance of opposition is seldom hypocrisy. Like positive and negative magnetic poles, Bohemian and bourgeois were—and are—parts of a single field: they imply, require, and attract each other.

We must remember that at the moment Bohemia was being established and explored, what was coming to be called "bourgeois society" was also just being formed and defined. Its nature and future were hotly debated. Precisely what was this newly so-prominent creature, the bourgeois? The polarity Bohemian-bourgeois misleads us most of all if it assumes we know where to locate the bourgeois and how to define him. Many people in the nineteenth century were less sure: the counterimage of Bohemia was one attempt to outline the bourgeoisie more clearly. Certain social types were recognizably not bourgeois: the established aris-tocrats, the proletarian poor. But there was a wide range in be-tween. The point was made humorously in a popular pamphlet of the early 1840s, *Bourgeois Physiology*: "My bourgeois is not yours, nor your neighbor's." For the soldier the bourgeois was any civil-ian; for the countryman it was the city-dweller on a Sunday outing. To the *grand seigneur* the bourgeois was anyone who dressed well but who was "not *born*, even though he may be seventy or eighty years old." The urban worker or artisan knew only one bourgeois: his boss. But the cabdriver called any fare "my bourgeois" (only while the customer occupied the coach, however; it was "Out of the way, you animal" once he had paid and climbed down). Artists had a particular way of using the word as a term of abuse, and the most insulting in the vocabulary of the studios. "Properly so-called," the bourgeois was the person enjoying a secure income and no debts, who passed through life comfortably with warm feet, cotton in his ears, and a walking-stick in his hand. This was the bourgeois exis-tence to which every small shopkeeper aspired.[4]

Such an account only hints at some of the more serious uncer-tainties. The most obvious had to do with levels of wealth. There were "little" and "big" (not to mention "middle") bourgeois, some relatively poor and others unquestionably rich. A careful study of the Parisian bourgeoisie in the early nineteenth century suggests that the bourgeoisie was an umbrella term hiding important con-trasts in incomes, expenditures, and behavior. Some owed their bourgeois status to long-standing family position, with property and station passed on over generations. Others were bourgeois of more recent origin, based in some cases on lucky speculations, in others on hard and shrewd work. Old bourgeois families might share the respect for stability and tradition characteristic of the Old Regime where their position originated, while newer bourgeois appealed to the virtues of activity, change, and progress. Rural bourgeois determined to invest their wealth in land contrasted with city people involved in business. The furrier or furniture maker who worked alongside his handful of employees had a different experience and often different politics from the big factory owner who did not know his workers, not to mention the banker or professor who did not employ others. Finally, some bourgeois were young and some old, an important distinction recognized by the pamphlet writer quoted above, for whom no genuine bourgeois existed under the age of fifty.[5]

Political attitudes and loyalties within the bourgeoisie were manifold and varied, but one straightforward set of questions recurred at many points in the nineteenth century: how separate was the bourgeoisie from other social groups, and how was it related to people above and below it? A certain way of thinking about politics, not originated by Marxism but strongly developed within it, asks us to regard the bourgeoisie as a class locked in struggle with other classes. The fact that the regime produced by the French Revolution of 1830 acquired the name "Bourgeois Monarchy," frightening many aristocrats out of politics and excluding manual workers from participation, was one major source of that way of thinking, and is often still cited in support of it. Looked at more closely, however, the July Monarchy (as the regime of 1830 is also known) reveals a different set of relationships. In the immediate aftermath of the 1830 Revolution, it seemed to take on the character of a broad coalition of bourgeois groups, rural and urban, small and large, united by hostility to the reactionary policies of the ousted Bourbon kings and their aristocratic supporters. Soon a division appeared, however, between two groupings—both bourgeois—called the Party of Movement and the Party of Resistance. The first, occupying the political Left, demanded a wide franchise, freedom of speech, press, and association, vigorous action against the hated Bourbon ministers, and an interventionist foreign policy. The second, more conservative, group resisted change and preferred restrictions on political debate and organization, a narrower electorate, and no foreign adventures. The political difference was also one of social orientation. The Party of Movement envisaged a politics open toward the lower tiers of society, where the world of small shopkeepers shaded off into that of artisans and craftsmen. For them, membership in the bourgeoisie still carried overtones of the old term *peuple*, the great mass of those who lived outside the Old Regime's system of privilege. The Party of Resistance, by contrast, carried on a politics open toward the upper reaches of social life. Their vision of the bourgeosie reflected the prerevolutionary image of the traditional urban elite occupying a special place in a hierarchically structured society. As things worked out, their victory over the Party of Movement during the 1830s led to an increasing policy of reconciliation between the July Monarchy and representatives of the Old Regime during the 1840s. By 1848, the so-called Bourgeois Monarchy faced a strong and determined bourgeois opposition.[6]

These opposing versions of how society and politics might be structured would continue to be fought over through most of the nineteenth century. They had their counterparts in the realms of consciousness and culture. Many people argued that the new society required a new mentality and a new form of art and literature. Yet, despite the explosion of Romanticism around 1830, nineteenth-century French culture continued to be dominated by the academicism and classicism established under the Old Regime. Traditionally, classicism had been the official culture of the royal court and the privileged groups—aristocratic and upper bourgeois—connected with it. To support classical standards in the nineteenth century was one way to link the new bourgeois society to the old aristocracy. It was (granted the roughness of the parallel) the cultural form of loyalty to the Party of Resistance. By contrast, Bohemia would be associated with a series of cultural forms— Romanticism was the first of them—self-consciously separate from the academy and classicism. With its orientation toward the lower parts of society unfamiliar with classicism and often excluded from the education it presupposed, Bohemianism would exhibit many parallels, some rough and some precise, to political tendencies like the Party of Movement. Both sought to keep bourgeois society open to new elements and energies.

The contrast between Bohemian and bourgeois raised questions about the nature and meaning of the new social and political forms that went beyond these issues of group or class formation. Central to it was a dilemma about the nature of modern individuality. The uncertainty arose out of fundamental changes brought by the French Revolution and amplified by economic transformation. Under the Old Regime, society had been organized on a corporate basis. Individuals belonged to the nation not as separate units but as members of intermediate bodies: estates, orders, guilds, communities, councils. The interplay of corporate groupings wove an intricate web of different positions within society. Where an individual fit into this pattern determined not only what taxes he paid and what courts he was subject to, but also what privileges and obligations he possessed and even what activities he could engage in. Individuals were not merely limited in their rights by tradition and privilege. Individuality as such was denied by many of the dominant assumptions and institutions: communal solidarity, collective privileges, tax exemptions, guild regulations and restrictions. Individuals were expected to fit some traditional mold; their personal development was supposed to be shaped and limited in accord with a model determined in advance.

Some people before 1789 escaped these constraints, to be sure. But only the Revolution announced their general elimination. The system of estates was to give way to a nation of citizens. Privileges and restrictions of all kinds were abolished. These measures did not transform French society overnight, but they set processes in motion that placed individual and social life on different foundations in the decades that followed. Society was reconstructed around individuals, not intermediate groups. All activities were, in principle, open to all citizens. The new arrangements were expected to benefit society as well as individuals. Personal capacities and productive energies that had been hemmed in or cut off by the restrictive force of tradition and privilege were now free to develop as far as their innate potentialities would take them. Society would grow more active, more wealthy, more diverse; individuals would be happier, more productive, more fully developed. Across the Rhine in Germany a probing analyst of change—the philosopher Hegel—identified the principle these new arrangements presupposed. He called it "free subjectivity," the unlimited right of each person to make his (less often her) personal development and interest the motive of his activity.[7]

But the new social forms brought many problems. The society of separate individuals no longer possessed a clear sense of common interest and purpose. It could easily become atomized, anarchic; free subjectivity could express itself as unrestricted selfishness and egotism. Hegel gave a detailed account of how these qualities operated in modern society. People treated each other as means, not ends, pursuing individual interest despite the damages it caused. Only those with some form of economic independence could acquire the education or training necessary to develop their abilities and compete with others. Class divisions were accented by extremes of wealth and poverty; the poor, excluded and demoralized, constituted a constant threat to society's stability and a visible denial of its claims to provide the means of self-development for everyone. In France, too, the recurring problems of modern life were seen to be closely tied to the fundamental place of individuality. Balzac's novels were accounts of the often destructive and damaging consequences of social atomization and individual egotism in modern life. "I claim that personality gnaws at the heart and devours the entrails of our society. In proportion to its increase, individuals isolate themselves; there are no longer links, no life in common any more." When each person made himself the center, society dissolved.[8]

These problems and dilemmas of individual and social development were the constitutive elements of Bohemia, both in the reality of its denizens' lives and in the image it projected. Bohemia was not a realm outside bourgeois life but the expression of a conflict that arose at its very heart. Bourgeois progress called for the dissolution of traditional restrictions on personal development; harmony and stability required that some new and different limits be set up in their place. Where were the limits to be drawn? At what point did personal cultivation cease to be beneficial or acceptable to the society that sponsored it? Bohemia grew up where the borders of bourgeois existence were murky and uncertain. It was a space within which newly liberated energies were continually thrown up against the barriers being erected to contain them, where social margins and frontiers were probed and tested.

One sign that this was the place Bohemia filled was that it drew together the strangely assorted grouping with which we began: artists, the young, shady but inventive characters. All shared—with the gypsies whose name they bore—a marginal existence based on the refusal or inability to take on a stable and limited social identity. All lived simultaneously within ordinary society and outside it. The real Bohemia had other components as well: eccentrics, visionaries, political radicals, rebels against discipline, people rejected by their families, the temporarily or permanently poor. But the three categories we encountered at the start were the ones most often associated with Bohemia, because certain people—we shall meet them—discovered that elements of their lives could be employed for a novel purpose: acting out the conflicts inherent in the bourgeois character. Exploring their discovery will allow us to define Bohemia in a more precise way: it was the appropriation of marginal life-styles by young and not so young bourgeois, for the dramatization of ambivalence toward their own social identities and destinies. Many non-Bohemians experienced the same ambivalence, but they did not devote their lives to living it out. People were or were not Bohemian to the degree that parts of their lives dramatized these tensions and conflicts for themselves and others, making them visible, and demanding that they be faced.

Defining Bohemia in this way allows us to grasp features of it that have been elusive or confusing before. First, there is neither mystery nor hypocrisy in Bohemians' simultaneous rejection of ordinary society and their longing to join it. Second, Bohemia emerges as a social phenomenon distinguishable from the literary and artistic subculture that provided many recruits for it, and with which it has usually been confused. To be sure, such a formulation will not neatly distinguish Bohemian individuals or forms of behavior from those that were not. But nor would any other definition. There is no action or gesture capable of being identified as Bohemian that cannot also be—or has not been—undertaken outside of Bohemia. Odd dress, long hair, living for the moment, having no stable residence, sexual freedom, radical political enthusiasms, drink, drug taking, irregular work patterns, addiction to nightlife—all were Bohemian or not according to how they were meant or how they were taken, Bohemian at some moments and not at others. The outward signs of Bohemia were important, but they were never sufficient to mark its frontiers. This uncertainty was essential, fitting Bohemia for its task of testing and probing the boundaries of bourgeois life, neither accepting them as already given, nor seeking to abolish them.

If Bohemia remains so resistant to clear classification, if its boundaries were so permeable, how can we write its history? Bohemia cannot be charted, graphed, and counted, because it was never wholly an objective condition. Since none of its elements belonged exclusively to it, we must sometimes let ourselves be led by those who experienced it—participants or observers, friends or enemies. The century after 1830 produced many such guides, some well known, others second-raters, some entirely obscure. By using them all as sources we do not mean to deny the differences among them. The best information often comes from the less remembered— Henry Murger, Alexandre Privat d'Anglemont, or Francis Carco— but sometimes the insights of a Charles Baudelaire, a Jules Vallès, or a Maurice Barrès confirm the exalted place each occupies in literary history. Nor can we fail to notice that all these commentators had their biases, their reasons for presenting Bohemia as they did. Their testimony remains essential because defining Bohemia's significance was a crucial way to participate in it. Bohemia arose where action and meaning, gesture and awareness, intersected. It was at once a form of life and a dramatized interpretation, both of itself and of the society to which it was a response. Its history illustrates what a well-known anthropologist means when he tells us that "Societies, like lives, contain their own interpretations. We have only to learn how to gain access to them"[9]

Art, youth, and criminality each transferred something of itself to Bohemia, now as reality, now as image. So did the genuine gypsy life that provided the name. We need briefly to examine the situation each faced in the early nineteenth century, as modern conditions forced its members out of old roles and into new ones. Their experiences reflected conditions that were in part common to Europe as a whole but that derived special qualities from the French context.

For artists and writers, the basic change is as easily summarized as it was often noticed: patronage gave way to the market. From the Middle Ages through the eighteenth century, artists survived through the support of patrons; their social position varied along a line that ran from servant or retainer to courtier, ornament, or state official. In the Middle Ages and Renaissance, artists had often belonged to guilds, but by the end of the Old Regime such organizations for collective well-being had mostly disappeared, leaving a painter's or writer's personal relationship to a private or public patron as the major determinant of his material position. During the nineteenth century, these relations receded with the aristocratic social order that had spawned them. Like other social groups, artists and writers found themselves participants in a commercial market, a world of buying and selling from which they had been mostly excluded or protected before.[10]

The change did not come all at once. Napoleon patronized some artists, as did the restored Bourbon monarchy that followed him. And in the 1850s and 1860s, the Bonapartist Second Empire paid regular pensions to some writers and supported others by making them senators (a post with few duties and a handsome salary). But during the nearly two decades of the July Monarchy, state patronage dropped to a low level, due in good part to the "bourgeois" king Louis-Philippe's indifference toward art and literature. Those years brought many discussions of the new position of culture in the world of commodities. There were both positive and negative reasons for this, as expanding literacy, urban growth, and increasing middle-class wealth enlarged the market for cultural products. In the mid-1830s, new-style newspapers showed how that market could be tapped, by reducing their prices and turning to advertising for added revenue. Literature contributed mightily to—and profited from—the success of the new papers, by means of serialized novels and other material that made up the *feuilleton* on the bottom half of each day's front page. That writers recognized both the opportunities and the dangers of their new position (for instance, the absence of effective copyright laws) was shown by the foundation of the Société des Gens de Lettres, a protective and mutual-benefit society for writers, in 1835.[11]

What did this new situation mean for the inner quality of artists' and writers' lives and works? Many were convinced that culture could only be debased by its entry into the marketplace. The world of commerce was too narrow to encompass the broad spaces of the imagination. Its values were utilitarian and earthbound, weighing down the aspiration toward beauty and exaltation that inspired poetry and art. The artist was deprived of the leisure necessary to develop his talents by the need to earn his bread. Nor was he given the opportunities to create on a large scale and produce the monumental work that had allowed genius to express itself in the past. He was condemned, according to a writer in *L'Artiste* during 1832, to do "salon or boudoir pieces; he gives his talent over to industry, to the caprices of fashion, to the whims of the buyers, the bourgeois." Some even thought this meant that the modern artist would lose those characteristics that set him off from others: imagination, color, impetuosity, finesse. He would dress in a business suit and grow just as materialistic and calculating as any lawyer or banker.[12]

Yet the change from patronage to the market also held out different possibilities. The decline of aristocratic social relations meant the liberation of some who had been oppressed by them, and the emergence of a society that encouraged all who could to develop their talents as members of a free community. Writers in

L'Artiste presented this vision of the relations between art and society at the same time others gave expression to the opposite view. Only under modern conditions could the artist really live from his work and thereby be free of the personal subjection that had oppressed and corrupted him in the past. "Today the artist is placed in the middle of society as a whole, he takes inspiration from the desires and sufferings of everyone, he speaks to all, he cries for all; he is no longer a retainer but a part of the people; he expects to be paid only for his work and the free products of his genius. His social position has therefore become more moral, more independent, more able to favor the progress of art." It was precisely the development of the market and the expansion of taste and interest to new parts of society that freed culture from the unfortunate effects of the older, more repressive form of social life.[13]

Although most histories of art and literature emphasize the first of these alternatives, the second also captures an important truth about what was happening to artists and writers in the nineteenth century. Whatever their personal troubles and discontents, figures like Hugo, Balzac, Berlioz, George Sand, Lamartine, and Delacroix were able to achieve not only success and recognition, but also a degree of liberation and independence that earlier artists, anxious to please a reigning prince or escape the strictures of a repressive government, could seldom enjoy. They represented the triumph of talent over circumstances to which many aspired. Artistic eminence—achieved by the expression of an individual's own inner qualities and talents—came to be emblematic of the emancipation and fulfillment the new society promised to all those who conscientiously developed their personal abilities. Conversely, not to succeed as an artist might be a sign of deep moral and personal failure.

It is this expanded significance of artistic life, rather than the specific issue of how market relations affected artists, that we see reflected in a famous expression of Romantic longing and despair, Alfred de Vigny's drama *Chatterton*. The story was of a poet's suicide, and Vigny had no hesitation in placing the guilt where he felt it belonged: on society. Society killed poets by failing to support them. It refused to "let them live according to the conditions of their nature." But who were these unfortunates? Vigny was careful to insist that they did not include the versatile man of letters, at home in the world and able to turn his facile talents to any subject. Nor did Vigny mean to claim that the truly great writer suffered the poet's fate. The *grand écrivain* possessed a power that made him master of himself and of others, keeping his sufferings to himself and holding a people in his hand. His life was not unhappy. It was otherwise with the person Vigny identified as the poet. His nature was purer and more rare; what defined it was not positive literary accomplishment, but a lack of capacity for anything other than his divine work. Born with feelings so deep and intimate that "ever since childhood they have plunged him into involuntary ecstasies, endless reveries, infinite imaginings," he could only survive through being cared for by others. "Inside his enflamed skull there takes shape and grows something like a volcano." He required "time to listen to the harmonies that take shape slowly in his mind, and that the vulgar noises of a positive and regular employment interrupt and infallibly cause to evaporate."

Vigny's image of the poet points toward a transformation of literary identity whose fuller unfolding would take place within Bohemia. He was aware that others might regard his plea as a demand that society support people whose claim to be writers was not based on their ability to produce poems but only on their dreamy and perhaps childish ambition. To which he replied: "And what do we know about it? Who gives us the right to snuff out the acorn by saying that it won't be an oak?" His defense of poets opened the domain of literature to those who inhabited it less through talent or achievement than through personality and mode of life.[14]

That redefinition was a phenomenon often remarked around 1830. People who claimed to be poets or artists in this way were not always taken as seriously as Vigny took them, however, and perhaps it is fitting that the person who seems to have been the first to describe these artists as Bohemians did it much more lightheartedly. His name was Félix Pyat, and he was a writer and dramatist familiar on the Parisian scene through most of the century; he later played a part in the revolutionary Commune of 1871. His account of modern artists as denizens of Bohemia appeared in a collection of essays on various aspects of Parisian life published in 1834 (and to which a number of other young writers, later well known, also contributed), *Nouveau tableau de Paris au XIXme siècle.*

Pyat built his description of artistic life around a paradox: at the same time that young artists were drawing apart from the rest of society, the claim to be an artist was becoming more and more widespread. Everybody claimed to be an artist nowadays, Pyat observed: princes, criminals, inventors, anyone who managed to touch Victor Hugo's hand. "One is an artist the way one used to be a property owner, it's the distinguishing mark of those people who don't have any." A crowd of young men made themselves up in outlandish costumes, adopted medieval dress and speech in the hope of being recognized as artists. But, in fact, they were only copying some common model and their antics therefore proclaimed their lack of art's essential quality: originality. Their mania for living out of their own time, "with other ideas and other behavior, isolates them from the world, makes them alien and bizarre, puts them outside the law, beyond the reaches of society. They are the Bohemians [*bohémiens*] of today."[15]

Pyat was not trying to invent a new term for artists and young camp followers; he merely meant to say that the people he was talking about were turning themselves into gypsies. Yet his description already contained most of the familiar features found in later accounts of Bohemia. The artist-Bohemians had a language of their own, the language of the art studios, constructed by adding some special syllable to the end of words; all those who were strangers to their own ways they disdainfully labeled "bourgeois," much as the Greeks had called all foreigners "barbarians"; they had a horror of everything that smelled of comfort, from umbrellas to gloves and shirt collars; their virtues were fraternity, equality, and freedom from self-interest; poverty was their golden calf, they idolized it; politics meant little to them, but they hated anyone who had prostituted his conscience; their greatest expenditure was of imagination, "they have so much of it." Their desire was for change and adventure, a life that moved from heat to cold, wealth to poverty; fie on the ties of family, the sweet chains of affection that brought charm to ordinary life.

Pyat found the perseverance of these young "artists," most of whom would never be real painters or writers, remarkable. Some would succeed, perhaps. "But what is it that keeps the rest of these good young people from returning to the world that calls out to them, to become there excellent notaries, very good lawyers, respectable fathers of families, with wives, children, business permits, income taxes, rents, and everything it takes to live long and happily in this life?" They were the victims of an epidemic disease that Pyat dubbed "artistism." The persons infected by it neglected their affairs and interests, cut themselves off from the world, and ran the danger of losing contact with it. They lived in an imaginary universe in which all colors were blue, and the suspect women they hung around with became worthy objects of poetic praise and attention. In some cases, abstinence from poetry or removal from Paris could effect a cure; for others, there was no remedy.

Pyat's sketch was acute and prescient. The features of Bohemia he listed were ones that Murger and others later made famous, and he linked them all to the disease of "artistism." But the idea of Bohemia would never have become so attractive and popular if it had retained Pyat's tone of skepticism. A more positive association between Bohemia and art was required. One source for it was the novelist and social reformer George Sand.

Because of her unconventional life and her insistence on personal freedom, George Sand has sometimes been seen as a Bohemian herself, an exemplar of the liberated female we shall find elsewhere in *la Bohème*. But her Bohemia was not specifically feminist, it was broadly artistic. She portrayed it in a novel about Venetian aristocrats and free-floating artists, *La dernière Aldini* (*The Last Aldini Woman*), the story of a singer, Lelio, who loves both a noblewoman and—years later—her daughter. Both women return his love and want to marry him; both times he saves them from the social disaster the marriage would have meant for them, renouncing his love and returning the aristocrats to their own world. His self-sacrifice shows that true nobility dwells in the artist and man of the people, but his refusal to accept the ties of love and family also stems from his citizenship in a larger nation of art that escapes locality just as it transcends social class. "The artist's country is the whole world, the great Bohemia, as we say." It is a world of deeper and stronger feeling, whose freedom and unconventionality are often mistaken for immorality by outsiders. On one level each world despises the other. "Let us mock the pride of the great, laugh at their foolishness, spend our wealth gaily when we have it, accept poverty without worry when it comes; above all let us preserve our liberty, enjoy life whatever happens, and *vive la Bohême!*" Yet Sand makes clear each world's attraction for the quality—freedom or stability—that only the other can provide.[16]

Like Pyat, George Sand found that the idea of Bohemia was deeply tied up with the relations between artists and nonartists. Her image included the gaiety and sexual unconventionality that were often to be associated with *la Bohème*; yet other features of her account did not survive. In accord with the political vocabulary of the post-Napoleonic era, the social group she opposed seemed aristocratic—they were the nobles, "the great"—and their opposite numbers were artists who belonged to "the people." In this she was further than Pyat and Vigny from identifying the classical opposite of Bohemia: the bourgeois.

For centuries, Europeans had recognized youth as a separate stage of life. Aristotle wrote about the special qualities of youth and its effect on politics, especially at moments of change in regimes. Since the Middle Ages, unmarried people in their late teens and early twenties had formed distinct groupings, with their own customs and activities, as well as taking a leading part in carnivals and festivals. These earlier ideas and practices fed the heightened and expanded awareness of youth in the nineteenth century. The young now called attention to themselves as participants in large-scale social conflict and historical change.

One reason for this was simply that there were more of them. The population of all European countries entered a phase of rapid

growth toward the middle of the eighteenth century; each birth co-
hort was larger than the previous one, making the proportion of
those between fifteen and thirty greater than it had been before.
The swollen numbers put pressure on society, since opportunities
for employment—particularly within the middle classes—expanded more slowly than the population. Balzac's image of Bohemia as youth waiting for society to make a place for them was by no
means the first literary vision to recognize this. In late-eighteenth-
century Germany, the sense that the young had nowhere to go contributed to the nervous anxiety and sense of exclusion that marked
the *Sturm und Drang* movement. Literary works like Goethe's *The
Sorrows of Young Werther* and Schiller's *The Robbers* depicted
young people driven to extremes of rebellion and suicide.[17]

Youth as such seemed to play only a small role in the real upheaval these images prefigured, the French Revolution. The special
needs of the young were identified with the aspirations of the whole
nation, and revolutionary festivals focused on the new order's ability to reconcile the needs of youth and age. Nonetheless, by absorbing youthful visions into the wider cause of renewal, the
Revolution also dramatized on the largest possible stage those tensions and aspirations that—at least in the middle classes—youth
felt and espoused most readily. In its aftermath, the social groups
and movements that sought to preserve or revive the Revolution's
message often identified themselves as actually or metaphorically
youthful. This was the case with the German student movement
after 1815 against which Metternich directed repressive measures,
and more generally with the groups around Mazzini in the early
1830s—Young Europe, Young Italy, Young Germany. Karl Marx
emerged out of a group calling itself Young Hegelians, a name that
recalled Hegel's description of youth as a phase in the life cycle
characterized by the impulse to "make war on the world." The importance ascribed to generational conflict led a Swiss writer, James
Fazy, to publish a book, *On Gerontocracy*, in 1829.

These issues were especially prominent in France around 1830.
The fact that the Revolution and Napoleon had offered opportunities for the young that succeeding regimes could not match

heightened the sense of generational identity and conflict. The development of Romanticism after 1815 was fed by these tensions. At the beginning of the July Monarchy, there was constant talk about "the generation of 1830."[18]

These young people experienced some conditions common all over Europe, notably the increased competition for entry into jobs, especially the professions. But much in their situation was specific to France. For one thing, Paris was a city like no other, at once a national capital, a focus of political and intellectual activities and ambitions, a center of manufacturing (based on handicraft methods that still dominated the Continent before 1850), and the scene of a large and highly self-conscious population of students. No continental city could match it for diversity and importance. London was larger, but England was still a relatively decentralized country; the capital was less important as a locus of industrial change than the new cities of the north, and it had no significant student presence. The students of the Quartier Latin preserved many ancient traditions within a larger urban frame that brought them into touch with the most vital historical currents of the time.

For generations, intellectual life in Paris had been deeply tied up with politics. During the eighteenth century, the writers and the artists of the Enlightenment had engaged in many conflicts with public authority and traditional values—in contrast to the situation in England, where the Enlightenment always shone in part by reflection from the Glorious Revolution of 1688. Romanticism, too, was a matter of public confrontation more in France than elsewhere, with figures like Chateaubriand, Hugo, and Delacroix coming to be identified with political opposition to the restored Bourbons during the late 1820s. Much more than in other countries, French Romantics expressed their opposition to tradition and convention through dramatic public behavior—medieval costumes, flowing beards, and disheveled hair. This was one form of the "artistism" Pyat described. The most noteworthy large-scale confrontation between French Romantics and the rest of society came in the famous "Battle of *Hernani*" in February 1830. At the opening of Victor Hugo's play, an organized and well-prepared body of young supporters established themselves in the theater. As expected, the play's attacks on classical standards and aristocratic morality drew loud protests from the regular audience. Hugo's followers, flamboyantly dressed and ready for the fray, outshouted them with cheers; by the end of the evening, they had triumphed.[19]

After 1830, the target of such confrontations with authority and society became the bourgeoisie, widely identified as the victor and beneficiary of the July Revolution. This political prominence made the French bourgeoisie unique in Europe: nowhere else did government rule in the name of that class. The corresponding political change in England, the Reform Bill of 1832, allowed greater middle-class participation in a regime still dominated by Whig aristocrats, an arrangement made possible largely because the commercial values of the middle classes had long ago spread into important sections of the nobility. In Germany (where the 1830 Revolution was only weakly echoed), the burghers were more scattered and locally oriented, as well as more dependent on absolutist princes and their bureaucratic structures. Only in France did the bourgeoisie seem capable of imposing its own form of organization on national life. The pressures that artists and youth felt all over Europe crystallized into an opposition between Bohemian and bourgeois more quickly and intensely in Paris than anywhere else.

Paris also nurtured the shady underworld that gave Bohemia some of its darker connotations. The city grew prodigiously, alarmingly, in the first half of the nineteenth century. From a number reckoned slightly over 500,000 in 1800, it mushroomed to twice that size by the mid-1840s. The new, mostly immigrant population, overwhelmingly composed of workers, was at the mercy of early industrialism's fluctuating and crisis-ridden economy. Often exploited and underpaid, repeatedly thrown out of work in times of crisis, unaccustomed to urban life, badly housed, hit with epidemic diseases (cholera was still a powerful killer in nineteenth-century cities), the new Parisians frightened the more established and better-off classes, to whom they appeared as strange and alien, and they were quickly seen as a threat to public order and political stability, a modern "barbarian invasion." The numbers who turned to crime at

moments of desperation were limited, but the line between criminality and the conditions that gave rise to it was not always visible;
the image of the working classes merged with the specter of *les
classes dangereuses*, the dangerous classes.[20]

Yet these poor, often marginal and desperate, workers also inspired fascination. The strangeness of their lives appealed to the
Romantic imagination, with its intimation that modern life set free
forces of all kinds, in whose novelty and uncertainty threat and
promise were inextricably intertwined. Like the artistic Bohemia
depicted by George Sand, the urban underworld drew outsiders toward itself, anxious to explore human possibilities that had emerged
nowhere else. Eugène Sue's *The Mysteries of Paris* described such
an exploration from outside. Its enormous success presaged a long
series of lesser accounts of "the underside of Paris." Violence and
strong emotion were part of the attraction; here behavior was permitted that respectability cast out. Beyond this was a suspicion that
necessity had mothered great inventiveness in these dark margins
of the city, even a kind of artistry. In *Notre-Dame de Paris*, Victor
Hugo described the *cour des miracles,* where deformed and crip-
pled beggars who filled Paris streets were transformed to health by
the removal of their costumes.

Similar, if smaller, groups had long been found in Paris, and one
traditional name for them was *bohémiens.* That usage was revived
in 1843, when Adolphe D'Ennery and Eugène Grangé achieved a
popular success with their play *The Bohemians of Paris.* Here Bohemians appeared (we saw at the start) as those "whose existence is
a problem, social condition a myth . . . who have no single occupation and who exercise fifty professions," not necessarily honest
ones. The play called attention to a phenomenon that merged traditional images of gypsies with new specters rising from the shadows
of modern urban life; it also emphasized how thin was the line between imagining and inventing on the one hand, and piercing the
limits of socially or legally sanctioned behavior on the other.[21]

The renewed currency D'Ennery and Grangé gave the word
bohémien, alongside the new form *bohème*, expressed a growing interest in the lives of actual gypsies. Scholars now believe that gyp-

sies originated in India; their appearance in Western Europe dates from the fifteenth century. There were many myths about their origins: the mistake embodied in the term "Bohemian" is paralleled by the similarly erroneous idea suggested by the common English word "gypsy" (and its allied terms in other languages) that their origin was in Egypt. Old suspicions about their penchant for criminality remained alive. But attention to gypsies and vagabonds was also encouraged by the Romantic fascination for the exotic, the uncivilized, the unclassifiable, the attempt to invoke the deeper levels of human nature, which reason could not grasp, nor organized social life satisfy. Shortly before 1830, Charles Nodier published a *History of the King of Bohemia and of His Seven Castles*, a heated but obscure account of a gypsy realm of pure personal fantasy. Soon after, a character in a story by Eugène Sue was described by *Le Figaro*'s reviewer as "*un bohémien*, a man of cursed and vagabond race, proscribed, wandering, condemned to death; murderer and smuggler, and yet endowed with a noble and generous character. . . . He is too beautiful and too colossal for the civilization that surrounds and smothers him."[22]

Set apart from a prosaic reality, the gypsy of Romantic imagination nonetheless stood for possibilities that were being created by modern society as well as for some that were excluded or repressed. This combination was captured very well by a writer in a popular illustrated magazine during 1851. By then, the gypsy image was perhaps already reflecting back some of the newer notion of youthful and artistic Bohemia it had helped to spawn, but its own features remained visible and independent. According to the *Magasin Pittoresque*, gypsy life was adventurous and carefree. Gypsies lived simply, and wholly for the moment. Modern conditions threatened to make their style disappear, as life became more organized and rigid. But their spirit, preserved in art, might bring new benefits all the same. As civilization advanced, drawing nations together, horizons would expand. People would become more open to what once seemed alien. Knowledge of foreign countries and customs would help everyone escape the narrow boundaries of their ordinary lives. "Then fantasy will have lost its purely poetical character to take on a social character: the gypsies of the old civilization will have become the messengers of the new."[23] The anonymous writer of these words possessed an important intuition: the very features of modern life that seemed to be squeezing fantasy into the corners and margins of existence were also preparing spaces for its liberation, much closer to society's center than gypsy life had ever been.

Nineteenth-century writers were quick to claim a long pedigree for Bohemia. Murger would trace its ancestors back into classical Greece, and follow the family tree through the whole of French cultural history. If some of that genealogy seems fanciful, other parts of it deserve to be taken seriously: medieval figures like François Villon did share features with modern Bohemians, while poor writers like the young Diderot and lesser eighteenth-century literary hacks and gutter poets were still closer in character as well as in time. The history of painting provides several examples of artists whose behavior dramatized their estrangement from the position in which social convention cast them: Caravaggio is one often cited case. During the eighteenth century, stories and plays about artists grew in number and popularity, some as satires of bourgeois cultural pretensions, others as cautionary tales about the dangers of becoming involved in lower-class life. Artists were also seen as socially problematic people, sometimes unable to accept regular conventions and obligations because (as a writer of 1792 put it) "their overlively and overexcited imagination naturally leads to a taste for freedom, independence, even wantonness of mind."[24]

Yet all this never added up to anything like Bohemianism as a general cultural and social phenomenon. The literary underground of the Enlightenment was defined by its exclusion from the Old Regime's system of privilege, a structure dominated—although not exclusively populated—by the aristocracy. Only in the nineteenth century did the bourgeoisie, with its peculiar combination of individualist ideology, revolutionary heritage, and longing for stability and tradition, assume the position in society that allowed Bohemia to take form as its reverse image and underside. Only then, too, did the vague but magnetic image of the artist devoted to his own imagination and self-development emerge as a symbol for the "free subjectivity" that postrevolutionary society claimed to liberate in everyone's life.

As we have seen, this "artistism" drew the metaphor of the gypsy Bohemian to itself almost as soon as it was first recognized. Pyat's term may have referred to any one of three groups that had a certain notoriety in the early 1830s. All were tied up with the Romantic movement. The first, the Jeunes-France, affected an exotic dress and manner partly inspired by medievalism. They grew beards, gave parties with outrageous and wild fare, claimed to drink punch from the skulls of their mistresses, surrounded themselves with poisoned arrows, animal traps, catapults. One unfriendly observer remarked on their "putrid gaiety" and macabre jokes. Rather different was the style of the "Bousingots," named for the waxed leather cap they wore. The Bousingots were mostly students, often known for noisy behavior, and a readiness to join in demonstrations and uprisings against the government. Their dress and behavior were much closer to that of the *peuple* than of the Jeunes-France. The Bousingots were often described as enemies of law and order and enthusiasts for absolute liberty. Tied up with both these groups was a clearer and more circumscribed one called the *petit cénacle*, a band of young writers and followers of Victor Hugo which included Théophile Gautier, Gérard de Nerval, Petrus Borel, and others. Around 1832, they were meeting in the Left Bank studio of Jean du Seigneur (who medievalized his name as Jehan Duseigneur), to read each other their work and provide mutual support. But they were also capable of more frivolous behavior. Gérard de Nerval went for walks in the Luxembourg Gardens accompanied by a pet lobster on a leash. Petrus Borel and some friends passed a summer camping in tents in a Paris garden, often scantily dressed, until the landlord evicted them. Both sides of their character were expressed during 1834–35, when Nerval and some new friends, Camille Rogier and Arsène Houssaye, lived together near the Louvre, in an ancient and dilapidated street called the rue du Doyenné. They decorated their rooms elaborately, gave splashy parties, and became a center of attraction for other young artists and writers, a kind of extension of the earlier *petit cénacle.*[25]

Although the members of these separate groups later followed contrary paths, the boundaries between them were often indistinct, and sometimes crossed. Some individuals seemed at times to belong to all three. Youth and attachment to the Latin Quarter made interchange easy, and they all moved in an atmosphere formed out of the enthusiasms and disappointments aroused by the 1830 Revolution. The Romantic movement had flowered in the previous decade, when hostility to the increasingly rigid and reactionary Bourbon monarchy was building up; the conservative policies of the new regime gave new life to the connection between cultural innovation and political dissatisfaction. Many people of fundamentally unpolitical orientations found themselves engaged in public questions with or against their wills. Nerval, whose quiet, dreamy nature made him an unlikely activist, was arrested on suspicion that he was part of a conspiracy in 1832. Some of his more political friends in the *petit cénacle* seem to have participated in insurrections together with groups of Bousingots. In 1832–33, Petrus Borel and Jehan Duseigneur were active in editing a paper called *La Liberté, Journal des Arts.* Its articles called for "the broadest and most complete liberty in the arts," the abolition of official institutions and restrictions. This anarchy—it was their term—was the only way to fulfill the principles that had inspired the 1830 Revolution. Borel said his brand of republicanism was that of a werewolf. "I am a republican because I cannot be a native of the Antilles. I need an enormous quantity of liberty." Paris, he said, possessed two dens of outlaws, "one of thieves, one of murderers; that of the thieves is the stock exchange, that of the murderers is the Palais de Justice." His friend Philothée O'Neddy (anagram for Théophile Dondey) declared: "Like you I despise from the depths of my soul the existing social order and above all the political order that is its excrement."[26]

This spirit of political challenge, tinged with the passions of actual revolutionary conflict, gave the artistic and literary circles of these years a tone of general cultural contestation. Literary activity dramatized a wider opposition to modern society and politics. That connection would recede for a while in the mid-1830s, as some of the people who had participated in these movements turned their backs on political causes, announcing for the first time the program of "art for art's sake." But, while it lasted, the earlier mood was responsible for much of the broad if ill-defined estrangement that Pyat defined in 1834 as gypsylike artistism. The closeness of the whole phenomenon to what was later a full-fledged *vie de Bohème* was testified in 1849, when Gautier reviewed Henry Murger's play of that name. Murger's Bohemia, he believed, recalled the one Gautier had known in the rue du Doyenné, with Nerval, Houssaye, and the others; both Nerval and Houssaye also later referred to that experience as Bohemian.[27]

For all their color and spirit, however, these movements of the years around 1830 constitute only the prehistory of Bohemianism, not its real foundation. The notion of Bohemia remained unfocused and sporadic until the late 1840s, when it gained a clearer and more permanent place in French consciousness. Pyat's association of artistic hangers-on with gypsy life had no impact (it seems to have remained unnoticed by all those who have written about Bohemia until now), and George Sand's slightly later appeals to Bohemian life also produced few echoes. There is no evidence that Gautier, Nerval, or the others ever regarded their life in 1834–35 as Bohemian at the time; what they said later was colored by the tones of a vocabulary not then available to them.[28]

This absence of Bohemia from French public consciousness is suggested by one particularly telling—albeit negative—piece of evidence. The years 1841–42 saw a great wave of popular pamphlets called *physiologies*, brief, often pungent and humorous, descriptions of various Parisian social types, characters, and practices. The eminence behind the *physiologies* was Charles Philipon, also publisher of the popular sheets *Le Charivari* and *Le Journal pour Rire*, where Daumier, Gavarni, and other noted cartoonists appeared. Philipon was a publicity genius, his antennae exquisitely sensitive to the opportunities provided by the growth of a new reading public and a new political consciousness. His *physiologies* were all the rage, several selling ten thousand copies and many others more than half that number. Among the most popular themes were the theater, the *flâneur* (the term for the curious, idle, and already seemingly omnipresent wanderer and observer of the Parisian streets), and a figure called *l'homme à bonnes fortunes.* It is a fairly safe bet that Philipon would have included a *Physiology of Bohemia* in his series if the idea had occurred to him or to any of his ambitious and sharp-eyed writers. But there was no such title in Philipon's collection. The word did not appear in the *Physiology of the Student*, where the themes of liberty, long hair, and easy love affairs with *grisettes* were prominent; it was missing from the *Physiology of the Poet*; nor was the term employed in the *Physiology of School Life*, even though that pamphlet had a substantial section on a type often tied up with Bohemia later, that sorry half-teacher–half-monitor, the *pion*, who occupied the lowest rank in the French school system. The *pion* appears here with features that later identified many *bohèmes*, product as he was of "that innumerable crowd of those who enter higher studies today without any personal wealth, and who leave their classes without any legitimate occupation, without a future, without being able to take up a liberal profession, and without knowing anything about a manual occupation." Faced with lack of success, he would let his hair grow, wear a funny hat, and become a rebel. But to the writer of 1841, he was not a Bohemian.[29]

By contrast, the early 1850s would produce a stream of publications explicitly devoted to Bohemia. These included a pamphlet in the spirit of the *physiologies* called *Paris-Bohème*, numerous Bohemian novels, at least one songbook, celebrations of Bohemia, and—a particularly important sign—the first full-fledged attacks on it.[30] Two circumstances account for this change: the return of political agitation and the renewed outbreak of revolution in 1848; and the appearance of the remarkable series of tales and sketches by Henry Murger. Those who have sought to reduce Murger to a mere popularizer of a notion already formed and established before his work—and they include most of those who have written about *la vie de Bohème*—have missed the special nature of the account he provided. It was he who clothed the image of Bohemia with elements that gave it the widespread appeal, and the peculiar evocative power, it retained for so long.

CHAPTER 2

A Country Explored: Murger

AT THE END OF JANUARY 1861, Henry Murger died in a Paris hospital. Poor and depressed, Murger in his last days cut a figure that prepares us for the oblivion into which he has fallen since. He was not a great writer. Yet his creations are alive in the minds of many who have never heard of him, for they people the single most influential image of nineteenth-century Bohemian Paris, Puccini's *La Bohème*. Puccini's figures, Rodolphe, Marcel, Mimi, Musette—to give them their French names—are Murger's characterizations of himself and his friends, and they were famous long before Puccini took them up. Though Murger's stories of Bohemian life attracted little attention when they first appeared in a small Paris newspaper during 1845 and 1846, he joined with a successful young vaudevillist, Théodore Barrière, to put his Bohemians on the musical stage in 1849. The play was an enormous success, filling the Varieties Theatre night after night and attracting much notice in the popular and established press. This was the moment when the image of Bohemia first caught the imagination of a broad public, focusing a bright light on Murger and his Bohemian companions. They had no difficulty recognizing themselves behind the characters on stage. Marcel spoke for them in the first act: "We are Bohemia"—"La Bohème, c'est nous."

Murger was well known throughout the nineteenth century. His play had at least five revivals by 1890, and the collection of his original tales and sketches published as a book in 1851 went through many editions. His death was marked by a large public funeral. A

subscription to provide a monument for him in Montmartre cemetery attracted gifts from most of the well-known literary figures of
the day as well as from dozens of more obscure people. No fewer
than three biographies saw the light in the years after his death, and
many newspaper articles tried to state what he had meant for his
time. An earlier spate of journalistic commentaries had greeted the
play of 1849, and a third round of attempts to place Murger in the
history of the nineteenth century took place in 1895, when a bust to
his memory was unveiled in the Luxembourg Gardens. As one biographer wrote after his death, "Murger is Bohemia just as Bohemia
was Murger."[1]

The contrast between Murger's sometimes glittering successes
and the sadness of his end was characteristic of his career and his
impact. In some ways, he was an odd person to represent the world
of youth and gaiety that his *Scenes of Bohemian Life* is often taken
to be. He did escape old age, dying at thirty-eight, but his person
was not attractive, and his life was seldom free of care. Ill for many
years with a strange disease called purpura, which gives the skin a
macabre color and apparently hastened his death, he was repeatedly in and out of the hospital. His ailments gave him uncontrollable
facial tics and caused his eyes to water. He was bald from his twenties (see figure 1). Marguerite Thuillier, the actress who created the
role of Mimi in 1849, complained that with his ill-fitting clothes and
his strange features, he looked like a scarecrow. Later, when he was
able to dress elegantly, she still found him unattractive: now he
looked like a tailor's dummy. The actress's eye caught the essential
in Murger's character: there was no social role he fit well.[2]

Murger was born in 1822, the son of a tailor who also served as a
concierge. (Those activities were fairly often linked in nineteenth-
century Paris because the sedentary work of cutting and sewing
could be combined with overseeing an apartment-house entry
door.) People like the elder Murger lived on the dividing line between the working class and the bourgeoisie, working with their
hands but inevitably involved in the more genteel style of life that
surrounded them. The building he served was inhabited by solid,
successful bourgeois, including a number of well-known and re-

1. Henry Murger, in a caricature by Etienne Carjat, 1856.

spectable artists: a painter, a playwright, and two families of musicians. Murger's mother felt the attractions of that bourgeois world and hoped her son would join it. He later remembered how she had dressed him in elegant clothes and found other ways to express her desire "to distinguish him from the other children of his class." Murger's father may have sympathized with these ambitions on some level, but a kind of fearful practicality made him most often suspicious that they would lead young Henri (as he still spelled his name) onto questionable or dangerous paths. Murger received little formal education—a circumstance many critics found revealed in his writings—never obtaining the *baccalauréat* that then as now provided a cultural emblem of membership in the respectable French bourgeoisie.[3]

Murger's mother managed to get him a post as messenger boy in a lawyer's office, probably hoping that it would lead through apprenticeship to some kind of career in the law. There his young companions were two clerks whose daytime work served to cloak and support their real ambitions—to become painters. Murger, too, felt called to the brush and palette for a time, until a friend convinced him that he was hopelessly untalented as a visual artist. His response was to turn his attention wholeheartedly to the poetry he had already begun to write. From this moment, Murger's visions for his own future fastened on literature.

His friends were young men with similar aspirations. Most of them came, like him, from families who lived on the margin between the middle and working classes, having little in the way of either education or material resources to support their artistic ambitions. Among them was the nucleus of the group that was to call itself the Water-Drinkers: Adrien Lelioux, a playwright; Léon Noël, a poet; the Desbrosses brothers, Joseph (a sculptor) and Léopold (a painter), sons of a cabdriver. They were linked to the sometimes hidden and mysterious world of political opposition to the Bourgeois Monarchy of Louis-Philippe, often gathering in one or another of the cheap Left Bank restaurants that were also known as hangouts for Polish political exiles and suspected members of republican secret societies. One of Murger's friends at the end of the

1830s was Eugène Pottier, a poet with radical sympathies (he later wrote the "Internationale"). At one time a monitor (*pion*) in Murger's school, Pottier influenced Murger for a number of years. Through about 1841, Murger's letters show the lively interest in politics that inspired his first published poem: "Apostasy," an attack on a former republican who had renounced the cause. But the new author expressed a different concern at that moment, when he accepted an older writer's suggestion to anglicize his first name as Henry, and put two German-style dots over the "u" in Murger. The purpose was to make himself appear more elegant and noticeable.[4]

Murger's first and greatest love was a woman named Marie Fonblanc, in many ways the model for his later heroines: spirited and fun-loving, but at the same time pale and sometimes given to melancholy. Alas for Murger, she was married, and it seems their liaison was never physical. But it was certainly marked by effusions of romantic and poetic feeling of the kind expected from young men who—like Murger—shared the unworldly passions that inspired such figures as Vigny's Chatterton. Murger gave Marie a copy of *Myosotis*, the posthumous poems by another writer who had seen himself in Chatterton, Hégésippe Moreau. An orphan who pursued his poetic career through perpetual poverty, Moreau worked sometimes as a printer, sometimes on literary odd-jobs; he wrote an ode to hunger and died at twenty-seven—from starvation, many believed.

Marie Fonblanc was also the first object of Murger's equally deep impulse for idealization. She was charming and intelligent, but the world she lived in was sordid and shady. Marie's husband may have had intellectual pretensions; he seems to have tutored students for the *baccalauréat*. But his later career spanned very different occupations, from police spy to forger to fence and bank robber. In July 1840, he and his accomplices were rounded up by the police. Early in the next year, Marie was arrested and imprisoned, too. Although acquitted, she had clearly been made to participate in actions for which her husband and their friends were convicted. Murger's attachment to Marie Fonblanc had brought him close to some of these people. He sometimes went to public dances with her and three women friends who were the mistresses of her husband's accomplices. One story tells how he proudly referred to them in public as *des femmes en velours*, women in velvet. In fact, all three were registered with the Paris police as professional prostitutes.[5]

At twenty, then, Murger was living in a world of young artists and would-be artists that shaded off into political radicalism on one side and criminality on another. But Murger, who later tried to purge Bohemia of its associations with radical politics and criminality, was moving away from them in the early 1840s. Although poor, often ill, and frequently depressed, he had a small but stable income as the secretary of a mysterious Russian émigré, Count Tolstoy, who acted as a kind of diplomatic agent for the czar. Murger reported on goings-on in Paris for Tolstoy, and during the revolutionary days of 1848, these duties involved him in information gathering of a sort that bordered on political spying. Well before 1848, Murger gave voice to the growing sense of distance from his earlier political radicalism that would make him disdain the actions and ambitions of the revolutionaries. Yet he remained friendly with people whose radical political convictions proved firmer and more lasting than his—a situation that was always characteristic of Bohemia.

Murger's associations with criminality, never more than chance, simply dropped from view in the early 1840s. In these years, he tried to break into the world of journalism and literature. The Paris press during the July Monarchy, fed by expanding population, growing literacy, and new commercial methods, was vigorous and lively. The big daily papers like *Le Siècle*, *La Presse*, and the more austere *Journal des Débats* were influential in politics and carried literary contributions (the *feuilletons*) by well-known writers like Balzac and Eugène Sue. Their pages were beyond the reach of an unknown like Murger, however. His ambitions focused on the *petits journaux* with smaller formats, more restricted budgets, and narrower, sometimes specialized audiences. Murger and his friends wrote for children's journals, judicial reviews, papers aimed at hat makers and milliners, and even for one printed on water-resistant paper intended for the patrons of bathhouses. In 1845, he became associated with one of the most important of the "small" papers, the *Corsaire-Satan*, a saucy, provocative sheet devoted to literature and politics. It seems to have been well known in the Latin Quarter if not in the rest of the city. Murger's Bohemian tales began to appear there in 1845 and 1846.

Even in this scaled-down world, Murger found little success. His ambition to be a writer was strong but vague and abstract: after giving up poetry for prose, he had no clear sense of what he wanted to write about. His attempts at plays and stories—whether historical fiction about the composer Pergolesi, or sheer fantasy, "The Loves of a Cricket and a Spark"—came to little. He had determination and the will to work, but his periods of sitting with pen in hand often left him with little more than titles and piles of discarded scribblings. From the first, he needed strong outside stimulation, and he sought it in enormous quantities of coffee, which kept him awake through the night but seldom brought him inspiration or results, and certainly contributed to his frequent illnesses. The pattern of working all night, stimulated by the caffeine that he knew was harmful to his health, would last his whole life. It was one habit that kept him from achieving the regular, stable existence outside Bohemia for which he continued to yearn.

Murger's mother had died before he was twenty, and in 1842 his father broke off relations with him when Henry refused to take a regular job the elder Murger had arranged. About this time—probably in 1841—he joined with the Desbrosses brothers, Lelioux, Noël, and some others to form the Water-Drinkers. Through mutual support, the group sought to protect its members' talent and potential for future development against the corrupting influence of doing hackwork for ready cash in the present. Murger later depicted these people as inspired by a stoic refusal to make concessions to bourgeois materialism, perpetuating the very isolation that oppressed them. In fact, the Water-Drinkers supported themselves with whatever jobs they could find; their fear and hostility in the face of corruption and materialism were joined to a desire to be recognized and accepted, albeit in a way that preserved their self-respect. The group lasted less than a year. Anxiety and jealousy

sharpened by poverty and isolation dissolved it in the spring of
1842. Murger remained friendly, if more distantly, with most of its
members, and he was deeply affected by the slow death of Joseph
Desbrosses, called *le Christ*, from tuberculosis, early in 1844.[6]

Meanwhile, the circle of his friends grew larger. In the summer
of 1843, Murger met Jules Fleury, a writer from the town of Laon
who would later achieve considerable fame under the name Champfleury. The two shared a room in the rue Vaugirard for a few
months, until their friendship cooled. Champfleury's ambitions
were much more focused than Murger's and his tolerance for the
marginal life considerably less. He worked with facility where
Murger found insuperable difficulties, and he found Murger's penchant for idealizing women of the Marie Fonblanc stamp positively
distasteful. (The contrast between them reappeared in the differing
attitudes of Rodolphe and Marcel to Bohemia in Murger's later
sketches.) Meanwhile, Murger grew closer to other young artists
who were finding clearer paths out of Bohemia than the Water-
Drinkers. One was Félix Tournachon, later to be famous as a photographer and publicist under the name Nadar. Nadar introduced
Murger to a young poet named Théodore de Banville. Through
Champfleury and Banville, Murger came to know the one genuinely
great writer to inhabit Bohemia in the mid-nineteenth century,
Charles Baudelaire. Others in his circle during these years included
Alexandre Schanne, son of a successful toy manufacturer who dabbled in drawing and music (the Schaunard of the tales); Charles
Barbara, a wealthy and well-connected young writer and tutor in
search of literary friends and excitement (he appeared in the stories
as Barbemuche); and two eccentric students who dabbled in mystical philosophy, Jean Wallon and Marc Trapadoux (combined by
Murger in the figure of Colline). These people were the nucleus of
the group that gathered with some regularity at a café Murger discovered on the Right Bank near the church of Saint-Germain-
l'Auxerrois, the Café Momus. Other, less regular, visitors to the
Momus in the years before 1848 included Nerval, the painter Gustave Courbet, and a young writer and journalist who would later be

identified with Bohemia almost as closely as Murger himself, Alexandre Privat d'Anglemont.[7]

Then there were the women. Mimi and Musette were real people, too. The original Musette was named Marie-Christine Roux, usually called Mariette, a well-known figure in the artistic and literary Paris of the early 1840s. Sought after as a model, she posed for the sculptor Clésinger and later served Nadar as subject for one of the first nude studies in the history of photography.[8] That she was Champfleury's mistress, never Murger's, perhaps suggests that she was drawn to the qualities that made for worldly success. Her other liaisons were often with wealthy and established men, and she eventually made a small fortune as a high-class prostitute before drowning in a shipwreck in 1863. Her gaiety and charm, combined with frank sensuality and promiscuity, as well as her egotism and eye for the main chance, are all clear in Murger's portrait; the same qualities appear, cast in a much harsher light, in Champfleury's acid *Adventures of Mademoiselle Mariette.*

Mimi was a different sort. Her name was Lucille Louvet, and Murger seems to have met her only in 1845, about the time he began to write his Bohemian tales. According to all accounts save Murger's, she was not very attractive physically, but then neither was Murger, and she may have reminded him somehow of Marie Fonblanc. Her origins were working class and she seems to have been married quite young to a cobbler. Separated from him, she had gone back to the life that had probably been hers before marriage, supporting herself with handwork—sewing, lace- or flowermaking—done at home. It was a characteristic occupation in the age when most manufacture was still literally that, organized by merchants who put work out to a network of people in country cottages or city garrets. Paris had become a center for the manufacture of fine articles requiring a certain level of attention and skill. Much of the labor required for them was provided by young women from the countryside, living away from their families. They were known as *grisettes*, perhaps after the gray cloth many of them wore, and a whole mythology had grown up around them.

From a middle-class perspective, the lives of *grisettes* often seemed attractive, independent and free from restraint. When Louis-Sébastien Mercier wrote about them in his *Tableau de Paris* toward the end of the eighteenth century, he recognized the dangers often faced by eighteen-year-old country girls alone in the city. But he thought their freedom and independence better than the restricted lives led by daughters of the Paris bourgeoisie, sheltered, hemmed in by respectability, and sometimes waiting endlessly at home for the suitors who never came. Many *grisettes* would find husbands in Paris, Mercier believed; if they were pretty—or lucky—wealthier ones than their hometowns could have offered. Nineteenth-century accounts regularly associated the *grisettes* with the Latin Quarter—it contained a quantity of cheap housing—and thus inevitably with the students who also lived there. The *Nouveau tableau de Paris* assembled by a group of writers in the 1830s (where Félix Pyat's account of artists and *artistisme* also appeared) depicted the ties that grew up between *grisettes* and students. Both groups were young, away from their families, and not tied to regular work schedules. Students who could lighten the *grisettes'* lives with good food or presents, and who could impress them with a show of elegance, could often win them as mistresses, the *Tableau* writers claimed. Such liaisons, brief or lasting, were not expected to be for life: the *grisette* who understood the world would find an artisan for a husband once her student had returned to his provincial home.[9]

By the early 1840s, the mythology of the *grisette* had become a staple of romantic fantasy: available, grateful and understanding, unencumbered by bourgeois morality, the *grisette* of popular literature was a perfect answer to the physical and emotional needs of lonely, sometimes idle, and often self-centered young bourgeois. In the most famous fictionalized portrait, Alfred de Musset's "Mimi Pinson," the *grisette* appeared as an embodied spirit of gaiety, fun, and pleasure, never so happy as when playing jokes, laughing at a party, or enjoying a good meal. "Mimi Pinson" also showed something of the other side of working-class life: its real poverty and suffering, and the deep loyalty its members felt toward those who shared its privations. Musset's Mimi had only one dress; she pawned it—with the embarrassing consequences that can be imagined—to help another young woman out of a tough spot. She and her friends never lost their sense of the social difference between themselves and the young students they took up with: it was expressed in the jokes they played, in their awareness of the different destinies in store for the two groups, and in the enjoyment of moments they shared out of sight of their middle-class men.[10]

What we now know about the real people on whom the literary image of the *grisette* was modeled confirms Musset's observations about the darker side of their lives. The romantic ties between *grisettes* and students—to the degree they actually existed—rested on a certain mutual lack of comprehension. Most *grisettes* still retained close ties with their families in the countryside and helped to support them by sending money home. If their sexual mores were less rigid than those of the urban middle class, this conformed to centuries-old communal behavior patterns that sanctioned and regulated sexual experimentation among young people, but on the expectation that if pregnancy occurred, it would be followed by marriage. In the age of early industrialism, these patterns were being strained and sometimes broken by the effects of population growth and economic transformation. But the romantic image of the *grisette* probably exaggerated the availability of young working-class women to Latin Quarter students and artists; it also confused sexual liberation and carefree promiscuity with the disorienting and disruptive effects of urban experience and economic necessity on traditional rural mores. Remember that Lucille Louvet had married very young and that her husband had somehow disappeared.[11]

One feature of the *grisette* mythology suggested these different truths: very soon the image of the *grisette* was projected into the past. After the 1860s, writers commonly attributed the disappearance of the *grisettes* to recent economic and social changes, assuming that they had still existed in the 1840s. In fact, however, Murger himself already described them as gone from the Parisian scene in 1846: *race disparue*, they had been replaced by a much more mercenary and hard-bitten type of woman called Lorettes, after the region of Paris some of them were thought to inhabit. In 1848, Alfred Delvau—a frequenter of the Bohemian milieu who later wrote a biography of Murger—published a book called *Grandeur et décadence des grisettes* in which he declared outright that there no longer were any. Delvau claimed to tell the story of the very last one. She passed unconcerned through a whole succession of lovers, but not out of carefree gaiety: the beginning of her amorous history had been betrayal by a man she truly loved. From that point unwound the path along which she would casually love and betray others.[12] That the *grisette* was already receding into the past in the 1840s tells us what kind of myth hers was. A fantasy image constructed out of the misunderstanding of one sex and class by another, it had to be projected into the past because it found few opportunities for realization in the present. It tells more about the Rodolphes of the world than about the Mimis.

This, then, was the Bohemian Paris Murger inhabited during the 1840s. How did he come to be its chronicler?

The first answer is negative: not out of love. The gaiety and underlying optimism displayed by the Rodolphe of Murger's *Scenes of Bohemian Life* do sometimes appear in Murger's own letters of the time, but more often poverty, hunger, and depression were the staples of his life. Murger's situation was seldom so grim as that of the Desbrosses brothers, whom he once described as passing half of each day not eating and the other half dying of the cold. But he was no stranger to discouragement and what he called "the painful anxieties of doubt." The money that sometimes came in from an article or a story was quickly spent. If life was a song, it was a sad one: "The refrain is always the same—poverty! poverty! poverty!" Recurring sickness and stays in the hospital added to the undertow of worry and fear. Several times during 1843 and 1844 Murger declared himself on the point of giving up his literary ambitions—suicide or joining the navy would be better than the life he was living, he complained. But he held out, supported by reserves of determi-

nation and an ability to bounce back every time some minor success
gave him a chance to believe things were improving. Early in 1845,
he was in touch with Arsène Houssaye, editor of the popular and
successful review *L'Artiste*, and he was beginning to get some
pieces accepted by the *Corsaire-Satan*. Combined with his work for
Count Tolstoy and his connections with a paper for children and a
fashion journal, these successes allowed him to believe that he was
"on the path toward the path."[13]

The idea of writing about Bohemia came slowly. When the first of
his Bohemian tales appeared in the *Corsaire-Satan* in March of the
same year, Murger seems to have regarded it as a casual and isolated piece of work: the second of the series did not see the light for
a year. Murger would not use the title "Scenes de la Bohême" (he
still kept the traditional circumflex instead of the grave accent he
later adopted) until the fourth installment, in July 1846. Only then
was it clear to himself or his readers that he was embarked on more
than a few casual sketches.[14]

Champfleury tells us that the editor of the *Corsaire-Satan*, Poitevin de Saint-Alme (his real name was the more plebeian Podevin),
had a liking for stories about goings-on among students and *grisettes*. In 1845 and 1846, several writers treated these subjects in
the paper. Murger was not the first to employ the term "Bohemia,"
or to point to the problems associated with it. In October 1845,
Champfleury published his story "Chien-Caillou" ("Dog-Pebble").
Its central figure was, he said, one of "that race of unfortunate Bohemians who remain Bohemians all their lives." Son of a tanner,
Chien-Caillou has become an engraver without acquiring the education or connections that might have given him stability. Innocent
and isolated, he is ripe for exploitation by an unscrupulous picture
dealer. Champfleury made Chien-Caillou's situation the occasion
for a set of disillusioned contrasts between the "poetic garrets" imagined in Romantic literature and "real garrets." The latter were
dirty, dark, stuffy, and lonely. Chien-Caillou becomes the lover of a
grisette, but she and her sister are evicted for not paying their rent;
the young artist, unable to trace them, dies of hunger and a broken
heart. In a second story, "The Pupil of Moreau," Champfleury

evoked the unfortunate but inevitable associations between the artistic and literary Bohemia and the criminal *bohémiens* of D'Ennery and Grangé. Another writer in the same paper, Édouard Plouvier, published an explicitly Bohemian story in September 1846. It took the form of memoirs by an eccentric and disillusioned writer, also of working-class origins, "Job the Dreamer." Most of the memoirs were in the form of aphorisms, among which was this one: "In the yearly statistics of suicides, why don't we count lovers who get married, poets who take a seat in the Chamber of Deputies or the Senate, young wits who go into journalism?" Some of Murger's early sketches were hardly less disillusioned about Bohemia; in one, a young *ouvrière*, Clémence, dies after being abandoned by her student lover.[15]

It is not clear what led Murger to extend his series to the more than two dozen episodes it eventually included. No doubt the stories acquired a certain following, but not a very large one. Only the musical play of 1849 and the collected edition of the tales that followed it in 1851 established Murger and Bohemia in the public's consciousness. In January 1849, he wrote to Victor Hugo, asking for help in finding some sort of government employment that would leave him time for writing without having to struggle as he had so far. "I am not complaining about what I have endured, poverty has been a good teacher for me and has taught me excellent things. Now it has nothing new to teach me and consequently is useless to me. We must absolutely separate from each other, for instead of making me work it keeps me from it today." We do not know how Hugo replied to Murger's request for aid, but he did not achieve a government post, then or later. It was not patronage, but Bohemia itself that eventually gave Murger the chance to join established society.[16]

His determination to take that chance is unmistakable in his writings, particularly in his self-portrayal as the poet Rodolphe. The Rodolphe of his play *Bohemian Life*—the first Rodolphe to be widely known—is clearly a temporary Bohemian. Although accustomed to laugh at the follies of society, he does not reject it in the way of Vigny's Chatterton. He is determined to "eat at the table of life," and describes his courage and wit as the "social capital" that will one day bring him good returns; his whole involvement with Bohemia unfolds as a transient withdrawal from the bourgeois existence planned for him by the wealthy uncle with whom he is living at the start. Even Mimi comes to recognize Rodolphe's ties to the bourgeois world: "He has been a poet . . . he will become a businessman." When she dies at the end—surrounded by all the pathos later to be made famous by Puccini's opera—Rodolphe exclaims: "O my youth! it is you that is being buried!" It is a cry from the heart, but also a declaration that Rodolphe's attachment to Bohemia is dying, too. So fully did Murger's old friends understand this that they pled with him to give his play a different conclusion—to no avail.[17]

The Rodolphe of Murger's newspaper sketches, collected as *Scenes of Bohemian Life* in 1851, is less clearly enmeshed in the web of his bourgeois destiny from the start than the figure in the play. Murger's readers first encounter him already living in Bohemia, apparently his original and natural environment. Yet here, too, the rich uncle is present in the background to signal the foothold in the bourgeois world Rodolphe retains. When he and Marcel decide to share a room, their explicit purpose is to escape from *la Bohème*, living respectably and steadily on some cash Rodolphe has unexpectedly come into, so as to produce the work that will establish them as recognized artists in official society. Their old habits defeat them then, but by the end both achieve success and abandon Bohemia, no longer living (as Marcel puts it) "on the margin of society, almost on the margin of life."[18]

When Murger wrote the preface for his collection in May 1850, he made its dominant theme the follies and dangers of remaining too long in Bohemia. That life was a necessary apprenticeship for artists who had no private means of support, but those who did not have the determination and good sense to bring it to an end would destroy themselves. They were *la Bohème ignorée*, the unknown Bohemia, a name that contrasted them with the true or official Bohemia that served as a regular passageway into established life. The unknown Bohemians—the largest segment of the overall population—were of two sorts. The first were those who refused on principle to do what was necessary to leave Bohemia behind, "obstinate dreamers for whom art has remained a faith and not a *métier*." Fanatically devoted to being poets, they could not see that they also had to be men and live in the world of material necessity.

These first unknown Bohemians were at least genuine poets and artists: the second part of *la Bohème ignorée* consisted of those who were not, who mistook a fantasy for a vocation. Among the literary figures who exemplified and encouraged this often unhappy and destructive confusion were some in whom Murger had once seen himself: Hégésippe Moreau and Vigny's Chatterton. They were the volunteers of art, hastening to inscribe themselves in the martyrology of mediocrity, finding even death welcome if one could only become a poet through embracing it. So convinced were they that society was at fault for their troubles that they were willing to turn art into a torture to prove it. Unlike Vigny, Murger in 1850 had no hesitation about ejecting these people from the ranks of art.[19]

These views are not what one might expect from the man usually taken to embody Bohemia. In Murger's own lifetime, many who knew him recognized how incomplete his identity with it really was. One associate from the 1850s later declared flatly that "Murger was not a Bohemian"—his dress was too respectable, his manners too worldly. At Murger's death in 1861, some of his old friends from the 1840s gave voice to the disappointment they had long felt with the anti-Bohemian attitudes worked into *Scenes of Bohemian Life*. Murger had come to resemble the soldier who, weak and unable to carry his supplies by himself, found a tired and abandoned old mule to help him, only to kick her into a ditch at the edge of town so no one would see him with her. Grasping at success, Murger had not been choosy about the means for attaining it, nor did he restrain himself from jeering at those who had fallen along the way.[20]

Yet Murger's repeatedly expressed desire to separate himself from Bohemia was never really fulfilled. He could move to the Right Bank, dress with care, give elegant musical evenings—and yet something always tied him to the marginal life he tried to escape. In the *Scenes* the firmest rejection of Bohemia is announced by Marcel, not Rodolphe. One writer who had followed Murger's career wrote after his death that he kept falling back into Bohemia, "as if gripped by a homesickness for disorder." The Goncourt brothers—no friends of Bohemia, as we shall see—told of meeting Murger in an elegant café where he announced his renunciation of *la Bohème*: he was moving bag and baggage into the fashionable literary world. But that entry in the famous Goncourt diary is from 1857, eight years after the success of his play marked Murger's exit from Bohemia in the eyes of others; the Goncourts had still regarded him as a leading Bohemian a year before, and they repeated this view at his death in 1861. Their comments are testimony that to renounce Bohemia was not to be free of it. Murger's many declarations of independence from Bohemia were part of the ritual of his subjection.[21]

Many things kept Murger from a solid bourgeois life—the pattern of working through the night, dosed with coffee; the recurrent illnesses. The whole complex meant that the contacts he obtained after 1849 with established publishers and periodicals like the *Revue des Deux Mondes* were not enough to provide him with a reliable income or a stable tenor of life. But there were deeper reasons why Murger could not escape from Bohemia. Consider the predominant fact of his literary career: he never succeeded in writing consistently about anything else. After the play of 1849 and the collected sketches in 1851, most of the rest of Murger's writings continued to mine the same Bohemian vein: *The Latin Country, Scenes of Youthful Life, The Water-Drinkers, The Last Rendez-Vous, Camille's Vacation*. There were in addition essays, reviews, some poetry, and an occasional piece of fiction or drama on some other theme. But the substance of Bohemian life always remained the central material of Murger's literary vocation. As Champfleury later put it, Murger's writings could only be slices of his own life. "From time to time he would cut an adventure out of his life the way one cuts a slice of pâté." His singular mania was that he "wrote only his life."[22] Why could Murger not find other subjects, and what does this tell us about his relationship to Bohemia?

Probably the most common opinion about Murger's depiction of Bohemia is that it was a romanticized idealization, somewhat like his description of Marie Fonblanc and her rather shady friends as *des femmes en velours.* So, in some ways, it was. Those who know Murger's characters through Puccini will probably not be surprised to be told that the real lives behind the story were considerably more sordid than they appear on the stage, the real Rodolphe, Mimi, and their friends neither so optimistic nor so generous and unselfish as their copies. It is Murger rather than Puccini who is responsible for these transformations: despite some simplifying, the opera follows the play of 1849 closely in spirit, language, and plot, right down to the death of Mimi, angel of consumption, in the last scene. For all the sadness of the ending, we in the audience know that Rodolphe will recover—his liaison with Mimi is finished, after all—strengthened by the maturative disappointments of youth.

Yet Murger was not always given to such romanticizing, and he recognized that poverty was tawdry and painful. The dejection and sourness of some of his letters creep into *Scenes of Bohemian Life.* The motto of Bohemia was hard: *vae victis,* woe to the defeated. (Marx invoked the same words apropos of the bloodily suppressed insurrection of June 1848.) Murger's harshness toward the "ridiculous stoics" and "martyrs of mediocrity" in *la Bohème ignorée* was equally unromantic. As he insisted at one point: "Every day is not gay in Bohemia."

But the real nature and limits of Murger's penchant for idealization appear most clearly in regard to the theme usually thought to embody it best: love. Far from being a poem of innocence and youthful devotion in the face of adversity, *Scenes of Bohemian Life* presents the amorous experiences of its characters as a tissue of infidelities and betrayals. Musette is responsible for some of these, to be sure. For her, love is an exchange of illusions. Her affection for the men who pursue her is only a love for the luxuries they can offer. Toward Marcel, she feels something closer to love, but the bond between them is not powerful enough to keep her from going wherever the winds of impulse lead.[23]

Musette is the most lively and colorful figure in the book, but she was never—in reality or in fiction—Murger's woman. The romantic center of the tales is Mimi. Her character is different: less volcanic, softer, as befits the recipient of Murger's sentimental fantasies. But the Mimi of the *Scenes* has little of the angelic aura she comes to assume in the play and opera. (Those qualities were assigned to her from a minor character, Francine, mistress of one of Rodolphe's friends.) Her physical qualities are fetching enough—delicate features, clear blue eyes, transparent skin, soft elegant hands—but the moment she appears, we are told that those hands have sharp nails, and that her features sometimes take on an "almost wild brutality" as likely to indicate profound egotism as deep feeling. She compares Rodolphe unfavorably to the richer lovers of other women in the neighborhood, and does not wait long before looking around to see if she can do better. Their life together subjects him to "the clumsy cruelties of the woman who is not in love." Physically excitable, she is often emotionally cold, so that Rodolphe's romantic enthusiasm has to melt layers of icy indifference to bring about the couple's fleeting moments of satisfaction and intimacy.[24]

This is not a portrait colored by romantic idealization. Why does Rodolphe put up with her? The answer Murger gives is clear. He lives willingly in the hell she creates, never carrying out his many resolves to break up, because "with it would end forever those fevers of youth and those agitations he had not felt for so long." The inferno Mimi creates for Rodolphe is a kind of artificially prolonged youth. At the time he meets her (Murger met Lucille Louvet only in 1845), he has believed such things were over for him. She revives them. Living in this aroused state of feeling has a particular importance for Rodolphe—that is, for Murger—one that becomes clear with another figure in the tales: the sculptor Jacques D. Jacques is one of those "who make passion a tool of art and poetry." For them, the mind can be active only when set in motion by the heart. His creations are little pieces of himself (slices of his life, as Champfleury would say of Murger). Memories are not enough: like the millstone without grain, his heart wears away in the absence of passion. When passion goes out of Jacques's life with the death of Francine, it is Rodolphe who gives him the prescription for recovery. To be able to work again, he must rekindle the flame in his heart: "Start up a passion and the ideas will come back to you." When Jacques protests that he loved Francine too much for that, Rodolphe comes back: "That will not prevent you from loving her forever. You will kiss her on the lips of another."[25]

We know, from his letters and stories, that all these comments apply to Murger himself. In 1842, he described himself as devoid of inspiration and anguished by doubt, "incapable of writing twenty decent lines for a miserable children's journal. For three months I've been searching for emotions, any emotions at all, like a tubercular patient who goes after the sun, and I can't succeed in warming myself in their sunlight. My brain is empty and nothing more moves in it than in a tomb."

Coffee was one lever Murger employed to get his imagination in motion. Caffeine and love were linked: Murger turned to both to rescue him from the lethargy of creative impotence. Rodolphe explains why he cannot choose some purer muse of poetry over Mimi, despite the unhappiness and suffering she has brought him: "Hadn't she often initiated him into transports that carried him so high in the ether of reverie that he lost sight of things on earth?" Life in Bohemia was a perpetual inebriation. There "each day brought a new elegy, a terrible drama, a grotesque comedy."[26]

Bohemia for Murger was the self-conscious prolongation of an aroused state of passion and excitement, a loosening of the reins that life in respectable society placed on the free movement of fantasy. In Bohemia, life itself served as the spur his otherwise immobile imagination required. There, his belief that deep feeling and a willingness to sacrifice made him a writer could be confirmed by the act of cutting slices from his life to serve up as literature. Living where "everyday existence is a work of genius" was no apprenticeship for Murger, but the substance of artistic possibility. The desire to claim a real artistic identity made him regard *la Bohème* as a temporary stage imposed by mere external, economic necessity, but in reality, its hold on him was internal and lasting. Here was one source of that "homesickness for disorder" that a contemporary identified as the root of his continual return to Bohemia, against all his renunciations.

Extending in time beyond the youth to which he attempted to confine it, Murger's Bohemia also included many who fell outside the category of young artists "with no other means of existence than art itself." There existed a whole class of "amateur" Bohemians: young bourgeois who turned their backs on respectable society in search of the thrills that came with living the life of chance. Most of them would return to bourgeois life and, warmed by some provincial fireplace, would recount their Bohemian adventures as others told about hunting tigers. Others, however, would be less lucky: rejected by their staid families, some amateur Bohemians might end up in a pauper's grave.[27] These people were supposed to be marginal in Murger's topography. In fact, however, they were more central than he wanted to admit. Some of Murger's main figures were such amateurs: Charles Barbara, whom Murger called Barbemuche, was independently wealthy and served as tutor in a rich, aristocratic family; Alexandre Schanne, the Schaunard of the stories, later abandoned Bohemia to take over his father's toy business. Even the Rodolphe of the 1849 play had many features of an "amateur" Bohemian.

The amateurs formed the opposite flank from the stoics and martyrs of *la Bohème ignorée*. Together the two extremes help us to see in what ways Bohemia's boundaries and purposes were wider than those suggested by Murger's description of it as a form of apprenticeship for poor artists. The amateurs were only peripherally involved in the aesthetic issues faced by fledgling painters and writers, but they were essential to another aspect of Bohemia, what we will call its moral structure. Basic to that architecture was a curious paradox: the Bohemians' simultaneous repudiation of and hunger for wealth and the comforts of bourgeois life. Several nineteenth-century critics pointed out that the rejection of wealth Murger's characters practiced was never wholehearted. Far from putting money out of their minds, they spent most of their daily energy in search of it. "It is a strange paradox when someone who publicly announces a proud disdain for the realities of life ends up making himself a slave to them. Contempt for the goods of this world has been, ever since Seneca, a philosophic and honorable sentiment— but on condition that one has authentic contempt for them and gives them up, and doesn't dream about them night and day and shed tears for their absence like a lover crying over his mistress." As another commentator put it (writing, like the first, just after Murger's death), the Bohemian contempt for wealth was like that of the fox for the grapes: "at bottom they desired nothing so much as riches."[28]

The moralistic haughtiness behind these judgments should make us cautious, yet it is easy to find passages in Murger's writings that confirm them. When Marcel appears with the pile of coins realized by selling the only picture on which he has worked for months (it ends up as a shop sign for a grocer), the Bohemians greet them with awed fascination, far beyond any enthusiasm the picture inspires. "Good day, gentlemen!" (Marcel); "One would think them alive" (Colline). "What a beautiful voice" (Schaunard, "making them sing"). "How pretty . . . one would think they were bits of the sun" (Rodolphe). Items of luxury provoke similar witty outcries of awed devotion. " 'To think that there are at this hour, in Paris, more than a hundred thousand cutlets on the grill,' observed Marcel. 'And just as many beefsteaks,' added Rodolphe." At one point, a display of fancy foods in the window of a *charcuterie* provokes a whole page of wishful, poetic appreciation. Admiring a turkey stuffed with truffles (lovingly described by Murger), Marcel observes: "I have seen impious people eat some without kneeling before it."[29]

Many of Murger's funniest incidents revolve around the fascination wealth and luxury exercise over his characters. If they were often without money, it was not because they had no means of earning it, but because they could not resist spending with princely abandon whenever it came their way.[30] To bourgeois critics of Murger in his own time, these features meant that his Bohemians were not sincere: their proclaimed disdain for pleasure and ease was a sign of their basic dishonesty. But hypocrisy is a hard charge to prove, especially against one so unattuned to cashing in on it as Murger. What all these instances of fascination with bourgeois enjoyments betray is not insincerity but a more genuine and deeper quality: ambivalence.

Some Bohemians, after all, genuinely accepted—indeed, insisted on—a life of poverty: the self-righteous but devoted denizens of the unknown Bohemia. Murger's relations with them were not simple. In the preface to *Scenes of Bohemian Life*, he decried their taste for martyrdom, rejecting their path in Bohemia as a dead end, a cul-de-sac. Yet he was more deeply—if less consciously—entangled with this side of Bohemia than these words suggested. Murger had been a member of the Water-Drinkers, relying on its members for friendship and support in the darkest days of his literary obscurity. Despite his criticisms of the group, one of his book's most vivid and magnetic figures—perhaps the only deeply compelling portrait— was one of them, the sculptor Jacques D. Based on Joseph Desbrosses, the friend whose death in 1844 left Murger so deeply shaken, Jacques D. also wore some features of Murger himself. Desbrosses had been at the center of the original Water-Drinkers. By contrast, Jacques is—like Murger—partly detached from the club: he has separated from them because their strict rejection of any activity aimed at gaining income instead of furthering art prevents him from supporting the woman he loves, Francine. She emerges as a kind of purified and idealized version of Mimi, closer to the romantic figure of the 1849 play or of Puccini's opera than to the Mimi of the tales: innocent, devoted, and marked for death by tuberculosis from the start. Jacques, who like Rodolphe is an artist whose creative spark cools in the absence of a real woman to animate his imagination, is too poor to have received much formal education; he has been rejected by his father; and, sensing that his illness is a mortal one, he seeks to experience youth ardently while he can. In the book, it is he, not Rodolphe, who exclaims, "O ma jeunesse! c'est vous qu'on enterre!"[31]

Finding these words in Jacques D's mouth suggests that they had more than one meaning for Murger: Nadar and the others were wrong to view them as purely egotistic. Of all Murger's Bohemians, Jacques D. is the only one with a deep commitment to genuine achievement in art. His belief in the power of imagination to preserve the dead Francine's memory endows his artistic energy with a quasi-mystical, almost Baudelairean intensity. Despite what Murger said about them in the preface, his link with the Water-Drinkers kept alive his image of himself as a serious artist.

This also appears in the title story of the collection called *The Water-Drinkers*, whose central character, Francis Bernier, is another surrogate for the author. Son of a family too poor to educate him but indulgent enough to spoil him, Francis is drawn to the Water-Drinkers but unable to make himself one of them. Torn between the moral purity and artistic single-mindedness they represent, and a stronger desire to use his own limited talents to carve out whatever place in the world he can, he enters the group for a time, hoping that its protective solidarity will shield him from the temptations of doing hackwork. But the lure of immediate material reward is too great. Bernier ends up as a mediocre artist, living easily, but no longer in touch with the moral and aesthetic aspirations that give strength and purpose to his former friends. As in *Scenes of Bohemian Life*, Murger here criticizes the Water-Drinkers in the preface but presents them with considerably more sympathy in the story itself.[32]

The form of artistic seriousness the Water-Drinkers embodied is related to their origin in a specific segment of society: the lower reaches of the middle class. Poor but respectable, accustomed to material privations but not to manual labor, excluded from the comfortable bourgeoisie but, like it, independent and individualistic, insisting on the necessity of self-restraint and hard work, people living at this edge of bourgeois life were sometimes suspicious of painters and writers because of their irregular and possibly suspect habits. In *The Water-Drinkers*, that suspicion leads the young men's families to disown them. Yet the group is never wholly cut off from their roots: a sympathetic grandmother keeps house for them. (Feminine encouragement for an artistic career was also found in Murger's own family.) Moreover, the Water-Drinkers demonstrate their continued loyalty to their families by organizing their artistic lives around precisely the virtues their parents bred in them. "We are cited in our families as models of disorder; they hardly dare mention our names before our sisters, and yet our existence is solid, calm, morally regulated. Our practices are those of a religious community, abstinence included."[33]

Such people felt the need for a group to preserve and protect these values because they were threatened by powerful forces outside their own milieu. Parisian life was full of temptations. Francis Bernier joins the Water-Drinkers to resist the corrupting pull of Paris's luxuries and pleasures. Their siren song weakens his will, leading him to exchange the substance of art for its shadow, tempting him to devote his talent to banal and frivolous but salable works. Similar moral anxieties are central to Murger's other stories. Claude, the student hero of *The Latin Country* (*Le Pays Latin*), isolates himself in Paris to shut out the city's corrupting atmosphere of wealth and luxury.

One reason the attitudes Murger's characters exhibit toward poverty and money seem inconsistent, even hypocritical, is that they reflect two different social and moral perspectives. Those who enter Bohemia from the upper reaches of the bourgeoisie, like Schaunard, Barbemuche, or Marcel, have known bourgeois comfort and even luxury; underneath, they still feel they have the right to know it again. They are the part of Bohemia that makes it appear as a rejection of social rigidity, a demand for personal liberty that borders on indulgence. But side by side with them are the others, often less well-off lower bourgeois, whose family values center on a dignified and respectable independence, preserved and maintained by hard work and a willingness to renounce gratifications that would have made saving impossible; this group makes commitment to poverty a vital element in Bohemia. They do not seek liberation from rules and constraints, but impose limits on themselves. What makes them draw away from society is not its rigidity; quite the contrary, they fear its indulgences and temptations, its powers of moral corruption.

Murger made clear the fundamental differences between these

two components of *la Bohème*, but his account by no means sealed them off from each other. He himself—both in life and fictionalized as Rodolphe—was one who felt the appeal of both perspectives. Murger's Bohemia was a meeting ground and crossing point, not only for individuals with different life trajectories but also for contrasting, but not mutually exclusive, moral attitudes. Within the bourgeoisie, wealth and comfort were attributed to hard work and saving; hardship and renunciation had success and betterment as their goal. This combination of orientations and attitudes, sometimes shared and sometimes exclusive, made the bourgeoisie appear now as a single category and now as a variety of separate and detached groups. Bohemia mirrored and intensified the moral alternatives of bourgeois life.[34]

The social dynamic that created these alternatives in Bohemia was matched by a psychological one. Murger's account contained patterns of youthful experience that have reappeared in more recent studies of adolescence. Some of his Bohemians—Schaunard is the clearest example, Barbemuche slightly less so—were in search of what Erik Erikson has called a moratorium, a temporary release from the demands of social maturation. For the whole category Murger called "amateurs," Bohemia was a moratorium. He noted that the flight to Bohemia had disastrous consequences for some, whose families abandoned them. But the Bohemians who suffered that fate were probably not the reprobates their parents feared. Twentieth-century psychologists have shown that youthful rebels—despite the way things sometimes appear to both them and their elders—characteristically do not abandon the values and attitudes imparted by their parents. Instead, they locate themselves at points of contradiction in their families' moral universe, questioning their parents' actual lives against a purified version of the values supposed to underpin them. Adolescent rebellions reject family values on one level in order to exhibit them more purely and single-mindedly on another.[35] The most striking illustration of this dynamic in Murger's narration is provided by the Water-Drinkers, whose lives exemplify the ascetic moral order upheld by their parents, in the world of art where their families believe such values can only be corrupted. The Rodolphe of the 1849 play, preparing his "social capital" in the Bohemia his uncle believes will only disperse it, is acting out a similar relationship to the values he will have to come to terms with as he constructs a mature identity.

Despite Murger's attempt to depict the return to ordinary society as the normal outcome of Bohemia, his emphasis on the dangers of falling by the wayside suggest deeper anxieties. There may have been more than a little self-analysis in his description of the leading member of the Water-Drinkers as one "who learned early how to vanquish all the rebellions of youth by opposing to them an inflexible *parti pris.*"[36] Murger, too, feared the consequences of youthful rebellion. His very ability to combine the two perspectives of indulgence and idealism suggests how deep were the conflicts that made arriving at a mature identity, and leaving Bohemia behind, so difficult for him. The child of a petit-bourgeois family, he nevertheless grew up among people who belonged to the higher reaches of the middle class. His mother valued art as a symbol of that neighboring world of ease and refinement from which her position excluded her but toward which she could aspire in the person of her son. His father may have felt the lure of such hopes for social ascent, but they also filled him with anxiety and suspicion. These contradictory messages were Murger's inheritance. The moral dilemmas they opened up—between easy wealth and honest poverty, between desire for achievement and fear of success—were central to his vision of the opportunities and pitfalls of the artistic life. Unable to resolve them, he devoted his life to displaying his loyalty to both poles, abandoning Bohemia only to fall back into it.

The central place Murger's writings occupy in the history of Bohemianism—like his own involvement in it—can be understood only if we recognize that for him these moral dilemmas constituted the deepest problems of the artistic life itself. One looks in vain for Murger's treatments of the burning issues that defined aesthetic commitment in the nineteenth century: classic versus romantic, traditional versus modern, nature versus artifice, beauty versus sublimity, color versus line. The organizing polarities in Murger's world were not these artistic choices, but wealth versus poverty, work versus enjoyment, duty versus indulgence, individual self-involvement versus society's demands. His own attempt to describe Bohemia as a stage of artistic apprenticeship was not a pretense so much as a move in the wider—partly unconscious—strategy that inspired it. The central experiences of Murger's Bohemia did not arise from the dilemmas of poor young artists struggling to achieve recognition in an age of market relationships. Instead, Bohemians appropriated their spirit and style of life for a different purpose: dramatizing the ambivalence many ordinary bourgeois felt toward their identities and destinies. This appropriation was the very definition of Bohemia. Murger filled in and completed the intuitions already given expression by Alfred de Vigny and Félix Pyat: that under modern conditions, the boundaries of the artistic identity were expanding. Postrevolutionary society, constructed around the claim to establish individualism as a social principle, made the artist's intense preoccupation with self-examination and self-development symbolic of wider issues common to many people. The image of the artist became the mirror in which a broader population faced and explored the uncertain moral boundaries that made their social identities problematic.

Many features of Murger's stories and tales were echoed and amplified by his readers, both sympathetic and critical: his association of Bohemia with a life of liberated fantasy; his display of the social contrasts and moral dilemmas underlying bourgeois existence; his representation of Bohemia as both a passageway into bourgeois society and a permanent form of separation from it. What joined these elements together and made Murger's presentation the classic account of Bohemian life was that within it, art merged with the life lived in its name. Bohemians were those for whom art meant living the life, not doing the work. This was the meaning of Murger's formula: "Their everyday existence is a work of genius." It was a notion whose potential for revealing some of the hidden impulses animating modern life and culture was only just beginning to be revealed.

CHAPTER 3

Politics, Fantasy, Identity: Bohemia in the Revolution of 1848

THE YEARS IN WHICH Murger's tales appeared corresponded to a moment of particular significance in the history of modern society. This was the era of widespread agitation and upheaval associated with the Revolutions of 1848. In February of that year, an uprising in Paris toppled the monarchy of Louis-Philippe, replacing it with the Second French Republic. The wave of revolution spread throughout the Continent, to Italy (where rumblings had begun earlier), Germany, and Central Europe, even threatening for a moment to wash up on the shores of England. But the moment when revolution seemed to sweep all before it was brief. By the fall of the year, the old governments began to recover their power in Germany and the Hapsburg dominions. French conservatives got reassurance soon after, when Louis-Napoleon Bonaparte—nephew of the first Napoleon and no friend of republican politics—was elected president in December. The Republic lasted in France for three more years: a period marked by much greater calm than had obtained during 1848 itself, but in which political agitation continued. Radical democrats and socialists made important gains, especially in the countryside, before the Republic succumbed to Bonaparte's *coup d'état* of December 2, 1851, and his subsequent proclamation of the Second Empire.

Despite its meager achievements, the crisis of 1848 made those who witnessed it face fundamental issues. In the previous decades, both liberal currents set in motion during the revolutionary and Napoleonic periods and more radical tendencies arising from early industrialization had provoked a series of smaller conflicts; when the revolutionary moment came, many visions and expectations about the nature of modern society and its potential future came into the open, and competed to define and lead the movement for change. The 1840s helped form Marx's theories. Other seminal figures owed much of their formation to these years, too: Richard Wagner, Jacob Burckhardt, Charles Baudelaire, Pierre-Joseph Proudhon, Gustave Courbet, John Ruskin. Because hopes were high, disappointments were deep when they came. Few people who experienced 1848 looked at life quite the way they had before, once its failure was confirmed.

In France, the political dimensions of the crisis were broader and clearer than elsewhere. The struggles that began in 1848 focused on a challenge to bourgeois rule that arose from the working classes and marched under the banner of socialism. A dizzying variety of socialist aspirations and programs appeared in Paris after February, some in the dozens of political clubs that sprang up, some in the official government commission on the problems of labor established in the Luxembourg Palace, others in the National Workshops set up to give employment and relief to the mushrooming legion of unemployed. The conflict between the Paris workers and the rest of the nation produced its sharpest confrontation in the bloody June Days, when thousands of mostly proletarian barricade fighters succumbed to a determined assault by militia forces and the army. For a time, it seemed as if the bourgeois social order sanctioned by the Monarchy of 1830 might be on the point of giving way to something else.

That it did not do so was an important legacy bequeathed by 1848 to the generation that lived through it. This was the first generation to experience revolution—and its defeat—in a declaredly bourgeois setting. They were the first Europeans who had to come to terms with bourgeois society's failure to transform itself into a different social order. Each generation since has spawned similar hopes for the transformation of society and faced a similar need to live with the disappointment. That need has created a political and cultural space that has often been occupied by Bohemia.

The reception given to Murger's portrait of Bohemia was shaped by the crisis that broke into the open during 1848. The newspaper publication of his tales and sketches during the previous years had caused little stir, whatever interest they generated being limited to the narrow audience of the *Corsaire-Satan*. In 1849, things were altogether different. Audiences flocked to the Varieties Theatre night after night to see his play, major daily papers published laudatory reviews, and some of them reported the remarkable box-office triumph for weeks afterward. Part of the success was certainly due to Murger's collaborator, Théodore Barrière, a talented theatrical craftsman with several earlier hits to his credit. But the reviews mentioned Barrière only in passing. It was Murger's characters that drew the audience's enthusiasm: the explosion of wit and fancy with which they confronted life, and the bittersweet attraction of the Bohemian world they brought into view. That it was still a relatively unfamiliar world is suggested by the fact that nearly every reviewer began by explaining what *la Bohème* meant, giving elementary definitions of Bohemia that would never be necessary again.[1]

The reviews of Murger's play also show that audiences were fascinated with the Bohemian world for political reasons. To some, *la Bohème* was attractive as an escape from nearly two years of revolutionary agitation and uncertainty, but to others it represented a reservoir of radical sentiments and energies.

It was in the first sense that the play was greeted by the best-known and most widely read drama critic of the day, Jules Janin, whose enthusiasm helped assure Murger's success. The critic for the stodgy *Journal des Débats* was aware that there were moral dangers in Bohemian life: warning against them, he quoted Lamennais (one of the idols of French youth): "There is a spiritual libertinism that uses up the mind just as debauchery uses up the senses." Yet, something won Janin to Rodolphe and Marcel, despite their questionable morals. Summing up the 1849 drama season, Janin imagined a debate between Politics and Poetry. Which was really dominant in the country that claimed preeminence in both? The chief exhibits in the case Poetry made for herself were Murger's Bohemians.

> At the Varieties Theatre we had *La Bohème*, and it is here that I have been waiting for you, O Politics, to show that even the youth of the Latin Quarter can get along without your counsels and your practice. O Poverty! It is in vain that you have infested these garrets, these attics, these poetic heights; it is in vain that you have wanted to rule on the mountain of Saint Jacques and thereabouts; between the Pantheon and the Luxembourg Gardens one finds a race of philosophers and poets, of lovers and idlers who have never read a single one of your red and bastard sheets, all filled with hate and vengeance! O happiness! The Bohemian who despises politics and who would give all of Proudhon for the corner of Musette's embroidered veil or of Mimi's shroud! Politics banished from the garret! banished from the studio! banished from poverty! even banished from the hospital![2]

Janin did not mean to claim seriously that the French had lost interest in politics; the debate ended in a standoff. Nonetheless, his vision of Bohemia as apolitical picked out elements within it that would often reappear.

In 1849, however, not everyone was prepared to accept such a perspective. A younger and lesser-known critic, Auguste Luchet, who contributed to the social-democratic *La Réforme* and identified himself as a Bohemian, exulted at the appearance of Murger's play. It called attention to a world that had hitherto remained invisible to the bourgeois, even though it existed in the center of Paris. To represent it on the popular stage was to transform vaudeville from a pastiche of fantasies and perfumed phrases to a revelation of hidden realities. "It is socialism—let's settle the word—entering like a conquest, flag and symbols blowing in the breeze, into the den of the emperors!" Bohemia was a living reproach to bourgeois life. It was the realm of liberty, pleasure, and truth. Its existence showed that idealism and devotion could find no home in ordinary society;

that the modern exaltation of work rested on domination by capital and the exploitation of real workers; that the position of many respectable fathers was rejected by their sons because it was founded on shadiness and deceit. True, Bohemia could be a passage into bourgeois life:

> Many leave it, to the salvation of your philosophy, tired out and enervated by the struggle. They are the insufficiently tempered ones. They soon become what you are, broad, heavy gray figures in the dingy world of exchange, dreaming of investments instead of their country, talking the language of the bank and not of virtue, hunting the poor instead of dogs, having their gods in their stomach and their souls in their pockets; perfect respectable people, in fact.
>
> But take care about those who remain inside! It is we who tell you.[3]

The Bohemia Luchet saw in Murger's staging was neither harmless nor unpolitical. Withdrawal from ordinary society led toward the radicalism and revolt that were still at the forefront of consciousness in 1849.

There was reality behind both images of Bohemia. During the 1850s, many no longer young men who had earlier lived extravagant and deviant lives in the milieux that spawned political radicalism made their peace with society. Some of them took over Janin's view as a way of coming to terms with their past. Before revolution broke out in 1848, however, the political associations of Bohemia had seemed to be uniformly on the Left. If any publication represented Bohemia during the 1840s, it was the newspaper *Le Corsaire-Satan*. Typical of the Parisian *petite presse* in its attempt to exploit the talents of young and unknown writers, it counted Champfleury, Privat d'Anglemont, and Baudelaire among its contributors. What set it apart from other papers was its self-conscious attention to the world of students, artists, and writers from whom its contributors—and perhaps a good proportion of its readers— came.

One theme that often surfaced in the *Corsaire-Satan* was the mutual interplay between literature and politics. A *feuilleton* of June

1846, "The Literary Movement" by Luis de Padilla, asserted flatly that "in our epoch the literary movement must necessarily follow the political movement." An article in January 1845 noted that Balzac's *The Peasants* was, "like all Balzac's work, written in opposition to the political influence of the bourgeoisie." Everywhere literature was becoming involved with the social side of political questions in a manner that led to criticism of the government. The writer even feared that literary people might be led astray by the attempt to handle political questions: the *feuilleton*, "having swallowed politics, will die of indigestion."[4]

Although the paper maintained a certain independence, its underlying political tone was consistently reformist and antibourgeois. An editorial published early in 1845 argued for electoral reform on the grounds that only a sufficient participation by "intelligence" could assure political stability. Those who did not meet the economic qualifications for voting should be granted suffrage rights if they had sufficient education. Later in the year, the journal noted that France often experienced political crises when the economic situation worsened, and speculated that a new round of agitation might arrive soon. Openness to political radicalism was also demonstrated by a series of sympathetic articles on the eccentric and flamboyant Fourierist missionary Jean Journet, in April 1846. The paper's editor, Poitevin de Saint-Alme, defended Journet when he was interned in a mental hospital.[5]

The Bohemian milieu of the 1830s and 1840s often intersected with the locales that nurtured radical politics. Champfleury told of first meeting the members of the Water-Drinkers in a café frequented by republican conspirators. Though not all the habitués took advantage of the chance to mix art and politics—the Desbrosses brothers talked only of art—other regulars sought out the back room, where a kind of altar of liberty, decorated with medallions representing noted political prisoners, served to consecrate the enthusiasms of the politically initiated. The publicist and photographer Nadar placed political concerns at the center of his recollections of Bohemia. One dominant figure was a Polish émigré called Karol (the son of a Napoleonic soldier and a Polish woman), who mixed an enthusiasm for poetry and philosophy with a determination to aid in liberating his native country. A patient and sweet-tempered man of gigantic proportions—like Nadar—Karol kept many of his Bohemian friends alive by sharing his money with them. His Polish patriotism was part of a general identification with all the world's unfortunate and oppressed. Balzac also recognized that Bohemia grew up in a political framework. The figures with whom he peopled *A Prince of Bohemia* were more likely to have aristocratic than populist sympathies, but it was politics that produced their separation from official society. Napoleon had been the last French ruler to comprehend what talented youth could contribute to the nation, and to employ them. The narrow vision of more recent governments kept the young isolated in their own sphere.[6]

The locales Champfleury and Nadar remembered were precisely Murger's. Earlier we noted his friendship with the author of the "Internationale," Eugène Pottier, and the republican inspiration of his first published work, the poem "Apostasy." A letter of 1841 recorded his interest in the political agitations stirring beneath the surface of events in Paris, and in the possibility of a popular uprising. By the mid-1840s, however, Murger's political interests were cooling down. In the summer of 1844, he wrote a criticism of those who sought to link art with political emancipation and the proletariat. If Champfleury's memory is to be trusted, he also wrote harshly about the more conservative "school of common sense" which suggests an estrangement from conservative bourgeois as well as radical politics. Nadar later criticized Murger for his inability to take a coherent position on the important issues of the day. He lacked the consistency and emotional commitment to a cause that made effective action possible.[7]

By 1848, this indifference was turning into frank hostility toward the Revolution and its supporters. Murger's mood during the spring of 1848 may have been soured by poverty, guilt, and illness. In April, Lucille Louvet died in a hospital. Murger had to be prodded by friends to visit her. The reason he gave was that he was too poor to buy her flowers, but the description of their relationship we already know from *Scenes of Bohemian Life* suggests other reasons for his detachment. In May, Murger himself was in a hospital, with an illness that was not purpura but probably syphilis. Some of these events may have contributed to the ill temper Murger displayed (at least according to one friend of the time) when he spoke of working-class club members as "conceited brutes." This was the time when Murger's reports to Count Tolstoy were finding their way to the Russian czar, eager for information about revolutionary Paris.[8]

The political tone of Murger's newspaper sketches also grew more ill tempered and hostile to the Left. In the early installments, he had noted the political features of the Bohemian landscape in passing, sometimes with humor, but without any animus. He gave voice to anticlerical feelings, and made fun of a bourgeois who feared newspapers because he blamed revolutions and inflated currency on them. And he referred to his Bohemian circle of friends with the Fourierist term "phalanstery." In one story, Rodolphe decides to attend a utopian banquet—but only in the hope of getting something to eat. "Causes come and go," he remarks, "but *effets*"—in French a pun for bills—"keep coming back."[9] Then in April 1849, Murger published "His Excellency Gustave Colline," the last in his series of tales and the only one that explicitly treated the Revolution. Humorously, Murger notes that the economic crisis brought on by bad harvests and the change in government amounts to a proclamation of "the right to idleness" for artists—it leaves them, like many other people, with no work. Most Bohemians respond by folding their arms and becoming disinterested spectators at the political comedy. Not so Colline. Murger describes him as concealing a gigantic ambition behind his mask of amiable indolence. His career in the Revolution revolves around one of the great themes of its critics: the change in government as a paradise for job seekers. Colline frequents a café patronized by journalists who have influence with the new regime. There he wins an ambassadorship in a billiard game. To be sure, his mission takes him to an obscure German princedom whose only industry is growing leeches. But behind this foolery is a strongly disillusioned picture of republican politics. When the tale appeared in Murger's collection during 1851, some of his old friends were incensed. Nadar asked Murger to remove it from the second edition. By the time it came out, the republicans had been rendered politically impotent by Bonaparte, and Murger, relenting, agreed.[10]

Murger's actual political attitudes remain uncertain, and may never have been very clear. The real-life model for Colline, who actually became politically involved during 1848, was Jean Wallon. But Wallon was a conservative. A Catholic mystic even when Murger had been close to him in the 1840s, he became an anti-democratic and antisocialist publicist after the Revolution broke out. If it was his ambitions that were satirized, then the object of Murger's barbs was not the republican Left alone. His sense of marginality led him through a variety of political positions, and his vagaries sometimes disappointed his more committed friends. But Murger's political plasticity may have been one feature of his personality that allowed him to draw together the separate and potentially hostile currents within Bohemia.[11]

That some who had been Bohemian rebels before 1848 might grow conservative in the face of real revolution was a possibility recognized by various contemporaries. One of these was Gustave Flaubert, who described a circle of young people with some resemblances to Murger's in his novelistic history of his generation, *Sentimental Education*. Flaubert labels only one of his characters a Bohemian, the writer Hussonet, who in the 1840s works for various marginal publications and dreams of success in the theater. He gaily tells how he had lived for a whole winter on nothing but cheese. But his instincts are conservative even then, and in 1849 he works for the antidemocratic Party of Order, writing pamphlets and propaganda. These activities are moves toward the more complete *embourgeoisement* Hussonet achieves under the Second Empire. By the 1860s, Flaubert sees his Bohemian—we cannot be sure who his models were, but Nerval's friend Arsène Houssaye fits the mold—as a powerful establishment figure, with great influence over Parisian theatrical and artistic life.[12]

A somewhat similar association of Bohemia with antirepublicanism was envisaged by an observer who hated bourgeois society with a passion equal to Flaubert's, but from a different point of view, Karl Marx. Marx was a foreigner, of course, but he had lived in Paris for a time in 1843–44, and he followed the French events of 1848 with close attention. Marx equated the movement toward socialism he promoted with the possibility that clear and well-defined social categories—classes—would become real historical actors. To him, Bohemia's social ambiguity was a breeding ground for revolution's enemies, not its friends. Those most willing to aid Bonaparte's assault on republican institutions were "decayed *roués* with dubious means of subsistence and of dubious origin, ruined and adventurous offshoots of the bourgeoisie, . . . vagabonds, discharged soldiers, discharged jailbirds, escaped galley slaves, swindlers, mountebanks, *lazzaroni*, pickpockets, *literati*, organ-grinders, ragpickers, knife grinders, tinkers, beggars—in short, the whole indefinite, disintegrated mass, thrown hither and thither, which the French term *la Bohème*." To Marx, even Bonaparte was a Bohemian.[13]

But Flaubert and Marx saw things from a distance. Flaubert wrote in the 1860s (he was, in addition, a person who feared and hated Paris, spending as little time there as he could, once his student days were past) and Marx from the beginning of his long exile in London. Most references to Bohemia's role by participants in the events of 1848 located it on the Left. This was especially true of two books published in 1850 and reviewed by Marx. Both were by former police spies who had penetrated into the republican secret societies, Lucien de la Hodde and Adolphe Chenu. The two men wrote to justify their own activities and to expose the world they had come to know under the July Monarchy. For both, Bohemian forms and styles of life were important elements in shaping the political milieu that nurtured revolution.[14]

Somewhat like Marx, but from a different point of view, Chenu and de la Hodde painted that world of republican secret societies as a realm where fantasy predominated over knowledge of real life. Both thought the politics of the Left were deeply colored by those two essentially Parisian experiences: literary passion and the life of the café. Republican groups met in dark taverns or wineshops; their members either cherished literary ambitions themselves or rubbed elbows with those who did. The combined influence of wine and poetry helped infect opposition politics during the 1840s with the fever of uncontrolled imagination. Even those among the republicans who possessed real talent and virtue were driven to extremes, either by intemperance or by the power of literary fantasy.[15]

Both authors explicitly identified this milieu as Bohemian, but it was Lucien de la Hodde who developed the theme more fully. He listed students, failures, workers, malcontents, and bandits as separate categories of conspirators, but Bohemians had a special place in that murky world. Driven by the desire to enjoy life without working, they dreamed up all kinds of expedients to support their habits and enjoyments—some clever, some cynical, some frankly criminal. They throve in the atmosphere of constant mobility and change that marked the modern city, throwing themselves into conspiracies and agitations because they sensed that a stable and calm society would make their own form of disordered life impossible. Their enthusiasm for political utopias was a natural extension of the contempt for ordinary life and its limits that ruled their existence.[16]

That both Chenu and de la Hodde used the term "Bohemian" may owe something to the notoriety gained for it by Murger's play. Their notion of Bohemia combined elements from Murger with the earlier image of a shadow world on the frontier between inventiveness and criminality. Both portraits also drew features from the same real-life exemplar. He was Marc Caussidière, the figure from the world they described who achieved the highest position under the Provisional Government set up in February 1848. He served as prefect of police. One reason Chenu and de la Hodde sought to portray him as a suspect figure was simple enough: it was he who had exposed them as spies.

By 1848, Caussidière was a veteran of revolutionary politics, having taken part in the famous uprisings of workers and republicans in Lyon in 1831 and 1834. Imprisoned for a time after the second outbreak, Caussidière remained active in opposition politics throughout the July Monarchy. During the 1840s, he was associated with the social-democratic newspaper *La Réforme*, not as a journalist but as a kind of traveling salesman, encouraging subscribers and drumming up support in various French cities. Much of this propaganda was carried on in provincial cabarets and restaurants, which Caussidière also frequented as a seller of wine and spirits. He was a blustery, colorful, expansive man, full of good feeling but often ready for a fight. As the opposition to Louis-Philippe and Guizot heated up, Caussidière's work of linking Parisian republicans with their provincial sympathizers gained a certain importance.[17]

When the government fell in February, however, Caussidière was not a prominent-enough figure to be given an important post by the new one. He obtained his position as police prefect by his own action, occupying the Prefecture during the confusion and fighting. The Provisional Government resisted giving him the title of "prefect," preferring the less official-sounding "delegate," but it did not attempt to remove or replace him. To aid in maintaining order, Caussidière set up new police units called "Montagnards" (after the radical party of the 1790s) and "Gardes Républicaines." Formed from barricade fighters and released political prisoners with some military experience, these troops were well known for their exotic appearance and their aura of revolutionary commitment. They frightened some good bourgeois, as Gustave Flaubert testified in *Sentimental Education.* Yet, Caussidière was surprisingly successful in achieving calm and good order with them. Crime was rare in Paris during that spring. He was especially proud of establishing order in the prisons, restraining gambling, limiting prostitutes to designated areas, and clearing the streets of acrobats and other performers who appeared there in large numbers. "I have made order out of disorder," was his boast.[18]

Caussidière's ties to the conspiratorial Left were important elements in the work he did for the Provisional Government, but they also got him into trouble. On May 15, a demonstration in behalf of Polish independence turned into a confused attempt to dissolve the Constituent Assembly elected in April, in favor of a new, more radical regime. The uprising was easily defeated, but it involved some leaders of the radical clubs. Since Caussidière was associated with

these milieux, he was suspected of sympathizing with the insurrection. His Montagnards and Gardes Républicaines were accused of
providing insufficient protection for the government in a crisis. On
May 17, he had to resign as head of the Paris police. Later, he
would be suspected of sympathy for the June revolt and would leave
France for exile in England.

While these events were taking place, Caussidière was the object
of considerable attention in the Paris press. The word "Bohemian"
was apparently not yet enough in people's minds for them to apply
it to him, but the features in his character observers underlined
were among those later conveyed by the term. The *Journal des
Débats* noted that his defense against the charges brought after
May 15 revealed "a gift for popular eloquence. From time to time
he has certain eccentricities of language that exceed the limits of
the picturesque; but, after all, we've heard lots of others in these
days." *Le National*, less conservative than the *Journal des Débats*
but directly in competition with *La Réforme*, was more hostile:
"Public tranquility cannot be allowed to depend on the ambitious
fantasies and crazy illusions of a few sick and infected minds."[19]

The personal ties and character traits that bound Caussidière to
the Parisian cafés and lowlife that nurtured conspiratorial politics
were magnified in the portraits by Chenu and de la Hodde. Chenu
told how the Prefecture of Police swarmed with "all the old barflies
with whom Caussidière had consorted throughout his life," causing
the prefect to regret the *vie de Bohème* he had shared with them.
The Provisional Government thus exhibited the noisy disorder, the
vulgar camaraderie of drink and rough horseplay, learned in tavern
life. De la Hodde added features to what he called "democratic Bohemia": its night-wandering escapades, its refusal of regular work,
its artistic pretense. This world was a dangerous training ground for
political leaders, not only because it was morally suspect, but also
because it fostered confusion between fantasy and reality. "In this
world of the imagination, in which the private man can lose himself
without harm, the citizen stumbles, the statesman loses all authority." Here were the elements for a portrait of Bohemian politics
that would be repeated many times.[20]

There was another part of the revolutionary landscape of 1848 that came to be identified with Bohemia—its plethora of utopian projects. At a time when modern society was younger, some hopes since tarnished still shone brightly; many people with a plan for saving the social world found an audience. Marx and Engels would pin the label "utopian socialists" on a rather restricted group of these theorists. The followers of such well-known figures as Fourier and Saint-Simon were small clusters within the droves of visionaries who filled Parisian streets and squares. The most famous description is by Alexis de Tocqueville:

> From the 25th of February onwards, a thousand strange systems came issuing pell-mell from the minds of inventors, and spread among the troubled minds of the crowd. . . . It seemed as though the shock of the Revolution had reduced society itself to dust, and as though a competition had been opened for the new form that was to be given to the edifice about to be erected in its place. Everyone came forward with a plan of his own: this one printed it in the papers, that other on the placards with which the walls were soon covered, a third proclaimed his loud-mouthed in the open air. One aimed at destroying inequality of fortune, another inequality of education, a third undertook to do away with the oldest of all inequalities, that between man and woman. Specifics were offered against poverty, and remedies for the disease of work which has tortured humanity since the first days of its existence.

The popular novelist Louis Reybaud called forth the same situation with still less respect: "All the monstrous or crazy ideas that mixed about in the catacombs of disdain and forgetfulness made their way all at once to the public square." Daniel Stern (in real life the Comtesse d'Agoult) observed more sympathetically that the ideas finding expression were those a repressive regime had refused any outlet before. Yet she, too, thought that these humane sentiments appeared in eccentric, even grotesque and sometimes incoherent forms. As the popular magazine *L'Illustration* said at the time: "There are utopias for every taste, every profession, every age, every sex, etc." Among the posters it mentioned was one demanding that public employments be reserved for penniless literary men.[21]

None of these observers associated the outpouring of utopian imagination with Bohemia, but others did. In December 1850, a writer in *Le Corsaire* (successor to Murger's old paper, now under a different and more conservative management) linked the whole complex of romantic extravagance in dress, appearance, and social fantasy with Bohemia. To have a Bohemia was characteristic of modern society's confusions. It was "the symptom of a certain agitation in people's minds, appearing above all in the moments just before and just after revolutions."[22] But the person who made the connection most extensively and effectively was Murger's old friend and apartment-mate, Champfleury.

In 1852, Champfleury published *Les excentriques (The Eccentrics)*, a collection of essays and sketches written just before and during the Second Republic. The subjects were themselves an eccentric group: discoverers of nature's secrets, squarers of the circle, conversers with great dead men, hallucinators. Only a few were political, but among them were some of those Tocqueville and the others had uppermost in their minds. There was the abbé Châtel, self-proclaimed bishop of the French Catholic Church, dedicated to reason and universal fraternity. In 1848, his enormous placards seen all over Paris proclaimed "Abolition and confiscation of all the misunderstood mysteries and doctrines of the past, to the benefit of reason." There was Rose-Marius Sardat, author of a plan to create utopia around small groups each led by a person over seventy years of age; and Jupille, determined to save humanity through vegetarianism. Above all there was Jean Journet, apostle of Fourierist communitarianism (see figure 2). Journet was a well-known figure in the years around 1848, noticed by newspapers, and defended (as we saw) in the old *Corsaire-Satan*. Converted to Fourier's ideas after a youthful involvement with the Carbonari (he was imprisoned for participating in an attempted insurrection) and Saint-Simon, from the mid-1830s Journet devoted himself to spreading the word. He abandoned the straitlaced and timid official Fourierist movement and operated on his own, selling his brochures for a few sous, when necessary giving them away. Sometimes, he sought out famous and influential people, pressing his ideas on them. At other times, he distributed his papers by raining them down from the balconies of theaters. The intensity of his devotion reduced common sense and accepted behavior to insignificance in his mind: more than once, he was confined in a mental hospital. Released, he traveled throughout France and other countries in the service of his utopian vision. Known to many literary and artistic figures of the day, he was for a time supported with a pension funded by Alexandre Dumas. Among his talents was a linguistic inventiveness used to launch imprecations against those he considered enemies of humanity: "plague of the human species," "cosmopolitan vampire," "stuffed sybarite." Champfleury's favorite was *omniarque omnivore*: all-ruler, all-eater.[23]

Journet had contacts with the Bohemian circles in which Murger and his friends circulated. He sometimes appeared at the Café Momus. His seriousness and intense asceticism were not unique in those precincts: the Water-Drinkers also sought to withdraw from the corruptions of society and found a purified community in a higher cause—art; and Murger's friends Wallon and Trapadoux were both devoted to religious mysticism. But others found Journet an irresistible target for practical jokes. On one occasion, they had an artist's model strip naked and perch on his lap. He dumped her off and hurried away, damning the corruptions of those who called themselves civilized.

Except for Journet, few of the visionaries and apostles active in the years around 1848 had ties with the life Murger made famous. Neither the requirements of artistic apprenticeship nor ambivalence toward bourgeois life determined their separation from society. Their estrangement was deeper, not conditional or assumed to be temporary, but inescapable, based on passions and beliefs that set them definitively on trajectories of their own. When Champfleury began to write about such people, he did not think of them as Bohemians. In fact, he complained that D'Ennery and Grangé's use of the term *bohémiens* was unfortunate because it led cardsharpers and con men to be confused with artists and other *bohèmes*. When

2. Jean Journet, in a lithograph by Courbet.

he published his articles together as *Les excentriques* in 1852, however, Champfleury was ready to forget this distinction. Now he located his whole gallery of eccentrics within Bohemia. His models were *bohèmes véritables*, true Bohemians, "often as mysterious as the sphynx, and always as indecipherable as the obelisk." He did not say exactly what made them belong to the type, but he did explain what made them stand out from other people in Paris. Their differences were expressed less often in clothing than in their physical features, their physiognomy, "which utopias, dreams, ideas have rendered bizarre." Citing the popular ideas of Swedenborg also employed by Balzac, Champfleury declared that "the body follows the path of the mind." Living in a different mental universe from their fellows made these Bohemian eccentrics look different, too.[24]

Champfleury's descriptions of his eccentrics as Bohemians may have been partly an attempt to capitalize on the interest in the term generated by Murger's play. But his portraits share an important feature with de la Hodde's and Chenu's depiction of Caussidière and other conspirators as Bohemians. Both viewed Bohemia as a sphere in which personal imagination and fantasy—about oneself and about society—were not restrained by the limits imposed in ordinary life. Conspirators like Caussidière lived in a world created by their own imaginations; this is precisely where Champfleury placed his eccentrics. In both perspectives, Bohemia was a realm of liberated fantasy. Life in the remote margins and dark corners of society allowed the mind a free play that the demands of a regular, orderly life constricted.

It was not in the agitated spring of 1848 that these links between Bohemia and revolution came into people's minds. There seem to have been a few—but only a few—references to Bohemia in the French press at that time. In April, one paper listed "a Bohemian existence" alongside prison slang and hands that bore the marks of barricade building as things prized by insurrectionists. In June and July, a short-lived newspaper called itself *Le Bohémien de Paris*; its politics were described as populist and ardently republican, but Bohemianism was not an explicit concern of its writers.[25]

The sustained interest in Bohemia as a source of revolutionary passions and energies emerged later, after the potentially most destructive social tensions had already been fought out.

The new notoriety Murger gave the term was not the only reason
for this. The conflicts at the center of the revolutionary struggles in
1848 itself either pitted those who controlled state power against
those excluded from it (a main issue behind the campaign against
the government that led to the violence in February), or else opposed the Paris workers to the rest of the nation (most obviously
the central question in the June uprising). Bohemia was at best
marginal to these events. But the fear of revolution did not end with
the return of relative stability during 1849. Political agitation continued, partly in anticipation of the presidential election scheduled
for 1852 (to prevent it was one reason Bonaparte staged his coup
the previous December). Within Paris, the improved economic situation and the defeat of June 1848 quieted the mood of the workers.
In this situation, the fear that revolution might be renewed came to
focus more than before on tensions within the middle classes, on
those bourgeois who held out against integration with existing society because it failed to match some purer vision they carried in
their minds. Whether those private visions would inspire public action was the question Jules Janin and Auguste Luchet debated when
Murger's play opened in November 1849. It was also the issue that
made Champfleury's eccentric prophets and de la Hodde's "democratic Bohemia" sources of anxiety. Did the free fantasy life of Bohemia generate energy to power utopian visions, or draw it away
into private enthusiasms? It was a question that could be neither
definitely answered nor ignored.

The dilemmas of Bohemian politics had still other sources. We can
identify and examine some of them through the career of Gustave
Courbet, one of the most remarkable participants in both Bohemia
and revolution during these years. In some ways, Courbet seems not
to belong in the company of those we have met in Bohemia so far.
He was an artistic talent of the first rank. His pictures were re-

3. Detail from a sketch by Courbet
showing himself (*center*) with Marc Trapadoux (*left*)
and Jean Ballois at the Brasserie Andler.

sented, even hated, by many of his contemporaries, but his abilities were noticed and valued early, too. Later artists and critics recognized him as one of the pioneers and founders of artistic modernism. The identity of Bohemian encompassed practically the whole of a personality like Murger's; it captured a much smaller part of Courbet's. Yet, his career suggests how the appropriation of art for self-dramatization, which opened the artistic life to nonartists, also made Bohemia a fitting and nurturing environment for certain forms of genuine innovation.

Courbet remained linked to Bohemia throughout his life. The Parisian cafés he frequented between the 1840s and the 1860s are among the locales chiefly identified with Bohemia through the middle decades of the century: during the 1840s, he consorted with the circle made famous by Murger at the Café Momus; for much of the 1850s, he was the central figure in an Alsatian beer hall often considered synonymous with Bohemia, the Brasserie Andler (see figure 3); in the later 1860s, he took part in the increasingly politicized café life of the Latin Quarter, where many future leaders of the Commune of 1871 were active. That Courbet remained voluntarily tied to Bohemia long after public recognition offered him an escape is a sign that for him Bohemian life possessed some essential attraction.

Courbet's family were landed farmers in the Franche-Comté. They were far from aristocrats, however. Although comfortable and respected, Courbet's forebears were simple local folk. During the revolutionary and Napoleonic periods, their politics had been decidedly on the Left: his maternal grandfather Oudot was a staunch Voltairean and supporter of the radical Republic of 1793. Courbet's father, Régis, a man of verve and high spirits, sometimes held local political office, and was known for a series of technical innovations and inventions aimed at increasing the yield of his lands. None of these paid off. Perhaps the elder Courbet was moved more by restless, overflowing energy than by clearly focused ambition. He was said to be an unstoppable talker.[26]

All these qualities made an imprint on Gustave Courbet. From the start, he seems to have been fiercely independent, convinced of his own talent, and deeply ambivalent about the path of social ascension toward which his family pushed him. Hoping to make him a lawyer, Régis Courbet sent Gustave to a strict school in nearby Besançon. The boy hated it, refusing to submit to its discomforts or discipline. Gustave was willing to break the connection to the land that had marked his family for generations, but not to let himself be molded by the rigid, predetermined pattern of education that made young men into typical bourgeois. It was while at Besançon that Courbet determined to become a painter. Within two years, he was in Paris, reluctantly supported by his family, and working to make himself an artist.

Courbet did not reject ambition. In Paris, he worked hard, copying the greats in museums, perfecting his technique, experimenting with styles, making connections. He lived frugally, determined to fulfill his family's hopes for the future as well as his own. His father's occasional reproaches were, he replied, "like the jab of a spur to an animal that's already pulling too hard." Gustave sent pictures each year to the Salon, the official government exhibition that provided artists with the public recognition and approval essential to finding buyers for their work. In 1844, he had his first acceptance, a self-portrait. He was pleased, but the success only intensified his ambition. "Small pictures don't make a name. I must paint a large picture that will make me decisively known at my true value. I want all or nothing." In 1849, he reassured his parents: "I am on the point of arriving because I am surrounded by people who are very influential in the papers and the arts and who are enthusiastic about my painting." He exaggerated the influence of his friends. But later the same year, his *After-Dinner at Ornans* won a gold medal, granting him the coveted privilege of exhibiting in the Salon without submitting his pictures to the official jury—increasingly hard-pressed and rigid in face of the mounting numbers of yearly submissions.[27]

But Courbet pursued his ambitions in his own way. He refused to attend classes where formal academic standards and techniques were taught (he did frequent some studios that provided models, but no instruction), nor was he willing to form his style after any living master. His *After-Dinner at Ornans* presented on a much larger scale the sort of intimate, domestic subject usually treated in the small dimensions of genre painting, raising the private and obscure to a status academic practice reserved for noted events of public history. The implied reversal of established hierarchies pushed the Romantic rebellion against classical standards in new directions.

Courbet's attack on tradition reached its full development in a new kind of realism. Saying just what Courbet's realism consisted in is not easy. Even those who applied the term to his art in his own day recognized its difficulties, since representing reality had been the purpose of painting in many times and places. But one thing was central to it: the absolute refusal of every form of idealization. The Romantics had rejected the academic demand that all artistic representation model itself on the timeless forms embodied in classical works. Yet their identification of artistic beauty with a purified vision inside an artist's mind only shifted the tension between artistic form and ordinary, everyday perception onto other grounds: in many ways, that tension was heightened rather than reduced. Courbet's realism sought to eliminate it, bringing art as close as possible to the direct reproduction of perception we associate with photography. Instead of the formal perfection aimed at in classicism, or the natural organic wholeness sought in Romanticism, Courbet's realism provided a visible world described by one recent critic as "broken up into innumerable irreducible particularities." Neither pattern nor ideal shaped the way individual people or objects were represented: every element was invested with "equal visual value." This was recognized by one of Courbet's contemporary detractors, who complained that his painting abandoned the ideal, defined as that essential element in all things that was "permanent, fixed, invariable, and therefore characteristic, submissible, and representable." Realism stripped objects of any link to a world beyond the visible and immediate present.[28]

Courbet's work was not without models in earlier painting—especially Dutch and Spanish artists outside the circle of classicism. But in addition to these exemplars in "high" art, Courbet patterned his work after the very different images and styles found in popular prints and illustrations. His figures were seen to have the flatness, rigidity, and naïveté found in the nineteenth-century approximation of the popular comic strip, the *images d'Épinal*. These awkward, unpretentious, innocently colored prints and painted lithographs, finished by part-time artists and sold by hawkers in small towns and countrysides throughout France, could be found in the homes of many ordinary people. Courbet's realism was not simply a revolt against inherited academic and learned traditions. It was also a direct strategy for linking high art with the tastes and experiences of the kind of simple country folk who were Courbet's own forebears.[29] The new style provided a pathway to artistic notoriety that accentuated Courbet's rural origins, his distance from the traditional world of art.

A similar manner of locating himself at a distance from urban, bourgeois Paris marked Courbet's personal style. He was famous for his rural patois, a colorful, explosive form of speech that gave pungency to his unconventional ideas and unrestrained feelings. Courbet's conversation had the flavor of rural songs and stories, like those collected by his friend and cousin Max Buchon, with their rough humor and barnyard expletives. The Brasserie Andler, which became Courbet's main hangout after 1848 (it was located near his studio in the rue Hautefeuille), was sometimes described as a rural village inside Paris.[30] That a major representative of Parisian Bohemia should have been so deeply colored by country life may seem surprising, given the usual assumption that Bohemianism was a quintessentially urban phenomenon. Yet, modern cities have always grown by drawing new blood from rural areas and small towns—a condition as true of the New York that made Greenwich Village a Bohemian center as of nineteenth-century Paris. Courbet was not the only major Bohemian figure to owe his sense of marginality to a need to keep in touch with his rural roots.

Courbet's origins gave him aesthetic and moral attitudes in common with the lower-middle class, from which an important segment of Bohemia was recruited. In artistic matters, the taste of rural people and of urban *petits bourgeois* was often similar. Both were said to prefer clearly outlined, uncomplicated, shadowless, and recognizable images like some Courbet would provide. Lower Parisian bourgeois like Murger and the Desbrosses brothers also shared with Courbet a mixture of ambition to move into the ease and luxury of the well-to-do, and anxiety about the moral laxity and corruption in established society. Courbet's beery, unbuttoned manner may seem very distant from the abstemiousness of the Water-Drinkers, but he shared with them a burning determination to make his way on his own terms, without any compromise. His goal, he told a friend in 1854, was the "unique miracle . . . to live from my art my whole life through without giving up a jot of my principles." It was the dream of the Water-Drinkers, never to be corrupted by the temptations of Paris, made good by the kind of talent none of them had. It seems significant that within the Café Momus circle, the people to whom Courbet was closest were Champfleury, a small-townsman (from Laon) who shared his interest in rural life and his determination to succeed, and Marc Trapadoux, the mystical eccentric who wrote the life of a Spanish saint and considered becoming a priest. Courbet remarked on Trapadoux's interest in the priesthood around the time he painted his portrait.[31]

One of the elements of his family heritage Courbet absorbed was its identification with the political Left. Politics were by no means always at the front of his mind; there were long periods—both in the 1840s and later on—when he seemed to have no political interests whatever. Yet the impulses that led him to be identified as a revolutionary artist—and to identify himself as a democrat and a socialist—were always present. He seems not to have taken part in any of the fighting during 1848, but he did design the masthead (modeled on Delacroix's famous painting of the 1830 Revolution, *Liberty Leading the People*) for a republican paper edited by Champfleury and Baudelaire. In 1849, he painted *The Stone-Breakers*, a portrait of rural poverty and hardship widely seen as bearing a political message. After he exhibited this and other pictures in the Salon that opened at the end of 1850, Courbet was repeatedly decried as the representative of radical democracy and socialism in art. Not only the subject matter but also the refusal of idealization at the center of Courbet's work marked him as the artist of the lowly, those for whom reality contained nothing more exalted than material needs and desires. To treat each object in a picture with equal attention, in a manner devoid of any ideal plan or vision, was the perspective of democracy: it recognized no distinctions of value, whether in aesthetics or society. This "exact representation of nature in all its triviality, without any choice or arrangement," Théophile Gautier declared, was natural to "the realist democratic school." In a letter of 1851, Courbet accepted these conclusions, declaring himself to be a socialist, democrat, and republican, "in a word a partisan of the whole revolution, and above all a *realist*." As he put it later: "The heart of realism is the negation of the ideal. . . . By arriving at the negation of the ideal and everything that follows from it I arrive fully at the emancipation of the individual, and finally at democracy."[32]

Looked at as a whole, the impulses and causes that moved Courbet seem difficult to harmonize: a longing for success and recognition; a blustery rejection of discipline; an identification with radicalism and revolution. What held them together in his psyche was their common derivation from a single animating center: his fierce individuality. Courbet's individualism was rooted in the determined independence of his peasant forebears, but it found expression as the searching, sometimes brooding quest for self-development characteristic of bourgeois society.

In Courbet's mind, to be an artist was inseparable from the full development of his personality: art was the vehicle of a wider self-development. In the credo he set down as a preface to the catalogue of works offered at his independent Realist Exhibition of 1855, he insisted that his purpose was not art for its own sake *(l'art pour l'art)*. He had become an artist in order to find "a justified and independent sense of my own individuality." He sought to interpret the ideas and spirit of his time in his own way, to be "not only a painter but also a man." Only thus could he create living art. A year or so earlier, he had written in similar terms to his friend and patron Alfred Bruyas, telling how he had refused an offer of favors from the Bonapartist government in return for his support. "I told him . . . that I was not just a painter but beyond that a man; that I did not paint to make art for its own sake but to conquer my intellectual liberty."[33]

Courbet's path to independence followed contours that suggest how young countrymen were being drawn into experiences that were modern, urban, and bourgeois, recasting the traditional desire for independence in terms of the more complex personal identities of modern life. Seeking to become an artist in Paris placed Courbet decisively on the modern and urban side of this divide. One sign of how directly he confronted it is in the series of self-portraits he undertook during the 1840s (and which he would continue in other forms later on). Occasionally, these show Courbet in a rural setting. But most of them show the young artist against a flat, uncommunicative background, emphasizing his isolation. Several place his eyes in shadow so that they do not look out at the spectator, as if they were absorbed in contemplation of some private or inner world. The shaded eyes link these self-portraits to one of Courbet's favorite themes: sleep. Sleep appears often in Courbet's art, as a moment "of entry into oneself and into nature without the obstructions and defense of the everyday waking consciousness." Such subjective self-preoccupation was part of the conquest of individuality that becoming an artist represented for Courbet.[34]

Hélène Toussaint has observed that Courbet's self-image in these portraits moves from elegant and dandyish to increasingly ragged and *débraillé*. He wrote about the most famous one, called *The Man with the Pipe* (figure 4), that it was "the portrait of a fanatic, of an aesthete, it is the portrait of a man disillusioned by the follies that have served for his education and who is seeking to seat himself in his principles." That quest led in difficult, even threatening, directions. Courbet told Bruyas in 1854: "In the society we live in, you don't have to go far to find emptiness. There are so many fools—it's so discouraging that one hesitates to develop one's intelligence, for fear of finding oneself absolutely alone." That sense of isolation was linked with the need to achieve a manner of painting whose originality would reflect Courbet's own personality and situation. "The more one distinguishes himself from others the

4. Courbet, self-portrait, called *The Man with the Pipe*.

harder it gets. To change a public's taste, its way of seeing, is no small thing; it is nothing less than to overturn what exists and replace it with something else. . . . Painting, when you think about it, is a state of frenzy, a continual struggle, a way of going crazy."[35]

To break free of authority and civilized social convention, Courbet found it necessary to abandon Paris from time to time. In 1850, he described this not simply as a return to the country but as entering into "la grande vie vagabonde et indépendente des bohémiens." This Bohemia may have been the literal one of the gypsies, but its ties to the one in Paris made the transition easy. It was at this time that Courbet exhibited in the Salon his portrait of Jean Journet (figure 2), Champfleury's archetypical Bohemian eccentric, and, like Courbet, a visible presence in Paris by virtue of qualities that marked him as an outsider there.[36]

In the notoriety that Courbet, like Journet, enjoyed, we come to a central and essential paradox in the persona of radical Bohemian outsider he constructed for himself. That identity expressed Courbet's anxieties and his deep sense of estrangement, but it was essential to his project of establishing himself—on his own terms—in the Parisian art world. Courbet's was a *succès de scandale*, but it was no less a success for that. The Salon of 1850, in which he showed the portrait of Journet, *The Stone-Breakers*, and *A Burial at Ornans*, made Courbet the most talked-about painter in Paris. The same works that marked him as a radical artist also "made Courbet's reputation, just as he had intended." He had discovered the fame that could come to a nineteenth-century artist through identifying himself fully with opposition to established social and cultural norms and practices.[37]

Courbet's social sensitivity is shown by the way he understood his own notoriety as a power that could put him into direct contact with the market for pictures, thus bypassing the traditional and official mode of organizing the relations between artists and the public through the Salon. Courbet never denied the importance of the Salon, and he continued to exhibit in it throughout his life. But, in 1855, he also set up his own private exhibition, making an immediate appeal to the public in a way that foreshadowed later practices by the Impressionists and their successors. Courbet's exhibition was conceived in direct rivalry with one planned by the Bonapartist government. In a letter to Bruyas, he told how he had repulsed the overtures of Bonaparte's intendant of fine arts, boasting that his private show would yield him forty thousand francs—much more than he could expect to earn in the official one. He even taunted the intendant, claiming that the government owed him fifteen thousand francs because of all the admission charges paid at previous exhibits by people who had come specifically to see Courbet's work. It did not matter, he insisted, whether they had come out of admiration or hostility.[38]

Courbet's appreciation of the way notoriety could be exploited by an artist whose underlying purposes were uncompromisingly serious shows how much more natural the existence of market relations in art seemed to him than to the Romantics of the 1820s and 1830s. For him, the market and the public who populated it were there to be exploited. A growing consciousness of the nature and importance of modern forms of publicity was visible at the same time in the Bohemian circles Courbet frequented in Paris. The audience for newspapers had been growing since the mid-1830s, and with it the opportunities for careers in journalism. The *petite presse* gave unknowns like Murger and Champfleury their start. The public it reached had different tastes and needs from the narrower readership of earlier, more expensive papers. Clear-sighted journalists like Charles Philipon were quick to learn how to appeal to it with a faster-paced, more assertive and amusing style of journalism often enlivened with lithographs or woodcuts. New forms of celebrity—popular novelists, elected political figures, even journalists themselves—provided expanded material for these sheets.

One of the aspiring young journalists whose careers were shaped in this world was Murger's friend and later biographer Nadar. After participating in an ill-fated attempt to liberate Poland in the spring of 1848, Nadar began a career as a political cartoonist. Gradually, he came to recognize the need for a more general kind of illustrated journalism, with pictures and short biographies of people who were coming to be known for this or that activity. The idea was clear in

his mind by the time Bonaparte's coup temporarily suspended political cartooning at the end of 1851. In 1852, there began to appear
the publications that soon became the *Panthéon Nadar*, a series of
brochures that combined group caricatures of well-known public
figures with brief, humorous biographies. The series was immediately successful, making Nadar himself famous. Out of this recognition that a new public sought contacts with new forms of celebrity,
Nadar moved from drawings and lithographs to a medium only then
becoming technically possible: photography. His portraits of practically all the celebrated in his time made up one of the great pio-
neer achievements in the early history of photography.[39]

Courbet knew Nadar and posed for him. He also seems to have
been struck by the *Panthéon* project; art historians now believe that
Nadar's groupings of the famous may have provided some inspiration for the great picture of 1854 *The Studio of the Painter*. Here,
in an extension of the series of self-portraits completed earlier,
Courbet showed himself at work. He was flanked by those who
helped him to understand his identity and achieve his goal at one
side, and those who provided material for him to paint on the other.
This was the main exhibit in the private showing of 1855: a fitting
centerpiece in the exhibition that demonstrated how aware Courbet
was of the new possibilities offered by the nineteenth-century public
and the forms of celebrity it made possible.[40]

Courbet's uncompromising devotion to his own individual development thus bound together the radical independence that set him
at odds with authority and tradition, and the self-conscious creation
of a persona whose very radicalism produced notoriety that could
be exploited for both artistic and commercial purposes. The man
whose art was identified with revolution knew how to navigate in the
world of the bourgeoisie. In fact, Courbet's relationship and attitude toward the bourgeoisie was a question directly raised in the
years he exploded into fame during the Second Republic. The picture mostly responsible for his sudden fame and notoriety was one
seen at the time as a kind of bourgeois group portrait, *A Burial at
Ornans*. Exhibited in the Salon that opened at the end of 1850, the
Burial was immediately recognized as something new in art—

Courbet called it his statement of principles—and it remains his most famous picture.

The *Burial* (figure 5) is a painting meant to be noticed: some ten by twenty feet in size, it contains over fifty near-life-size figures. Save for the gravedigger, who kneels near the edge of the trench, all are standing in positions determined by their place in the procession just arriving at the country grave site. The people are real inhabitants of Courbet's native town, including a number of his relatives; most posed for him there during 1849. Except for those in some sort of religious dress, most are in black. Several of the women and one man are weeping, but most of the faces are composed, apparently unconcerned, and many are painted with a relentless and unflattering fidelity. The priest and other church officials are especially notable—and were immediately criticized—for their heavy, everyday, secular appearance, their red faces and bulbous noses. The major elements of Courbet's realism are forthrightly proclaimed: its apparently haphazard composition, its equal attention to each individual figure, its absence of shadow, its insistent refusal of every form of idealization. To many contemporaries, the picture was simply ugly, even grotesque.

The political and social meanings in Courbet's picture were widely discussed when it was exhibited. Yet the reactions showed anything but agreement. Critics found—and still find—fundamentally different ways to view the scene. To some, the painter's intentions were to discredit religion and authority by presenting its representatives in a ridiculous light; one critic castigated Courbet for "the ignoble and impious caricatures of the judges, the local constable, and all those whom you have put round the open grave." From a different point of view, this sense of the picture's meaning was shared by Courbet's cousin, the socialist writer and active 1848 revolutionary Max Buchon. In his view, the picture revolved around the figure of the gravedigger, in real life a humble peasant whose central position in the canvas served as a modern, socially pointed version of the ancient truth that all were equal in the face of death. His place here was a kind of revenge for the degradation modern

5. Courbet, *A Burial at Ornans*.

life visited on the poor, as Courbet had shown it in his *Stone-Breakers.*[41]

To others, however, the picture had neither a destructive nor an antireligious meaning. One of these was the social philosopher Pierre-Joseph Proudhon, with whom Courbet established close relations in 1853, and many of whose ideas the painter took over or shared. To Proudhon, the picture's message was highly moralistic and even religious. It was not Courbet who degraded the meaning of such sacred occasions as funerals: it was modern society's own selfish materialism that robbed life of meaning. By refusing to idealize the scene, Courbet had simply drawn attention to the reality and the sources of modern sacrilege; in doing so, he called men back to the human dignity religion once embodied. The picture was like a sermon, an incitement to a moral ideal.[42]

A third view was put forward by Courbet's friend Champfleury. He agreed with Proudhon about the picture's fundamental commitment to objective, realistic depiction, but denied that any moral message could be read beneath the surface. Painting's mission was not to expose the social system, and Courbet had not sought to prove anything in *A Burial.* Yes, the picture showed the ugliness of modern life, but it also showed its beauty, the humanity and power in its acceptance of the ordinary. "Is it the painter's fault that material interests, small-town life, sordid egoism, and provincial pettiness have marked the faces with their claws, have made the eyes dim, have wrinkled the foreheads and stupefied the mouths? Many bourgeois are like that; Courbet has painted bourgeois." The achievement of the picture lay in its fidelity to the subject: "It is the modern bourgeoisie, full-length, in all its ridiculousness, its ugliness, and its beauty."[43]

Each of these views carries authority because all come from people close to Courbet and sympathetic to him. To find one or another definite political message in Courbet's painting can be justified by his declarations that he was indeed a committed democrat, socialist, and revolutionary. But he nowhere said that *A Burial at Ornans* embodied particular political views. He was "above all a realist" and many of his subjects—landscapes, flowers, portraits, nudes—

are hard to fit into an explicitly political conception of painting. The question to ask about the various interpretations of the *Burial* is not which of them to choose but how, separately and together, they help understand Courbet's relationship to what he represented there.

Champfleury was not the only contemporary to describe the people depicted as bourgeois; yet that way of regarding them is not without problems. For one, these bourgeois were country people. Some critics referred to Courbet's subjects as "country bourgeois" or "half-bourgeois." Moreover, their economic and social positions were diverse: some were hardly more than rural workers, one was a shoemaker, and they were depicted side by side with comfortable landowners and village officeholders. The central place of the gravedigger—in real life, a humble vineyard worker—makes the point Max Buchon insisted on: this was a community whose cohesion depended on the membership of its lower elements.

Such was the world out of which Courbet himself came: its dimensions defined his own social identity. Among those present are his father and mother, his grandfather, his three sisters, his cousin Buchon, and his good friend the musician Alphonse Promayet. Even though the painter left himself out of the scene, we are in the presence of many elements for yet another self-portrait. It is also a portrait that highlights many important features of French society at the time: in particular, its fluidity of social boundaries and identities. The truth about many people who claimed bourgeois status in the mid-nineteenth century was that they were not far removed from their origins in the popular classes or from the rougher life of the countryside. The aesthetic of the picture underlines that social perspective. By refusing to idealize the individuals or to depict them in a manner that continued the traditions of earlier styles associated with the French royalty and aristocracy, Courbet emphasized that the position even of the scene's notables remained tied to popular life. Rejecting the standards imposed by the traditional forms of aesthetic hierarchy weakened the force of social hierarchy, too. These were bourgeois too close to ordinary folk to support aspirations upward, toward aristocracy.

To read *A Burial at Ornans* in these terms is to tie it firmly to the language of contemporary social perception and debate, particularly as it was sharpened by the revolutionary crisis of 1848. In 1850 appeared the *History of the February Revolution* by Alfred Delvau, an eclectic young socialist who had served as an aide to the prominent politician Ledru-Rollin. Delvau was also a familiar figure to Bohemian circles in Paris: in addition to the little book on *grisettes* quoted above, he wrote an account of café life that Courbet illustrated, sympathetically described the conditions of poor street artists and carnival performers, and wrote a biography of Murger. In his view, the central issue of French politics in the mid-century was whether the bourgeoisie would recognize or try to deny its links with the common people. The bourgeoisie was bound to the *peuple* "by a kind of moral plexus, an original tie, a primordial nerve." During the July Monarchy, however, elements of the bourgeoisie had tried to constitute a new aristocracy, cutting its connections with those beneath. The spirit of this new regime was egotism and money worship. Yet, Delvau did not "want to calumniate the bourgeoisie too much, because, risen out of the people, it must return to it one day." Similar sentiments were often voiced by Proudhon: "The present, firmly established distinction between the two classes of workers and bourgeoisie is simply an accident of revolution. The day when the common people constitute the majority . . . will be the day when they both fuse forever."[44]

For Courbet as for Delvau, the immediate political implication of this social perspective was that the bourgeois should continue to uphold the Revolution, supporting a strengthened republic with a determined social program. The people gathered for the *Burial* include several unmistakably ready to carry on this political task. Close to the center appear two men dressed as "Republicans of 1793," representatives of the radical social democracy produced by the most advanced phase of the Great Revolution. In the background appear Max Buchon, whose radical politics we have already noticed, and Jean-Antoine Oudot, the maternal grandfather whose republicanism and Voltairean convictions Courbet admired. Oudot had died a year before; to include him was to make a clear statement. This bourgeoisie was Courbet's own class, and it contained the sources of his politics.

At the time Courbet painted and exhibited the *Burial*, these political questions were central to the future of the Second Republic. After the defeat of the June 1848 uprising in Paris and the election of Louis-Napoleon Bonaparte in December, much of the nation's political activity moved into the countryside. Bonaparte's term was for four years, and according to the constitution, he could not succeed himself. The possibility of choosing a new and different president, one genuinely committed to the Republic and social reform, existed, if only the mass of voters outside Paris could be organized. That organization was undertaken in many rural regions with remarkable success, as the interim elections of 1849 and 1850 demonstrated. Central to the campaign was a group called *démoc-socs* or—like Caussidière's police—Montagnards after the radical deputies of 1793. The movement they hoped to organize was an alliance of rural and small-town bourgeois at the head of a larger grouping of poorer citizens best characterized as *peuple*. It was a politics based on precisely the sense of commonality between bourgeoisie and common people Delvau invoked. That Courbet's painting could be seen to carry such a message is revealed by the comment of one fearful critic who found in it "four black pallbearers sporting *démoc-soc* beards, Montagnard turnouts and hats *à la Caussidière*."[45]

A Burial at Ornans is a criticism of the bourgeoisie, to be sure, but it is a criticism from within, an attempt to bring the social sources of Courbet's own personality into harmony with his sense of how the values and energies they contained could be absorbed and continued. The tensions animating Courbet's work are not those between the bourgeoisie and another class (as a recent study of Courbet has imaginatively but I think wrongheadedly argued) but inside it. They are the same tensions Courbet acted out in his life. As Courbet's recent biographer observes: "Bourgeois individuality evokes unresolved conflicts, for that is its nature. [In *A Burial*] Courbet is at once realistically defining his rural-bourgeois origin, his sense of community, and his achievement of individuality."[46]

Courbet's *Burial* brings us back to his ties with Bohemia. It cannot be called a Bohemian painting—not even in the sense that some of his self-portraits and his portrayal of Trapadoux can be and have been. But it is the art of a man for whom Bohemia became a crucial field of self-expression. Courbet's roots in the world of the *Burial* were responsible for much of the inner conflict he felt in Paris, helping to shape his search for individuality at once toward success and toward rebellion. In the painting the ambivalence he and his fellow Bohemians dramatized in their lives became the subject of his work. His career shows that Bohemia could shelter artists more powerfully gifted than a Murger, provided they pursued art not only for its own sake, but also as a way of coming to terms with the dilemmas of individuality that artists and nonartists alike faced in modern society.

CHAPTER 4

The Poet as Dandy and Bohemian: Baudelaire

ALL BY ITSELF, Charles Baudelaire's involvement in Bohemianism would be enough to signal Bohemia's important place in the development of modernist literature. Undeniably a great poet, Baudelaire was also a remarkable translator (of Edgar Allan Poe) and critic, of both literature and painting. He provided continuity between the Romanticism of the early nineteenth century and the schools of symbolism and decadence that ushered in the twentieth. His inexhaustible imagination creates a universe both sensual and visionary, where many boundaries of ordinary experience dissolve. Yet, he was insistently and self-consciously oriented toward the real challenges of his time—the experience of great cities, the implications of bourgeois ascendancy, the spread of democracy, the promise and threat of revolution.

Baudelaire was never a Bohemian by choice. He hated the tawdry unkemptness, the dirt and disorder, of Bohemian life, and especially its ready confusion of art with such a life. His preferred personal style was elegant, refined, aristocratic, self-contained. Above all, he cared about real poems and pictures, the finished products of artistic imagination; his idea of the artistic life emphasized the disciplined training required to produce them. He was drawn to Bohemia neither by the lack of personal resources Murger thought led artists into it, nor by the suspicion of urban refinements that fueled Courbet's ambivalence. Yet, there is no doubt that from his twenties to the end of his life Baudelaire lived in Bohemia: he shared its friendships, frequented its circles and cafés, partook of the messy, *débraillé* style he despised. His explorations and dissections of the range and meaning of Bohemian life, although never so persistent or direct as those by Murger and others, were searching and deeply probing.

There is something strange and mysterious about Baudelaire's Bohemianism—as about much else in his history. Once, when trying to paint him, Courbet remarked on the rapid evanescence of his person, a mobility of identity that frustrated the attempt to capture his image. It seems that Baudelaire experienced much of that frustration himself: the boundaries of his selfhood were never stable and assured. Baudelaire exploited his instability, his sense of being within and beside himself at the same time, in many of his poems, sounding the depths of psychic mysteries with a fascination only intensified by the pain of exposing wounds and raw nerves. One of his most haunting autoportraits is as a self-torturer:

> I am the wound and the knife!
> I am the blow and the cheek!
> I am the limbs and the rack,
> Both the victim and the torturer!

Living in the Bohemia he hated was part of this self-torture, confronting himself with his own painful and deeply rooted conflicts. Yet, to invoke the psychological language of masochism would be to cloud over the element of conscious and determined exploration in Baudelaire's Bohemianism. He was drawn to Bohemia—as to much else that caused him pain—by the intuition that it encompassed an inescapable feature of the relations between art and reality under modern conditions.[1]

Baudelaire took an oblique and backward path into Bohemia, passing through a persona in many ways its opposite: the dandy. Baudelaire defined dandies as those who had "no profession other than elegance . . . no other status but that of cultivating the idea of beauty in their own persons." They polished their personalities into hard reflective surfaces. "The dandy must aspire to be sublime without interruption; he must live and sleep before a mirror."[2] For a brief time in his early twenties, Baudelaire lived in a manner that approached these formulas. Enjoying a sizable inheritance, he rented an apartment in an elegant seventeenth-century house on the Île Saint-Louis, the Hôtel Lauzun, toward the end of 1843. His high-ceilinged rooms were luxuriously fitted out and he dressed in a style that matched them.

By this time, the notion of the dandy already possessed a considerable history. Although the word was used to describe someone with pretensions to elegance in the 1760s (remember the feather in Yankee-Doodle Dandy's cap), its career really took off during the Napoleonic Wars after 1800. That was the era of the most celebrated and imitated of all modern dandies, Beau Brummell. Brummell's name remains alive today; it is harder to recall the person behind it. He was, as his reputation suggests, a model and dictator of fashion, the person whose manner of dress and behavior all those who aspired to social recognition had to follow. Yet his own styles were not foppish and extravagant: on the contrary, they marked a simplification of current ideas about male dress. His trousers were straighter, his coattails shorter than those common before. What distinguished him was the cleanliness and polish of his costume. The elegance he represented depended on care and judgment, not excess.[3]

Brummell achieved his position in a self-consciously aristocratic society; his power depended on the influence he exercised for a number of years over the prince regent, the man who later became George IV. Yet Brummell's own claims to aristocratic position were weak. His father was secretary to Lord North, but his grandfather had cut a much more meager and shadowy figure, something between a valet and a hotelkeeper. Brummell did not seek to hide the obscurity of his origins. On the contrary, he emphasized it, cutting his siblings despite their successful and fashionable marriages, and making his ancestry out to be lowlier than it was. Brummell was, like others in his country and generation, a self-made man. His dandyism was molded of the aristocratic externals: appearance, bearing, pretension, disdain. These were the elements of upper-class life most easily appropriated by one who had no claim on the deeper and subtler web of family tradition and connections. His was a model of aristocracy that rested on pure, intensely cultivated personality. He stood "on an isolated pedestal of self."[4]

These features of Brummell's person suggest why it was that dandyism appeared at the moment when aristocracy was losing its grip on European society. When the barriers to entry into the aristocracy were relatively permeable, the need for clear external signs of belonging to it was all the greater, and the association between aristocracy and personal cultivation made it easier for aristocrats to absorb the new energies coming from below. In fact, much of Brummell's reputation was created by the new periodical press aimed at the upwardly aspiring middle classes. Dandyism reconstructed aristocracy so that it could become a vehicle for the modern exaltation of the individual self. "Like those philosophers who establish a higher obligation above the law, dandies, by their purely private authority, set up a rule higher than the one that governs those circles that are most aristocratic and most attached to tradition; and by the acid of their humor and the solvent of their grace, they manage to impose this rule that is, at bottom, nothing more than the audacity of their own personality."[5]

The last comment comes from Brummell's first French biographer, the chief literary representative of dandyism in mid-century Paris (and a longtime friend of Baudelaire), Jules Barbey d'Aurevilly. In Barbey's hands, the image of the dandy came to represent an exalted vision of independently developed personality. Brummell had been "a great artist in his fashion; only his art was not some special one, exercised at a particular time. It was his very life." Central to this image of life as art was its self-containment. Brummell's power was in the effect he achieved over others, but he was never really dependent on them, as a performer may be on his audience. He placed himself inside a labyrinth, fascinated others from afar: "He preferred astonishing others to pleasing them." He loved and sought pleasures, but even in drunkenness he never abandoned control over himself. "His indolence allowed him no enthusiasms, because to have an enthusiasm is to get passionate about something, to care about something, and to care about something is to show oneself inferior to it." Such images were the stuff of idealization; reality was not so sublime. Brummell himself may have presented a figure recognizably close to such an ideal in the days of his greatest celebrity and influence; by 1816, however, he had been out of favor at court for several years and he was forced to flee England for France to escape his creditors.[6]

The notion of dandyism first entered France at about the same time, riding a wave of Anglophilia that greeted the end of the Napoleonic Wars. The figure of the dandy altered to fit the demands of its new environment. To put it simply, the cultures and styles of the various classes were more at odds with each other in the country that had experienced revolution than in the one that had avoided it. From the start, dandyism became a counter in the campaign of the French aristocracy to reassert its traditional preeminence. For the *lions* and *incroyables* who represented dandyism in France, its purpose was to exalt modes of dress and behavior self-consciously opposed to the values of utility and equality spawned by the Revolution. This presence of dandyism in the public life of the day grew still more marked during the crisis of 1830 and its aftermath. Revolution might oust the aristocracy from political dominance, but its supporters took their revenge by demonstrating their superiority on the boulevards of the city. What characterized the French *lions*, Barbey himself observed in 1836, was the ferocity of their hatred for the upstart bourgeois.[7]

This meant that dandyism in France never really possessed the qualities of indifference, imperturbability, and self-containment that Brummell was able to give it in England. Political passion robbed the French dandy of his Olympian detachment. This was certainly the case with Barbey himself during the mid-1830s, when he sought to embody the dandy ideal in his own person. One of his ideas of happiness was to thrash an insolent cabdriver. There were other reasons why Barbey's dandyism failed to measure up to his idealized account of it. The son of a Norman family with a long pedigree but only moderate wealth, Barbey took up journalism to supplement his income. Still, he didn't have the cash to support his dream of refinement and elegance. He would spend hours on his toilette, getting himself up finely and constructing a facade of luxury; but the mask was thin. Behind it lurked a sense of hollowness, of falseness, which Barbey described in his private diary. "Here I am back in my solitude. My room in disorder, bottles opened hurriedly at the moment of leaving and left that way, give off the odor of what they no longer contain; clothes all over the furniture, books and papers strewn about! This life weighs on me. No attachments, no home life, a nomad's tent that can be folded up in a few hours and carried away." The round of dressing up and visiting fashionable places appeared endless, but there seem to have been a fair number of days when Barbey went without eating because he could not afford to buy dinner in the pretentious restaurants he frequented. He appears to have taken his meals in a cheap student café for a time.[8]

From the start, then, French dandyism tended to collapse the distance separating it from the opposite theater of self-dramatization, Bohemia. Years later, Barbey denied that he had ever been Bohemian himself. Bohemia represented "one of the most contemptible features of a society without stability." He had felt poverty indeed, but "I never abandoned my white gloves." Perhaps by then he had forgotten the sordidness of his earlier life and his earlier self-image as a nomad in a tent. By the late 1840s, Barbey had given up his primary identification with dandyism. He returned to the Catholicism abandoned in his youth, and in his novels celebrated his native Normandy and its heroic aristocracy.[9]

Other famous dandies of the time reveal similar problems and tensions. One of the most celebrated was Roger de Beauvoir, for a time Baudelaire's neighbor in the Hôtel Lauzun. Beauvoir was a talented poet and writer, but his life-style brought him more fame than his works. Possessed of a sizable fortune, he was the central figure in a noted group of bons vivants and men-about-town during the 1830s and 1840s. Several other writers created characters based on him, including Balzac. His carefree life took a harsh and troubled turn, however, when he made what turned out to be a disastrous marriage to an actress who had been his mistress. The two were incompatible, and their quarrels soon expanded into public confrontations and lawsuits. By the mid-1850s, Beauvoir had grown bitter and depressed; his old elegance was gone and he passed much of his time in Bohemian haunts and cafés. He became a friend of Murger, and at the latter's death in 1861 wrote a letter to *Le Figaro*, asking that Murger's last mistress receive some financial aid.

Beauvoir's dandyism would have revealed its inner tensions and weaknesses even if it had not ended in descent toward Bohemia. He exercised his talent for turning life into art variously, but one field of ingenuity was particularly remarked by his contemporaries: his debts. Beauvoir's fortune was large enough (his claim to aristocracy went back only a generation) to support him independently until his death in 1866. But there were many moments along the way when insouciance or extravagance left him unable to pay his bills. In nineteenth-century France, a creditor could obtain a legal judgment against a debtor, after which a bailiff seized the latter's goods to pay the claim. Especially after 1850, bailiffs seem to have been frequent visitors at Beauvoir's house. His manner of dealing with them was unforgettable. On one occasion, he had a servant talk the representative of the law into climbing up ten feet onto a wooden horse, used to display a suit of medieval armor, in order to examine a saddle said to be worth much more than the debt in question. Once the bailiff was there, the ladder he had climbed quickly disappeared; the poor man was left stranded for several hours. Another time, Beauvoir asked a deputy how much he earned for keeping watch over the dandy's goods: five francs a day. Beauvoir offered him ten, plus meals, to work for him. Offer accepted: Beauvoir dressed the compliant man (who turned out to have a talent for acting) in a Turkish costume and established him, mute, smoking, and eloquent of gesture, in a corner to add interest to his parties.[10]

These pranks might be just as funny had some other cause inspired them. The fact remains that they were the fruit of Beauvoir's clash with the economic morality of bourgeois society. He was subject to the ordinary rules of credit and debit, but before giving in he made them look ridiculous next to his own capacity for living by the sheer force of imagination. It was precisely the power those rules and their representatives could finally claim that made him generate the theatrical facade of superiority to them. Not aristocratic independence and indifference, but the clash between aristocratic values, focused into a cult of individual personality, and the encroaching world of bourgeois morality defined the space in which the French dandy flourished. In a similar way, Barbey d'Aurevilly's veneer of luxury and elegance was polished as a shield against the power that bourgeois values and mores were gaining.

Notwithstanding the contrast between the dandy's aristocratic elegance and the Bohemian's unkempt shabbiness, the two often came together. When Honoré de Balzac populated Bohemia with young men not yet able to make their mark in French life, he had his mind on aristocrats excluded by the Bourgeois Monarchy of Louis-Philippe: the chief model for his Prince of Bohemia, La Palferine, was Roger de Beauvoir. Murger himself sometimes liked to affect dandified styles, and on one occasion convinced a friend to join him in dressing up to the hilt—only to go off at once to one of his favorite dingy bars. Flaubert's Bohemian, Hussonet, is also described as dandyish in appearance. Through the century, representatives of Bohemia and dandyism regularly joined in a series of pairings. Alfred Delvau told about one such couple often seen in a cabaret frequented by artists and writers during 1849–50. It consisted of Rodolphe Bresdin, the talented but eccentric and perpetually down-and-out engraver who had served Champfleury as model for Chien-Caillou a few years before; and Louis L'Herminier, who Delvau thought had been one of Balzac's models for the elegant La Palferine: a personage who illuminated his surroundings with his wit and "perfumed them with the flowers of his incomparable elegance." Another explorer of Bohemian haunts, Philibert Audebrand, told of a similar pair during the 1850s, Marc Bayeux and Charles Coligny. "If they shared the same kind of life, that is the same chance existence, the same love of inactivity, the same appetite for celebrity," they contrasted with each other in personal style. "One was handsome and given to elegance, the other prided himself on being ugly and affected a careless exterior." According to

Audebrand, the two friends had taken opposite sides in the barricade fighting of June 1848—the dandy Coligny with the forces of order, the Bohemian Bayeux with the rebels. During the 1870s, the Bohemian-dandy symbiosis reappeared, as we shall see, in the more famous pairing of the unkempt and (for a time) radical writer Jean Richepin and the elegant practitioner of psychological fiction Paul Bourget. Still later, it would be found in the circle around Paul Verlaine, in the 1890s.[11]

Baudelaire's aspirations to dandyism—and his entanglements with Bohemia—can now be seen in full relief. To Baudelaire, dandyism meant something beyond elegance, even beyond self-cultivation: the triumph of personal artifice over nature, which was a central tenet of his aesthetic. In "The Painter of Modern Life" (where he projected his own vision of how art should present contemporary experience onto the illustrator Constantin Guys), he rejected the materiality of nature and the potential violence of natural impulses: "Everything that is beautiful and noble is the product of reason and calculation." Fashionable dress, personal decorations, even cosmetics he praised as means of rising above nature, symptoms of "the taste for the ideal that floats on the surface of the human brain." Women, expert in those arts, were bearers of the aspiration to improve and adorn nature. Elsewhere, in the intimate journal *My Heart Laid Bare*, Baudelaire typically reversed himself about women, identifying them with the raw natural impulses of hunger, thirst, and sex; the dandy was now the opposite of the woman, precisely because she was the creature of nature. In "The Painter of Modern Life," dandyism was "a kind of cult of the ego which can still survive the pursuit of that form of happiness to be found in others, in woman for example." Its independence of such ordinary, natural satisfactions brought dandyism "close to spirituality and to stoicism."[12]

Baudelaire's image of the dandy was more elaborately idealized and rarefied than Barbey d'Aurevilly's, with which he began. Perhaps for that reason it was also more difficult to embody in real life.

Baudelaire gave many hints in his writings why dandyism escaped him. For one thing, dandyism flowered in periods of social transition, "when democracy has not yet become all-powerful and when aristocracy is only partially weakened." It was "the last flicker of heroism in decadent ages . . . a setting sun." In these images, Baudelaire recognized his own aspiration to dandyism as a doomed attempt to stand against the most powerful currents of his time. He saw himself as already infected by the viruses of the democratic age. Writing about the aristocratic poet Théophile Gautier, Baudelaire praised him for his detachment, which shielded him from any taint of vulgarity; Baudelaire himself lacked this self-possession, and his inability to hold back the antagonisms he felt toward philistines lowered him to their level. "Recriminating and indulging in opposition, and even demanding justice, is there not in all that a certain degree of 'philistinization'? How easily we forget that to hurl insults at a crowd puts us ourselves amongst the rabble [*c'est s'encanailler soi-même*]."[13]

Baudelaire's penchant for such undandylike behavior was not limited to literary polemics, but displayed itself in the political sphere. At most moments in his life, Baudelaire hardly seems a person of strong political passions. Most of his writings ignore politics altogether, and several warn of the dangers that come from mixing politics and literature. Yet he supported and publicized the working-class poet Pierre Dupont, and in his famous essay "The Salon of 1846," insisted that criticism become "partial, passionate, political." Above all, Baudelaire was deeply caught up in the Revolution of 1848. Not only in February, but even in the radical days of June, Baudelaire was on the barricades, always with the rebels; between times he wrote for two political papers. In 1849, Murger's friend Jean Wallon expected Baudelaire's poems to be "socialist verses." In fact, his political notions were neither clearheaded nor stable, mixing conservative sentiments with radical impulses in a murky but heady brew. In February, personal passions were near the surface: he exhorted a crowd to go after his stepfather General Aupick, a dashing soldier who had married Baudelaire's widowed mother at a time when the seven-year-old seemed to have her all to himself. In June, a lust for excitement and even danger surfaced: one of Baudelaire's friends told of meeting him just after the insurrection had been defeated. He was "nervous, excited, febrile, agitated. . . . I had never seen Baudelaire in such a state." His exaltation drew him toward martyrdom. "They've just arrested Flotte," he said. "Is it because his hands smelled of powder? Smell mine!"[14]

Years later, Baudelaire looked back on what he called his "intoxication in 1848" with detachment, but never with indifference. The Revolution, he observed, "had only been amusing because everybody built utopias just like castles in Spain." This placed his own enthusiasm under the sign of liberated fantasy we have seen others associate with 1848. To Baudelaire, such intoxication flowed from regions that were far removed from the aspiration to refinement and spirituality. Literary reminiscences played a part, but they were given force by a taste for vengeance and a *"natural* pleasure [Baudelaire's emphasis] in destruction." The reciprocal madness of the bourgeoisie and the people in June was associated with a "natural love of crime." The contradiction between such impulses and the dandy's self-contained elevation of artifice above nature was explicit: "Can you imagine a dandy talking to the people, except to make them ridiculous?"[15]

One might expect that once the revolutionary excitement waned, Baudelaire's interest in politics must have receded. Sometimes he spoke as if it had. In 1852, he declared that Bonaparte's coup of December 2, 1851, had "physically depoliticized me." The effect was only temporary, however. In 1859, he wrote to Nadar: "Twenty times I have persuaded myself that I would never again be interested in politics, but every time an important question arises I am taken up with curiosity and passion." Yet, Baudelaire's was never the political passion of a straightforward and loyal republican, of the sort Nadar might hope to find in him. In 1865, in his last comment on politics, he wrote: "As for me, when I agree to be a republican, I do evil knowingly. Yes! Hurrah for the Revolution! Always! In spite of all! But me, I am no dupe, I have never been a dupe. I cry *Hurrah for the Republic* the way I would cry: *Hurrah for*

Destruction! Hurrah for Expiation! Hurrah for Punishment! Hurrah for Death!" He would be happy to be the victim, but willingly play the torturer, "in order to feel the revolution in both manners." The republican spirit, he concluded, was a kind of infection, flowing in modern veins like smallpox or syphilis.[16]

What ultimately made dandyism an unstable identity for Baudelaire was his susceptibility to passions that broke through the shield of indifference. Politics was not the only form such passions took. Closer to his heart were the passions that animated art itself.

Baudelaire made the tie between passion and art clearest in "The Painter of Modern Life." Here he praised Constantin Guys (always covered with a thin veil of anonymity as Monsieur G.) for possessing the true dandy's character and worldly understanding. But the dandy "aspires to cold detachment, and it is in this way that M. G., who is dominated, if ever anyone was, by an insatiable passion, that of seeing and feeling, parts company trenchantly with dandyism." The dandy was blasé by policy: this the artist could never be. Clearly, Baudelaire thought of himself as animated by the same artistic passion for seeing and feeling. That passion took one special form that emphasized how far it was from dandyism: a love of the crowd. The dandy was the opposite of the vulgar crowd, as the isolation of truly aristocratic artists like Gautier showed. Not so the painter of modern life: "The crowd is his domain, just as the air is the bird's, and water that of the fish. His passion and his profession is to merge with the crowd."[17]

Baudelaire sometimes had reservations about his closeness to the ordinary inhabitants of cities, but here it was the source of positive pleasure. The idler given to passionate observation found it an immense enjoyment "to choose his dwelling in the multitude, in the ebb and flow, the movement, the fleeting and infinite." Baudelaire plunged into the depths of Paris in search of experiences that could fulfill his "passion for seeing and feeling." He loved the city for its bandits and prostitutes, its "monstrosities blooming like a flower," because every departure from the norms of ordinary life opened up a space where the imagination could expand to its own limits. This vagabond search for experience, unimpeded by fixed and regular

habits of life, was precisely what Baudelaire understood by Bohemianism in *My Heart Laid Bare*, the one text where he specifically
identified himself with it: "To glorify the vagabond life, and that
which may be called Bohemianism: the cult of multiplied sensation."[18]

Here we are no longer in the presence of the dandy Baudelaire of
the Hôtel Lauzun but the other Baudelaire: the penniless inhabitant
of dingy hotels, the friend of prostitutes, the celebrant of inebriation, the explorer of drugs. That these features of his life came to
dominate it had much to do with the tangled relationship between
Baudelaire and his family. After passing his *baccalauréat* at the age
of eighteen in 1839, Baudelaire rejected their attempts to turn him
toward a diplomatic career. He lived for a time in the Latin Quarter,
passing his time with a typically rowdy and adventurous group of
students and others with intellectual pretensions—none of whom
apart from Baudelaire himself ever made a mark on the literary
world. He began to experiment with drugs, and probably contracted
the syphilis from which he died in 1867. Before long, his companions, with their skeptical opinions and profligate behavior, frightened Baudelaire's mother. Caroline Baudelaire was a romantic and
intermittently indulgent but also anxious and conventional woman.
Her union with the much older man who was Baudelaire's father
had been a matter of convenience; her second marriage, to the
dashing and handsome but entirely respectable General Aupick,
was a love match that also fulfilled her longing for a stable and regular life. Her son's refusal or inability to conform to a similar model
alternately provoked horror and pity, making it impossible for her
ever to regard him as a responsible adult.

In 1841, she and General Aupick arranged to remove Baudelaire
from his dangerous environment by sending him on a journey to
India. Whether he ever arrived there is debated. Probably he went
only part of the way, to Réunion in the Indian Ocean; certainly he
returned to France at the beginning of 1842. A few months later,
his twenty-first birthday brought him the inheritance that supported
the elegant life of the Hôtel Lauzun. This was the time when Baudelaire acquired a mistress with whom he had a deep and mysteri-

ous relationship for many years, the mulatto actress Jeanne Duval. She was the Black Venus who inspired many of his most erotic poems; both on her later testimony and others, however, their liaison was never physical. Jeanne's presence in the Hôtel Lauzun, together with Baudelaire's continued closeness to people like those he had known before, hardly reassured his anxious family. Their fears about his future were not without foundation: in two years, Baudelaire succeeded in spending not just his sizable income, but a good part of his capital as well. In 1844, the family obtained a court judgment declaring Baudelaire incapable of managing his own affairs and appointing a legal guardian to control his finances. From then on, he received only the monthly income on his remaining inheritance, and was unable to touch the principal.

Now the carefree and expansive Baudelaire disappeared; perhaps his own extravagance might have done away with that side of him before long anyway. What replaced him was the driven, haggard figure who stares bleakly at us from the contemporary photographs. A suicide attempt in 1845 led to a momentary reconciliation with his family; once the harmony broke down, Baudelaire's existence took on a permanent dreary instability: living in hotels or furnished rooms, full of projects that seldom came to fruition, perpetually short of cash. This is the Baudelaire we meet in his letters, unendingly pleading to his mother for money to help him escape from his sordid and disorderly life. In 1847, he complained that he had been forced to stay in bed for three days because he lacked clean linen to put on or wood for his stove. In 1851, the confusion of his life made productive work impossible. In 1853, the same; poverty and disorder prevented him even from keeping appointments. In 1854, his question to himself was: could he dress in the morning, or did he have to stay in bed for lack of clothes? In 1855, he had to change his residence six times in one month, living where plaster fell off the walls, sleeping amid fleas, unable to receive his letters. Repeatedly he told his mother that a few weeks of a stable existence—supported by extra money—would allow him to put his projects enough in order so that he could start a new life. It never happened.[19]

By the end of the 1840s, Baudelaire was firmly installed as a part of recognized Bohemian Paris. Among his close friends and associates were Courbet, Champfleury, and the arch-Bohemian Alexandre Privat d'Anglemont. Baudelaire could be seen at Momus, the Brasserie Andler, and other Bohemian locales. He appeared, next to Murger, in Champfleury's fictionalized account of that world, *The Adventures of Mademoiselle Mariette*. That he still tried to dress well, one observer noted, made him stand out from the other Bohemians, but did not separate him from them. Champfleury recalled that during the 1850s, Baudelaire's appearance could change radically from one day to the next, his perfumed hair, redolent of refinement and beauty, suddenly replaced by a bizarrely shaved scalp, with head and shoulders hanging in despair.[20]

One of Baudelaire's literary passions gave added prominence to his Bohemian features: his sponsorship of the American writer Edgar Allan Poe. Baudelaire discovered Poe around 1847, when a translation of his story "The Black Cat" appeared in a French newspaper. In 1848, his own first Poe translation appeared, "Mesmeric Revelation." It was during 1852—following Bonaparte's *coup d'état*—that Baudelaire began to give sustained attention to Poe. He had first learned English as a child from his mother, who was born in England; improving and refurbishing his knowledge of the language, Baudelaire now translated enough Poe stories to fill a volume published in 1856. Baudelaire's involvement with Poe rested on a deep identification. The American was, to use a term that fascinated both men, Baudelaire's double in the more thoroughly modern and democratized land across the sea. Both wrote literature of mysterious and tortured self-examination; both experienced the isolation and misunderstanding common to modern writers.

In his essays on Poe's life and works, Baudelaire intimated many points of similarity between the two writers. The typical American's view of Poe called up his "unkempt poet's life, his alcoholized breath that would have caught fire in a candle flame, his vagabond habits." Yet Poe was "a being created to breathe in a more aromatic world." His appearance was not unkempt by choice; on the

contrary, he often appeared "handsome, elegant, correct." One
editor who visited him was "struck beyond measure not only by the
perfection of his manners, but also by his aristocratic physiognomy
and the perfumed atmosphere of his modestly furnished apartment." That such a man was reduced to a life of poverty, and suffered a death from alcoholism that was "almost a suicide," was the
fault of the society that—in France, too, as the recent suicide of
Baudelaire's friend Gérard de Nerval showed—could make no
place for troublesome and unconventional poets. "For Edgar Poe
was an embarrassing man. Apart from the fact that he wrote with a
fastidious difficulty and *in a style too far above the common intellectual level to be paid well* [Baudelaire's emphasis], he was always
stuck in money troubles and often he and his sick wife lacked the
most necessary things."[21]

In this portrait, Baudelaire highlighted the features of correct-
ness and elegance the common image of Poe neglected, but he
found virtues in the other side, too. One trait that made Poe larger
than life was his drunkenness, and Baudelaire was at pains to justify
it. That so solitary and unintegrated a person should flee to drink
was not surprising. It was an escape from grudges, anguish, insults,
a kind of "preparatory tomb." But the bottle also contained something essential to Poe as an artist: most of his best pieces of writing
were either preceded or followed by a bout of unrestrained drinking. Observing this unlocked the secret of Poe's drunkenness:
"There exist in intoxicated states not only dream linkages, but also
mental connections that need the medium that gave birth to them in
order to reproduce themselves." Poe's drunkenness was a mnemonic device, "a method of work, an energetic and fatal method,
but appropriate to his passionate nature. The poet learned to drink
the way a careful literary man practices making notebooks. He
could not resist the desire to find again the marvelous or terrifying
visions, the subtle conceptions he had met in a previous storm; they
were old acquaintances who drew him imperiously, and in order to
link up with them again he took the path that was most dangerous
but most direct."[22]

Baudelaire nowhere described Poe as a Bohemian: he was too intent on rescuing him from images of immorality and disorder to allow the word. Given the portrait he drew, however, it is not surprising that some who read it did. One of these was no less than the chief representative of dandyism, Barbey d'Aurevilly. In 1858, in an article entitled "The King of the Bohemians, or Edgar Poe," he admitted Poe's talent as a writer, but insisted that he was a perfect Bohemian. From Barbey, now a self-conscious Catholic, the term was no compliment. For him, Bohemianism was a characteristic product of the materialistic society that had abandoned any shared spiritual commitment for the anarchic principle of pure individuality. Poe's writing represented that principle to perfection. It was characterized by sensual egotism, a determined disdain for tradition and education, and "the search for emotion without restraint, or at any price." Poe embodied the Bohemian condition, the man estranged from belief in anything outside himself, and who therefore "lived intellectually by the random occurrence of his thought, his feelings, or his dreams." His death, in a gutter after a drunken bout, was "the Bohemian death, fruit of Edgar Poe's Bohemian life." Barbey explicitly rejected Baudelaire's suggestions that society was to be blamed for Poe's fate. What he took from society was greater than what he objected to in it: he was, in fact, a pure emanation of the spiritless modern sinkhole of isolated egotists that had reached its most fully developed form in America.[23]

Baudelaire was deeply wounded by the article. He regarded Barbey as one of his few real friends, and felt that the attack was directed against him. The quarrel was made up, but not before Barbey repeated his insistence that Poe was a Bohemian, indicating that he intended the term to apply to Baudelaire, too. Referring to a poem by Baudelaire's friend Théodore de Banville with the line "Vive la Sainte Bohème," he concluded: "You even use it about yourselves." The tone of Barbey's remarks aside, his view of what Bohemia meant was not so far from Baudelaire's. "The search for emotion without restraint, or at any price," was only a negative way of saying what Baudelaire meant by "the cult of multiplied sensation." Like Barbey, Baudelaire recognized that the principle of modern life and art was individualism, which he discussed at length in "The Salon of 1846." The dandy focused his energy on the cultivation of his own person.[24]

Despite Baudelaire's distaste for many features of Bohemia, it seems that he accepted Bohemianism as one pole of attraction and repulsion in a field where dandyism was the other. Baudelaire saw human life—and notably his own—as determined by a series of binary oppositions, dialectical pairs whose contradictory character collapsed in the real flow of experience. The images of himself as "the wound and the knife . . . the victim and the torturer" provide one illustration. Much more famous is the comment in *My Heart Laid Bare*: "There exist in every man at every moment two simultaneous postulations, one toward God, the other toward Satan." This declaration has often been cited as a frame for comprehending Baudelaire's seemingly contradictory impulses toward spirituality and eroticism, refinement and dissipation. In some ways, dandyism and Bohemianism, with their respective associations of aristocracy and the crowd, can be located in such a vertical system of aspirations and desires, too.[25]

But the polarity that most illuminates the relationship of dandyism and Bohemianism in Baudelaire's mind is the one with which he begins his personal reflections in *My Heart Laid Bare*: "On the vaporization and the centralization of the *Self*. Everything is there." Baudelaire compared the *Moi* to water, expanding to become vapor, then contracting back into itself. These polar forms of selfhood corresponded to the figures of the Bohemian and the dandy. Taken together, they defined both the psychology of creativity and the conditions of personal development.[26]

Many times Baudelaire depicted the artist as a virtuoso of self-diffusion. Merging with the crowd, he multiplied himself through fragmentation. He was "a kaleidoscope endowed with consciousness . . . an ego athirst for the non-ego, and reflecting it at every moment in energies more vivid than life itself, always inconstant and fleeting." The poet was "like those wandering souls who go looking for a body, he enters as he likes into each man's personal-

ity. For him alone everything is vacant. . . . The man who loves to
lose himself in a crowd enjoys feverish delights that the egoist
locked up in himself as in a box, and the slothful man like a mollusk
in his shell, will be eternally deprived of. He adopts to his own all
the occupations, all the joys and all the sorrows that chance offers."
The sexuality of his entry into others was not merely implicit. Indeed, ordinary love was a paltry thing compared with such "divine
prostitution of the soul," giving itself unhesitatingly to whatever
and whoever came along. But the experience also applied to relations with inanimate objects in nature. A tiny sail losing itself in the
monotonous blue immensity of sky and sea on an autumn afternoon: "All these things think through me or I through them (for in
the grandeur of reverie the ego is quickly lost!)."[27]
   All forms of intoxication partook of this evaporation, diffusing
the self in a foreign medium and preparing it to receive the shape of
things outside. Baudelaire in one prose-poem exhorted his readers
to flee the burden of time—like Poe—through drunkenness:
"Drunk with what? With wine, with poetry, or with virtue as you
please. But get drunk." He sought political involvement as *ivresse*
because it was a means of expanding the self by identifying it with
the larger world of movement and action outside. But the most intense intoxication was found in drugs. Baudelaire experimented
with drugs at various times in his life, both in groups and by himself, and he wrote about his own and others' experiences in two
essays: "Wine and Hashish," and "Artificial Paradises." He had
many cautionary things to say about drug taking, but he always
maintained that resort to drugs reflected the human being's desire
to rise above himself, to escape "the heavy shadows of ordinary
daily existence." "The frenetic taste of man for all the healthy or
dangerous substances that exalt his personality, testifies to his
greatness. He always aspires to warm his hopes and raise himself toward the infinite." So effective were drug-induced states of self-
vaporization that in them "the contemplation of external objects
makes you forget your own existence, and you soon confuse yourself with them." What was merely a metaphor in poetry became a
reality: you compare your desires or feelings to a tree or a bird; be-

fore you know it, you are the tree or the bird. Contemplate the smoke that arises from an opium pipe: "The idea of a slow, continuous, eternal evaporation takes hold of your mind. . . . By a singular equivocation, a kind of transposition or intellectual *quidproquo*, you feel yourself evaporating, and you attribute to your pipe . . . the strange ability to *smoke you*."[28]

This evaporation of the self—into crowds, into nature, into causes, into other people, into states of natural or induced reverie—was an essential part of artistic creativity. To be able to recreate the world of experience the artist had to have identified himself so fully and intently with the world outside that he could reproduce objects in it from within himself. Art did not proceed directly from nature but from an image imprinted on the brain. It was mnemonic, animated by "the absorbed intenseness of a resurrecting and evocative memory, a memory that says to every object: 'Lazarus, arise.' " It was in pursuit of the experiences that could stock this memory that Baudelaire would glorify vagabond Bohemianism, "the cult of multiplied sensation."[29]

Pervasive as these ideas were in Baudelaire's consciousness, they were matched and opposed by the equally numerous images of *concentration*, a quality shared by the artist and the dandy. In an essay about Delacroix, Baudelaire characterized his favorite modern painter's style by its conciseness and unostentatious intensity, "the habitual result of concentrating all one's spiritual forces toward a given point." Baudelaire quoted Ralph Waldo Emerson, "The hero is he who is immovably centered," a notion he found closer to the Stoic Seneca than to Bostonian Puritanism. "The maxim that the chief of American Transcendentalism applies to the conduct of life and the sphere of business can be equally applied to the domain of poetry and art. One could just as well say: 'The literary hero, that is the true writer, is he who is immovably centered [*concentré*].' " This centering was partly concentration in the mental sense. Beyond that, it meant a single-minded direction of personal energies, a disciplined summoning of the will. The centered individual was fully himself, his needs and actions shaped from within and not by anything outside: "The man of genius wants to be *one*, therefore solitary." Baudelaire associated this distillation of self with work that formed and strengthened the will, and with the calculation and artifice that the dandy and the poet substituted for nature. Sexual love was its opposite because it gave the self over to dependency on another. "The bothersome thing about love is that it is a crime where one cannot do without an accomplice." More pointed and desperate: "To screw is to desire to enter into another person, and the artist never goes outside of himself."[30]

Every form of pleasure appeared in Baudelaire as a departure from the centripetal imperative of self-concentration. Pleasures that dissolved the ordinary boundaries of the self were means of escaping the restrictive boundaries of time. But work was another escape from time. "At every instant we are crushed by the idea and the sensation of time. And there are only two ways to escape this nightmare—to forget it: pleasure and work. Pleasure uses us up. Work fortifies us. Let us choose." These were the terms in which Baudelaire's ultimate rejection of drugs was cast: their experience of instant gratification killed the desire for work. "Let us admit for a moment that hashish gives, or at least augments, genius; those who say so forget that it is in the nature of hashish to weaken the will, and that it thus gives on one side what it takes away on the other, namely imagination without the ability to profit from it." Quoting a contemporary writer, Baudelaire concluded: "The great poets, philosophers, and prophets are those beings who arrive by the pure and free exercise of their will at a state where they are at once cause and effect, subject and object, hypnotizer and sleepwalker."[31]

Baudelaire sometimes insisted on his right to contradict himself, but these contradictions were regular and methodical: vaporization and centralization were fundamentally different experiences, but both had to be constantly pursued and finally unified by the artist. The person who first lost himself in the world in order to impress its shape on his spirit had then to condense his being into himself like vapor returning purified from the surrounding air. Then he was ready to give forth a distilled vision that was both nurtured by external reality and born wholly from within. Multitude and solitude had to be "identical terms, and interchangeable by the active and fertile poet." Delacroix showed how the circle could be squared. He sought the privacy of a secret place, not for debauchery, but "for inspiration, and there he gave himself over to veritable drunken bouts of work. 'The one prudence in life is concentration; the one evil is dissipation,' says the American philosopher we have already cited." In the end, the self-intoxication of the artist had to arise not from impressions or sensations nurtured by anything outside himself, but from the heady experience of creative work itself.[32]

If "the cult of multiplied sensation" was one side of artistic creativity, therefore, it was never the whole of it. Baudelaire insisted on what it left out in several places where he discussed writers identified with Bohemia in his time. In 1861, the year of Murger's death, Baudelaire wrote a preface for a novel about Bohemian Paris by Léon Cladel, *Les martyrs ridicules*. The ridiculous martyrs of the title were idealistic young men who sacrificed their lives to unrealistic visions of literary greatness. They bore considerable resemblance to Murger's *Bohème ignorée* (he, too, refered to them as *martyrs ridicules*), but Cladel treated them with still more skepticism and reserve. In one scene, his two main characters attend a revival of Murger's play (one was being given in 1861) and on the way home converse in language that exactly reproduces the play's dialogue, even unconsciously calling each other by the names of its characters. In Cladel, however, Rodolphe finds himself confronted not with the faithful Mimi, but with the flighty and egotistical Musette.[33]

In his preface, Baudelaire admired the "sinister power of caricature" this scene revealed. It was not Murger who deserved such treatment, but his followers, those who "do not know with what bitter raillery Murger spoke about Bohemia." These writers marched under the banner of realism, a term Baudelaire employed both as a jab at Courbet (from whom he had become estranged during the 1850s), and as a reminder that Murger stood for the equation of literature with "slices of life." Believing that art could be an immediate reflection of spontaneity and feeling, these Bohemians justified their disorderly and undisciplined lives in the name of pursuing experience. "From their absolute confidence in genius and inspiration they derive the right not to submit themselves to any training. They do not know that genius (if indeed one can name the indefinable seed of the great man in this way) must, like the apprentice acrobat, risk breaking his bones a thousand times in private before dancing for the public; that inspiration, in a word, is only the reward of daily practice."[34]

Baudelaire believed that people of real talent were turned away from the path of literary achievement by the impulse to identify art with the life Murger had written about. One of these was the poet who often symbolized the misunderstood and estranged genius to the mid-nineteenth century, Hégésippe Moreau. Baudelaire described him as a poet of talent whose real merits one would never know, because he had refused the work that might have developed his abilities. He had not needed to work, because the public viewed his chaotic life—similar in externals to that of real poets like Poe and Nerval—as the sign of his poetic nature. Living like a nomadic Arab in the midst of civilization, "his unhappiness was counted in his favor as work, the disorder of his life as misunderstood genius." He lived as a child of nature, doing as he liked, singing when the impulse took him, like the birds. His views about literature "permit the poet to consider himself a prating bird, light, irresponsible, untrappable, and moving his house about from one branch to another."

In part, the impulse to view art in this way came from Moreau himself, but it also arose from his public. Many people felt they did not deserve the fate society meted out to them, and it made them feel better to believe that all unrecognized and misunderstood people were kept from success by their qualities, not their defects: by the depth and strength of their feelings. Thus, Moreau was able to make himself into "a kind of ideal persona, damned but innocent, dedicated to undeserved suffering from his birth." He stood for the unrecognized talents and unrealized strivings in everyone.[35]

In other words, the Bohemian identification of art with a certain mode of living, rather than with work, had its strongest roots among nonartists. The bourgeois, fearful of real visionaries like Poe but cozy with the likes of Moreau, encouraged the equation of genius with an inner core of passion and sentiment. Romanticism's image of the passionate, isolated genius had originally been a reproach to the bourgeois society that gave him no nurture. But since 1830, the Romantic attack on the bloodless grayness of modern life had been avenged by writers who learned to turn its own weapons against it. Leaders of the counterattack had been the literary schools of moral uprightness *(honnêteté)* and common sense. In the works of writers like the dramatist Émile Augier, the bourgeoisie had appropriated Romanticism for its own purposes. Was poetry the realm of true feeling? So be it—what feelings were more true than the healthy passions of love for family and society? Poetry could flow as easily out of the sentiments that cemented respectable life as out of those that weakened it. In one of Augier's plays, an ordinary bourgeois woman exclaims to her lawyer husband at a moment of tenderness: "O poète! je t'aime!" Baudelaire expressed his horror of this scene in several essays. To equate art with mere feeling satisfied the bourgeois' need to find poetry in their everyday lives. In the end, such a view made it impossible to say where ordinary life left off and art began.[36]

The surprising conclusion was that the most characteristically Bohemian attitude toward art—its identification with feeling and sentiment—was precisely the bourgeois view. Both neglected the conditions of real artistic production for some form of pure natural feeling. In bourgeois writers like Augier, this feeling could be found within ordinary life rather than, as for Murger's followers, at its margins. But both invited the confusion of art and life. The Bohemian project of living life in the name of art dissolved real artistic production in the life that was substituted for it. Thus, it allowed the bourgeois to believe either that poetry was as well represented by lawyers as by poets, or that all poets were like Moreau, self-indulgent do-nothings, to be pitied, exploited, or made fun of as the occasion arose.

It was to counteract this simultaneously Bohemian and bourgeois tendency that Baudelaire often insisted on the difference between ordinary feeling and the special enthusiasm that arose from acts of the imagination. "Sensibility of the heart is not absolutely favorable to poetic work. An extreme sensibility of heart can even harm it." The aspiration to a higher form of beauty was a strictly mental excitement, "an enthusiasm altogether independent of the passion that is intoxication of the heart. . . . For passion is *natural*, too natural not to introduce a tone that is wounding and discordant into the domain of pure beauty." The point had particularly to be made against "the partisans of inspiration in spite of all," those writers whose confidence in the power of spontaneity allowed them to believe that the jottings emanating from their disorderly lives would turn into real poetry. The exemplary upholder of this distinction was no other than Poe, who, far from trusting to innate talent or free spontaneity, insisted on the part science, work, and analysis played in literary composition. One of Baudelaire's earliest Poe translations had been the essay "The Philosophy of Composition," in which Poe presented "The Raven" as a poem constructed out of pure rational calculation. Poe worked hard to assure that his will could control the appearance and return of those happy visions and poetic inspirations whose precious rarity made them seem to come from some source of grace exterior to men. "He also submitted inspiration to method, to the most severe analysis."[37]

This attempt to place the poetic imagination under the sign of an enthusiasm that could be cleanly separated from natural sentiment and controlled by rational analysis marks the point where Baudelaire's conception of art departed furthest from the Bohemian "cult of multiplied sensation." Read in isolation, these passages would suggest that Baudelaire regarded his own artistic enterprise as wholly independent of the Romantic search for real feeling and experience. Indeed, that is just what his many celebrations of dandyism and aristocracy in literature were meant to suggest. Artists he greatly admired—Constantin Guys, Gautier, Delacroix—were free of any taint of Bohemia. By now it should hardly be necessary to insist on the point that the same was in no way true of Baudelaire himself. The theory of art as nurtured by a special aesthetic passion separate from natural feeling was a kind of wish fulfillment, a projection of Baudelaire's idealized but unrealized self-image. He admitted as much in his description of an opium-dreamer who was none other than himself: "He completely confuses dream with action, and his imagination heating itself up more and more before the enchanting spectacle of his own nature corrected and idealized, substituting this fascinating image of himself for his real individuality, so poor in will, so rich in vanity." One of his last comments on the relations between his own art and life was the most honest: "Into this horrible book I have put all my *heart*, all my *tenderness*, all my (travestied) religion, all my *hatred*, all my *bad luck*. It is true I will write the contrary, I will swear up and down that it is a book of *pure art*, of mummery and acrobatics, and I will be lying like a con man."[38]

Because he remained mired in his sordid and exasperating life, his vision of escaping from it through work never achieved the calm and self-containment he saw in Gautier or Delacroix. Instead, it became the center of an obsession. The dingy hotels, ever-present creditors, energy wasted on financial tricks and expedients, all left him feeling debased, wasted, unproductive. In his later years, Baudelaire was possessed by the need to counteract the effects of indulgence through a life of extreme regularity and devotion to work. "To be cured of everything, poverty, sickness, and melancholy, I lack only one thing," he wrote in one journal entry, "the taste for work." His obsession with work as a cure for his ills sometimes took on Franklinesque features: "Work for six days without respite." "Nothing is done save little by little." "The only way to forget time is by making use of it." The respectable bourgeois who decried the immorality of Baudelaire's poems would have smiled warmly on these maxims.[39] Baudelaire sought to associate himself so intensely with the image of the "immovably centered" artist precisely because his own life was so painfully stretched out between the extremes of self-indulgence and obsessive work.

*   *   *

Along the line joining those extremes we must locate Baudelaire's involvement with Bohemia. His was not the only *Bohème* pulled between indulgence and asceticism: the relations between Murger and the Water-Drinkers moved between the same alternatives. "The cult of multiplied sensation" recalls Murger's description of Rodolphe's attachment to Mimi as a self-conscious determination to keep alive the heated agitations of youthful passion. And the link Baudelaire established between the Bohemian trust in spontaneity of feeling and the bourgeois equation of literature with sentiment fits easily into the often recognized chain of connection between Bohemia and bourgeois life. For him, too, Bohemia was less a genuine departure from the ground of bourgeois experience than an accentuation of certain of its features; the tension between work and indulgence, *travail* and *jouissance*, was part of bourgeois life, too.

For Baudelaire, the injunction to live life for the sake of art could never be turned around to substitute personal drama for the finished products of mind and hand. Yet, part of him remained within Bohemia, caught up in the condition Barbey d'Aurevilly defined as the basis of Bohemian art when he designated Poe as its monarch: the radical individuality of modern life. Baudelaire was intensely aware that modern art had to rest on individual experience. The nineteenth-century artist, he believed, could neither draw on nor attempt to impart any shared system of values of the sort that had sustained imagination in an earlier age. Modern painting and poetry had to create meaning out of the confrontation of an individual consciousness with the world of direct experience. It was "a suggestive magic containing at once the object and the subject, the world outside the artist and the artist himself."[40] Because modern art had only the resources of individual personality to invest in the transcendence of everyday life, it had to employ dark energies that had seemed inimical to art before. The visionary possibilities of every form of intoxication, alcohol, drugs, sexuality, politics, had to be cultivated despite the dangers to personal integrity they posed and the inescapable loss of control they brought in their wake. Baudelaire took on the most problematic and challenging of the consequences that arose from art's turn to individual experience: that artists had now to construct the ideal out of the very elements of existence that threatened to corrode and dissolve it. This was the burden of artistic modernity, which Baudelaire shouldered more self-consciously than anyone else in his time. Here was the real heroism of his life: not his aspiration to a self-contained dandyism, but his acceptance of the Bohemian need to live for the multiplication of sensation, with all its attendant sordidness and degradation. His discovery would loom ever larger as successive artistic movements found themselves retracing the same paths. It was Baudelaire—the Baudelaire who found himself in Bohemia against his will—who lurked behind the modernist avant-garde's later discovery that the boundary between art and the life of art could no longer be maintained.

CHAPTER 5

The Other Bohemia and Its Uses

MURGER BEGAN HIS *Scenes of Bohemian Life* with an attempt to reassure his readers. His Bohemians had "no relation with the Bohemians whom some boulevard dramatists have made synonymous with crooks and assassins. No more are they recruited among the bear trainers, sword swallowers, sellers of safety chains, professors of con games, participants in the social depths of commerce, and the thousand other mysterious and cloudy producers whose principal industry is not to have any and who are always ready to do everything save the good." Murger's disclaimer reminds us that the term *bohémien* had been part of the vocabulary that described the Paris underworld for centuries. Murger and his friends were always concerned to distinguish their form of deviance and social descent from this other one. Nadar, who contested Murger's sense that Bohemia ought to be a place from which to enter bourgeois society as it existed, also insisted that neither poverty nor temptation had ever pushed him and his friends outside the confines of law and morality. Yet the barrier between the two forms of Bohemia was not so rigid and impassable as Murger and Nadar wanted to believe, and we can sometimes get a glimpse of the other side.[1]

In December 1849, while crowds were applauding Murger's play at the Varieties Theatre, several Paris newspapers carried the following story. A man of about thirty with a thick beard and a worried look appeared in criminal court. Charged with destroying property and vagrancy, he gave his name as François-Auguste-Armand-Achille Daille-Lefebvre. Asked his profession, Daille-Lefebvre re-

125

sponded *artiste dramatique*—he was an actor. The property involved was a large show window said to be worth twelve hundred francs. He readily admitted to breaking the window. But the accusation of vagrancy stuck in his craw: "What does it matter! Who knows better than I that I am a Bohemian? [*que je suis bohémien*]." Why had he broken the window? To get arrested. At least in prison he would eat. The value of the window meant nothing to him, he insisted: twelve hundred francs or twelve sous, what was the difference? "I am a dramatic artist, I demand to live from my art; but as you know, since February 1848 the arts have fallen into the mud, into the crud, into the ————. [Nineteenth-century papers would print *crotte*, but not *merde*.] People don't want to raise them up again and France will die from that. What have artists become? Beggars! Bohemians!" Here Daille-Lefebvre called his judge's attention to the lottery to aid poor artists then being advertised all over Paris. "The arts are lost; I am an artist. Do with me as you like: put me in chains or tell the Odéon to open its doors to me, and then we'll see."

This was not Daille-Lefebvre's first brush with the law. Two years earlier, he had broken another window, and served a sentence of three months. This time, the presiding judge ordered a psychiatric examination; its conclusion was that he was not mad, and capable of standing trial. He was sentenced to a year. What sort of "dramatic artist" was he? Not one of a recognized sort, it seems. Ten days after his sentencing, the court received a letter from the Association of Dramatic Artists informing the judge that careful inquiries showed he had never belonged to any association or organization of actors. Had he really been one, he could have addressed himself to their relief committee. Its chairman proudly insisted that no real theatrical artist would have had to employ reprehensible and unworthy expedients in order to survive.[2]

Yet there is little reason to doubt Daille-Lefebvre's claim to be a theater performer. At his trial, he named the leader of the troupe for which he had worked and described it as giving performances in the Parisian suburbs. (The prosecutor had laughed at that.) We know little enough about such troupes, but Privat d'Anglemont, whose career will draw our attention later in this chapter, described some of them in an account of the down-and-out sections of Paris whose interpreter he became at the beginning of the 1850s. "Intellect is represented there by two or three worker-poets; by those who write topical songs for poets who recite in the squares; and by some *auteurs dramatiques* or play-cutters [*coupeurs de pièces*]. Their *métier* consists in abridging popular melodramas." These latter took the plays that were making a splash at the time, gothic dramas, Napoleonic epics, revolutionary tableaux, and "made them available to the marionette theatres that go about the fairs. Some of these *dramaturges expurgateurs* have made quite a reputation in this sort of work, by taking out the most number of scenes while still leaving the main lines of the story intact." Daille-Lefebvre was an actor, not an author, but the world Privat described cannot have been either socially or culturally very distant from his. It shows us a different kind of artist and a different kind of Bohemian—equally self-conscious, it should be noticed—from those for whom Murger sought to reserve the term.[3]

Strictly speaking, Daille-Lefebvre did not belong to the group of shady characters and criminals Murger sought to exclude from his official Bohemia. Yet his life as artist and Bohemian was such that criminality more than once seemed to him a preferable alternative. We must also remember the laugh with which the prosecutor greeted the name of the acting company: he probably believed that the claim to represent art masked more questionable activities— from begging to real crime. Other people held this view, and it was enshrined in popular books by Victor Hugo and Eugène Sue. The ease with which itinerant street artists could be confused with ordinary beggars and criminals appears again and again in the single source that tells us much about such people: the records of their brushes with the law.

Nineteenth-century representatives of authority looked on these marginal figures with a suspicious eye, and the courts often treated them harshly. After 1848, the severity may have been colored by fear that popular performers were spreading subversive doctrines.[4] But the treatment was just as severe when its grounds were not political. In August 1843, a family of street entertainers were hauled into court because some of their children were accused of begging. The father, Lemêle, gave his occupation as *saltimbanque—physicien—sauteur—équilibriste*; he was an acrobat who performed in streets and at provincial fairs. But in his reply to the charge that he was training his children to become beggars, he placed his family's activity in a wider sphere. "The artist receives a salary," Lemêle insisted, "he does not ask for charity. Every day you see musicians in cafés and restaurants, playing the violin, the guitar, the triangle, who receive the reward of their talent according to the idea people have about it. Would you flatter these honorable virtuosos with the name of beggars? Well, my child does the same." The defense was rejected. The two children were taken from their parents and placed in a house of correction, one for four, the other for five years. The severity of the sentence reminds us how rigid and cruel nineteenth-century justice could be. It also suggests how alien the lives of street performers must have seemed to upholders of law and order. What was art to Lemêle was somehow a threat to society and morality in the eyes of his judge. We begin to understand why Murger insisted on the distinction between his Bohemia and the other one.[5]

The story of the Lemêle family was repeated many times. Just the next month another father was accused of encouraging his daughter's mendicancy by allowing her to exhibit a dancing monkey in the Palais Royal Garden. To the father, his daughter's activity was part of a respectable calling. "I did not think there was any profession more honorable than that of artist," he protested. In July 1846, a mother and her daughters were arrested. The court reporter described them as "a whole family of Bohemians." (The word was *bohémien*, but they were not gypsies; they lived regularly in Paris and had ordinary French names.) They did not deny that they begged, but they also sang. The mother insisted that singing in the streets was their regular occupation; they had always done it; and if it seemed less than respectable to the judge, it was real work—hard and tiring—to those who engaged in it.[6]

Musicians and acrobats were not the only street artists who occupied this equivocal social space. In November 1846, a thin, yellow-complexioned, and raggedly dressed man appeared in court, also accused of begging. Yet his crime was more complex. He had been going from door to door, attempting to sell poems written on a topical subject: the effects of a series of recent floods. He had not been altogether honest; thinking the verses would sell better, the writer claimed they were the work of the popular poet Béranger. Although he admitted to lying about the authorship, the would-be poet stoutly rejected the charge of begging. "If selling the product of one's own talent and imagination is begging, then I no longer have any sense for my mother tongue." This was not the first time he had tried such verses: the idea of writing lines on topics of current public interest had come to him earlier, and he had written about fashionable marriages and notable political events. The mysterious unnamed poet claimed to have served as a private tutor for a time, "but I am no longer wanted anywhere." Hence, he had tried to make use of his talent and imagination in another way. Perhaps only chance or eccentricity separated him from the world of the *petite presse*.[7]

Selling verses house to house was not uncommon in mid-century Paris. In the summer of 1849, a woman writer—*femme de lettres,* in the court reporter's language—was accused of mendicancy for hawking her own writings from door to door. Her dress and manner were respectable, even elegant, and she was let off. Some who were not may have been simply begging under the cover of literature, like a certain Gilles, who asked people for money to get his songs published. But others clearly belonged to a popular culture that developed outside of official channels, like the poet who in the summer of 1850 described himself as going about "from village to village, to offer verses, songs, compliments, for festivals, engagements, baptisms, marriages, burials, and other occasions." He also provided poetic copy for businesses of all kinds, including cake decorators.[8]

In 1846, a seventy-five-year-old man described as "the dean, without question, of all the writers in Paris" appeared in court as a defendant. He was not a journalist or novelist, however, but a public letter-writer. His specialty was drawing up petitions for people desirous of some official favor or consideration—such as having taxes reduced. He was said by some who knew him to have been one of the defenders of the Tuileries Palace against the revolutionary insurgents on the famous night of August 10, 1792. But he was accused of fraudulent representation: claiming to be able to help his clients through an influence in high places that he did not in fact possess. The journalist who wrote up his case found his appearance evidence that he had been able to salvage nothing from the shipwrecks of his life. He carried his whole fortune on his person. On his head he wore an old-fashioned wig, so decayed and disordered that it allowed his rare shocks of gray hair to poke through. "The knot of his cravat is in a problematic state; his coat, of an impossible shade, betrays long and loyal service, and his fantastically shaped hat is additionally remarkable for the long goose feather" that drooped down into his beard.[9]

Murger was aware that the possible linkages between such forms of Bohemian existence and his own were not merely linguistic. In one story, Rodolphe competes with just such a public letter-writer for the job of composing a tombstone epitaph. Murger warned that one of the dangers of remaining too long in the *Bohème ignorée* was that "either one can no longer get out, or one tries to get out by dangerous stratagems, and ends up falling into a neighboring Bohemia, whose form of life belongs to a different jurisdiction than that of literary physiology." No doubt he knew about cases like those of the ex-students who in 1849 were sentenced for running an illegal business as examination stand-ins. Finding themselves without resources, the young men had set up a tutoring service for candidates to the *baccalauréat*. Little by little, they had begun to take the exams for their clients.[10]

Unlike Murger, some successful writers did not shy away from recognizing the ties between the two worlds. Baudelaire several times associated himself symbolically with clowns, acrobats, and other lowlife performers, and in a book about *saltimbanques*, published in 1853, his friend and fellow poet Théodore de Banville upbraided successful artists who turned their backs on street performers. To Banville, these lowly figures embodied something characteristic of all artists. "What is the *saltimbanque*, if not a free and independent artist who accomplishes prodigies to earn his daily bread . . . without the hope of ever getting into any academy?" Banville saw, if Murger did not, that these marginal artists also had to turn their everyday existence into a work of genius.[11]

For some young writers during the 1850s, the passage through Bohemia meant something much closer to joining this lower world than to taking on the features of Rodolphe and Marcel. What drew them in that direction, and what does their experience tell us? One was a figure who enjoyed considerable notoriety as a journalist for a few years, Charles Pradier. Pradier seems to have written only for small, usually fly-by-night papers, but he was noticed by more established ones. An article in the popular *Le Siècle* in March 1855 told what was unusual about his mode of making a literary career: he hawked his verses in cafés and squares. He was careful to obtain an official license first, thus saving himself from run-ins with the police. His care to stay within the law, together with the suggestion by several commentators that he had some formal education, suggests that his social origins may have been fairly solid. But his desire to make a literary career led him to depart from them. One contemporary described his thinking as follows: "Is the intellectual worker [*ouvrier des choses intellectuelles*] fatally condemned to poverty and the hospital? No! The poet armed himself with a courageous resolve—I shall go into the public square, he said to himself, I will speak to the people, they will buy my poetic products, the way they buy the thousand products of Parisian industry hawked in the open air."[12]

Pradier seems to have embarked on this course around 1852. Perhaps it brought him some success, since in 1855 he was able to start up a weekly newspaper. Its name was *The Bohemian, Le Bohème*, and it lasted from April 1 to the end of June, with a final appearance at the end of December. The first issue proclaimed Bohemia to be a realm in which art was treated as a sacred priesthood, a divine mission for which its faithful stood ready to make every necessary sacrifice. But the same article also contained a more radical and challenging image, depicting Bohemians as smugglers, or at least as travelers made to act like smugglers by the official guardians of society's cultural entry points. Their attempts to storm the heights of public acceptance were resisted by those who had already found a place there. The Bohemians needed all their vitality and energy for their struggle against "the monopolizers of publicity" who policed the world of literary legitimacy.[13]

This identification of Bohemians with radical outsiders appeared in some of the paper's other articles. Pradier published verses about the sufferings of poets by an unknown writer, Piconel, whom he described as the father of eight children. The talent Pradier discerned in Piconel's verses had not prevented the poor man from finding his way onto the official list of indigents for the hard-pressed twelfth *arrondissement.* A later article by another writer, Eric Isoard, identified Piconel further as a simple worker who made four francs fifty a day doing designs on cloth. (The salary was relatively high for Paris workers, but hardly enough to provide well for Piconel's large family.) Pradier compared his own attempts to sell his poems in squares and cafés with similar efforts by Piconel. The implication that Pradier and Piconel were socially similar was joined to the old theme of Vigny's *Chatterton*, that society failed to reward artistic talent.[14]

The same theme appeared again in *Le Bohème*, in an essay about modern novels by Paul Saulnier. It told of a rich and successful writer returning to his elegant apartment after an evening of pleasure. There he opens a door to a small alcove to reveal, bent over a table, the poor down-and-out poet who is the real author of his books. The moral was explicit: modern literary reputations rested on money and the exploitation of other people's talents. The modern taste for sensationalist stories and cheap thrills made literature an impossible career for the person devoted to art itself. Only those willing to exploit the debased tastes of the public could succeed.[15]

These radical themes suggest that Pradier's Bohemianism was more estranged and disillusioned than Murger's. Yet they were not the dominant message broadcast by *Le Bohème.* Its contributors also wrote in favor of moderation and reconciliation. For example, the writer who identified Piconel as a simple worker, Eric Isoard, also serialized parts of his novel *Les faux bohèmes* in the paper. "The counterfeit Bohemians," false litterateurs, were the real enemies of serious young writers. Using their exclusion as a pretext, they "do nothing but make insults, drink, and scandalize respectable people, and all that *from the point of view of art*, as they have the insolence and the self-possession to say." They claimed to represent freedom of thought and the intellectual life, but all they really stood for was the tobacco pipe.[16]

We do not know what personal relationship existed between Isoard and Pradier, but their basic attitude was the same. Both were critical of the literary establishment only to the degree that it excluded them, and not because of any deeper alienation. Pradier made this clear in an article at the end of April, "Fathers and Sons." A successful father displays all his wealth and enjoyments to his son, arousing his desire to share in them, only to conclude that the heir may not touch a scrap until the old man is dead and gone. This was the position in which the current monarchs of thought placed their literary progeny, inspiring them with ardent aspirations only to frustrate them. The younger generation therefore had to create its own means of access to the public, little papers devoted to making a place for new talent, like *Le Bohème*. Yet, as Pradier made clear, the desire of the "sons" to find a place at their spiritual fathers' tables only testified to the younger generation's desire to resemble and follow the older one, not to create a different world of their own. The sons of Pradier's vision had no new literary program to offer: they were simply the reproduction, on a smaller scale, of those who had inspired them, "in thought, in style, in color, in content, in form." Those who now drank the adulterated wine of the cheap bars were only waiting to realize the fairy dream of sitting instead at the elegant tables of the boulevards.[17]

Much the same set of ideas and attitudes appeared at the same time in another short-lived Bohemian paper that called itself *Le Sans le Sou* (*The Pennyless*). About its editor, Constant Arnould, little is known. He may have been related to the better-known

Arthur Arnould, a friend of Jules Vallès and a participant in the Commune of 1871. One of the paper's contributors—according to Vallès, at any rate, who wrote a sketch of his life—was a vagabond poet and writer called Fonton. Fonton once tried unsuccessfully to sell some of his poetry among the peddlers outside the Louvre, before falling into the life of poverty and homelessness that placed him in the catalogue of heroism and defeat Vallès would call "The Irregulars of Paris."[18]

Le Sans le Sou lasted from November 1854 until the following May. So limited was its budget that it was not printed (except for two issues); instead it was handwritten and reproduced by lithography. Like *Le Bohème*, it started out by expressing hostility toward *les grands de la littérature*, who had forgotten their own cold and hungry youth and refused to help those who struggled with poverty now. "We rise up against your blind despotism, and if necessary our courage will be greater than our power." To the young, the paper's message was courage and work. "O you Bohemians of thought! Cast your wheat no longer on the rocks, we offer you a bit of fertile ground." The paper's enemies were those literary parasites who exploited the poverty and obscurity of their less fortunate colleagues, like speculators gambling on stock-market prices. Its heroes were the martyrs of thought and art invoked so many times in the nineteenth century, Hégéssipe Moreau, Gilbert, Chatterton.[19]

Yet *Le Sans le Sou*, like *Le Bohème*, drew back from the possible radical implications of these sentiments, and ended up identifying itself with respectability and moderation. An article at the end of April insisted that the paper was the friend of beggars but not of evildoers. In the latter category were "those counterfeit Bohemians [*faux bohèmes*] for whom alcohol is the muse," those whose only talent was in making fun of the bourgeoisie, and who preferred scandal to enthusiasm and faith. Such people made the public suspicious of all writers. "The true poet gets drunk on three things: feeling, ideas, and color." The sentiments were so close to those appearing in *Le Bohème* at the same time that Charles Pradier wrote to *Le Sans le Sou* suggesting that the two papers collaborate.[20]

In the end, therefore, the willingness of these papers to associate with the Bohemia Murger sought to exclude did not distance them very far from him. They, too, thought of Bohemian existence as a temporary necessity imposed on young artists and writers, a form of life they would be only too willing to give up once their careers were launched. That neither Pradier nor any of the writers associated with *Le Sans le Sou* ever made careers comparable to those of Murger or Champfleury (not to speak of Courbet or Baudelaire) may have something to do with their talent—or lack of it. Perhaps, too, the very fact that by the early 1850s a number of the original Café Momus circle had achieved some sort of literary or artistic acceptance encouraged a younger generation to define Bohemia in a different way. Also, unknown young writers faced different conditions under Louis-Napoleon Bonaparte's Second Empire from those of their predecessors under the more liberal July Monarchy. The empire's program of social peace, i.e., the prevention of revolutionary troubles like those of 1848, meant close control over the press and narrow restrictions on political activity. Only toward the end of the 1860s would liberalization allow oppositional politics and literature to come together as they had during the 1840s. In the interim, those who found their needs met by some kind of Bohemian identity were bound to be more isolated than their predecessors, and in need of new strategies. The subtitle of Pradier's paper *Le Bohème* was *journal non politique*. Perhaps the identification he and others felt with genuine social outcasts provided a substitute for the sense of social distance that freer contact with radical political movements had provided before. We may be tempted to doubt the authenticity of the threat against the established order contained in either Bohemianism, given the careerism it was usually intended to serve. But we should not be too harsh. Nineteenth-century society was capable of great cruelty and rigid self-righteousness; the Bohemian demand that it open itself to outsiders was an insistence that it prove itself true to its own liberal principles, that it keep the promises it made.

*   *   *

There was one person in nineteenth-century Paris who created his identity around the connections between the two Bohemias. He was Alexandre Privat d'Anglemont. Privat was a newspaper writer with a large following, a famous character about whom stories were often told in the popular press, a friend of Banville and Murger and Baudelaire. And he was a recognized arch-Bohemian. Murger is reported to have told him: "You are not a Bohemian, you are Bohemia." The *mot* was often recalled. At Privat's death in 1859, a writer in *Le Figaro* complained that people had repeated the saying to Privat so often he ended up believing it, to his detriment.[21]

There are a number of reasons for Privat's identification with Bohemia, beginning with his fabled poverty. One story told how some thieves had tried to rob him at night on a Paris street. He looked at them in astonishment: "But I am Privat!" he exclaimed. According to one version, this was enough to have the thieves dissolve in laughter at the idea he might have any money; they stood him to a drink. Other versions had him coming up with seven francs, or getting his nose broken. Whatever the truth, the tale points to another feature of his life: he was a renowned noctambule, prowling around in the streets and squares long after respectable people were safely locked into their apartments. It was these wanderings that made Privat famous, for they were the basis of the series of articles on the obscure industries and unknown occupations of mid-nineteenth-century Paris that he published in the newspaper *Le Siècle* beginning in 1852.[22]

Privat's life was and remains full of mystery, although some of the questions were finally answered by diligent archival research published in 1976. We know now that he was the illegitimate child of a mulatto woman in Guadeloupe. Although some people in his time thought the name "d'Anglemont" had been adopted after Privat arrived in France, it was somehow connected with his family in the West Indies. Born in 1815, he was sent to study in France at the age of ten. Attending school first in Nantes, and then at a famous lycée in Paris, Privat obtained his *baccalauréat* in 1833. His history as a student suggests that the poverty so often associated with him was indeed a fable. In fact, his family owned considerable property, and Privat received a regular allowance (comparable in amount to Baudelaire's income after 1844) from an elder brother who remained in Guadeloupe. The money provided little stability, however, since Privat seems usually to have spent it immediately on meals and drinks for down-and-out friends and acquaintances.[23]

According to Théodore de Banville, Privat had a passion for telling the story of his life, recounting it over and over again to whoever would listen. But he never told it the same way twice, so that nobody every really knew anything about him. By universal agreement, he was a great master of the farcical mixture of teasing and pretense known in French as *blague*. He claimed to have written a learned article on Egyptian art, but some friends made him tell the truth by luring him into the place de la Concorde on an excuse, and challenging him to read the characters on the obelisk. Banville believed that all this obfuscation was in the service of his desire to discover the hidden secrets of Paris: in order to gain entry to all the darkest corners of the city, he had to hide his real person from others, and just to make sure, he had taken the radical tack of actually forgetting or not knowing who he was. Privat was a *Luftmensch*: he lived in the air of fantasy. If Bohemia was the country in which reality gave way before the power of the imagination, then Privat was indeed the arch-Bohemian.[24]

His Bohemianism also had more conventional and straightforward aspects. Some of his earliest literary projects, which he outlined in a letter requesting help from Eugène Sue in 1843, are very close to the ones that later made Murger famous. He planned two novels. One was to recount the lives of girls who started out working in various Paris manufactures, and who then became the *grisettes* of the Latin Quarter before going on to lives as prostitutes, kept women, or actresses. His second project covered another main area of Murger's topography: "the life of poverty, hunger and rage of that intelligent, laborious, and educated race, the problematic existences of all the young men who have their arms broken by secondary education and who have no occupation. They are those whom our unhappy civilization leaves only two outlets: power or the hospital. In their lives one finds wonderful eccentricities, unknown joys, and above all prodigious ways of making do. I know them, I have lived there, I live there still. I have seen more talent, wit, and learning expended there to get a dinner than it takes for all the diplomats to change the face of the world." These young men lived by selling their intelligence, even writing things to be signed by others. Like the *grisettes*, therefore, they were prostitutes, putting their minds up for sale just as the young women put up their bodies.[25]

There is much that is remarkable in this letter from an obscure young man to a well-known writer. But most jarring is the contrast between the accents of anger and revolt in which Privat described the lives of his proposed subjects, and the surprisingly pragmatic use to which he intended to put them. Privat d'Anglemont identified so strongly with the prostitutes of the intelligence that he was writing to Sue in an effort to sell himself. The subjects were interesting and would attract the public, he thought. And he offered to write them up so that Sue could put his name to them. Sue seems to have replied, asking Privat why he did not simply write his books and publish them under his own name. In answer, Privat expressed a fear that people would not take seriously such an exposé by an unknown writer. It would be dismissed as the grumblings of a disgruntled *bohème*. Privat claimed in a later letter that he had already written more than forty stout octavo volumes, all published under other people's names.

It seems unlikely that there was any truth in this claim. Privat was only twenty-eight, he was a master of *blague* (remember the boast about his knowledge of Egyptian art), and we know in addition that he was sometimes the beneficiary of false literary attributions. Some poems of Baudelaire appeared in *L'Artiste* under Privat's name. But other young people did sell their talent in the way he described. Several well-known figures, notably Alexandre Dumas and Balzac, were said to have stables of ghostwriters who helped them turn out the articles and book chapters for which editors paid them well. Murger in one story had Rodolphe write a review to be signed by "an influential critic." Walter Benjamin, in his study of Baudelaire, made this phenomenon central to Bohemian

Paris, citing the story from Pradier's *Le Bohème* we noted before. Others have concluded that Bohemia was at base a phenomenon of literary proletarianization. Its opposition to bourgeois society was the revolt of a class who had no choice but to sell their labor.[26]

Such a view of Bohemia may have fit some of its members. But that it cannot point us to the major and recurrent themes of Bohemian life is one of the main arguments of this book. Pradier and the other writers in *Le Bohème* were concerned about moral relationships within the bourgeois literary class, not the situation of people likely to be excluded from it permanently. Their appropriation of styles and figures found at lower social levels dramatized an ambivalence that presupposed their right eventually to sit at the table of their fathers. Privat, too, located himself not among a class excluded from membership in the bourgeoisie, but in one that had been raised up into it in a manner that bred false hopes. He was one of those whom education had prepared for a literary career that, he feared, did not exist. "Instead of sending us to school with scholarships, the government would do better to teach us to play the drum" in an army band—at least they could then look forward to retirement in the Hôtel des Invalides. He claimed to have supported himself by playing the violin and horn in cheap cafés on the outskirts of Paris, and by painting signs for bakers and wine merchants.[27]

It is hard to know whether these last claims are evidence that Privat had shared the life of people like Daille-Lefebvre, or whether we are simply in the presence of more of his famous capacity for *blague*. However that may be, Privat seems never to have written the works he proposed in his letter to Eugène Sue. What he did write was the series of explorations of the underside of Paris that made his reputation, and where we shall find the best expression of his social consciousness. Privat's *Paris inconnu* was not so unknown as his title claimed, having been explored by Sue, Hugo, Banville, Delvau, and others. But it fascinated nineteenth-century readers, anxious about revolution and deviance, at once drawn and repulsed by the mysteries lurking beneath the surface of city life, and aware that new forms of industry and urban rebuilding projects threatened to do away with a world that still looked, behaved, and smelled like a remnant of the Middle Ages. Privat's accounts of the Parisian *bas-fonds* were especially timely in that they came just at the moment when the new streets and buildings of the Napoleonic Second Empire were beginning to destroy some crowded old sections and give the city a different, more modern face.

It is uncertain how much Privat lived in this world, but he certainly felt a resonance with it. Like the Latin Quarter of students and poor writers, it was a realm where all things seemed possible, where no stable principle of reality set limits to the power of fantasy. As he put it: "After having studied Paris in every direction, I have come to formulate my deepest belief in the following way: if somebody told me that there exists in some far-off street a man who makes knife handles out of old moons, I would believe it. Paris has used up all my capacity for astonishment. I no longer comment. I look, I listen, and I say: it is possible. I have seen everything in my travels through the city of miseries. I have met men of genius, Columbuses who, in order to eat during the day and sleep at night, are obliged to discover a new America every morning." Privat's discoveries were people whose everyday life was a work of genius. They shaped the world in the image of their imagination.[28]

Those who populated this "vagabond Bohemia" (as he called it) were a legion: "ambulatory musicians, street singers, tooth swallowers, fire eaters," plus "all the *métiers inconnus* that are followed without any licence . . . makers of fantastic and incredible things, people who live from occupations whose existence no one suspects." In such a pandemonium of activities, variety might seem the only common principle of existence. Yet, a fair number of Privat's people shared one specific feature: the ability to live, as one of his readers put it in a letter Privat published, like the peasant gleaners of fields.

Privat described the most typical night people as those who "live on leftovers from the banquets of the earth's fortunate, they gnaw bones like dogs and content themselves with the crusts and other pieces that are tossed aside." Among these urban gleaners were of course the *chiffonniers*, the ragpickers about whom Baudelaire also wrote. Privat sympathetically described their lives and their social organization, telling how they were recruited, what divisions existed among them, how their *métier* was passed on between generations. Others included a collector of dog and cat manure, who stored it in an attic where he went to harvest the worms it spawned to sell for fishbait; the *boulanger en vieux* (used-goods baker) who gathered stale bread to sell as dog and cat food, later discovering that he could also bag solid pieces and sell them as soup croutons; Madame Vanard, widow of a chemist who did away with himself, but not before teaching her enough to let her live by collecting lemon peels to be made into perfume and liqueur; and Matagatos, the cat killer, who wandered the streets at night searching for unwary felines, which he would slaughter, selling the fur for clothing and the meat to be made into rabbit stew. When customers at some of the cafés he serviced became suspicious, he collected rabbit heads from butchers so that the bistro owners could convince customers that they were getting the genuine article.[29]

This list may raise a suspicion that the *grand blaguer* may have been having his readers on. He would have believed the story about making knife handles out of old moons—did he expect others to believe it as well? What is more important than his veracity is what Privat thought about his people, and what he tried to make others see in them. Privat did not invent the notion of *métiers inconnus*; their existence was known in one way or another to many people. But the dominant view was that these people were in fact engaged in criminal activity. Murger referred to "the thousand mysterious and murky producers whose principal industry is not to have any, and who are always ready to do anything save the good." In one trial during October 1852, a Paris judge asserted flatly that people in the lower reaches of society claimed to follow a multitude of occupations but none of them was real; all were invented on the spot as defenses against the charge of vagrancy.[30]

Privat's reportage aimed to show not only that the *métiers inconnus* existed, but also that they were legitimate and socially productive. To Privat, the people he described were neither deviants nor criminals but honest folk who responded to the challenge of poverty. They had had "an idea," an inspiration about how to use something other people had abandoned, or do something no one had thought worth trying before, and they had developed it with determination and hard work. "If a man has found a way to make a name for himself, in whatever industry, that man has necessarily made use of a greater sum of intelligence and activity than his confrères." And Privat was careful to show that a number of them had made good. Several (including Madame Vanard, the lemon-peel collector) had arrived at relative comfort, and Privat was particularly pleased that business increased for some of them because of the publicity he gave. The message was clear: the "vagabond Bohemians" who inhabited the margins of Parisian society may have had odd demeanors and indulged in apparently mysterious activities, but if one took the trouble to examine them, one could see they were neither criminals nor rebels. At heart they were all good bourgeois.[31]

Not quite all. The squalid, teeming, and isolated back streets of the Left Bank, the old Halles market and other overcrowded neighborhoods, bred their harvest of disease, incurable poverty, and crime. Privat illustrated all this with statistics as well as personal observation, and he upbraided the modern society that allowed such conditions to exist. He was on the side of improvement. He had great praise for a kind of spontaneous urban renewal project in Montparnasse called the Villa des Chiffonniers. Here ragpickers had built huts in an open space that afforded them fresh air and a view, a marked improvement over the dark and infested streets where they had been living. The children were healthier, the adults calmer and more civilized. Crime had practically disappeared. "Sainir, c'est moraliser," Privat concluded: cleaning up brings moral improvement. Placed in good conditions, the poor developed virtues of fraternity and self-help that allowed them to solve common problems resolutely and successfully.[32]

There is something surprising about Privat, explorer of what was left of medieval Paris, turning out to be an advocate of urban reconstruction. Yet that is precisely what he was. Certainly he appreciated the romantic charm of the old city, and in one essay even argued that wit and imagination only flourished along crooked streets: people who lived on straight streets were dull. But confronted with the crime and disease of the old Left Bank, Privat became an enthusiast for urban reconstruction. Rebuild the quarter! Cut the rue des Écoles through the whole area! Not piece by piece, as the municipal administration wanted to do it, but in a single blow, from one end to the other! This would provide light and air, clean out the Augean stables. It would place people whose isolation from the rest of society left them barbarous in healthy contact with the city as a whole, changing them from urban savages to civilized human beings.[33]

Thus the message Privat brought in regard to the parts of Paris that bred sickness and crime paralleled his vision of the *métiers inconnus*. Both appeared to him as candidates for social integration. Just as dedication and success showed that Madame Vanard and the *boulanger en vieux* were productive members of modern society, so would the rebuilding of Paris cause those more deeply buried in the depths of Paris to join civilization. Privat descended into the other Bohemia not to separate himself from respectable society but to reconcile diverse social levels with each other. His image of himself is well represented by a comment he made about the artists among the poor quarters he visited, the "painters of shop displays and orchestra musicians of cheap cafés." They were "much loved by the people because they are good company and are known as warmhearted jokers. The best part of humanity prizes them because, after all, they form the upper aristocracy of the working classes. They are not yet bourgeois, they are no longer workers; they occupy the extreme limit and form, so to say, the link to join the two castes together. They are independent, free and proud." Privat's portrait of the other Bohemia was an image of himself.[34]

Privat d'Anglemont's views about the obscure people who worked in the shadowy depths of Paris were not unique during the nineteenth century: they had been anticipated, and they would be repeated. Privat described his subjects—both the exploited young

writers he sketched for Eugène Sue and the practicers of the unknown occupations—as *existences problématiques.* The term
meant both that staying alive presented a problem for them, and
that understanding how they managed to survive was puzzling for
outsiders. The word and the idea were current earlier, and provided
the subject for a chapter, "Les existences problématiques," in the
same collection of *Nouveau tableau de Paris* that contained Félix
Pyat's study of Bohemian *artistisme* in 1834. Here the author,
Frédéric Soulié, took the phrase to refer to those who had no visible, or legitimate and admissible, source of income. The category
ranged over the whole social scale, from procurers to cabinet ministers; but most were lonely people who lived quietly and out of
sight in some attic or dark corner of the city. Several of the features
Soulié attached to them appear in Privat's sketches. One was their
inventiveness. Their imagination produced new products, new
ideas, new fads. Did new styles and enthusiasms appear by themselves, like children under cabbage leaves? "Not in the slightest;
the problematic existences create them, the problematic existences
create everything. It is the man who has nothing to eat who sees,
imagines, gives birth. . . . Everything great, useful, splendid, belongs to *l'existence en problème*, for the problematic existence has
its genius side." Those who would invent new styles of painting or
music, or figure out how to build a tunnel to London, belonged to
the category of problematic existences. Their lives were difficult,
and they needed courage not to turn themselves into "hawkers,
street singers, or knaves," while preserving their inspiration
through the trials of poverty and shame. Among them were the
ones who Soulié said had once been called the "copper wheel, or
clockwork man of letters," the impoverished young litterateur who
accepted ten francs for the articles that some more fortunate author
would then sell for two hundred to a big newspaper, and which
made the second writer famous.[35]

So closely were these qualities associated with *la Bohème* that a
popular pamphlet writer of the 1860s, Gabriel Guillemot, recast
the whole idea of Bohemia in terms of them. Claiming that the figures with whom Murger had populated his tales were no longer to

be found in Paris, Guillemot proposed to use the term (since it still drew the interest of the public) for "all those whose existence is a problem, all those who live by expedients." Guillemot admitted that the category was broad; the boundaries that separated it from eccentrics and the mentally unbalanced were hard to discern. Some people crossed the thin line that distinguished Bohemia from fraud and crime. But more insistently than Soulié, Guillemot made clear that Bohemia—defined in his way—had no essential tie with the condition of poverty that a Murger or a Privat had assumed was natural to it. There were Bohemians at every social level, from princes and dukes on down: whoever built his (or her, since there were women, too) existence on a show of wealth, position, knowledge, or talent that was in fact the product of pretense or illusion was a Bohemian.[36]

Guillemot was not the only observer to expand the frontiers of Bohemia toward the top of society. In 1859, a writer in *Le Figaro* used the title "La grande Bohème" to suggest that shady characters living from irregular expedients could be found in the upper reaches of social life as well as in the world Murger had sketched. A year before Guillemot published his pamphlet, the brilliant anti-Bonapartist journalist Henri de Rochefort used the same title to sum up his picture of self-seeking and corruption among the supporters and hangers-on of the Second Empire. Later in the century, a short-lived newspaper, *La Bohème Financière (The Bohemia of Finance)* and a novel, *La Bohème bourgeoise*, would even suggest that the taste for disorder and happy-go-lucky living from day to day had migrated into the higher social levels of business and stock-market speculation.[37]

These developments illuminate some essential characteristics that shaped Bohemia from the start, ones hard to discern behind its more superficial features. Both Murger and Privat devoted themselves to exploring areas and segments of society that seemed exotic, marginal, and threatening to many respectable people. A major conclusion in their reports, however, was that the oppositions and contrasts between these worlds and the lives of good bourgeois contained the seeds of reconciliation and synthesis. Inventiveness, imagination, and the liberation of originality from tradition were some of the major qualities that the nineteenth-century middle classes pointed to in claiming superiority over the more elegant and stable world that their industry was replacing. To make everyday existence a work of genius was precisely what the avatars of progress aspired to do.

That some preferred to deny these parallels suggests that Bohemia offered the rest of society a special service of which few on either side were usually conscious. It gave powerful symbolic aid to bourgeois who needed to emphasize tradition and stability; for them, Bohemia was a way to project onto others the features of social disruption and moral uncertainty that rapid historical change called forth, to inoculate themselves against the negative effects of the dissolution of tradition that society as a whole was bringing about. To expand the boundaries of Bohemian *existence problématique* upward along the social scale was only to say that the original frontiers had been drawn too narrowly. Bohemia was a revelation of tendencies nurtured by society as a whole, as revolution and innovation caused inherited structures and assumptions to give way.

We can see something of what was at stake if we compare Privat's positive portrayal of the lower depths of Paris with the image of its inhabitants we find in the prosecutors and judges who sought to discipline them. Judges often had the same suspicions about *saltimbanques* and street performers as they did of people who claimed to practice some new or unheard-of *métier*: both might be masks for illegality or simple begging. Declaring that these activities had no legal footing, the judges particularly insisted that they were not *états*. The word *état*, meaning civil status as well as state, is one of those linguistic legacies that echo with premodern assumptions about social activity and organization. Nineteenth-century people who used it to refer to everyday occupations were invoking a traditional vision of society as made up of activities and functions that could be catalogued and listed in advance. The *états* that they believed deserved recognition in the present were the ones handed down by tradition and usage. To require that an activity be an *état* was to imply a standard of social membership that shaped individuals according to preexisting ideas about what productive work was, and what activities society required. In the *Bourgeois Physiology*, a businessman posing for his portrait taunts the artist to "admit that what you do is not an *état*."[38]

Some of the street performers themselves, faced with this attitude, responded in ways that suggested a different notion of what made individuals part of the social whole. That their work was fatiguing, and that it added to the pleasure of those who rewarded it, were proofs enough that their occupations were real and socially useful.[39] Privat's vision moved along similar lines, more self-consciously developed. The *métiers inconnus* not only provided necessary services and used the resources of society more efficiently than officially recognized occupations, but also allowed individuals with original inspirations to develop their abilities, thus fulfilling society's claim to open itself to the talented and diligent, whatever their origins. Here, as elsewhere, Bohemia revealed its inner association with those elements and tendencies in middle-class life that stood for openness and innovation, against the attempt by others to preserve and defend values and expectations rooted in the Old Regime.

The specifically modern, forward-looking character of Privat's work was partially veiled by his own sense that the people he was describing seemed to belong to an earlier age, that in some ways they were left over from the Paris of the Middle Ages. But to define society in such a way that sectors and activities once regarded as marginal became central was an essential and recurring strategy in the modern displacement of tradition. A similar process was at work in Courbet's development of a determinedly modern style of painting, through incorporating elements earlier associated with the primitive and undeveloped techniques of popular art.

Like Courbet, and Baudelaire and Murger, Privat's ties to Bohemia testify to a need to make his work not just a manner of entering society and earning a living, but a way of exploring the dilemmas of personal identity. His confession that the experience of Paris left him with no basis for knowing where reality left off and pure imagination began recalls Baudelaire's comment: "I go to bed proud to have lived and to have suffered in some one besides myself. Perhaps you will say: Are you sure that your story is the real one? But what does it matter what reality is outside myself, so long as it has helped me to live, to feel that I am, and what I am?" Like Baudelaire—and their mutual friend Alfred Delvau, who sometimes made a similar confession—what Privat was seeking in his night walks about Paris was his own self.[40]

That it should have been Privat d'Anglemont who sought that self most single-mindedly among the shadowy characters and problematic existences of the city is not surprising: of all the people associated with Bohemia in the mid-century, he was the one whose own marginality was the most material and inescapable. For Privat, we remember, was not wholly French by origin: he was the descendant of black slaves, transported from Africa to the Caribbean by relatives and ancestors of the whites among whom he now lived. Privat seldom referred to his black roots in his writing, but in one story he recounted an African myth that made blacks the children of God and whites the progeny of the devil, reversing the racial hierarchy presupposed by most Europeans. That specifically black or African themes were not more prominent in his writings may reflect in part the fairly extensive possibilities of integration into French society and culture actually open to him, and in part the ability of native French images of exploitation, prostitution, and oppression to substitute for ones Privat knew from his childhood. He nowhere seems to have compared the Paris underworld to those other "barbarians" and "savages" (in European eyes) who were his own people. But on some level the link must have existed in his mind. To reveal the virtues and qualities of the one—to insist on the contributions they could make to civilization once the conditions that separated them from the rest of society were removed—spoke also against the ideas most people held about the other.[41]

To the end, there remained something unassimilable about Privat, something that tied him permanently to Bohemia, just as Courbet's loyalty to his rural roots kept him at a permanent distance from the Paris he yearned to take by storm. Banville's suggestion that Privat's identity was problematic because he had purposefully

cast it off, lest it interfere with his explorations of the underside of
Paris life, probably missed the point. Finding a stable and permanent identity in modern France was not really possible for Privat.
His status as an outsider was too powerful and conflicted. The master of *blague* and obfuscation was engaged all his life in seeking
himself and hiding from himself. Just for that reason he became an
important example for others who carried the burden of designing,
even of imagining, an identity whose structure and boundaries society could never completely define, the burden of Bohemia.

CHAPTER 6

Friends and
Enemies

BOHEMIA ENTERED INTO PRIVATE HISTORIES, but it also had a public use, as a screen on which problems of morality and politics could be projected and played out. To define Bohemia, to locate it in the larger topography of society, was to take a stand on hotly debated social and moral issues. Such discussions could break out at many moments, occasioned by a book, a play, or a political event. But the great moment for public self-examination in the Bohemian mirror at mid-century was the demise and funeral of Henry Murger at the end of January 1861.

Murger's last years had continued the combination of success and disappointment that marked his earlier career. He gained a certain reputation as a writer, appearing in prestigious organs and receiving the Légion d'Honneur in 1859. His play, *Bohemian Life*, had a revival in that year. He spent much time in a country house not far from Paris. But his literary production remained small and his financial position precarious. He was often ill. When the end came, he died like many of the century's poor, in a hospital. A few days before his death, Napoleon III's minister Count Walesky sent five hundred francs to help pay the medical expenses, but it was too late. The government then agreed to pay for the funeral.

However tawdry Murger's death, his funeral was a great public occasion. *Le Figaro*, for which Murger had written occasionally, publicized the event, calling it a *rendez-vous d'honneur* for all those who supported the cult of "talent, youth, and unhappiness." The response was enormous—some would later even say exaggerated and inappropriate. *Le Figaro* claimed that more than two thousand people attended and that the procession had more than one hundred carriages. Even if those figures were inflated, Murger's public funeral was far grander than the recognition accorded many better writers. *Le Figaro* listed the names of some 250 luminaries who attended, mostly from journalism, literature, theater, and the arts. The paper also started a subscription for a monument. Hundreds of people contributed, some as individuals, some in groups. By mid-February, the sum raised was fifty-five hundred francs, rising to over sixty-five hundred during March. Within weeks of the funeral, at least a dozen newspaper and magazine articles about Murger appeared. Three of his old friends from the days of the Water-Drinkers announced that they were at work on his biography. In fact, two biographies of Murger appeared by 1862, joined by a third a few years later. Léon Cladel's *Les martyrs ridicules*—and Baudelaire's preface to it—were by-products of the attention focused on Murger's death, too.[1]

Some of this remarkable outpouring of interest seems to have been inspired by Murger's personal qualities, his kindness and sympathy for others. The editor of *Le Figaro* declared that he was a man without an enemy. But that claim, however understandable, was not quite true, as we shall see. What made Murger of so much interest was that he stood for Bohemia. Most of the articles occasioned by his death took Bohemia for their subject. The indefatigable Jules Janin, still appearing in the *Journal des Débats*, praised Murger, quoted his analyses and descriptions of Bohemian life, and identified some eighteenth-century precursors. Armand de Pontmartin in the *Revue des Deux Mondes* emphasized Murger's inability to grow out of Bohemia (describing him, we noted earlier, as "seized by a homesickness for disorder"), and pointed to the contradiction between his characters' apparent devotion to poverty and their real obsession with money. But Charles Coligny, writing in *L'Artiste*, insisted that Murger had aspired to citizenship in the bourgeoisie. If he had not transformed himself as completely as his character Rodolphe, at least he had palpably changed. It was not his fault if others had "plagiarized *la vie de Bohème* on the shady side." These comments all suggest once again that Bohemia stood for both assimilation to regular life and resistance to it. The size of the funeral, and the list of contributors to the subscription for Murger's monument, testified to the same breadth of appeal and uncertainty of meaning. Alongside writers, students, and many unidentifiable people, the names included figures later to be active in the Commune, two stockbrokers, and one fencing master.[2]

But the Murger funeral was not altogether the festival of murky harmony it seemed to be on the surface. The sharp dissonances of opinion that lurked underneath soon came into the open. Veiled hostility toward Murger was expressed right away, first by the conservative journalist Francisque Sarcey. Everyone had loved Murger, Sarcey admitted, but there was great danger in taking his life for a model. Society could be healthy only if ruled by a single moral standard, and the claim to be a writer or an artist did not justify undermining it. Sarcey was more directly hostile toward *Le Figaro*, claiming that the paper was taking Murger's death as a chance to make publicity for itself. A sharper rejection of Murger—also linking him to the offbeat journalism of the *petite presse*—came from the Catholic publicist Louis Veuillot. To him, the Bohemians Murger had represented were a tribe of pseudo-artists, parasites without talent who hid their incapacity behind a facade of eccentricity. When they could no longer conceal their failure, even from themselves, they blamed it on the defects of society. What fit Murger to be Bohemia's chronicler was his mediocrity. "Endowed with a stronger imagination and a more lively feeling, Murger would have considered the Bohemian as a rebel, the rebel as a legitimate reformer of society, and he would have fallen into some revolutionary extravagance. Neither his passion nor his powers went that far." Instead, he had painted a quaint and melancholy canvas that, far from frightening the bourgeoisie, had been taken up by them because it was just what they wanted. Murger showed the artists and writers who lived on society's margins for the clowns and madmen they were, making them the court fools of the democratic age. No wonder, Veuillot observed (with considerable exaggeration), that the subscription list for his monument was "full with the names of *agents de change* [stockbrokers]."[3]

A similar condemnation came from a rather unexpected source, the writer and art critic Théodore Pelloquet, whose brief biography of Murger appeared in 1861. Pelloquet had known Murger and the whole Café Momus group during the 1840s, and was himself fairly often associated with Bohemia. According to one writer, Pelloquet later went mad. Around 1860, in any case, his sympathies were strongly with the establishment; he seems to have wanted to put whatever distance he could between himself and his Bohemian past. Murger's *vie de Bohème* was no poem of youth, he insisted, but an unhealthy kind of life, often false and vicious, "where youth rouges itself up like an aged coquette, where the carefree life is a pretense and hides not poetic idleness but the cowardly indolence of people without courage and without talent." Bohemians travestied the costume of poets and artists to escape honest work and to make themselves unlike the bourgeois they mocked, but who were mostly worth more than they. Pelloquet took up Armand de Pontmartin's observation that the declared rejection of wealth in Murger's tales was contradicted by the unmistakable fascination displayed for it. Pelloquet seemed to attribute Murger's defects to his modest social origins: he idealized Bohemians because he had too little education and experience to have known any more suitable heroes.[4]

Pelloquet's denunciation of Murger seems to have derived some of its passion from the force of rejected identification and sympathy. If so, then it serves to remind us that associations made in Bohemia, especially by the young, were subject to dissolution when the contrasting personal and social threads they had temporarily woven together unraveled. Exactly what Bohemia represented to those who had once been there depended on where they had subsequently moved. Two quite different perspectives appeared in the other two biographies of Murger inspired by his death.

The first to appear was the *History of Murger, To Serve as a History of the True Bohemia*, by "Three Water-Drinkers," the poet and artist Léon Noël, the writer Adrien Lelioux, and the photographer Nadar. In fact, only the first two had really belonged to the Water-Drinkers. Nadar had met Murger after the group disbanded, but he shared with the others a nostalgia for the world of the 1840s, with its hopes for a society transformed by republicanism and social harmony. The political message had to be dissembled under the Bonapartist empire, but the old values of fraternity, poverty, and liberty were asserted clearly enough.[5]

The Bohemia the trio remembered was neither weepily sentimental, disordered, nor impotent. It consisted of young men proudly fighting against poverty and determined to make the contribution to society for which their talents fit them. The real Water-Drinkers, they insisted, had been far from the stoic rejection of success, the uncompromising refusal to live an ordinary life of which Murger accused them. Of course, Bohemia had to be left behind. The question was what attitude one took toward it afterward. The wholehearted and *arriviste* enthusiasm of Murger's conversion to the bourgeoisie amounted to a pitiless rejection of his own self, an attack on the noble and generous aspirations of youth. At the end of *Scenes of Bohemian Life*, poetry, love, courage, and gaiety had been drowned in the cold sea of reality. Rodolphe and Marcel's willingness to embrace success by whatever means they encountered was "a negation of the whole poem." It led to an unsympathetic abandonment of those who had stumbled or fallen along the way. Was the drama of Bohemia to be but a spectacle for the curious, leaving behind no tempering of the soul, no widening of horizons? Murger was to be praised for giving a picture of youth that (the three authors thought) was a model of loyalty, devotion, and honest work. But he lacked the moral determination and intellectual consistency necessary to grasp the meaning of what he had described. He feared conviction, lest he be called upon to act on it. His willingness to have Rodolphe bury his youth with Mimi was a sign of this weakness; it had caused great pain to his old friends.[6]

Even with the politics heavily muted, this was a criticism of Murger from the Left. But the Three Water-Drinkers were not revolutionaries or rebels. By 1861, all were regular members of society, having made their place by hard work and—at least in Nadar's case, as a photographer—imaginative strategies. What was at stake was the relationship between their present existence and their former one. They belonged to the generation of 1848, the first that had to face up to bourgeois society's failure to transform itself into something else. That failure threatened to divide their personal histories into two disparate parts, one linked with hope, the other with resignation or submission. By affirming Bohemia as a passageway into society, and as the source of persisting moral conviction, they made it an emblem for continuity. They joined the bourgeoisie, but they brought their youthful visions with them.

That Bohemia raised similar issues of disruption and continuity in regard to both individual identity and social membership appears also from the third of the biographies written after Murger's death. The author of this one was Alfred Delvau, the friend of Baudelaire and of Privat d'Anglemont, who wrote about *saltimbanques, grisettes*, and the underside of Paris. His interest in popular culture led him to study Parisian argot. In his history of 1848, he made a plea for the bourgeoisie to affirm its roots in the *peuple*, but by 1861 Delvau was coming to see his own relationship to bourgeois life in a way that put him at odds with the Three Water-Drinkers. He announced this in an article in *Le Figaro* of February 17, 1861, less than three weeks after Murger's death; the title—hard to put into English—was *"Les mangeurs de bourgeois."* Delvau's target was those who persecuted the bourgeoisie.[7]

Like other writers, Delvau described the modern idea of the bourgeois as hopelessly vague: every part of society gave its own definition. Yet this did not preserve the bourgeois from his many implacable *mangeurs*: dreamers, vaudevillists, young poets, painters, apprentice novelists. What was remarkable, in Delvau's view, was that the bourgeois did not return the *blague* and mockery directed against him. Why not? "Because he started out by being you before becoming himself, because he had heart before he acquired his tummy, because he had debts before he had bonds, because he had long hair before he had a trimmed lawn, because he had mistresses before he had a wife." The bourgeois did not reject his detractors because he saw himself in them: "He is the conclusion to a book of which you are the preface."

When Delvau's own biography of Murger saw the light a few years later, it contained many of the same notions, now specifically cast as a criticism of Nadar and the others. But making this attack obviously made Delvau uneasy: his life of Murger is so riven with ambivalence that it comes near to collapsing under the weight of its internal contradictions. True to his own democratic and populist history, he agreed with many things his rivals had said about Murger, but his conclusion placed them among those *mangeurs de bourgeois* he upbraided.

In the first part of the book—a chronicle of Murger's career, followed by an account of his strictures against the Water-Drinkers and other determined Bohemians—Delvau seemed to come out just where Nadar and the others did. To speak as Murger had was "to fire on one's own troops." Delvau compared Murger to the *garde mobile* of 1848, the legion of unemployed working-class youths who had been among the most ferocious opponents of the radical June uprising. "People have not called Murger a bourgeois, but he was one." Given his experiences, he should not have been the one to shoot down his former comrades, left behind in the *peuple*. But was that execution necessary in itself? The answer was yes.

Delvau now told what had been wrong with Bohemia. Its denizens pooled their illusions instead of their powers, dreamed about life in place of living it. The danger posed by Bohemia—now reawakened by Nadar and his partners—was that others would be misled into a life of unnecessary suffering. Murger had understood that Bohemians in politics, whatever their heroism, had been useless to any cause because they were wrapped up in illusions. He had saved himself from the abyss of unreality, as had many others, Nadar and his friends included. Those who remained behind had suffered a fate not to be imitated. It was regrettable that Murger had provided models of irresponsibility and laziness: those who couldn't pay their debts shouldn't make any. This criticism of Murger, however, arose naturally out of the later histories of his characters who, like Musette and Schaunard, had become good bourgeois and "think exactly as I do."[8]

Delvau reported attending a revival of Murger's play in 1865. He was disappointed, the drama no longer spoke to him. It is hard to say whether his disillusionment stemmed from his identification with bourgeois life, or his bad conscience about turning against his earlier loyalties. In either case, the memory of Murger evoked an ambivalence that he found difficult to resolve.

Although critical of Bohemia in ways the Water-Drinkers were not, Delvau resembled them in his attempt to define the continuity between Bohemia and bourgeois life. Both attitudes must surely have been represented among those whose participation made Murger's funeral a grand occasion. His ambivalence corresponded to the experience of many people who had exchanged an adventurous youth for a sober middle age. The theme of Bohemian conversion—and continuity with the bourgeoisie—appeared elsewhere in this period. Early in 1867, *Le Figaro* published a brief tale, "La conversion d'un Bohème," whose moral was that a Bohemian could fulfill his dreams only by accepting a stable, regulated life.[9]

Bohemia evoked clear and unambiguous hostility, on the other hand, from those social elements who identified most strongly with the traditions of order and stability that, like Catholicism and hierarchy, still survived from the Old Regime. Francisque Sarcey and Louis Veuillot represented this position in 1861, as had Barbey d'Aurevilly in his castigation of Poe a few years before. To understand these enemies of Bohemia, their worries and anxieties, we turn now to the two contemporaries who dedicated themselves to attacking Bohemia with the greatest determination: the brothers Edmond and Jules de Goncourt.

The Goncourt brothers may be little read today, especially outside of France, but they occupy an important place in cultural history. Their famous *Journal*, a literary and personal diary assiduously kept during five decades—first by both brothers, then after 1870 by the surviving Edmond—remains an unparalleled source of information and gossip about Parisian intellectual life from 1851 to the 1890s. Their novels, besides providing fictionalized transformations of many events and people chronicled in the *Journal*, pioneered literary realism and the use of theoretical psychology in fiction. In their linked roles as writers, publicists, and art collectors, the Goncourt brothers contributed to the rise and development of important aesthetic movements, including Impressionism and Art Nouveau. Behind their unusual career was a personal relationship that has not yielded up its secrets, and a stance toward culture and society compounded of originality and stodginess, ambition and distance, desire for acceptance and hostility to most of those around them. Reading the Goncourt brothers can be distasteful and exasperating, but even the most hostile, self-important of their writings are often arresting and provoking, revealing facets of nineteenth-century experience hardly visible anywhere else.[10]

Born in 1822 and 1830, both brothers experimented with drawing and painting in their youth, turning to plays and prose at the end of the Second Republic and the start of the Bonapartist empire. The first novel on which they collaborated was published on the day of Louis-Napoleon's coup, December 2, 1851. Because its enigmatic title, *In 18—*, seemed provocative, the novel was seized by government authorities—the first in a train of irritations that set the Goncourts against the regime. Early in 1853, they were prosecuted for including some racy Renaissance poetry in one of their publications. For most of their career, the Goncourts felt themselves to be outsiders within Paris, a sentiment that was strengthened as their literary efforts failed to receive the recognition they craved.

During the first years of the Second Empire, the brothers lived in the world of the *petite presse*. They wrote for and edited a weekly paper, then a daily. When these failed, the pair turned to a series of historical studies about the eighteenth century. Edmond and Jules were deeply drawn to prerevolutionary society, whose art they passionately collected and sponsored. The two Goncourts had many ties with Bohemia, strengthened by their sense of being outsiders, and emphasized by many personal relations. Several figures well known as Bohemians participated in the Goncourts' journalistic projects, including Nadar and Murger. But we also learn from them about Bohemian figures who would otherwise be difficult to identify or even trace.

One of these was Alexandre Pouthier, a marginal painter who had been a school friend of Edmond. He came to represent the character and fate of Bohemia in their most elaborate anti-Bohemian novel, *Manette Salomon*. In the *Journal* of 1852, they described him as "salvaged from the far depths of Bohemia" to work on their weekly *L'Éclair*. Edmond remembered him as a schoolboy with radical enthusiasms, happily running through the streets to announce the start of revolution. He experimented with hashish and displayed a happy-go-lucky unconcern about the future, enchanted with life despite his uncertainty about where his next meal would come from, "always persuaded that his last coin will give birth to little ones tomorrow." The brothers—especially Edmond—were often sympathetic to Pouthier, but by the late 1850s the *Journal*'s references to him grew less indulgent, describing him alternately as a clown and a parasite. They mocked his artistic projects, particularly his desire to paint a Christ who stood for modern humanitarianism. When Pouthier resisted their efforts to find him a stable job, they attributed his reluctance to "the Bohemian's horror and persisting instinct against orderly classification, against being signed up, against social work." They found in him an inclination toward "the barracks, the hospital, the phalanstery, all those assemblages where one relieves himself of his initiative and will-power." Despite his middle-class origins, his aspirations were toward the gutter and lower-class society.[11]

The Goncourt brothers' growing hostility to Bohemia had several sources, the most obvious of which were social. Their family belonged to that segment of the bourgeoisie that had risen into the aristocracy through the legal profession in the last century of the Old Regime. The noble particle "de" had not been in their name more than a couple of generations, but they were passionately devoted to it. After one visit to a working-class bar (in Murger's company) during 1857, they described the experience with undisguised revulsion and contempt. "Yes, that is the people, that is the people, and I hate it, with its poverty, its dirty hands, the fingers of its women stuck with needle holes, its louse-infested pallets, its slangy speech, its pride and its meanness, its work and its prostitution, I hate it for its crude vices, its naked prostitution, its hovels full of amulets. My whole self rises up against these things that are not of my class [*ordre*], and against these creatures that are not of my blood." The brothers were not without their—limited—sympathy for the poor, and Edmond wrote harsh things against the official repression of the Paris Commune in 1871. But their lines bristling with hatred of poverty and quivering with unconscious fear of social descent represent the Goncourts' deeper impulses very well.[12]

The brothers' preference for life under the Old Regime shared elements with other nineteenth-century conservatives and reactionaries. Modern life was to be condemned for its confusion and disunity, its abandonment of any principle of political or social authority, its vulgar materialism. A culture dominated by literary and artistic realism—practices that had always been part of the best European art, but in proper subordination to higher aims—was one that abandoned aspirations toward the ideal in favor of "the gross instinct of the common people." Eighteenth-century society had not been perfect. Just as the equality introduced since 1789 was a lie, so was the earlier lack of equality an injustice, but at least it had worked to the benefit of well-brought-up people.[13]

The Goncourt brothers first gave expression to these views in a series of historical writings about the Old Regime and the Revolution completed by 1855. Those writings received a cool reception. Disappointed, the two traveled outside France for several months, returning to Paris in May 1856. On their return, their feelings about the defects of modern social and cultural life began to focus into a hostility toward Bohemia.

Visiting cafés and other hangouts, the brothers quickly rediscovered some of their old associates, among them Murger. One of the earliest *Journal* entries following their return reports on these renewed contacts. "When Murger wrote *Bohemian Life*, he did not suspect that he was writing the history of something that was to become a power in five or six years' time—and yet it has. At the present moment, the world that runs after the five-franc piece, that freemasonry of publicity, reigns and governs and denies entry to every well-born man: 'He's an *amateur!*' And with that word they kill him." What the upstart writers of Bohemia were trying to establish amounted to the rule of socialism in literature. The people who gathered in a well-known locale, Le Divan Le Pelletier, were literary odd-job men who had set themselves up as judges and executioners. "The piece to write is a play, *The Men of Letters* [*Les Hommes de Lettres*], against Bohemia. It reigns, it is ripe. The paradox to prove is the following: knowing Latin does not make one know less French."[14]

Behind this new determination lay the Goncourts' long-standing sense of social superiority, sharpened by their failure to gain recognition for their literary efforts. The men of letters were now described as being like prostitutes, spitting on the bourgeoisie, denying the latter had heart or force or spontaneity. But the truth was that the only thing that mattered in Bohemia was business. Their criticisms, their tirades, their friendships, their *blague*—all were tactics and maneuvers. "Beggars male or female, they march toward fortune or toward the publisher with a mechanical logic, a sublime and comic insensibility, a complete lack of heart and honor." In the heavy, stale atmosphere of the Brasserie des Martyrs in Montmartre, the brothers found the ignoble world of Bohemian gossipmongers. "No idea, no party, no banner waved," what lay at the bottom of every conversation was only hunger for the franc.[15]

In May 1857, the brothers reported that a writer often linked to Bohemia, Aurélien Scholl, had approached them on behalf of a kind of association of people united in search of success. Writers, painters, sculptors, doctors, even priests, were coming together to gain control of organs of public opinion and thereby aid each other's careers. It is hard to know whether any such group was really in the works; it fit the Goncourts' expectations so well that they mav have made it up, or Scholl may have proposed it to them as a tease. In any case, during the fall of 1857 the brothers placed themselves at the center of a similar but opposite informal circle whose aim they described as "the counterrevolution against Bohemia." Part of its purpose was to provide material for the play Jules and Edmond were writing. Present were a number of their friends, including—more to their surprise than ours—Murger.[16]

The Goncourts had known Murger at least since the early 1850s. In 1852, they reported on his life in the country, at the little village of Marlotte. They enjoyed making him (and almost everyone else) look silly, and told how his mistress interrupted an embrace to ask him how much the *Revue des Deux Mondes* paid per page. Later, they commented on his teary eyes, his barrack-room language, and his openhearted but weak-minded desire to declare everyone talented. Presumably, the Goncourts had actually read Murger's *Scenes*, but there is no evidence for that in the *Journal*; their attitude toward him bears no trace of the cautionary views about Bohemia that inspired his 1851 preface to that book. In May 1857, they described him as the only Bohemian who counted elsewhere; his conversion came, for them, that October, when, at a gathering of their group of "writers with gloves," Murger made his profession of faith. "He renounces Bohemia and passes, with arms and supplies, to the men of letters of the *monde*. He is the Mirabeau of the affair." At a series of *soirées* in the following December, Murger told the brothers about his down-and-out life during the 1840s, his work for Count Tolstoy, and about the real figures behind some of the well-known fictional denizens of *la Bohème*.[17]

None of this gained Murger the brothers' admiration or sympathy. The *Journal* entries regularly carped at Murger for the meagerness of his talent, the deficiencies of his education, the poverty of his imagination. As he neared death, the brothers saw in his passing both his personal demise and the end of the life he had painted, "debauchery of night work, periods of poverty and periods of excess, venereal diseases not attended to, the hot and cold of the homeless life, eating one meal and skipping the next, glasses of absinthe as consolation for the pawn shop." It was a life that used up those who led it, a life in revolt against the needs of body and mind, "which makes a man of forty-two [Murger was in fact only thirty-eight] take leave of life in tatters, without enough vitality to suffer, and complaining of only one thing, the smell of rotten flesh in his room: his own." Even after his death they did not let up. The government had behaved shamefully, paying for Murger's burial while it allowed better writers to die of hunger. The fuss made about Murger and the size of his funeral showed the injustice of public recognition and reputation. Murger was a self-indulgent egotist who became a parasite because he refused to work hard enough to develop what talent he had. He was not of the brothers' world, "he only knew Parisian. He did not know enough Latin."[18]

The Goncourts' dislike of Murger was compounded of social prejudice and a view of how life and literature should be related that had something in common with Baudelaire's. Emotional excitement was dangerous for the imagination. "One only gets ideas [*conçoit*] in silence and as it were in the sleep and repose of mental activity. The emotions are contrary to the gestation of literary works. Those who imagine or invent should not live. It requires days that are regular and calm, a bourgeois condition of the whole being, a cotton-capped self-communion, to bring to light what is great, tormented, nervous, passionate, dramatic. People who spend themselves too much in their passions or in nervous energy will not complete their works and will end up exhausting their life in the living of it." The brothers identified themselves not only with a social position and a century that were distant from Bohemia, but also with an aesthetic psychology that called into question the literary potentiality of those who made their everyday lives a work of genius.[19]

These were the ideas behind the work against Bohemia the Goncourts began during 1856. Called *The Men of Letters*, it first took form as a play, finished in the fall of 1857. To their great disappointment, Jules and Edmond could not get the work produced. They rewrote the play into a novel with the same title, eventually publishing it at their own expense in 1860. Perhaps their difficulty in finding first a producer and then a publisher shows people's reluctance to become associated with a project that seemed calculated to offend the Parisian literary world. Similar worries probably affected the Goncourts' decision to give the book a less provocative title. Beginning with its second edition it was called after its central character, Charles Demailly.

Charles Demailly was the brothers' first real literary success. It combined many of the best features of their work—the interest in psychology, the realistic account of Parisian life, the description of evolving movements in modern culture. Contemporary psychiatric theories received colorful exposition, helping to account for the main character's descent into madness. No doubt many readers were at least equally attracted by the fictionalized appearance of well-known Parisian literary figures, including Nadar, Théodore de Banville, Champfleury, and Barbey d'Aurevilly. The Goncourts never considered themselves realists in anything like the slice-of-life manner Champfleury had associated with Murger, however. Their own ambitions for the novel are better represented by their description of its main character's literary goal: to interest the public "through the psychological development and drama of emotions and mental catastrophes."[20]

The chief catastrophe is that of the book's hero, a young writer who, like the Goncourt brothers themselves, lives in the world of Paris writers and journalists and, like them, too, feels intellectually and personally above that world, seeking to escape from it into serious literature. Charles Demailly keeps a diary, several of whose entries are reworkings of passages from the brothers' *Journal.* A typical one confessed: "Didn't sleep at all last night, and I get up like a man who spent the night gambling. . . . It is only one act, the play I submitted to the Odéon, but it is a way of coming before the public." Not only the feverish desire to become known, but even the language, matched the Goncourts' own outpourings of unsatisfied ambition during the 1850s. What blocks Demailly's hopes and leads to his demise is precisely the power they were blaming for their own frustrations, Bohemia.[21]

The Bohemia of *Charles Demailly* is "a new species" of writers, attuned to the contemporary world of publicity and display and devoid of links to the past and its traditions. "Risen behind the charming book of one of its own, *Voyage Around a Five-Franc Coin*, Bohemia, this impecunious people, bridled and whipped by need, did not make its entry into art at all in the way of the previous generation, the men of 1830." The older group had belonged almost totally to the comfortable upper bourgeoisie. But the people chronicled in *Scenes of Bohemian Life*—everybody would get the joke in the Goncourts' substitute title—are driven so strongly by the exigencies of making a living that "their appetites held their beliefs up for ransom." The natural habitat of Bohemia is the world of the *petite presse*, particularly that of the Second Empire, in which government restrictions on political journalism leave no targets for gossipmongers but the only aristocracy possible in the nineteenth century, that of the spirit. The difficulties and deprivations of their lives instill in Bohemians "the hates of a proletariat," ready to shout like the crowds of 1848, "Down with people who wear gloves!"[22] Their typical paper is called *Le Scandale*.

Charles Demailly is shown another literary environment when he is befriended by a lyric poet, Boisroger, modeled on Théodore de Banville. Boisroger introduces Demailly into a circle where writers dress carefully and speak with restraint; in contrast to the group around *Le Scandale*, most address each other with the polite *vous* instead of the familiar *tu*. Until then, the Goncourts write, Charles had not been aware that lack of pretense and genuine feeling came increasingly together as one rose into the higher reaches of the literary world. Boisroger has familiar views about literature and life. He believes that "the emotions are contrary to the creative powers of the imagination. You need calm, regular days, a bourgeois condition of the whole being, . . . to give birth to the great, the tormented, the poignant, the dramatic. Those who spend themselves in passion and movement will never produce a passionate book." These ideas are paralleled by Boisroger's social views: social distances had to be preserved, because "from the moment that two classes find themselves in contact, it is the lower class that devours the higher one."[23]

Demailly seeks passage out of Bohemia by way of a novel. This book within the book shows its readers what the Goncourts saw at the core of Bohemia: the history—fictionalized but aimed at the essential, à la Balzac—of the French bourgeoisie. The class's evolution is encapsulated in three generations of its representatives. The family's founder, a no-nonsense, square-jawed, and determined example of economic man, makes a fortune in revolutionary land speculation. On that tough but ample foundation, the second generation arises, no longer oriented only toward money, but fired by the enthusiasms and aspirations of the passionate days of Napoleon. Formed by military training, devoted to human solidarity, caught up in the political struggles of the Restoration, this generation of the family is molded in a pattern that transcends its own narrow horizons, giving it "the healthy and attractive virtues of the eighteenth-century bourgeoisie." Alas, not so the third installment. The nineteenth-century bourgeois is a man in a hurry, cankered by the effects of too much knowledge even at twenty, born old but never allowed to ripen, "summing up in his person the cold ambitions, the impatience for success, the dry calculus of interest, the moral sense deranged by the counsels and temptations of scandalous fortunes, all the practical skepticisms of modern youth."[24]

In *Charles Demailly*, the Goncourts' analysis of modern life appears in the mouth of a doctor Charles consults at the onset of an illness. The doctor—modeled on certain real French physicians and psychiatrists—conceives his task not just as curing his patients but as treating the *mal du siècle*. Why are so many people ill? Because the nervous system is overloaded as never before. "The appetites for well-being, the demands of careers, of position, of money, of domestic luxury, the unbridled competition in everything, the unbridled production of everything, have produced a prodigality in effort, in will, in intelligence, in a word the exaggerated expenditure of human faculties and passions. The activity of everyone, from the top of the scale to the bottom, has been doubled, tripled, quadrupled. We are all of us overexcited."[25]

Like others who subscribed to this diagnosis, the Goncourts believed that the condition they identified was especially harsh on those who worked with their heads, because the contents of men's minds were being constantly disrupted, subjected to blows and counterblows, fortunes that rose and disappeared, dynasties that lasted only ten years. The century of momentary eternities was a terrible devourer of men's beliefs, their hopes, their lives. It is not hard to see how Bohemia typified this modern world. The over-heated life of constantly aroused passion and unremitting inventiveness described by Murger was one special form of the bourgeois existence responsible for the *mal du siècle.* The preference for calmness and regularity insisted on by Boisroger in the novel, and by the brothers themselves in their *Journal,* was the indicated therapy.

Just as Bohemia was one special case of modern life, the nature of modern femininity was another. Demailly's novel was to include women as counterparts of the men in each generation; the Goncourts presented only one woman, but she, too, was the distilled essence of her age. That she occupies a central place in the story is part of its hero's downfall, for here as elsewhere the brothers insist on their conviction that the writer or artist must never marry. Yet marry Charles Demailly does. His choice falls on a young woman whose person and career are the incarnation of femininity in her age. Marthe is, to begin with, an actress, a person whose charms are on display for all who will pay to see them, whose life is a pretense, focusing her energies on self-advertisement. Yet she is respectable, no loose woman, but a *fille à marier,* a condition guaranteed by her determined and watchful mother.[26]

With her reliance on publicity, Marthe finds her counterparts in the Bohemian world of *Le Scandale.* Her attraction to Charles testifies to her eye for talent and the main chance, but her intellectual and moral hollowness puts real loyalty beyond her reach. She betrays Demailly with one of his old Bohemian companions (for whom the original was probably Aurélien Scholl); her final treachery is to provide her lover with letters Charles had written to her during their engagement, *jeux d'esprit* in which he had practiced his wit by making fun of his friends. Their publication brings back Charles's earlier illness and leads to his final collapse. The circumstances surrounding these developments reveal the Bohemians as disloyal, unprincipled, selfish, and scheming. In such an atmosphere—this is the moral of the tale—no serious writer can survive.

The identification of Bohemia with the control of public opinion for self-interested and commercial aims continued to be one of the brothers' pet hates. In 1872, when the artist Fantin-Latour painted two pictures of literary and artistic figures including Rimbaud, Verlaine, and many important Impressionist painters, they described him disdainfully as "the distributor of glory to the beer-hall geniuses." But the Goncourts were just as much in need of publicity, and in search of public recognition, as any of the Bohemians they despised. It is one of their unconscious ironies that they sought to gain a reputation by writing—like none other than Murger—scenes of Bohemian life. Indeed, their obsession with recognition and publicity related them all the closer to Bohemia. In *Charles Demailly*, the ultimate revelation of Bohemia's moral bankruptcy appears in the willingness of Charles's old friends to ruin him by publishing his private letters. Presumably, the point was that such betrayals were miles away from the principled conduct of writers like the Goncourts. Yet, what else was the famous *Journal* but a collection of observations and confidences serving as a reservoir for the brothers' thinly veiled revelations in their writings? Many details in the story of Charles Demailly's failed marriage were based on the experience of the Goncourts' friend Mario Uchard, who had married the actress Madeleine Brohan in 1854 and separated from her by 1858. Numerous readers could recognize Uchard and his estranged wife in the guise of Charles and Marthe, and Uchard was deeply hurt by the use the brothers made of facts he believed had been told them in confidence.[27] The Goncourts' literary practice was less pure, and more indebted to slice-of-life realism, than they wanted to admit. Perhaps this is part of the reason why writing *Charles Demailly* did not purge them of their need to confront Bohemia. Several years later, they wrote an even more elaborate and ambitious anti-Bohemian novel, in which the simultaneous unmasking of Bohemia and its most determined pair of enemies went still further.

The Goncourt brothers wrote *Manette Salomon* between 1864 and 1866, and it appeared first in newspaper serialization in 1867. Much of the interest of the novel was and remains its exploration of the world of French visual arts in the years when debates about classicism and Romanticism were giving way to the emergence of modern painting in the work of Manet and the first Impressionists. The book contains long and often thoughtful discussions of the situation faced by painters of the time, and of the attempts being made to evolve an art appropriate to the new conditions and requirements of modern life. These aesthetic questions were placed in a framework of social and psychological themes the Goncourts had sounded earlier, among them the character of modern femininity and the nature and meaning of Bohemia. The last topic drew especially on the story of their old friend Alexandre Pouthier. The results lack the visionary coherence and literary power of their friend Gustave Flaubert, yet *Manette Salomon* provides a portrait of nineteenth-century artistic life and an image of Bohemia unequaled in its combined hostility and insight.

The novel is the story of three lives from the 1840s to the 1860s. The title character is a Jewish model. (Several independent sources confirm that Jewish women sometimes worked as models in the mid-century.) The original for Manette seems to have been Lia Félix, sister of the well-known actress Rachel and for a time the mistress of one of the brothers' friends, Paul de Saint-Victor. Saint-Victor became one of their sources for the details of Jewish life and practice included in the book. Like Mario Uchard earlier, he was hurt and angry to find his conversations exploited in a published work, all the more so because he himself was partly the source of the second protagonist, Coriolis, an artist and like Saint-Victor a Creole. The third figure, Anatole Bazoche, was based on Pouthier.[28]

Of the minor figures, Chassagnol was a particularly significant one. Modeled on Paul Chenavard, a well-known figure in Bohemian haunts of the mid-century, he stands for the Bohemian who expends his life in passionate talking, leaving no energy for real accomplishment. "Out of his fevered and morbid eloquence that grew as it became more exalted, there rose up the night-time orator, the speaker whose theories, paradoxes, aesthetic ideas, seemed to get drunk on the excitement of wakefulness and on the gaslight, a sort of genius of Parisian speech, arising when others go to sleep, at the end of a café table, his elbows on the dirtied newspapers and cast-off lies of the day." Yet, curiously, Chassagnol served to present views the brothers themselves held. He criticizes the official artistic establishment, but he also castigates artists who believe that society owes them sustenance even though they do nothing worthwhile, the "ridiculous martyrs" who mistakenly think that society, not themselves, is dishonored by their wretched lives.[29]

Anatole's history provides the framework for the others'. "Much less called by art than attracted by the artistic life," he is drawn by "those Bohemian vistas that seemed so enchanting when viewed from a distance," the perpetual carnival of poverty, indiscipline, joking, and models. Anatole's love of practical jokes and teasing gives him the nickname of *la blague*; he represents the vulgar, skeptical, childish, and decadent modern humor that refuses to take anything in life seriously. But his impulses as an artist are conventional and academic, as bourgeois as any grocer's. He burns to win the *prix de Rome*, the official approval "of which Bohemian natures, despite all their shows of independence, are more desirous and avid than all the others."[30] Failing to win the *prix*, and unable to complete his project of a *Christ humanitaire*, Anatole turns increasingly to hackwork, even painting dead bodies for an undertaker. Chassagnol makes him see the emptiness of his life, and he decides to leave Paris. Traveling to Marseille, he meets his old friend Coriolis. The lives of the two now become entwined.

Unlike Anatole, Coriolis has a real calling, talent, vision, and a willingness to struggle. The Goncourts have him inherit enough money to protect him from having to live by hackwork. Recognizing the dangers posed by the twin temptations of women and the desire for material comfort, he insists on living in a poor student quarter, and he chooses Anatole for a companion so as to have conversation and social contact without having to take a mistress.[31]

Coriolis's desire to do ever better work leads him to search for a model, and thus to Manette; she is perfect, physically beautiful, at home in the world of art, and proud of the work she inspires. Even after she and Coriolis become lovers, her independent spirit keeps her from moving in with him. But her attitude changes as his growing success and recognition open up the vista of a more comfortable and regular life both for herself and for their child. Meanwhile, he becomes ever more fatally attached to her.

Recovering from an illness after a stay in the country (which allows the Goncourts to describe the development of the famous Barbizon school of Millet and others, with its attempt to bring French painting into more direct contact with nature), Coriolis begins to evolve a specifically modern kind of art. This is not dull and ugly realism in the manner of Courbet (who is not named, but certainly intended), but a continuation of Delacroix, freed from the delusions of Romanticism. The new art will depict "a century that has suffered so much, the great century of the disquiet of science and the anxiety of truth. . . . A failed Prometheus, but a Prometheus all the same."[32] But that failure overcomes Coriolis, too. His personal need for Manette grows, first during his illness, and then increasingly as her soft and reassuring material presence comforts him when he is fatigued, contrary, fearful of the future, tormented in his imagination. Pregnancy and motherhood change her, too, and her desire to see her son well cared for leads her to think more about Coriolis as a money earner. At the same time, the Jewish side of her personality now becomes prominent, expressed in domestic rituals and ceremonies and in the alien character of her relatives—much more obviously Jewish in speech and appearance than she.

Coriolis is prey to Manette's changed needs and desires because his own artistic efforts have been frustrated. His paintings are condemned in the Bohemian press. Comparing himself with those whose work is praised, "he felt himself born under one of those unhappy stars that predestine the whole existence of a man to struggle, consecrating his talent to contestation, his works and his name to the dispute of battle." Obsessed with death, he falls back into his old illness. His household is taken over by Manette's relatives, muttering Hebrew blessings into the cooking pots. He agrees to sign a contract with a picture dealer, assuring the family a regular income, but condemning him to a schedule and a kind of work dictated by commerce. When eventually he and Manette marry, he is an altogether broken man.[33]

Coriolis's fall—the descent of the modern artist—is framed by the further decline of Anatole, his friend and parasite. Anatole, who had come to depend on Coriolis when the painter seemed to be on the road to success, remains part of the ménage during its stay in the country, but once Manette's domination over Coriolis is strong enough, she engineers his expulsion. The details of Anatole's demise, taken directly from Pouthier's history, include a period of sharing a room with a policeman in a dingy district of central Paris, and whole days without getting out of bed. The Goncourts' comment on this fully embodies their analysis of the psychological and social meanings of Bohemia:

> Anatole presented the curious psychological phenomenon of a man who does not have possession of his individuality, a man who does not experience the need for a separate life, for his own private life, a man who by taste and instinct attaches his existence to the existence of others by a kind of natural parasitism. He was carried along by the force of his temperament toward all those assemblages, all those aggregations, all those forms of regimentation that mix up and dissolve the initiative and person of each in universal commonality. What attracted him, what he loved, was the café, the barracks, the phalanstery.

More and more he abandons himself to "that slope where many men raised in a bourgeois manner, but who by their social preferences, their relations, their meeting-places, descend little by little toward the common people, immerse themselves in its habits, there to forget and lose themselves." No longer seeking work as an artist, Anatole appears now in a different guise, as "the pure Bohemian, the ragpicker of Paris, the man with no other ambition than his nourishment and subsistence, the man who lives from day to day, begging from fortune, at the mercy of chance, and in the grasp of hunger." His life becomes nothing but—the quotation is from Privat d'Anglemont—"a long series of todays."[34]

In this condition, Anatole experiences the discouragement that comes to many aging Bohemians. Yet his story concludes not in despair but in a kind of apotheosis. A sympathetic friend finds him a job—feeding animals in the zoo. There, in the last scene of the novel, Anatole knows peace and contentment. "He slides into the being of the creatures that are there. It seems to him that he exists a bit in everything that flies, that grows, that runs. The day, the spring, the bird that sings, sings in him." A sense of animal happiness filled him with "one of those material beatitudes in which the creature seems to dissolve in the living whole of creation." From time to time, "the former Bohemian rediscovered the joys of Eden, and there rose up in him, in an almost heavenly fashion, something like the happiness of the first man in the presence of a virgin Nature."[35]

The depictions of Bohemia in *Manette Salomon* and in *Charles Demailly* share many motifs—the image of *la Bohème* as a conspiracy of petty and scheming second-rate journalists, the dangers to serious artists and writers inherent in the conditions of modern commercialism and publicity, the pitfalls created by modern womanhood and by a culture that does not protect people from their own animal natures as eighteenth-century society had. In both novels, too, Bohemia lacked the quality that let some suspicious people tolerate it, if reluctantly—namely, its status as a culture of the young. To the Goncourt brothers, Bohemianism represented not youthful experimentation or apprenticeship, but a permanent condition that revealed the deepest perils and defects of modern life.

Some of the notions to which this image of Bohemia was attached in *Manette Salomon* resemble themes of other writers. Privat was specifically invoked, and the portraits of Anatole Bazoche losing his personality—in the crowd, in animals, in nature—recall Baudelairean images of evaporation or self-diffusion. (The Goncourts were always hostile to Baudelaire, who seemed to them essentially Bohemian.) But unlike Baudelaire, they related this psychological phenomenon to a rejection of hierarchy and social distinctions. This allowed them to present the modern form of life crystallized in Bohemia as the embodiment of a paradox: despite its claims to foster and defend the individual person, modern society was no bastion of individuality; quite the contrary, since to eliminate hierarchy and distinction as principles of social organization deprived the individual of the solid attachments and defenses necessary for independence. Anatole's life illustrates this doctrine. His Bohemian rejection of regularity and discipline seems to be inspired by a vision of individual liberty and free development, but hidden in this hatred of *la distinction* was the yearning for humanitarian, socialist solidarity that rose from the heated imagination of the crowd. At its deepest level—finally reached in the last pages of the novel—what such a person longs for is distinction's ultimate contrary: unity with the undifferentiated animal nature that it had been the project of eighteenth-century culture to dominate and spiritualize. The nineteenth century released all the low currents against which the social bulwarks of the Old Regime stood fast: economic materialism, the primitive social impulses of the lower classes, the debilitating and spiritless domesticity of modern women. For a country like France, to trade its traditional culture for these denatured social forms was, in the Goncourts' view, to open itself to domination by those foreign and barbarous elements waiting to overtake it from within: the Jews.

Even those artistic natures who, like Coriolis, instinctively tried to protect themselves against these dangers were likely to succumb to them. Given no point of attachment by an uncomprehending and hostile society, they would be drawn by the force of their own unchecked animal needs toward the slippery slope that led to loss of their manliness and independence. The fate of art was sealed if it was condemned to inhabit the world that nurtured Bohemia.

The social fears and attitudes expressed in these visions of decadence and collapse resembled those of other, less desperate, conservatives. The idea that the attack on social distinctions and aristocratic privileges in the name of equality and personal satisfaction would eventually turn against the individualistic principles in whose name it was mounted lay behind the analysis of Alexis de Tocqueville, the great mid-century historian and social theorist. In his history of France under the Old Regime and in his dissections of nineteenth-century society, Tocqueville warned that the middle-class attack on aristocratic society was destroying the social stability required as much by the bourgeoisie as by the nobles. Once it had triumphed in the realm of politics, the principle of equality would challenge every distinction on which the social order depended, notably that between rich and poor. Socialism, and a society made prey to selfishness and unrestrained passion for material satisfactions, were the dangers looming in the path of a country that sought to abolish the traditional social differences. No stable society could be organized on the principle of individualism. Both Tocqueville and the Goncourts saw the experiences of 1848 as essential revelations of these deeper tendencies in nineteenth-century life.

Yet, as we have seen, the brothers Goncourt were more deeply entangled in the world of Bohemia than their hostility to it suggests. Were they ever aware how much their own practices resembled those of the scandalmongers they attacked? We still know too little about them to be certain, but this question goes to the heart of one of the great enigmas about them, namely the relationship between Edmond and Jules. They shared a remarkable range of activities and attitudes, of which their literary collaboration, common household, and enthusiasm for the society and art of the eighteenth century were only the most visible and publicly known. Few people in Paris ever saw them apart until the day of Jules's death in 1870, and Jules once said that one separated from the other had only halfway sensations, half a life. In 1866, the *Journal* compared them to two women "whose health is identical, whose periods come at the same time. Even our migraines develop on the same day."[36]

The commonality of feeling extended to a shared hostility toward women. Both brothers had sexual relations with women, but neither seems ever to have had a real emotional tie to one. Both in private and public they declared that writers and artists were unsuited for marriage, and that the best mistresses were either married women in search of consolation, or uneducated women of the lower classes, both cases that assured limits on the duration or depth of the affair.

They followed their own advice, involving themselves with women only sporadically and keeping their emotional distance. On some occasions, they seem to have shared a mistress.

But this surface of perfect agreement hid contrasts between Edmond and Jules. Eight years older, Edmond was expected to look after his brother after their mother died in 1848. Yet, it was the younger Jules who came to dominate the fraternity. The favorite of his mother, Jules was thought to be the more talented. He seemed more at home in the world, entering a room confidently while Edmond hung back in the doorway. He usually gave his opinions in the first person singular, while Edmond dissolved himself in the plural "we." Moreover, Jules seems to have been the real source of many of the brothers' social attitudes, including their misogyny. He was never tempted by marriage, whereas Edmond was, having considered establishing a family at the end of his student days. Edmond described himself as a person of strong feelings, whereas Jules's feelings were held in check by conscious will. Jules thought Edmond's character bore traces of his birth in German-influenced Lorraine (Jules was born after the family moved to Paris): he was often ruled by passing desires, the sentiments of "a man weak in the face of pleasure, who has need of discipline, who desires to be carried along by another." Moreover, Edmond's natural impulse "would be toward the bourgeois dream of a communion of life with a sentimental woman." Edmond described the same features of his own personality with less restraint. "There is an underlay of piggishness in me which seems not to have achieved its development."[37]

It seems likely, then, that the hatred of domesticity found in the *Journal* and novels had different roots for each. For Jules, it was a direct expression of his own feelings, at least as he allowed them to be known to himself and others. For Edmond, on the contrary, the mysogyny and determination to avoid intimacy were a kind of discipline, partly self-imposed, partly imposed on him by his brother. The Goncourts' antipathy toward women, with its fear of passivity, of being dominated from outside, subjected to a different nature, responded to a tension between the brothers. It was a way of making certain that their partnership was not endangered by Edmond's attraction for a less strenuous, less self-denying, and less productive life. He said as much in 1895. "Searching through my memories, I do not find in myself, during my whole youth, any desire to become a personality of the first rank. I had only the ambition for an independent life, in which I would occupy myself idly with art and literature, but as an amateur and not, as it turned out, as a galley-slave of glory." Between the brothers themselves, Edmond represented that part of their collective personality revealed in Charles Demailly's or Coriolis's destructive need for sentimental and continuous intimacy.[38]

One of the brothers' projects reveals especially well how these inner differences and tensions related to their career as a whole: the Academy they endowed in their will. The Goncourt Academy remains a prestigious bestower of literary recognition in France. By endowing it, the brothers intended to create an alternative to the official honor conveyed by the government-controlled French Academy. As a private foundation, it could reward suspect or controversial work, passed over by the public one, but genuinely responsive to the needs of the time. It was, in their own terms, a kind of counter-Bohemia, a source of public recognition that would be in the hands not of the plebeian writers who dominated public opinion, but of respectable and educated but independent judges named, in the first instance, by the brothers themselves in their will. Once set up, it would guarantee that the Goncourt name would survive as a presence in French letters. Yet, the manner of its survival testified to the brothers' recognition of their own uncertain status. If their talents as writers were not recognized, still their reputation would be assured by their place as patrons. It was a striking, if unintended, affirmation that their literary position was just what it seemed to their Bohemian enemies—and what Edmond seems originally to have desired—that of wealthy amateurs.

The Goncourt Academy had a further meaning in the brothers' intricate drama. The project was agreed on between them before Jules's death. To carry it out was Edmond's pledge of loyalty to his brother's memory. But that pledge was also a commitment for Edmond that he would preserve the Goncourt capital for the Academy. In other words, he would not allow himself to have any heirs with a claim on the money. His dream of a sentimental union must never become reality: Jules's views about marriage and domesticity were to retain their salutary discipline over Edmond, even from beyond the grave. Thus, each brother's personality and place in their relations contributed to the partnership in its own way.[39]

But the dominant force was Jules, and it would seem that it was especially from him that the brothers' deep hostility to Bohemia arose. Pouthier, we recall, was Edmond's friend, and the *Journal* suggests that Edmond continued to regard him with a combination of indulgence and interest quite different from Jules's caustic wit. It was Jules who suggested at one point that the brothers rid themselves of Pouthier by taking out a classified advertisement: "For transfer: a parasite who has served his purpose." But in 1877, with Jules dead, Edmond made an addition to one of the already written reports on Pouthier's idleness. "Really, I esteem him more than many others," Edmond admitted, for his generosity and directness, and in spite of his vulgarity. Prostituted, banal, Pouthier was still "full of delicate feelings, incapable of envy."[40] So the brother who was attracted to bourgeois sentimentality and the comforts of an ordinary life was also the one more sympathetic to the figure who stood for Bohemia. Like so many others of its enemies, the brothers' hostility to *la Bohème* was so strong in part because it had to overcome an attraction too threatening and dangerous to admit.

Something more needs to be said about the brothers' anti-Semitism. They were not political anti-Semites, and dislike of Jews was, for them, only one of many at least equally strong aversions. Nonetheless, to insist on Manette Salomon's Jewishness emphasized their view that Bohemia, too, was a foreign presence, part of the century's overall abandonment of genuinely French forms of life. The same association between anti-Semitism and anti-Bohemianism reappeared later in the nineteenth century. Edmond knew, and in general approved of, the rabid anti-Semitic publicist Édouard Drumont, whose punchy and influential scandal sheet, *La Libre Parole*, first made anti-Semitism a major force in French public life during the 1890s. Drumont's anti-Semitism—like that of the whole movement he represented—was part of a wider hostility to modern liberal society, with its individualism, its openness to change, and its democratization of life, a hostility that the Goncourts had expressed for the most part in other terms. Animus against Jews was one way to express a yearning for social forms that were smaller in scale, more intimate, tied to the traditions of a community that still enjoyed the social unity and cultural solidarity that modern fragmentation and the need for overarching large-scale organizations were destroying. Anti-Semitism had support among the descendants of groups that had once enjoyed greater authority, the aristocracies. But it often appealed to lower social strata who felt that modern conditions threatened whatever stability their traditional ways of life still possessed—small farmers, artisans, the lower-middle class. Anti-Semitic politics and publicity were therefore often hostile to the activities and interests of the liberal bourgeoisie.

It was in terms of just such hostility that Édouard Drumont linked his anti-Semitism to anti-Bohemianism. When Henry Murger's portrait bust was unveiled in the Luxembourg Gardens in the summer of 1895, several Parisian papers took the occasion to say something about the world he represented. Drumont's article in *La Libre Parole* made it clear that the youth Murger portrayed was not the *jeunesse*—Catholic, serious, antirepublican—he looked to for renewal. Murger had indeed made a place for himself in literature, by linking together the poetic images of the old Latin Quarter with the romantic figure of the artist. The result had served a particular social function, however. It helped to create the mythic world of illusions required by the bourgeoisie in its campaign to make the whole of French society serve its purposes. Young bourgeois needed working-class girls as pleasant diversions until they could acquire a position and marry someone of their own class. They practiced a form of exploitation similar to the bourgeois treatment of workers in industry, and parallel to the clever employment of working-class crowds to further the ambitions of bourgeois politi-

cians. The history of the bourgeoisie was the story of how it corrupted and exploited everyone else in France, a work that had to be
hidden by some sentimental veil. Bohemia was that cover. Now,
however, those people who had been exploited by the bourgeois
were beginning to get back at them. Artists were passing off jokes
as paintings, the duplicity of bourgeois deal making was being exposed, and the morals of the republican leadership were everywhere under attack. "Besotted by the prostitute, robbed by the
Jews, menaced by the worker, the Voltairean and masonic bourgeois begins to perceive that he is in a bad way. He has killed off
every ideal and all faith within people's souls; he has corrupted
everything around him, and all the corruptions he has sown are rising up before him like the avenging furies to push him into the
deep." Thus were the effects of its Bohemian past being visited on
the liberal bourgeoisie.[41]

It would not be fair to the Goncourts to assert that the anti-
Bohemian and anti-Semitic social visions of *Manette Salomon* had a
necessary connection with the protofascist rhetoric of Drumont.
Nonetheless, anti-Bohemianism and anti-Semitism came to be
linked during the nineteenth century because both were forms of
hostility to the modern liberal pluralism that was entering life as the
bourgeois transformation of society continued. Those who rejected
Bohemia with greatest consistency and determination were not the
defenders of modern bourgeois values, but the conservative enemies of bourgeois society.

CHAPTER 7

"A Fatal Scent of Liberty": Bohemia and the Commune of 1871

BOHEMIA PLAYED A ROLE in the most bitter social struggle of the nineteenth century, the Paris Commune of 1871. The Commune punctuated the transition from the mostly authoritarian social peace of the Second Empire to the troubled parliamentarianism of the Third Republic, its drama of utopian aspiration followed by civil war providing one last chance for the hopes and fears of the 1830s and 1840s—and even some actors who still survived from those years—to appear on the public stage. The Commune lasted for only six weeks, from mid-March to late May, but its memory remained alive into the twentieth century. The number of dead in the last bloody week probably reached twenty-five thousand, with many more arrested and deported afterward. The bitterness of the civil conflict was increased by the fact that it followed in the wake of France's humiliating defeat by Prussia in the war of 1870. By contrast with the public face of expansive self-confidence Paris wore during the Bonapartist empire, the class hatred and desperation released in the spring of 1871 signaled to some the collapse of civilization itself.

That the origins and character of the Commune owed something to Bohemia is an assertion seldom found in modern studies, most of which concentrate on its place in the history of socialism and the working classes. But contemporary observers were quick to insist

181

on the Commune's Bohemian features. Only a few weeks after its demise, an article in the prestigious and influential *Revue des Deux Mondes* depicted the Commune as "la fin de la Bohème," the end of Bohemia. The author was a popular and fashionable philosophy professor, later a member of the French Academy, Elme-Marie Caro. The Commune differed from earlier French revolts, Caro thought. Until then, hardly any non-working-class participants had joined the rebel ranks, apart from professional barricade fighters and conspirators like Armand Barbès and Louis-Auguste Blanqui. This latest barbarian incursion had counted at its head "a crowd of names belonging originally to the civilized world, to letters, sciences, and the schools." Literary men had been especially prominent. To Caro, the rage and despair in which the Commune ended were the logical outcome of the moral disorder and indiscipline that had infected French intellectual life during the nineteenth century, and of which Bohemia had served for more than two decades as the sign and banner.[1]

That *la Bohème* had been preparing such a harsh and destructive destiny for its votaries had been hidden through most of its history, Caro believed, by two factors. One was the charm and inoffensive gaiety with which writers like Murger had infused their accounts of Bohemian life. The other was the separation long maintained, he thought, between Bohemia and politics: until five or six years before, he said, Bohemia had remained a purely literary movement. (Within the compass of the Second Empire, this was true enough.) Yet, Caro was convinced that the direction in which Bohemia had evolved should have been apparent from the start. Even Murger's insouciant Bohemians had displayed the weakness, pretension, and disorder that became the moral basis of politics for the Commune's literary leadership, and the vision of Bohemia led many young imaginations astray with its "false and vile ideal of a free life." Bohemia's age of innocence had therefore been short. Poverty had given way to envy, and once Bohemian morality was transplanted into the more heated medium of politics, the unfortunate harvest had quickly ripened.

Caro dated the politicization of Bohemia from the last years of the Second Empire, giving as examples Henri de Rochefort's paper *La Lanterne* (1868) and Jules Vallès's journalism and books, notably the collection *Les réfractaires* (1865). Alongside them, Caro cited a current of atheist and materialist criticism (perhaps best represented, although Caro did not say so, by Raoul Rigault). These writers and others like them had taken part in the café life and clandestine meetings where the social hatred that would break forth in the Commune had been nurtured. Educated leaders had sought to raise themselves by exploiting "lower-class hatreds." Many of them had succeeded. Caro did not have to remind his readers that Rigault and Vallès had become members of the Commune, Vallès as minister of education and Rigault as police commissioner. His audience probably knew, too, that Vallès's *Le Cri du Peuple* had been the most widely circulated and influential Communard paper, with Rochefort's *Le Mot d'Ordre* not far behind. If they did not know precisely whom he meant by "a few misunderstood and jealous sketchers," they had no trouble identifying Gustave Courbet as the "painter mad with pride" in Caro's list of Bohemians who had become Communal officeholders.

Caro's article was the most extensive and serious attempt to link the Commune with Bohemia, but there were others. A popular collective biography of the Communal leadership published soon after its defeat described Charles Longuet (chief editor of the official Communal newspaper and later Marx's son-in-law) as, in his appearance and manner, "the most perfect example of a Bohemian one could meet." The same book cited Rigault as "one of those Bohemians that the Commune placed in a position requiring at once knowledge he absolutely did not have and a bearing, a dignity, for which he had not the slightest care." Jules Forni, author of a biography of Rigault published in 1871, described his Bohemian Latin Quarter life in detail and repeated Caro's account of how the literary Bohemia had become political; echoing Caro's comments about the moral repugnance of Bohemian life, Forni concluded that the threat it presented intensified when it came into contact with working-class dissatisfaction and hostility—the danger still existed that "the workers will once again become the sacrificial victims of the Bohemian."[2]

Similar notions were sometimes expressed without the Bohemian label. Two weeks before the Commune fell, a newspaper generally sympathetic to it complained that the government could only be discredited by the "dissolute airs and wine-shop postures" affected by some of its leaders. From a frankly hostile perspective, Lecomte de Lisle castigated the Commune in an 1871 letter as "that league of all the *déclassés*, the incapable, the envious . . . bad poets, bad painters, journalists *manqués*, novelists from the lower depths." Witnesses at the official government inquiry about the causes of the revolt also suggested that class hatred had been exploited by café orators and "beer-drinkers who talked politics." Both the theme and the label reappeared in a newspaper article of 1872 that found the common origin of many Communard leaders in cafés, dubbing them "the great men of the cheap bars" *("les grands hommes d'Estaminet")*. Among these were Courbet, Vallès, and Gambetta, the latter "the admitted chief of the intellectual and gambling Bohemia." Others said to frequent Bohemian locales included Gustave Flourens and Prosper Lissagaray, as well as the journalists Eugène Vermersch and Auguste Vermorel.[3]

Opponents of the Commune were not alone in dubbing their enemies Bohemians: its defenders occasionally depicted the representatives of the government at Versailles in the same terms. Although rare, this usage serves to remind us that writers like Gabriel Guillemot had suggested that Bohemia extended beyond insignificant down-and-outers to those who lived morally questionable lives on the higher levels of society. This notion of an upper-class Bohemia received wide currency when Henri de Rochefort attacked the Bonapartist regime's moral corruption, pinning the label *La Grande Bohème* on all its supporters and hangers-on. Rochefort's satire was probably what lay behind the pamphlet by "Jacques Bonhomme, rural elector," blaming the Commune on the overblown position Paris occupied within France and on the empire's intellectual and moral degeneration, which it christened *Bohemiasis Napoleonica.* Rochefort's gibes also resembled some of Marx's, who had associated Bohemia with counterrevolution as early as 1851. In *The Civil War in France* (1871), he referred to "the exodus from Paris of the high Bonapartist and capitalist *Bohème*," and spoke of the "phantom Paris" believed in by the moderate minister Adolphe Thiers, "the rich, the capitalist, the gilded, the idle Paris, now thronging with its lackeys, its blacklegs, its literary *Bohème* and its *cocottes* at Versailles" and elsewhere. To Marx, the real, the working-class, Paris of the Commune was not Bohemian.[4]

So it was not. Is there any reason, then, to take Caro, Forni, and the others who associated the Commune and Bohemia seriously? It is tempting to dismiss them all: their purpose was to tar a political cause they feared and hated with the brush of moral decay. Yet in fact there was a Bohemian side to the Commune, and it provides a context within which to consider the nature of Bohemian politics in the nineteenth century.

Conservatives like Caro were not the first to see the radical journalism of the 1860s as Bohemian. Young writers in the Latin Quarter papers that helped lead the movement of opposition to the Second Empire during the 1860s themselves called up the legacy of Bohemia. Some of them were critical of that inheritance, however, and those who were willing to enter into it defined *la Bohème* very differently from people like Caro.

Their vision of Bohemian life, with its conflicts and ambiguities, appears in the pages of the radical weekly *La Rive Gauche.* One of the best-known of the new anti-Bonapartist papers of the 1860s, *La Rive Gauche* led an excited and harried existence in the years after its founding in November 1864. Pursued by the government and the police, the paper found some of its writers and editors in jail, and had to move its offices to Brussels to survive. Both Marx's future sons-in-law, Paul Lafargue and Charles Longuet, were among its contributors. The paper often supported the anarchist visions of

Pierre-Joseph Proudhon, but it was not sectarian: in 1866, it published in translation Marx's "Inaugural Address to the International Workingmen's Association."

In their very first issue, the editors of *La Rive Gauche* sought to define their relationship to the Bohemian traditions of their native Latin Quarter. Urban growth and economic change had so altered the Left Bank that the old Quartier Latin seemed to have disappeared. For a time, the students had acquiesced in Rodolphe's willingness to see the end of his youth in Mimi's death, they said, burying their convictions and satisfied to "put Murger and Musset on their tables next to their law books." Now that time was ending. However much modern egotism and political discouragement had sapped the old traditions, French youth still had heart and spirit. They would show their seriousness and determination.[5]

A month later, one of the paper's editors discussed Bohemia still more directly. The writer was Aimé Cournet, a young author with a law degree and radical convictions, then attempting to support himself with various sorts of literary hackwork. Cournet had been attending some lectures on Henry Murger in a popular series in the rue de la Paix; the *conférencier*, Émile Deschanel, had talked Murger down, telling scabrous stories about his immoral life. Cournet did not want to defend Murger, but he had his own views on what was really wrong with Murger's *Scenes of Bohemian Life*. Not a single page of Murger's book was true, he said, but not for the reasons that bourgeois critics usually alleged. Its real fault was that "behind all that grotesque joy, at the bottom of that existence embroidered with suspect mistresses and equivocal escapades, one never perceives that which makes Bohemia proud, that which makes Bohemia heroic: work." Murger had tried to make up for this defect in the preface, which warned his readers against the pitfalls of the life he described, but that only served to make his account incoherent. "The book of Bohemian life remains to be written."[6]

Cournet's comments were fully in harmony with the general tone of *La Rive Gauche*, a paper frank in its rejection of religion and capitalist society, but moralistic and *sérieux*. In its appeal to duty and *dévouement*, it was typical of other Left Bank publications of the 1860s. One, *Le Critique*, began its career in July 1866 with an attack on "the literature of fantasy"—"all literature that has sensual excitation for its goal." The fantasy writer was a kind of literary tightrope-walker. "Bohemian of letters, he lives from day to day, seizing on whatever can provide material for an article." His purely mercantile literature corrupted taste and morality, mocking those who were devoted to human improvement. Political commitment offered an antidote to the literary temptations of sensuality and corruption.[7]

The attitudes revealed in the Latin Quarter papers of the 1860s remind us that since Murger's day two contrasting moralities had coexisted within Bohemia. Cournet's identification with a heroic life of work echoed the ascetic principles of the Water-Drinkers, who like him kept themselves at a distance from bourgeois life because they feared its softness and corruption. This stance did not always entail commitment to radical politics, but its generally leftist implications had been reaffirmed by Nadar, Lelioux, and Noël in their biography of Murger. Both Cournet and the writers in *Le Critique* set themselves against the other form of Bohemia—the one we identified with Murger's amateurs—which sought spontaneity and indulgence as a liberation from the rigidity of bourgeois life. Only by depicting the two as mutually exclusive could Cournet acknowledge his own membership in Bohemia. Yet the barriers between them had never been as rigid as Cournet supposed, and they would prove to be permeable now, too.

After Cournet's attack on Murger's image of Bohemian life in December 1864, *La Rive Gauche* seemed to lose interest in the subject until late June 1866, when the twenty-six-year-old Aimé Cournet died—appropriately enough, of tuberculosis. (*La Rive Gauche* was not the only paper to notice Cournet's passing: the more established *Courrier Français* also ran an obituary.) An extensive and anguished article praised him for fighting to his last breath in the name of atheism, socialism, and the Revolution, and characterized his heroic life and its miserable end as a protest against existing society.[8]

The author of the obituary was Paul Lafargue, never known for calm or restraint (Marx once threatened to break relations between Lafargue and his daughter if he did not moderate his behavior toward her), and hurt and upset by his friend's suffering and demise. He saw Cournet as one in a series of misunderstood and despised representatives of youth and intelligence whom the nineteenth century had rejected and driven to death. Among these were Musset and Murger, who, Lafargue insisted, had never deserted the humanitarian cause. (Lafargue also invoked Hégésippe Moreau, whom even Murger had warned his readers not to take for a model.) The fate of these people demonstrated the worthlessness of existing society.

Lafargue went on to expound the rudimentary social theory that underpinned his interpretation of Cournet's life. Men came into society with an absolute right to live, and to develop themselves physically and intellectually. This right preceded all social duty. "These revolutionary, anarchist, and incendiary principles declare and authorize the struggle of man against man, of the poor man against the rich, of the hungry man against the idle and satisfied." Modern society provided sustenance only for the limited number of the poor who met its needs; the rest could be left to starve. Only the bourgeois could give his passions free rein without fearing vengeance: the poor man could never satisfy his. "I love women," Lafargue burst out, "and you only allow me to have a woman made ugly and deformed by work. And when my heart and head are filled with an image of a woman who is beautiful and rich, she despises me—I am too low for her. If, enraged, I take her, I violate her—you send me to the galleys. Damn you!"

In associating Aimé Cournet with a frankly anarchist and revolutionary Bohemia, Paul Lafargue was true to his dead friend's own views and feelings. But Cournet had insistently distinguished his Bohemia from the indulgence and egotism he saw in Murger; that distinction now dissolved. Lafargue's Bohemia called up a vision of vengeance, a fantasy of violent personal gratification animated by resentment of society's refusal to meet the sensual needs and desires of its members. The contrast between these two forms of Bohemian consciousness reflected the differences between the two men, but Cournet and Lafargue had been close personal and political friends. The two Bohemias lay closer to each other in real life than the opposition of their moral postures suggested.

Other boundaries also dissolved in Lafargue's tortured necrology. What "poor" did he have in mind when he proclaimed a Hobbesian war between the poor and the rich? Whose voice was raised in the cry of frustration and despair metamorphosed into a threat of rape? Somehow in Lafargue's mind the plight of the working class merged with that of Bohemian poets like Hégésippe Moreau and young radicals with law degrees like Aimé Cournet. His rage erased the line between the different experiences of working class and bourgeoisie that socialist theory presupposed.

The fluid barrier between stoic self-discipline and the demand for gratification reappears with other figures from the same milieu. One of these was Eugène Vermersch, a poet and popular journalist well known in Paris during the 1860s, and a contributor to two prominent Communard papers, Vallès's *Le Cri du Peuple* and *Le Père Duchêne*. Born in 1845, Vermersch was only nineteen when he began to write a series of Murgerian comments about life on the Left Bank: his *Letters to Mimi about the Latin Quarter* shows him living the life, surrounded by students and *grisettes*, walking the streets, sitting in cafés. The only note of criticism is the by-then conventional complaint that the old Quartier Latin has disappeared in the face of urban growth, the influx of nonstudents, and the triumph of materialism. Murger had voiced similar plaints in the 1840s.[9]

During the Commune, Vermersch seems to have devoted most of his energies to *Le Père Duchêne*, a paper that he started up and edited together with Maxime Vuillaume and Alphonse Humbert. Modeled on Hébert's famous sheet of the 1790s, the paper used popular slang and a gallery of stock characters to advocate the Communal and popular cause. Unlike a more ideological admirer of Hébert, Raoul Rigault, the paper's editors were politically flexible and eclectic, associating with both antiauthoritarian and neo-Jacobin elements. Vuillaume, the only one of the editors to have left detailed recollections about the Commune, told that *Le Père Duchêne* made money for its supporters: the news dealers who put up the original five hundred francs necessary to launch the journal received ten thousand francs back on their investment, he claimed, while he and the other editors were brought "a good sum" every day. Although he did not know for sure, Vuillaume suspected that Vermersch used some of his share to recommence a long-standing on-again, off-again affair with an actress. In May, not long before the Commune's end, Vuillaume and several of their friends dined with Vermersch and his mistress at a brilliant *soirée*, with impeccable service, shining dishes, and sparkling crystal. The conversation was political, focusing on a plan to overthrow the Communal government in favor of a directorate that would include the *Père Duchêne* group and their friends.[10]

When the Commune fell, Vermersch escaped to London, where he died in 1878. He remained in touch with many exiles and published a radical paper for a time. He also wrote a series of revolutionary pamphlets, *Opuscules révolutionnaires*, on the subjects of force, dictatorship, the right to steal, the strike, and revolutionary propaganda. In these writings, his social thought emerges as an amplified and intensified version of the ideas Paul Lafargue expressed when Aimé Cournet died: the conflict of bourgeoisie and proletariat was irreconcilable, and since their struggle could end only with the triumph of one or the other, neither side could renounce the use of force; every individual possessed an inherent right to have his basic needs fulfilled, and if society deprived someone of this right, then he was no longer subject to the law and had a perfect right to steal. Vermersch recognized only one appropriate and effective weapon in the social struggle: violence. Strikes by workers were pointless; the only worthwhile form of revolutionary propaganda and education was the kind that taught battle formations and the use of weapons. These lessons, he wrote, were of infinitely more use than "to write a 1,000-page volume on Capital or to give thirty speeches in provincial towns."[11]

What Vermersch's writings shared with his politics was a common demand for the satisfaction of personal desires: Bohemia and revolution were both paths to individual gratification. Yet, the opposition to discipline and restraint he often expressed was countered by his declared allegiance to the great theorist of revolutionary organization and discipline, Louis-Auguste Blanqui. Vermersch's Blanquist sympathies, clear in his support for direct action, also underlay his insistence that a long revolutionary dictatorship would be necessary after the defeat of the bourgeoisie, first to complete the destruction of the old society, then to construct and organize the new. The contrast between this Blanquist *dirigisme* and the rejection of restraint in Vermersch's assertion of the right to steal suggests that he harbored opposing and unsynthesized impulses toward individual liberation on the one hand and authoritarian control on the other. For him, as for the writers of *La Rive Gauche*, existing society was pernicious sometimes because it was too rigid and restrictive, and sometimes because it was too undisciplined and corrupt.

That same duality appeared in the career of one of the officials of the Commune most often and explicitly identified with Bohemia, Raoul Rigault. Rigault was a more consistent Blanquist than Vermersch; he was also a more unrestrained and flamboyant Bohemian. Born in Paris in 1846, the son of a councilor in the Prefecture of the Seine, Rigault received a double *baccalauréat* in letters and sciences, and studied mathematics in preparation for entering the École Polytechnique. But from about 1865 he began to devote himself mostly to radical politics and journalism. Involved in various political projects of a Blanquist cast, he was several times arrested and imprisoned. Rigault sought to develop links between revolutionary student groups and Parisian workers, particularly the traditionally radical artisans of the faubourg Saint-Antoine. (He seems to have been less interested in the more industrialized workers of the suburbs, modeling his politics here as elsewhere on the *enragé* of the 1790s, Hébert. According to Vuillaume, Rigault objected when Vermersch and the others called their paper *Le Père Duchêne*, wanting to reserve the Hébertist title for himself.) At the center of his thinking was atheism, and he carried on vigorous antireligious propaganda. Those who knew and observed him often remarked on one peculiar feature of his radicalism: his personal campaign against linguistic residues of religion and tradition. He refused to say the word "saint," referring to the old artisan district simply as "Antoine" and the Left Bank thoroughfare as "boulevard Michel." In place of "cross," he said "guillotine." A friend named Leroy became "Loi."[12]

To his contemporaries, these linguistic provocations were part of the extreme and dramatic behavior that won Rigault his reputation as an arch-Bohemian. They helped make him one of the best-known characters in the Latin Quarter at the end of the Second Empire. According to his biographer Jules Forni, he could often be seen there, arguing, posing, coughing, spitting, drinking, making speeches, ogling girls, looking down his nose at the police, and staring down priests. His dress was determinedly unkempt and unclean. "Anyone in his entourage who dared wear a white collar was immediately marked down as a Jesuit."[13]

One remarkable feature of Rigault's short life (he was killed during the repression of the Commune in May 1871) is the contrast between this image of the *bohème débraillé* and the figure he presented during the six weeks of the Commune's life. Far from serving as an advocate of libertinism or even social relaxation, Rigault was a force for rigid revolutionary morality. "Revolutionary laws are never severe enough," he is reported to have said. Soon after he took over the Prefecture of Police (it was called the "ex-Prefecture" during the Commune, but, as several people remarked, its functions remained the same), Rigault issued a decree banning all games of chance because they led to "all the vices, even to crime." He did not slough off all his old habits overnight, continuing to frequent cafés and drink with his old friends. But his manner of dress seems to have altered radically, becoming careful and even elegant. A photo from the spring of 1871 preserved in Rigault's dossier at the Paris Police Archives shows him with carefully brushed hair and beard, calm and severe; other contemporary images concur (see figure 6). His severity was directed at those he considered the Commune's enemies, and notably against priests, whom he continued to pursue. (Interrogating one, he asked who the priest's

6. Raoul Rigault as Communard Police Prefect,
in a contemporary lithograph.

employer was. "God," came the answer. Where did he live? "Everywhere." "Write it down," Rigault instructed his secretary. "X, calling himself the servant of one called God, a vagrant.") Loyal to his friends, Rigault was largely responsible for saving the painter Renoir's life after Renoir, innocently sketching one of the approaches to Paris, created suspicion he was a spy. But he also pressed for the prosecution and execution of several hostages, and even some supporters of the Commune thought him unnecessarily harsh and bloodthirsty.[14]

Rigault's passion for police work had grown out of an interest in the spies the Bonapartist regime set on republican and socialist political groupings in the 1860s. After the Second Empire fell on September 4, 1870, he became an official of the Prefecture for a time, and wrote a series of articles exposing Bonapartist spies. Both Rigault's long-standing fascination for the police and the severity and determination he brought to his duties recall the most prominent official of the revolutionary provisional government to be explicitly identified with Bohemia in 1848, Marc Caussidière. Like Rigault, Caussidière also served as revolutionary police prefect. He, too, had been a famous café fixture before the outbreak of revolution, as well as a member of secret societies. Caussidière once in office also turned out to be a vigorous advocate of social order, favoring a puritanical morality and boasting that he had "made order with disorder."[15]

Rigault was not as morally rigid as Caussidière, but both were Bohemians whose attitudes and behavior altered markedly once revolution endowed them with authority. Blanqui himself seems to have understood something of the process at work in such transformations. Arguing for the arming of the whole male population of France to fight the Prussians in September 1870, he insisted it was wrong to limit arms bearing to those who could demonstrate a regular means of support. The "supreme test" of combat would turn even vagrants into new and purified men. "Rehabilitated in their own eyes by the solemn contact with the society that had stigmatized them, they will become the most pitiless repressors of those evil natures that resist reconciliation. Never will any police have been so severe."[16]

When Caro characterized the Commune as "la fin de la Bohème" in the *Revue des Deux Mondes*, he contrasted the discipline and order that reigned in respectable society with the irregularity and indulgence characteristic of Bohemia. The histories of Rigault and the editors of *La Rive Gauche* show how much Caro's account left out: the unkempt and indulgent life could be closer than he realized to the ethic of severity and work, and the one was sometimes transformed into the other; the moral principles that struggled within Bohemia were not unique to it, but were exactly those that competed to define bourgeois society as a whole—the claim to individual liberation and satisfaction on the one hand, the identification with duty and work on the other. Perhaps the fear and hostility a conservative bourgeois like Caro felt toward Bohemia arose unconsciously from a repressed recognition of this inner similarity.

Both the sources and significance of the Commune's Bohemian ingredient appear more fully in the career of Jules Vallès, the most prominent and self-conscious Communard Bohemian. Born in 1832, and therefore ten or more years older than the other people we have so far considered, Vallès was only a year from his fortieth birthday at the time of the Commune. His influence in the spring of 1871 was greater than that of Rigault or Vermersch, both as a member of the Communal government and through his newspaper, *Le Cri du Peuple*, which seems to have reached a daily circulation of 100,000 during April and May. His identification with the Commune continued after its defeat. He wrote a play about the uprising from his London exile in 1872, and the third volume of his autobiographical trilogy, *Jacques Vingtras*, finished a few years later, recounted the history of the Commune and of his participation in it. That book, *L'insurgé* (*The Insurrectionist* in its English version), remains a useful and often cited source for Communard history.

Vallès is often presented as the representative of a new kind of

Bohemia. Compared with Murger's realm of carefree poets and artists, Vallès's *Bohème* was darker, harder, more separated from ordinary society; it was more likely to retain a permanent hold on its denizens, and more fully allied with political opposition, even with revolution. Here the smoldering hatreds of permanently *déclassé* ex-bourgeois, unable or unwilling to find a point of entry into ordinary society, waited for the moment when they could contribute to a general conflagration.[17] In the *Jacques Vingtras* trilogy, Vallès presented the Commune as the longed-for outcome and the dramatic fulfillment of his own passage through Bohemia, and he made his discovery that earlier pictures of Bohemia were false and deceptive an important stage along the way. Vallès first adopted those images, taken from Balzac, Gautier, and Murger, but his experience of continuing poverty and disappointment in the early years of the Second Empire led him to realize that these earlier writers had known hunger and despair, too. "They lie, then, when they sing the joys of the adventurous life, of nights spent under the stars. Writers, professors, comic and tragic poets, they all lie!"[18]

In *L'insurgé*, Vallès depicted Murger's funeral as a critical moment in his decision to write the truth about Bohemia. He had taken time off from his job as clerk in a Parisian district mayor's office to march in the procession. But the sentimentality and official mock-concern struck him like a blow: "I felt my guts knot up in anger." Later, he identified that rage with the first stirrings of a book he would write, *Les réfractaires*. "I who am saved shall write the story of those who are not, the story of the beggars who have not found the bowl." Vallès said he had intended to "sow revolt without seeming to, without anyone suspecting that, beneath the tatters that I will hang up like those in the morgue, there is a weapon to be seized by those who have kept their rage or haven't been degraded by poverty." In place of the Bohemia of cowards earlier writers had depicted, Vallès would show one populated by men who were "desperate and threatening." The Vallès of *Jacques Vingtras* was one of these. He might be forced into compromises with the bourgeois: "But you will pay us for it, stupid society! you who starve the learned and the courageous when they don't want to be your lackeys!" When the day of battle came, Vallès would have thousands of rebels behind him: "I shall have become . . . the commander of the [bourgeois] frock coats at the side of the [working-class] smocks."[19]

Yet Vallès's purposes and motives, even as he depicted them in *L'insurgé*, were not always so clear. Describing his work on *Les réfractaires*, he spoke in different terms:

> I took the pieces of my life and sewed them to pieces of other lives, laughing when I felt like it, grinding my teeth when memories of humiliation made my flesh crawl over my bones like the meat of a cutlet as the blood pours out under the knife.
>
> But I've saved the honor of a whole battalion of young people who had read *Scenes of Bohemian Life* and who believed in that carefree, rosy life; poor dupes to whom I shouted the truth.
>
> If they still want to taste that life, it's because they're nothing but potential sawdust for a barroom floor or fair game for Mazas prison. When they reach thirty, suicide or insanity will grab them by the neck, the hospital guard or the prison guard will grab them by the arms, they will die before their time or be dishonored at their time.
>
> I shall not pity them now that I've ripped the bandages from my wounds to show the kind of gash made in a man's heart by ten years of lost youth![20]

Was Vallès's purpose to invoke the revolutionary potential of Bohemian life or to warn people away from entering it? Did the paths of Bohemia lead to a struggle worth joining or to a preordained defeat?

Vallès's personal history between 1848 and the fall of the Bonapartist regime does not provide an easy answer to these questions. His revolutionary credentials were of long standing. As a schoolboy, he greeted the 1848 Revolution with enthusiasm. Still only nineteen at the time of Louis-Napoleon Bonaparte's *coup d'état* at the end of 1851, he attempted to organize resistance, and when it failed fled the capital. His father, fearing the family and the younger man's future would be compromised, then had Jules shut up briefly in a mental asylum. In 1853, Vallès became involved in an anti-Bonapartist plot, and spent six months in prison as a result. During the mid-1850s, Vallès lived in the precincts of literary poverty, supporting himself with a small allowance from his family and with whatever jobs came his way. He served as secretary to Gustave Planche, a critic well known for his independent and often biting commentary as well as for his Bohemian life-style. Vallès worked for various small and ill-paying papers, including, like Murger, one printed on water-resistant paper for the patrons of bathhouses. He also seems to have tried out jobs in schools and in commerce both in Paris and elsewhere.[21]

Then, in 1857, Vallès made himself known in Parisian literary circles with a booklet on a surprising subject: the stock market. It was an astounding debut, seemingly as unconnected with Vallès's past as with his future. Called simply *L'argent (Money)*, the book consisted mainly of a description of the functions and arrangements of the Paris Bourse. The dangers of speculation were noted, but so were the services rendered to industrial progress by the centralization of capital. Some critics doubt that Vallès wrote the whole of the work himself, and point out its resemblances to Proudhon's recently published *Manual for the Stock-Market Speculator.* But whereas Proudhon's work was clearly intended as an exposure of the egotism and immorality of modern finance, it is much more difficult to say what Vallès's intentions were.[22]

No doubt much of his praise of the stock market and of wealth was bathed in irony. Vallès chose to appear, as one reviewer at the time observed, as "the disillusioned person who no longer believes in anything but money." But he spoke from the gut. "I have tried out literature; in that *métier* I have lost two organs, my heart and my stomach." Vallès was not burning his verses, he said, but he was fleeing his old friends the misunderstood poets, the martyrs of thought, the false great men who belonged rather in the lunatic asylum than in the Panthéon. Vallès said "Vive l'argent" with despair, but he said it. To praise money was to recognize that every worthwhile human achievement partook of "that mental power, that *je ne sais quoi* of the unexpected and the strong that makes millionaires." Poverty made even great writers—witness Jean Jacques—sad, bitter, cynical, and mean.

> The stock market is the City Hall of the new republic. It is there that we gather in the sacred instrument of independence: fortune. It is there that the genius of France will break out henceforth, far from tribunes and soldiers. It is there that a discouraged generation, saddened by inactivity, avid for emotion, can come to re-temper its heart. In that war of interests, in that noise of jumping millions, of whistling locomotives, of cities that are born as in books written with the pen or the sword, I see a moving poetry, serious and profound, that I would call, let God condemn me, the *sacred poetry* of the nineteenth century.[23]

Although students of Vallès quibble about whether there is more ironic social criticism or bitter self-rejection in *L'argent*, all seem to agree that the work was a declaration of independence from the romantic glorification of literary poverty represented by Murger's *Scenes of Bohemian Life*. The author of *Jacques Vingtras* would have approved such a judgment, but there remain good reasons for questioning it. A yearning for the five-franc piece that decorated the cover of Vallès's book had been a commonplace of Bohemian literature from the start. Vallès's career before the Commune expressed an ambivalence very much like Murger's. As his biographer Roger Bellet has recognized, much of his work in this period suggests a conflicted but recurring impulse to make his peace with society.

The notoriety he gained with his first published book gave him entry to a number of papers, among them the popular and well-paying *Le Figaro*. His income from writing was sometimes impressive (in one year, he made over twenty thousand francs from *Le Figaro* alone), and he hired an assistant to make fair copies and read proof. The helper was Victor Noir—Vallès referred to him as "mon Noir," my slave—a struggling journalist whose murder by one of Napoleon III's relatives nearly sparked a revolt in 1870. Yet

Vallès was never sufficiently comfortable with his success to live and work in a stable enough way to make it last. More often than not, his writings continued to mark him as an outsider.[24]

In these years, Vallès was struggling to weave some sort of literary success out of the tangled web of hostility and desire that tied him to ordinary life. If any single quotation can encompass his state of mind, it may be this one from the article "The Dead," first published in *Le Figaro* on November 1, 1861. "Messieurs! There is a misunderstanding between us! In every man who takes up a pen, a palette, a chisel, a pencil, whatever, the bourgeois sees a useless person; in every bourgeois, the man of letters sees an enemy. Sad prejudice, foolish opinion, unhappy antagonism. Our cause is the same, the valiant cause of the parvenus! This day and place [All Saints' Day, when people visit cemeteries] are well chosen for sealing the alliance between young literature and the old bourgeoisie. You have your dead, we have ours. Let us mix our immortals over their tombs."[25] This image of social unification in the face of death would reappear, invested with still more psychic intensity, in Vallès's writing during the Commune. The salient element in this tortuous plea for reconciliation is, however, the jarring claim—so reminiscent of *L'argent*—that what brings artists and bourgeois together is their common status as parvenus. Was Vallès joking? Was he appealing to the bourgeois or insulting them?

The conflicts in his mind demanded that he had to do both. We can see this in the revised version of Bohemia he presented in the essay inspired by Murger's funeral, the title piece for his collection that appeared four years later, in 1865, *Les réfractaires*. The term *réfractaires* originally referred to those who had refused military service during the first Napoleonic empire. The group to whom Vallès now applied it sought freedom in a different way: individuals who, "instead of accepting the place the world offered them, desired to make one all by themselves, by the force of audacity or talent; those who, thinking themselves big enough to arrive at the burning goal of their ambition by the sole force of their desire, deigned not to mix with the others and take a number in life." They had cut through the fields instead of taking the high road; and they ended up in the gutters of Paris. Leaving aside that unhappy ending, we can see how this definition joined *réfractaires* and bourgeois as parvenus. Both insisted on being self-made men, creating positions in society by the power of their individuality.

Included in Vallès's Bohemia were some whom Murger would have accepted and others he had sought to exclude. The catalogue listed those "who have done everything and are not anything," who had been to all the schools and had no degrees or diplomas; professors who had cast off their robes, lawyers turned into comedians, priests become journalists. Here were the fools and geniuses who searched for perpetual motion, the secret of flight, the blue dahlia, the white blackbird; and those who "thirst only for noise and emotion, but who still believe they have a mission to accomplish, a priestly duty to fulfill, a banner to defend." Resisting the world's attempt to make them teachers or notaries, they departed into a separate life, strange and sad. They carried their pride before them like a torch, hid their anguish and shame in the cloak of their eccentricity, willing to pass for madmen in order that others not attribute their raggedness to poverty. Living on the margin of *la vie sérieuse*, they shared in all the follies and all the festivals, paying for their drink with *bons mots,* telling stories, reciting verses. Some were only there as visitors—Murger would have called them amateur Bohemians—bourgeois or gentlemen playing at art or lowlife, descending to the haunts of the *réfractaires* to share *la soupe et l'émotion.*[26]

It is hard to see how Vallès in 1861 could have regarded this description as an incitement to revolution, even a hidden one. There were intimations of revolt; but they were overpowered by something more pervasive and sadder: the sense of defeat. The difference between the suffering poor and the *réfractaires* was "the difference between the slave and the vanquished." They organized resistance, but against hunger. The revolutionary image Vallès found for them was that of the Vendée, the province whose rejection of Parisian domination during the 1790s had taken the form of nostalgic clericalism and royalism. Like the people of the Vendée, the *réfractaires* were prey to isolation, illusion, and defeat. "From this troubled life with its false joys there arises, alas, an unhealthy vapor, not an odor of debauchery but a fatal scent of liberty." After a day of trailing through the mud, the *réfractaires* came together at night, to plunge up to their necks in wine and talk, flaunting their paradoxes, proving their merit to one another, pouring out their hearts in a cloud of heroic but useless fantasy, imagining things never done and books never written. "People call them roués, but they are dupes; or débauchés, when they are mad." They ended up in a hospital, as suicides, in the provinces. They might make a powerful army if only their country knew how to use them. But the reality of their lives was shipwreck, and Vallès's final cry summed it up: "Man overboard!"

Nothing is more pervasive in Vallès's writings throughout his life than the sense of identification with the defeated, the *vaincus*. He devoted one essay in *Les réfractaires* to victims of the book, "Les victimes du livre":[27] those who have been oppressed by the tyranny of print, persuaded to form their lives after some literary model, which causes them to distort themselves or torture others. Vallès included among them "almost all the danger-seekers, banner-wavers, apostles, tribunes, soldiers, conquerors, conquered, the martyrs of history, the executioners of liberty." The list overlapped the catalogue of *réfractaires* at many points, redefining the latter not as victims of their individual talent, pride, or audacity, but of illusions that culture imposed on them. Vallès defended and cherished the individuality of the *réfractaires* despite all its dangers; just for that reason he sought to liberate himself and others from the tyranny of culture. Especially in his politics, Vallès consistently rejected models derived from the past. He was determined to be free of them even at the cost of rendering himself isolated and vulnerable at his most wholeheartedly revolutionary moments.

Writing in a radical Lyon newspaper in 1864, Vallès warned against continuing the errors of the Jacobins. Their classicism had led them to stifle their individuality and the needs of their time under the weight of inherited tradition. Men of the nineteenth century should not model themselves on ancient survivals. "It is necessary to be oneself, to cast the heavy books and banners far away, to affirm one's own personality, be it weak or strong, and not sacrifice the character and rights of the individual either to the need for glory or to reasons of state." Two years later, he lamented the unitary and centralizing course modern revolutions had taken, and called for reaction in favor of the individual personality and against regimentation. Even faith in revolution must not be allowed to "devour the personality." It was this individualist and anti-Jacobin sentiment that tied Vallès to Proudhon. Vallès read and praised Proudhon during the 1860s, but the attraction he felt had little to do with Proudhon's specific views about the proper way to organize society. What drew Vallès was Proudhon's insistence that the paths of revolution not be clogged up with the heroic debris of the past. Proudhon had summed up his rejection of pedestals and altars, Vallès said, in a single sentence: "After persecutors there is no one I hate more than martyrs."[28]

Like Proudhon, Vallès often spoke on behalf of the poor and oppressed. But for both men the central tenet of the faith in revolution and even in what they called socialism was the defense of individuality. Thus, Vallès's sense of being a loner, an *irrégulier*, as he called himself in a series of letters published in 1868, applied not only to his feeling of distance from established bourgeois life, but also to his manner of joining the political struggle against it. "I am an irregular, like many men of determination and people of heart who have never been able to go anywhere without finding others who wanted willy-nilly to submit them to a discipline or attach them to a flag. Some, the number is growing every day, have preferred to march all alone." It was a difficult way of life; feared by those who belonged to a party or a school, the irregular was "caught between two fires," as likely to be attacked by those he counted friends as by the common enemy. Yet this was the price of liberty and it had to be paid.[29]

The phases of Vallès's personal odyssey are well represented by the titles of the *Jacques Vingtras* triology: *L'enfant, Le bachelier, L'insurgé*, for the passage from childhood to rebel led through the world of education. That personal story was also the history of Vallès's family. His father, son of a peasant with a little land, had sought to enter the bourgeoisie by a path often recommended in nineteenth-century rural France, the path of learning. The French educational system expanded in the nineteenth century, and many primary- and secondary-school teachers, especially in rural and small-town districts, were drawn from peasant families, attracted to the career by the promise of bourgeois respectability and comfort. Yet the career patterns and the marriages of schoolteachers show that few of them ever rose to the ease and position they craved; their hopes of social ascension were usually aroused only to be dashed, and most remained in the social milieu of their origins.

Jean-Louis Vallez (Jules adopted the different spelling) was a perfect example of the difficulties such people faced. He married the unlettered daughter of poor peasants, so that even his home life displayed the conflict between his aspirations and the weight of his origins. His early career was beset by troubles, poverty, shame, even unemployment for a time. These were the formative years of Jules's life, and if we can trust the account in *L'enfant*, they were gray indeed; the father seems to have been persecuted and disdained by both students and colleagues, who thought themselves socially superior. Jules never forgot the indignities to which his father was subjected, the dressings-down he received from superiors, the tears of shame he hid, the great weight of sadness that the son felt pressing down on his own shoulders. Relief came only in visits to peasant relations, free of his father's frustrated ambitions. The lesson seemed clear: to escape peasant status through education only led to new forms of degradation; the subjection inherited by the rural underclass was confirmed, not canceled. This burden of pain and guilt was the origin of the ambivalence that simultaneously drew Vallès toward the educated bourgeoisie and drove him to revolt against it.[30]

Acceptance of defeat and punishment was the great theme of Vallès's childhood as he reports it in his autobiographical novel. The first sentences of *L'enfant* tell that Vallès had no memory of any caress, any cuddling or indulgence, from his mother: his memories were of being regularly beaten. She made promises to obtain good behavior, he writes, only to break them; her peasant ideas of appropriate manners and proper clothes were inappropriate in school, where he was shamed and derided. These humiliations helped to fuel the fire of revolt; at the same time, they contributed to his sense of belonging to a group whose humanity was defined by its histories of rebellion and defeat. In 1864, Vallès described the people of his native province, La Velay, in these terms: "Strange race whose sons all carry in their hearts a terrible need for liberty, and even the instinct of revolt, so much so that their life is always agitated and they die in the shadows, one by one, crushed by their own power, victims of their ferocious pride." Vallès thought he belonged to a people of *réfractaires* by birth.[31]

As we know, Vallès was by no means the only denizen of Bohemian Paris in the nineteenth century whose sense of marginality in the city was rooted in rural France. Vallès felt much sympathy for Gustave Courbet, sensing in him both sides of his own dilemma: the instinct for revolt and the ambition to be accepted. In 1866, Vallès wrote an article recalling the strong impression that Courbet's socially charged *The Stone-Breakers* had made on him when it was first exhibited in 1851. At the same time, he praised some of Courbet's more recent (and less provocative) landscapes, which, he thought, showed how an artist who had been derided for his "odor of the stable or of Bohemia" could produce works that were tender and gay, of a pure and healthy air.[32]

The climate of growing political confrontation during the last years of the Second Empire heightened the tone of conflict in Vallès's writings. Yet the idea of defeat remained central to him, and he continued to shift tortuously between confrontation and reconciliation. At the end of 1868, Vallès published an impassioned memoir of the *coup d'état* that had brought Napoleon III to power seventeen years before: it had been a body blow to a whole generation, "many went mad from it." Those who had been twenty in 1845 had known what it was to live and hope. Vallès's generation hardly had a chance to experience either: "We left the lycée in 1850; in '51 we were already beaten." The following years with all their disappointments taught much about the difficulty of struggle. Vallès was ready to write on his banner "To live working" without

adding—as the Lyon silk weavers had in 1834—"or die fighting."
He was removing himself from the field of battle. His memorial to
1851 was "a *réfractaire*'s letter of adieu."[33]

Vallès did not abandon politics. His writing led to prosecutions
by the Bonapartist regime and to several short terms in prison. As
the empire's crisis grew more apparent, Vallès recalled the revolutionary traditions of the Parisian *peuple*. They would do their duty
when the time came; out of the city's streets, a Third French Republic would arise. Yet oppression and humiliation were not limited
to one class. The bourgeoisie was less distant from the people than
it seemed because it "includes many ruined people," and his own
audience, Vallès believed, consisted of "those young men who are
tied to the people by their origins, and to the bourgeoisie by their
education." He continued to ask for an end to "this misunderstanding that has for a long time separated the artists and the bourgeois,
divided the fathers from the sons."[34]

The Second Empire fell—defeated by the Prussians—on September 4, 1870. The Paris Commune was not established until the following March. In the intervening months, republicans and socialists
(Vallès prominent among them) worked to keep the new regime as
close to the earlier revolutionary traditions as they could, even attempting insurrection on two occasions. But the uprising that led to
the Commune was not the product of organized planning, despite
the many conspiracy theories that grew up in its wake. Paris had
been under siege during the fall and winter; to counter it, arms had
been widely distributed. After the armistice on January 28 and the
election of a National Assembly in February, moderate leaders like
Adolphe Thiers wanted to disarm the populace. The army's attempt
to remove cannon from the northern districts on March 18 provoked a spontaneous uprising, frightening the government's leaders into abandoning the city for Versailles. Those who found
themselves in control of Paris—much to their own surprise—were
not the radicals of the Republican Central Committee but the much
more diverse National Guard Central Committee. This group, work-

ing together with the district mayors, arranged the elections that produced the Commune government on March 26.[35]

A regime that arose so unexpectedly was bound to be subject to contrasting attempts to capture and define it. Two issues became particularly important. One was whether the Commune was primarily a government of revolutionary national defense on the model of the Jacobin regime of 1793–94, or primarily an expression of some form of communitarian cooperation (socialist or not) opposed to Jacobin centralism. Although the question was never posed so clearly for many Communard participants and sympathizers, this alternative provided the line along which the Commune divided into two factions over the issue of establishing a Committee of Public Safety at the end of April. The majority, in favor of the Committee, contained a large number of Jacobins and Blanquists; the minority included followers of Proudhon and members of the International Workingmen's Association. The second critical issue concerned the class basis of the Commune's support. The uprising on March 18 was supported by both bourgeois and working-class groups, the former radicalized by defeat, the siege of Paris, and widespread fear that the National Assembly would restore the monarchy; the elections of March 26 brought out many voters in middle-class districts. In the weeks after, however, most better-off Parisians ceased to support the Commune, and many fled the city. The Commune became an increasingly working-class regime. Some leaders recognized that the government would have to draw on continued middle-class support if it were to have any chance of surviving the attack from Versailles, yet its bourgois supporters dwindled and became isolated.

These issues provided the frame for Vallès's activity in the six weeks of the Commune's life. His first feelings were of profound release and joy. "O great Paris!" he wrote in *Le Cri du Peuple* on March 26. "Cowards that we were, we were already talking of leaving, of putting ourselves far from your faubourgs—we believed them dead! Pardon! Country of honor, city of salvation, bivouac of the Revolution! Whatever happens, even if we have to be defeated again and die tomorrow, our generation has its solace. We are repaid for twenty years of defeat and anguish." Vallès felt that he could finally breathe the air of liberty for which he had so long yearned.[36]

Yet the revolutionary rebirth did not wash Vallès clean of his past. The hostility he had always felt toward those radical currents he identified with regimentation grew more important once the various revolutionary factions were actually competing for power. Those with whom Vallès felt most in harmony were the advocates of liberty in all its forms. He was enthusiastic for working-class political figures like the shoemaker Édouard Rouiller, whose innocence of grammar went along with a general contempt for discipline, and whose carnivalesque espousal of autonomy included a conviction that a few good drinks cleared the head. Toward the valiant old Jacobin conspirator Delescluze, Vallès felt a certain sympathy, but his admiration was mixed with suspicion of a republic that "had roads traced out, military frontiers and outposts, combat cadences, regular stops for martyrdom." For sectarians like Vermorel, Vallès felt a more straightforward hostility, hating the attempt to turn the heroes of 1793 into a new calendar of saints, and to imprison the Commune in a straitjacket of Robespierrean revolutionary virtue. Vallès's opposition to censoring Le Figaro—resented on the Left for its disillusioned and sometimes cynical comments on republicans and socialists—made him suspect to some Communards.[37]

Vallès's journalism in the spring of 1871 continued to sound the old themes: the desire for reconciliation, the identification with defeat, the foreboding of disaster and death. There were two bourgeoisies, Vallès explained: one, inactive and corrupt, was beyond saving; but the working bourgeoisie, upright and worthy, toiling side by side with the people and willing to get its hands dirty, was the sister of the proletariat, by virtue of its courage and, even, its anguish. "For it has its anguish, its risks of failure, its days of reckoning. . . . How many I know among the established and the well-placed who have troubles like those of the poor, who ask themselves sometimes what their children will become, and who would exchange all their chances for happiness and profit against the certitude of a modest employment and an old age without tears!"[38]

Vallès called for this unification with promises and with threats, expansively and by wheedling. But his pleas reached their greatest intensity in an image of violent, sacrificial death. If the two classes were not united in struggle, they would be joined in bloody defeat. Who knew what fate was reserved for the Commune, he asked at the beginning of April. A surprise attack could deliver it up to the infamous men of Versailles, and give the revolutionaries over to death. They would fall by the dozens, and their bones would pave the cellars of the Hôtel de Ville. "And in the ferocious joy of that quick revenge, all the shades of difference will be confounded by deportation or assassination; the bayonette and the club, the cannonball and the bullet will strike red and blue alike; in the same sewer, behind the demolished barricade, will flow together the blood of men in [bourgeois] frock coats and men in [working-class] smocks."[39]

Even before the popular revolt of March 18, Vallès had spoken of the possibility of a replay of earlier defeated uprisings: "How base you will seem, O June Days; how small you will appear, O Second of December!" Certainly not all Vallès's images of struggle were thus bathed in the backlight of defeat. He called for organization and action, envisaged the final victory of revolution, described the people of Paris as noble, proud, and heroic. But the image of these fighters as already and necessarily defeated, *vaincus* like his *réfractaires*, kept coming back. In an article called "The Red Flag," Vallès defended the popular symbol against those who made it an object of loathing and fear. "Poor red flag, great calumny. People have made it into the standard of murderers because it has the color of blood. But this blood is that of the people, the blood of the martyr, and not the blood of the executioner. The people has nothing else to give. Blood is its gold and its purple; it has opened its veins, that's all, and soaked its banner with them."[40]

The retrospective account of the Commune in *L'insurgé* also associated the Communard revolt with an impulse for self-sacrifice. Raoul Rigault—who died in the last days—had shown his readiness well before, always just as prepared to expose his breast to bullets as he was to "show his rear end" to the forces of order. Several of the Commune's working-class participants revealed the same psychology to Vallès. He recounted the story of a worker from Nantes who went to Paris in the hope of finding work, and "where I may also find a way to give my life, poor as I am, if it can stop up a breach, one morning of revolt." His case reminded Vallès of the stone cutter (later a street vendor) Mabille, who also dreamt of sacrificing himself to start a rebellion: "Ah! If the blood could flow!" Thinking to write a history of "the defeated of June," Vallès had visited former barricade fighters and their relatives. He found families where images of the catastrophe were piously preserved. Why, he asked, did these poor people "believe in the necessity of sacrifice, in the fatality of the hecatomb?" His own mood was no different in the last days. He was ready to give himself to the only duty left, "to go and stand next to the flag, like the officers around the mainmast when the ship goes under."[41]

Vallès's identification with the revolutionary people of Paris in 1871 thus echoed his earlier visions of Bohemia, with their peculiar mixture of self-assertion, rebellion, and the acceptance of suffering and defeat. It is not too much to say that Vallès joined the Commune in the expectation of its defeat, that on some level he even desired it—as a confirmation of his conflicted desire to join society and reject it, at once to rise through education and literary talent, and return to the soil of his ancestors.[42]

Despite many reports of his death, Vallès survived the bloody repression of the Commune, hid out for a time, and then escaped to London, where he had a fitful, frustrating, and unhappy exile until the official amnesty granted all Communards allowed him to return to Paris in 1878. He read modern socialist writers (including Marx, whom he found difficult and obscure) and moved closer to organized politics. During the last years of his life, a revived *Le Cri du Peuple* became a major organ of the French radical Left; before that, in 1881, Vallès wrote an admiring preface for a book by the socialist leader Benoît Malon, *The New Party*, in which he said, "I hold for the hotheads against the moderates, for the workers in smocks against the uniformed Bohemians, and I declare that I believe only in the Revolution."[43]

Vallès had proclaimed his separation from nonpolitical Bohemians before. But the distance was greater now than during the 1860s. In the same year, 1881, he wrote a pair of articles about his old friend André Gill, the famous cartoonist whose biting satirical drawings had been important weapons for the political opponents of the Second Empire. Gill had been a loyal Communard, but in the following years he seemed to lose his bearings and drift from one political camp to another. Finally, in 1881, he had a breakdown and entered a mental hospital. Gill's fate touched Vallès closely and he reacted from the depths, but his response was neither sympathetic nor generous. What had led to Gill's breakdown was, said Vallès, his rejection of continuing political commitment. He had refused to be moved by Vallès's descriptions of the health-giving air one breathed in the fields of battle, the pride that flowed from doing one's duty to a higher cause than the self. Vallès, for his part, was enlisted in the great social army. "For my account, every time a personal wound made me bleed, I put myself by the side of the flag. . . . Poverty itself, deadening and vile poverty, does not stain the imagination of those who have conviction." Vallès had always known that the life of the *irrégulier* was full of perils; now his fear of them had overcome his distaste for organization and discipline. The *réfractaire* was giving way to the party member.[44]

Vallès was already moving in this direction when he made the villain of his play *The Paris Commune* the only explicitly Bohemian figure in it. Drawn to radical workers by his jealousy and envy of successful bourgeois, the journalist Racatel is loyal only to his own ambition and hunger for power; during the Commune, he gives information to the Versaillais, weakening the Communard position and causing the death of some supporters. Vallès was coming to believe some of the things about Bohemia that the philosopher Caro had said of it—from the opposite political perspective—in 1871.[45]

Yet Vallès never wholly cut his ties with Bohemia. His declarations of party loyalty in the last years of his life were contradicted by the identity of *irrégulier* that structured his self-portrayal in

Jacques Vingtras. Like the other figures considered in this chapter, he was torn between a sense of membership in the bourgeoisie and a contrary consciousness of exclusion and hostility that could not be firmly attached to any other class identity. In Bohemia, every social identification was undermined by a residue of refractory individualism.

If there is to be a definition of Bohemian politics, this must be its starting point. What made a political style Bohemian was not its connection with a form of dress or behavior, with artists' studios or cheap cafés. A Bohemian political style was one formed by ambivalence toward membership in the bourgeoisie, and whose successive expressions were the dramatizations of that ambivalence. Many non-Bohemians felt similar tensions and conflicts, but to the degree that they identified themselves with a clear party or doctrine— whether republican or socialist, Proudhonian or Jacobin—they adhered to a politics defined in external, objective terms rather than the Bohemian theater of the self. The careers and pronouncements of a Lafargue, a Vermersch, or a Vallès show how such external identifications could be resisted, limited, or distorted by the Bohemian style. If the political attitudes of these Bohemians were sometimes egocentric or confused, they were still deeply felt, and sometimes—certainly in the case of Vallès—courageously tested and lived through. The powerful ambivalence toward bourgeois life that fathered Bohemia was never more sharply outlined than in the spring of 1871.

PART II

PUBLIC WORLDS AND INNER LIVES

CHAPTER 8

Publicity and Fantasy: The World of the Cabarets

DESPITE THE CLAIM made in the *Revue des Deux Mondes* in 1871 that the Commune marked the end of Bohemia, the final decades of the nineteenth century found *la Bohème* very much alive. These were the years when the *fin de siècle* shaded off into the *Belle Époque*, the labels evoking respectively the period's anxiety and its glitter. The new age was bigger, brasher, harsher; it built larger and more complex structures of all kinds—taller monuments (the Eiffel Tower was completed in 1889), faster-growing cities, more extensive networks of roads and railroads, larger armies, bigger bureaucracies, more highly organized political parties. The Franco-Prussian War and the Commune ushered in an age of intensified rivalry between the European nations, with industrial competition and political maneuvering feeding the contest for empire, the struggles and alliances that would bring on the First World War. At home, political conflicts grew more vocal and often more violent, as radical challenges from the burgeoning forces of the Left competed with new attempts by conservatives to gain a mass following. The mood was one of forcefulness and confidence on the one hand, but of tension and worry on the other. Some who experienced the age's unprecedented scale and power sought novel forms of escape, or tried to meet the powerful public pressures by calling forth hidden energies from the shadowy reaches of social and personal life. It was the time of Nietzsche's impassioned and sometimes reckless speculations, of Freud's attempt to plumb the depths of personal and social irrationality, of Max Weber's analysis of how modern rationalism and progress had constructed an iron cage around the individuals they had earlier promised to liberate. Bohemia was transformed, too.

For many Frenchmen during the Third Republic the mention of Bohemia would have called up an image of the cafés and cabarets of Montmartre. Murger and his friends had made the Café Momus famous, and later locales continued the association of Bohemia with shadowy bars and beer halls—places with names like Chez Dinochau and the Brasserie des Martyrs, both on the Right Bank, and Courbet's Alsatian Brasserie Andler in the Latin Quarter. Yet there was something novel about the Montmartre establishments known as Bohemian haunts in the 1880s and 1890s, beginning with Rodolphe Salis's Chat Noir (Black Cat). These were public places of entertainment, and the Bohemians found there were assembled not to segregate themselves from the workaday world outside, but to attract and entertain a clientele that was largely respectable and bourgeois. The new establishments testified to a new kind of symbiosis between *la Bohème* and the bourgeoisie, and to the existence of a broad public seeking a taste of Bohemia.

Both the cabarets and their audiences had multiple and complex origins. As a start, we can approach them through the career of an individual most directly responsible for their creation. His name was Émile Goudeau, a well-known figure during the 1880s and 1890s, whose notoriety is preserved less in his books, no longer read, than in the square named for him—place Émile Goudeau—in the Montmartre he helped to make popular.

Born in Périgueux in 1850, Goudeau went to Paris at the age of nineteen, equipped, like so many provincials in search of a literary career, with his *baccalauréat,* dreams of success, and little else. He obtained a low-level job in the Finance Ministry, and tried to pursue his literary ambitions on the side. In 1878, Goudeau started up a literary café and theater called the Hydropathes. The word, which seems to have been linked to the title of a popular waltz, may have appealed to him because it made a pun on his own name; some people at the time also saw in it a distant echo of Murger's Water-Drinkers. The organization and activities of the Hydropathes provided the model for the more popular and lasting Chat Noir, established three years later in Montmartre by Goudeau and his friend Rodolphe Salis. Goudeau managed to publish a book of poems in 1878, called *Fleurs de bitume (Asphalt Flowers)*, followed during the 1880s by two accounts of the Bohemian life he had led: a novel, *La vache enragée* (to eat *la vache enragée* means to go hungry in colloquial French), and a memoir, *Ten Years of Bohemia*.[1]

That Goudeau's writings contained many echoes of Murger's tales is not surprising: in part, his life in Paris was consciously modeled on them. "Like a good reader of *Bohemian Life*, the neophyte Parisian set himself up in the Latin Quarter, as tradition demanded." There he fled from the boredom of his menial clerk's job, rubbing elbows with the quasi-celebrities and half-glories who hung out in the cafés. The ideas this life bred, however—at least as Goudeau reported them later—were closer to ones we can associate with Privat d'Anglemont or Jules Vallès than to Murger. He saw himself as a product of the educational system established by Napoleon I, a structure full of both promises and booby traps for provincial families with social ambitions. Believing what official propaganda told them, country fathers naïvely paid the costs of educating their sons. But the *baccalauréat* was not the magic ticket to a better life it was made to appear. Unfit for manual work, and bereft of the connections required for real success, the provincial graduate was a puzzle and a burden to his family. His only way out was to accept a lowly place in some bureaucracy. There his bourgeois pretensions were respected, but the work was boring and pointless, the salary less than that of a skilled worker, and the need to put up a respectable front meant there was hardly enough money even to buy food. Goudeau discovered, like many before him, that life was not always gay in Bohemia.

Yet there was something new in Goudeau's sense of the dangers and pitfalls of Bohemian life. His experience of Bohemia lay in the shadow of France's defeat by Prussia, was darkened by the signs of the harsher, more conflict-ridden age it portended, colored by Darwinian naturalism and pessimism. *La vache enragée* contains a gallery of more or less traditional types—the students and young girls, the aspiring poets (some marked for fame, others not), the disappointed graduates, the café philosophers—but the central figure in the tale is one no earlier exploration of Bohemia prepares us for. His name is Hercule Trimard, called Tignassou; the nickname refers to his disheveled hair, but his defining characteristic is deformity: he is a humpback. Anatomy was—or long claimed its right to be—destiny. Rejected by his father for his ugliness, Tignassou is drawn to religion. In the Church, he hopes to find a respected position and a chance to rise above the vulgarity of ordinary life. But when he is told that his deformity disqualifies him for the priesthood, the cripple's anger and hurt pride produce a "lack of resignation" that makes his seminary teachers reject him, too. Apprenticed to a shoemaker but too clumsy to learn the trade, in his isolation and despair Tignassou finds a vocation for himself as a revolutionary, identifying with "the poor, his brothers," and substituting democracy for his earlier Christian devotion to the lowly. At this point, Goudeau's hero departs for Paris.

Tignassou's politics are based on what we may call a biological theory of the conditions of revolutionary purity. Until his own time, he believes, every revolution was spoiled by the subsequent corruption of its leaders; success turned the party heads into satisfied conservatives. Revolutionary aspirations could be fulfilled only if new leaders emerged. There was but one group that could be depended on to remain social outcasts, physical misfits, and they must therefore become the Revolution's leaders. Hearing Tignassou's discourses, one of his friends conceives a name for the paper he wants to start: *The Crooked Line: Organ of the Humpbacks, the Bandy-legged, the Rickety, the One-armed, and the Deaf.*[2]

The image of a once idealistic provincial, drawn into Bohemia by the effects of physical deformity, conveyed what was new about Goudeau's view of marginal life in Paris. Tignassou was a kind of

Darwinized transformation of Baudelaire's image of the poet as albatross—deformed by the power of imagination. Bohemia as Goudeau described it was formed not around the idealism of Murger's younger artists, the imagination of Privat's miniature entrepreneurs, or even the unrelenting individualism of Vallès's *réfractaires*; its spirit was shaped by material necessity and by the cult of the stronger that now invaded society. The youth of the Latin Quarter who populated the cafés and garrets of the 1870s had all been affected by the shock of war and defeat by Bismarck's Germany. "The idea of intellectual and physical force that the iron chancellor relaunched into the world entered violently into their young brains; military service made it grow, physical training gave them all a brutal manner unknown to their elders." Their dreams of revenge and frustrated energies fed a malignant fever. The most thoughtful of the figures in Goudeau's account are driven toward madness as their youthful hopes and ideals meet the deforming power of Darwinian competition for survival, Schopenhauerian pessimism, and the sheer volume and complexity of modern life and knowledge. Goudeau's vision of Bohemia in his generation prepares us well for the confrontation, irrationality, and violence that mark French politics in the 1890s. And, like the Goncourt brothers, Goudeau was prey to early stirrings of the anti-Semitism that gave this new political brew its peculiar acid power in the anti-Dreyfusard campaigns.[3]

One might expect a Bohemia injected with such large doses of naturalism and pessimism to be immune from the earlier pattern of *embourgeoisement* found in the likes of Murger and Privat. Not at all. Even the humpback Tignassou finds his way to respectability. The ex–aspiring priest is seized by a thirst to save himself in whatever way he can. His path back into society leads through the world of shady commerce and marginal *métiers inconnus*: one day on the northern side of Montmartre, Tignassou comes upon an enormous pile of old flasks and vases, a cache accumulated by ragpickers and scavengers, social misfits who perished in the repression of the Commune. By selling this forgotten treasure from the depths of Paris, Tignassou begins his ascent. Warned off the stock market by a glass manufacturer who tells him it is dominated by Jews, the humpback turns to a different kind of speculation: he sets up commercial ventures based on ideas thrown off by inventive but impractical poets. (The real-life inspiration for this turn in Goudeau's story was Charles Cros, a poet who had in fact made some remarkable inventions, including a form of color photography and a telephone.) The apostle of the outcast and misshapen now becomes a knight of commerce, prospers, marries (a girl whose desire to be an actress had been defeated by the length of her nose), and grows fat.[4]

A similar trajectory marks the career of *La vache enragée's* second main character, Lynar, the poet who befriends the humpback in Paris, clearly modeled on Goudeau himself. At first, the success of the newly respectable ex-rebel pushes Lynar along in a descent from literary poverty into "the black Bohemia" of idleness and desperation, eventually into a hospital. Asked by an attendant what his religion is, Lynar replies: *"Zutiste.* I believe in *zut."* But this descent into nihilism marks the critical point for Lynar; in the countryside, he shakes himself free of the legends of misunderstood poets like Hégésippe Moreau on whom he had modeled his life before. "You have to imitate the sublime Orpheus, who returned living from hell." It is a hard climb. The return to Paris renews his desire for the old life of night wandering, "the rough liberty, the riskiness of Bohemian life with its fill of the unexpected." But he knows that he has taken the right road. Lynar defends *les bohèmes de lettres* against those who poke fun at their willingness to exchange Bohemia for comfort and position once the chance comes. From the time of the medieval troubadours, writers had always wanted to enter into the aristocracy; and nowadays the elite of society is no longer warlike but *financière.* Just as Goudeau's portrait of Bohemia made it harsher than earlier ones, more subject to material pressures of all kinds, so was his justification of the return to bourgeois life more materialistic, too, more frank and unblinking.[5]

Lynar's path out of Bohemia, like Goudeau's own, leads him through a literary cabaret "destined to become famous." In his memoir, *Ten Years of Bohemia,* Goudeau showed how the tone and atmosphere of these cabarets arose. The spirit that reigned in the new locales was one of *fumisme* or, as Goudeau sometimes said, *fumisterie*—"a kind of disdain for everything, an inner spite against creatures and things, that translated itself on the outside by innumerable acts of aggression, farces and practical jokes." *Fumisme* was meant to express an attitude common to Left Bank students and Bohemians of the 1870s. Less desperate than the *zutisme* into which Lynar fell before his return to regular life, it was still a refusal to treat the official world with seriousness and respect—an attitude with many precedents: the constant joking and raillery of Murger's characters, the seemingly boundless *blague* for which Privat was famous. At the Chat Noir, the traditional *blague* of students and artists took on new forms: the staff of the cabaret was dressed in the green robes of the French Academy; as patrons arrived, they were greeted with exaggerated politeness, addressed with noble titles, and treated with extreme, caricatured respect. Bohemia was literally turned into theater, acting out its estrangement from ordinary life but also masking it, channeling its energy to appeal to the bourgeoisie as patrons and consumers of literary and artistic work.[6]

Goudeau never hid this commercial purpose. From the start, the cabarets were a mode of advertising for the poets and artists associated with them. In *Ten Years of Bohemia*, Goudeau explained that his original idea had been that the *fumisterie* of Bohemia could be transformed from an expression of social hostility to a mode of bringing obscure poor poets out of their garrets and into the light of public recognition. His purpose in organizing the Hydropathes was "to cause some notions of poetry and art to penetrate into the brains of the young students destined to become the *haute bourgeoisie*; to reveal to them some books they had not known about." This education of the audience for art and literature was to be accompanied by an education of the writers themselves: "to force young poets to join the battle, like the troubadours of old, like them and different from them, in that the troubadours went around knocking on the lordly doors of feudal castles, while today you have to make yourself known and appreciated by addressing yourself, if not to the suffrage of all, at least to the restricted suffrage of the able bourgeois, kings of the epoch." Bohemia was no longer a form of withdrawal from ordinary life in the name of art or experience, nor a realm of *réfractaires*. It had become a form of publicity.[7]

That Goudeau's establishments actually functioned in this way is confirmed by observers and documents of the time, independently of his novel and memoir. Observers in the Paris press immediately remarked the public nature of the Hydropathes Café set up in the rue Cujas. This was no narrow poetic coterie, one writer pointed out, with its windows closed to outside influences, but a vast hall, capable of containing several hundred spectators. (Goudeau claimed there were six hundred on some nights.) The police feared so large a gathering and kept a close watch on it. Soon, however, the commissioner saw that the evenings were harmless and allowed them to be open to anybody who wanted to come. The activities consisted of dramatic readings of poetry or prose, alternating with songs, the lyrics for some of which were original, and some drawn from known writers, including Baudelaire. These were real performances, not private readings or expressions of spontaneous poetic inspiration. Ten years after the group began, one observer attributed its demise to the discomfort certain writers felt at having to perform the same piece over and over again; some felt limited or demeaned by such behavior and left. Still, more than one well-known writer owed his success to the Hydropathes' meetings.[8]

The commercial and publicity purpose of the society was clearly expressed in its newspaper, *L'Hydropathe*, which was published between January 1879 and the spring of 1880, and where members of the group could print stories, songs, poems, and drawings or woodcuts. Each issue featured a specific member: his picture, often in amusing caricature, would appear on the cover, and inside, an article would introduce him and praise his work. Goudeau adorned the first number. The caricaturist André Gill was featured in the second. These were followed by issues shining spotlights on Paul Vivien, Félicien Champsaur, Jules Jouy, Alphonse Allais, Charles Cros, François Coppée, and others. Not all these figures were equally unknown in 1879, and part of Goudeau's strategy seems to have been to enlist artists who already had some reputation to help others emerge from obscurity.[9]

The model provided by the Hydropathes was followed closely by the Chat Noir, when Goudeau and Rodolphe Salis opened it in 1881. In the Montmartre location, the place of the students was taken by a wider category of *amateurs*. Salis—who provided the capital—was the son of a liquor manufacturer who had tried to become a painter; for him, an artistic cabaret was a synthesis of his youthful ambitions with his family heritage, and he played a lively, spirited role, sometimes performing himself. A month later, the accompanying newspaper, also called *Le Chat Noir*, appeared, with Goudeau as editor. As with the Hydropathes, newspaper and café each provided publicity for the other. The paper (much more elaborate and successful than the minuscule *L'Hydropathe*) conducted campaigns in support of up-to-the-minute artistic trends (Impressionists and Symbolists particularly), and a column listing recently published books informed readers that some of the titles were "for sale at the Chat Noir cabaret." In addition, the paper gave regular publicity to Montmartre itself, comparing it favorably with distant and obscure Paris and campaigning to have it recognized as a free city. Other neighboring establishments were recommended, too. Salis repeated the same themes in impromptu speeches he gave at the café. What Goudeau called his "system" included a kind of unofficial Montmartre chamber of commerce—reason enough for the eventual official decision to name a square after him.[10]

The success of the Chat Noir was enormous, so much so that its original purpose was transformed: the cabaret itself became more important than the publicity it gave to writers and artists. In 1885, the establishment moved from its small quarters to larger ones in what is now the rue Victor Massé. The move itself was an enormous publicity stunt, a loud and bizarre parade complete with costumes, music, and elaborate ceremonies for bringing pieces of furniture and decorations from the old hall to the new one. From the start, Goudeau's *fumisterie* had included exaggerated claims that all the celebrities of the day were *clients assidus*; before long, the pretense became truth. Visitors to the Chat Noir in the next decade were a roster of famous names: Maupassant, Huysmans, Edmond de Goncourt, Robert de Montesquiou, Toulouse-Lautrec and other painters, many political figures, apparently including General Boulanger and the Prince of Wales. The entertainment expanded beyond the original songs and poems to include a famous shadow theater; the grandeur and elegance of the new Chat Noir showed that Goudeau's and Salis's project contained potentialities they had hardly suspected at first. But the continuity, even with the Hydropathes, was clear. Many of the performers were the same. The spirit of *fumisme* continued, as did the "system" of linking the cabaret to its performers' careers: those who appeared also published books of poetry or songs and used their appearances to further their search for public recognition. In addition, the Chat Noir sold portfolios of prints and etchings. Some of its imitators became picture galleries where the works of young artists could be made known to the public of potential purchasers.[11]

Goudeau was able to give form to a new phase in the history of Bohemia because conditions were ripe for it—and not just the ones he pointed to in his books. The establishment of the Chat Noir and similar places reflected wider changes in French—and particularly in Parisian—life. Two parallel developments that had started in the 1850s now began to have their full effect: the extraordinary economic and demographic growth of the capital, and the rebuilding projects initiated by Napoleon III and his prefect, Baron Haussmann. The new avenues and boulevards that Haussmann planned, replacing as they did the crooked old streets of crowded and disorganized districts, made Paris more integrated, its outlying quarters more accessible. Montmartre's growing importance depended on such improvements. At the same time, the old neighborhoods with their quaint buildings disappeared from the central sections of the city; so did some of the traditional mix of social classes that had given Paris a romantic aura for so long. Montmartre, with its rustic character and its cheap cafés, retained these elements longer than other sections, and remained a place where the marginal forms of social existence could still be seen and experienced.[12]

Haussmann's rebuilding of Paris meant that it was becoming increasingly the domain of the middle class, as manual workers were displaced toward the new suburban districts like Belleville, and sections of the bourgeoisie were enriched through the direct profits and economic fallout of urban reconstruction. These transformations underlay another one, to which contemporaries were highly sensitive. The structure and forms of commerce were changing: the end of the Second Empire and the beginning of the Third Republic witnessed the birth of the modern department store. The department stores, beginning with the Bazaar de l'Hôtel de Ville and the Bon Marché in the 1860s, were not simply bigger than earlier retail establishments. They owed their existence to the possibility of reaching a different kind of consumer market—broader, more spread-out, and more anonymous. Located for the most part on the new, expanded boulevards, the big stores depended on the greater ease of movement to bring them customers. They abandoned the direct and personal relationship to their clientele that characterized the smaller, more traditional neighborhood establishments of the July Monarchy. The earlier forms of commerce had presumed that a lady or gentleman only entered the shop of a tailor, a hat- or glove-maker, when she or he intended to purchase a specific item, but the new stores were open to anyone who wanted to browse or buy: purchases were encouraged by means of striking displays. The department stores traded not merely in goods, but, as one historian of these changes has said, "in spectacle, adventure, fantasy." One observer compared the interior of the Bon Marché to "a gigantic fairy extravaganza in a music hall." Commerce became a mixture of business and theater.[13]

The same changes that altered the market for clothing and household goods also changed the relations between cultural producers and their audience. Émile Goudeau's idea that a literary cabaret retaining the aura of Bohemia could serve to introduce aspiring writers and poets to prospective consumers of their works was the cultural equivalent of the department store. Like the Bon

Marché and its imitators, it mixed products of various genres, traded in a mélange of commerce and fantasy, and maintained a policy of *entrée libre*. Its form presupposed that the economic position of writers and artists, like that of tailors and hat makers, was coming to depend less on their relations to a small group of identifiable enthusiasts, and more on access to a wider and more anonymous market. Goudeau may have felt the connection. In the very first number of the *Chat Noir* newspaper, his humorous Parisian travelogue referred to one of the big stores, Les Grands Magasins du Louvre, as a "fairy palace" full of attractions. It may be that Goudeau gave the Louvre Department Stores this free plug in the hope it would advertise in the *Chat Noir*; if so, he was disappointed. But the sympathy was there, all the same.[14]

The increasing reliance of writers and artists on the market for cultural products, rather than on direct patronage, was not new, of course. Observers during the 1830s had decried the end of state and aristocratic patronage and the reduction of cultural products to commodities. The commercial success of writers like Balzac and Eugène Sue, and the formation of the Société des Gens de Lettres as an organization to represent the financial interests of authors under the July Monarchy, show the degree to which market relations had become important even before 1848. Bohemia had grown up in this new world; some of its children, like Nadar, had invented and explored new forms of publicity, and Courbet, as we saw, learned that even unfavorable publicity could create interest and income for artists. To the Goncourts, Bohemia had been the typical product of the new relations, a "freemasonry of publicity" organized to promote the self-interest of its members.

Yet in many respects the market for cultural products had remained very traditional, and incompletely organized, before the Third Republic. Publishers' contracts with authors still often provided only flat fees, rather than royalties, so that an author's income from a work did not depend on how well it sold. Zola, who saw the decline of this system around 1880, described it as a gamble that either author or publisher was fated to lose. Even those who lived

from the market knew that patronage remained a significant re-
source through much of the century. Official recognition was often
a necessary preliminary; in the visual arts, for instance, the state-
organized Salon was the principal means by which artists gained access to the public. When Courbet set up his own exhibit in 1855, in
part because he believed it would be financially more beneficial than
participating in the Salon, he was foreshadowing later developments. But only under the Third Republic were there significant se-
cessions from the Salons, beginning with the Impressionists, whose
first independent exhibits in 1874, 1876, and 1877 were practically contemporary with the literary experiments of Goudeau and
Salis. Visual and literary artists were reacting to the same changes
in the commercial possibilities of their work, sensing a new opportunity to appeal directly to the public rather than through the inter-
mediary of official or personal patronage.[15]

The slow rise in literacy and the growth of a consumer public
took place side by side with a series of more rapid and violent
shocks, upsets caused by particular crises in social relations. One of
these occurred when the Revolution of 1830 threw artists who had
benefited from the largess of the Bourbons on the mercies of the
marketplace. That is one reason why the problem of art as a market
commodity received so much attention at the beginning of the July
Monarchy. A different sort of crisis seemed to have occurred in
1877–78, when the conservative monarchists who had dominated
the Third Republic in its early years were decisively defeated. The
crisis was initiated on May 16, 1877, when the upright and stodgy
president of the Republic, Marshal MacMahon, dissolved the National Assembly in an attempt to frustrate the increasingly powerful
republicans led by Léon Gambetta. In the elections that followed,
the republican leaders worked to arouse the country against the policies and machinations of their clerical and royalist enemies, and
they succeeded. Voters in both towns and rural districts rejected
the men of substance who had long claimed to dominate French political life by right of personal or family standing. The result was
what Daniel Halévy called *La fin des notables*, the political defeat of

that mixture of old aristocracy and bourgeois wealth that had served as a main support of social and cultural conservatism throughout the nineteenth century.[16]

In *Ten Years of Bohemia*, Émile Goudeau specifically related the Hydropathe society's founding to the atmosphere of hostility created by May 16, 1877. The crisis had been "a sad and truly anti-literary moment," leading several magazines to cease publication. Artists and writers needed new ways to reach their audience. In the election of 1877, Gambetta (who had many literary contacts, and was sometimes dubbed a Bohemian himself) appealed against the conservatives to what he called the *nouveaux couches sociales*, the broad middle and lower-middle classes hitherto excluded from politics. Generally speaking, that description fits the clientele of both the department stores and the new literary cabarets. Their participation was helping to reshape the worlds of consumption, of politics, and of culture.[17]

The significance of publicity was now being felt in all realms of life. Gambetta's election campaign of 1877 was one of the first examples of large-scale public politics, with slogans, speeches, and nationally recognized issues. The importance of publicity to politics was underlined even more in the famous Boulanger crisis of the late 1880s. In an atmosphere colored by scandals involving high government officials, General Georges Boulanger, a dashing and ambitious military hero, became the gathering point for many who were dissatisfied with the Republic. His followers were a motley crew, including monarchists and clericals on the Right and radicals and socialists on the Left, but by 1888 it seemed he might lead them in a coup. (His flight in the following year and suicide in 1891 ended the affair.) One of the ways in which Boulanger's backers were able to unite his diverse following was by using new kinds of publicity, described by contemporaries as "American." The crisis was partly the creation of an extensive and very well-financed advertising campaign, using not only newspapers, songs, posters, and broadsheets, but also Boulanger portraits, ashtrays, banners, and souvenirs.[18]

Goudeau's system of literary publicity belonged to this world, and it may well have had a direct influence on other ventures in journalism and publishing. In 1892, a journalist and impresario named Fernand Xau—recently enriched from his successful presentation of Buffalo Bill's Wild West Rodeo in France—began publication of a paper destined to become one of the Third Republic's most popular, *Le Journal*. It was not only a general newspaper, but a self-consciously literary organ, in which works of Émile Zola, Anatole France, and many others were serialized. Xau's project seems to have been explicitly aimed at the new reading public constituted by the educated lower-middle class, and even some of the working class. As its first issue proclaimed, it was "composed to be seen and written to be read." As with the *Chat Noir*, extraliterary activities surrounded *Le Journal*. Xau bought a townhouse in the rue de Richelieu to serve as the seat of his paper. In it, he placed not only the journal's editorial offices, but an elegant public restaurant and theater. Customers were attracted by the cuisine and the elaborate decorations, particularly the large wall paintings executed by well-known illustrators of the time. But they were also drawn by the prospect of being able to rub elbows with the writers whose works the paper sold in hundreds of thousands of copies every day. As with Goudeau's ventures, the restaurant and the paper each provided publicity for the other. Writers whose names appeared in the columns of the paper could be seen, perhaps even approached, in the restaurant.[19]

The story of *Le Journal* suggests that those who were willing to follow Goudeau's lead and devote themselves to reaching and organizing the emerging and expanding market for cultural products were often rewarded. But the new conditions deeply troubled others. Their worries were expressed in 1895 by the writer Rachilde (whose husband, Alfred Vallette, edited the literary periodical *Le Mercure de France*) when she heard that a poet, Gabriel Randon, was to read his work at another Montmartre cabaret, the Quatz'-Arts. "The news is terrifying, because it is a summary notification on the present state of mind of society in regard to poets. Without the platform provided by the beer hall, without histrionics, society will not listen." Any poet who desired to live from his writing had no choice but to participate in the cabaret system.[20]

Rachilde's anxiety may have made her exaggerate the dangers, but other evidence suggests that commercial relations more and more influenced artistic and cultural life at the end of the nineteenth century. The *fin de siècle* was the classic age of the advertising poster—another consequence of the expansion and transformation of the market for consumer goods. All kinds of products were touted on posters, from bicycles and railroad travel to department stores, printers, milk and chocolate, soap, cigarette papers, beverages, and ink. Several of the most successful poster artists were linked to the Montmartre cafés and cabarets. Théodore Steinlen and Adolphe Willette were associated with the Chat Noir almost from the beginning, publishing drawings in the newspaper and producing posters and decorations for the cabaret. When a singer who had performed there, Aristide Bruant, set up his own cabaret and newspaper in 1885, Steinlen joined up with him, contributing illustrations and articles for the paper and helping to bring Bruant the notoriety that would make him one of Montmartre's best-known figures.

But the most famous images of Bruant, indeed of anyone connected with the Chat Noir, were those by Henri de Toulouse-Lautrec. (Lautrec's striking portrayal of Bruant, with his broad-brimmed black hat and flowing red scarf, remains familiar today. I shall have something to say about the reality behind that image in a moment.) In the 1890s, Lautrec turned his attention to other Montmartre establishments, notably the famous Moulin Rouge dance hall, opened in 1889, where he painted publicity posters for the popular performers Jane Avril, "La Goulue," and others, perhaps his most remarkable subjects. But Lautrec had begun his career as an advertising illustrator in the precincts of the Chat Noir, producing his very first lithograph for Bruant in 1885. Earlier artists, such as Daumier, Gavarni, and Constantin Guys, had used lithography to capture the fast pace of modern life, but none of them had willingly turned his talents to advertising. It is a vivid testimony to the conditions of *fin-de-siècle* cultural life that so serious an artist as Toulouse-Lautrec seems to have recognized immediately that the medium of advertising posters and lithographs was appropriate to the qualities of modern life he found represented in Montmartre.[21]

Inside the Chat Noir—cabaret and paper—one could find both explicit and implicit evocations of Bohemia. The first issue of the newspaper contained a poem, "Ballade de joyeuse Bohème." It located the contributors to both café and journal in the land of poverty chosen for art's sake. Art was a difficult, and to many an odd, choice in a materialistic world, the poet proclaimed, but he would stubbornly cling to it, making himself "painter, poet, or ham actor [*cabotin*]." The trio of roles described the cabaret's activities very well. It also made clear that the form of art represented by the Chat Noir was not restricted to clear and defined vocations.[22]

The most visible commentary on Bohemian life in the cabaret had a different tone. It was a large painting by Willette—who regularly contributed cartoons to the newspaper—executed some months after the opening. Its title was *Parce Domine* (*Lord, Have Mercy*) (see figure 7). The scene represented, in Goudeau's description, "the life, gay and murderous at the same time, of the poetic troubadours and eccentrics" who formed the cabaret's nucleus, symbolized by Pierrots and Pierrettes. Those carnival figures were Willette's constant cartoon subjects, their wistful lightheartedness and vulnerability characteristic of the culturally and socially marginal people with whom he identified. Willette was not the only person to link Pierrots with Bohemia, for the Goncourt brothers had made them the favorite subject of Anatole Bazoche, too. In *Parce Domine*, they wind their way downward from the heights of Montmartre to the Seine below. At first—we are following Goudeau's reading of the scene—they appear young and fresh, next becoming frenetic adolescents, then growing old along the steep incline of their lives. Always keeping a glass in one hand and a song on their lips, on their pale faces they nonetheless wear mourning for their illusions. Those who continue finally fall into a ditch—of sickness, madness, or suicide; those who turn aside find the pathway to salvation. It was a sad scene, Goudeau concluded, and a warning to the

7. Adolphe Willette, *Parce Domine* ("Lord Have Mercy"), decor for the Chat Noir cabaret.

cabaret poets, "the Bohemians who raise their glasses while they launch their songs: Brothers! Turn off while there is still time!" *Parce Domine* was an allegory on the dangers of growing old in Bohemia.[23]

That sort of melancholy is not what we expect in a locale of popular entertainment, and it is not what many clients sought there. The Chat Noir's atmosphere also breathed a very different spirit, that of sensual indulgence and sexual innuendo. When Goudeau and Salis arrived in Montmartre, the quarter was already known as a hangout of prostitutes. Many stories and comments in the paper took off from the world of prostitution, with its pimps and customers. Often the drawings by Willette and Steinlen were provocative and sensual, the figure of the black cat itself sometimes standing for physical arousal. Some of the writers and performers associated with the venture did their work along the same lines. At least one, Félicien Champsaur, wrote stories that were little more than high-class pornography.[24]

Important as that side of the Chat Noir's activities was, however, it was matched by the more serious tone suggested in Willette's painting. The cabaret offered its patrons the very different experience of anxiety and preoccupation with death. Probably the most effective and popular of the original performers, both at the Hydropathes and at the later cabaret, was a young musician and poet called Maurice Rollinat. His performances included singing his settings of poems—many of them his own, but some of the most memorable (according to those who heard them) by Baudelaire. His subjects concerned suffering, evil, and death, and his manner was described by one admirer as "a heart-breaking and diabolical neuroticism," causing his hearers to feel pass over them "the shiver of the unknown and the terror of death."[25]

One of the Chat Noir regulars who felt the fascination of Rollinat was the Catholic writer Léon Bloy, a person of hypersensitive feelings whose path from literary poverty and disorder to an intense and mystical Catholicism kept him permanently in a state of ferocious conflict with existing society. During the late 1870s and 1880s, he and the ex-prostitute he wanted to marry shared a common project of repentance. Bloy contributed regularly to the *Chat Noir* newspaper during its early years, where his dour, glowering writings created a surprising contrast with the lightheartedness and sensual indulgence that usually surrounded them. In September 1882, Bloy wrote an appreciation of Rollinat, whose miraculous combination of music and poetry, "at once earthly and angelic," he thought had the power to fill up the abyss that separated reality from the dream. Whenever Rollinat performed, "that passing and strangely troubling lucidity that every great aesthetic upheaval starts up inside the human brain rose within me." His hearers participated in the profound hidden life of "the sinners of art," famished for the infinite and trying to find relief in some mere earthly passion. Rollinat's music and poetry wove a powerful spell around "that heap of modern hearts tossed about by the power of fantasy in a banal locale." Other observers gave similar accounts of Rollinat's impact. Even Barbey D'Aurevilly, at first suspicious about the idea of setting his old friend Baudelaire's poems to music, wrote a favorable article about him when he heard Rollinat perform in 1882.[26]

Rollinat's success turned sour in the next few years, as reviewers found his published collection of poems artificial and mediocre, invaded by the *cabotin* spirit that made his performances a success. But his presence at the Chat Noir, like that of Bloy and others, suggests that the transformed Bohemia Goudeau and Salis installed in Montmartre still contained some of the same alternative postures and attitudes that had structured it since the days of Murger and the Water-Drinkers. There was another familiar element in the Bohemian compound of the Chat Noir as well, politics.

From the beginning, politics was an important component of Goudeau's projects and activities. One reason that the Paris police worried about the gatherings in the Latin Quarter was the political content in some of the presentations. One member of the group, Paul Mounet, made a strong impression with his raspingly delivered militant poem "The Ironworkers' Strike" ("Le grève des forgerons"). Sometimes he dressed up in a working-class costume to make his recitation more effective. Goudeau recalled that young political aspirants of all shades of opinion had been among the original members of the group, although they had gone off in their own directions once its dominant literary tone became clear. At the Chat Noir itself—most clearly in the newspaper—politics continued to be an important subject, but it was usually treated in the spirit of *fumisterie.*

The cartoons poked fun at politicians of every stripe—Gambetta, Marshal MacMahon, and the socialists in turn. An early political column reported that the existing French electoral districts were about to be abolished—so that voters could be more properly classified according to height. The issue of the paper for October 28, 1883, announced that Jules Grévy had carried out a *coup d'état*—on November 2, a date still five days off! Despite the Chat Noir's refusal to take politics seriously, its constant interest in political affairs conveyed the strong current of populist, antiofficial feeling animating its *fumisme.* That atmosphere made it possible for some figures with genuine radical commitments, such as the poet Jules Jouy and the illustrator Steinlen, to operate there.[27]

The complicated mix of political messages that emanated from the Chat Noir is nowhere better exemplified than in the career of Aristide Bruant. Bruant's songs had their roots in the slangy popular language of the Parisian working class, and they expressed much of the suffering, anxiety, and instinctive rebelliousness of the poor and exploited. His powerful directness, his ability to convey raw emotion, and the magnetism of his raucous and penetrating voice, all helped to make him the single best-known figure in the world of Montmartre cabarets and cafés. But the appearance of political commitment his subjects conveyed turned out to be deceiving.[28]

Bruant was born in the Loiret in 1851, into a solid bourgeois family that had fallen on hard times. His education was interrupted by his father's death; in 1863, he became apprenticed to a Parisian jewelry maker. After serving in the French army during the Franco-Prussian War, he returned to Paris and a few years later began to work as a clerk in a railway office. It was at this time that he began to frequent cafés where popular songs were sung, and to read poetry. At first, he seems to have been shocked by the brutality of popular Parisian language, but its humor and forcefulness won him over. He began to perform his own songs in public, progressing from obscure cafés to more prestigious ones by the end of the 1870s. And at the Chat Noir he began to achieve the recognition he enjoyed for most of the rest of his life.

When Salis moved his cabaret to its larger premises in 1885, Bruant took over the old location and stayed behind to run it himself. He called it Le Mirliton, a name that meant both a primitive flute and a doggerel verse. The tone of the two establishments was very different. In its new quarters, the Chat Noir grew elegant, its clients treated with exaggerated politeness. Bruant adopted the opposite style. His clients were glowered at and insulted. On entering, some were greeted with a musical insult, in which Bruant led the audience: "Oh! la! la! Cett' gueule, cette binette! Oh la la! cett' gueul' qu'il a . . ." ("Oh, boy! What a muzzle! What a puss that one has!") Special insults and provocations were meted out to women and to groups who caught Bruant's eye.

From the time he opened his café in 1885, Bruant published his own newspaper, also called *Le Mirliton*. Filled with poems, music, cartoons, and stories, it was sold at the cabaret, as were the published collections of Bruant's lyrics. These evoked the world of street life, the uncertain spaces where poverty and Bohemia came together. The envoi of his most famous collection, *Dans la rue*, proclaimed the central message: "T'es dans la ru', va, t'es chez toi!" ("You're in the street? Go on! You're at home.") The refrains often evoked some particular place or district in working-class Paris: Montmartre (which Bruant pointedly spelled Montmertre), Belleville, Montrouge, la Glacière, Batignolles. Much of the language was popular argot, and Bruant even published a two-volume dictionary of modern Parisian slang to aid those who could not understand it.

Both the style and atmosphere of Bruant's cabaret, and the content of his lyrics, made him seem to be a figure of the political Left. His published collections were often noticed in the socialist press, and there is evidence that his songs were sometimes sung at socialist and anarchist gatherings. One was particularly popular, his evocation of the Lyon silk weavers, the famous *canuts*. It proclaimed that the beautiful cloth they wove for the rich and great did not help them to cover their own nakedness: "Et nous, nous sommes tous nus," was the repeated refrain. So strong was the impact of this lyric that it was taken to have been a product of the still-remembered silk workers' revolt of 1834. Bruant's paper, *Le Mirliton*, did not treat politics in the same spirit of mystification and raillery found in *Le Chat Noir*, but adopted a tone of sympathy for the oppressed. It was for this reason that the illustrator Steinlen—unlike his friend and co-artist Willette a man of determined radical commitment—left the Chat Noir and published his sketches and comments in Bruant's journal.[29]

But it would be wrong to take Bruant's apparent radicalism altogether seriously. No doubt he felt some kind of identification with the poor, but he always kept his distance. When his songs dealt explicitly with politics, this sometimes became mockery: one told of a radical workingman who insisted he was a socialist but admitted he could understand nearly nothing of what the orators had to say. Bruant's usual subjects were not workers as such but the *miséreux*, the tattered, homeless, and degenerate who exploited each other, got in trouble with the police, and did not know where they would sleep the next night. In their experience and consciousness, Bruant found not social awareness and self-help, but sudden outbreaks of uncontrolled passion—fear, jealousy, violence, and revenge. Bruant did not seek working-class subjects out of political interest or instinct, but with a traditional romantic attraction for a world of color and movement, focused through a filter of Zolaesque naturalism that highlighted the brutish and animalistic underside of modern life.

Bruant's own attitude toward his songs and monologues is probably well represented by the views put forward in a pamphlet written by a friend and associate, the former police official Oscar Méténier, in 1893. Bruant wrote a favorable description of Méténier as an afterword to the work, and published it under his imprint, Le Mirliton. The pamphlet insisted that *le peuple* had taken Bruant to heart

but went on to say: "The characteristic of Bruant's particular success is that he has known how to make himself the idol of the poor
and at the same time gain the acceptance of the others, the highly
placed people and those he calls *les fins-de-siècle*. He has on his
side both the oppressors and the oppressed." Mêténier quoted another appreciation of Bruant, describing his achievement as revealing the humanity of people—whores, pimps, murderers—who
seemed so morally corrupt that respectable folk could not believe
they had anything in common with them. Bruant's portraits created
"perhaps, and in spite of our repugnance, a certain solidarity between those people and ourselves." That seems a fair judgment, but
Bruant's writings also confirmed the view most middle-class people
started out with, that moral corruption and poverty went together.[30]

Bruant actually mounted a political campaign on one occasion,
and its story is revealing. In 1893, a politician (and poet) called
Clovis Hughes found himself running against a young lawyer who
would later be a prominent political figure, Aristide Briand. Hughes
took advantage of the similarity in names to pretend that his oppo-
nent was Bruant. Five years later, Bruant took the mistake seriously
and ran as a candidate for the National Assembly in the twentieth
arrondissement of Paris. He described his program as one of "republican, socialistic, and patriotic protest," calling for support from
"all the enemies of the capitalistic feudality and cosmopolitan
Jewry." This mélange of themes might have held together ten years
earlier at the time of the Boulanger crisis, but now the combination
of socialism, patriotism, and anti-Semitism was being broken up by
the increasing clarity of working-class and socialist consciousness,
and its separation from the nationalistic rhetoric of the anti-Dreyfu-
sards. Bruant's program located him on the Right, not the Left. In
fact, not a single socialist organization supported him, and he lost
badly.[31]

The socialists' instincts were correct, for the end of the 1890s
saw a new note in Bruant's lyrics: a defense of order and tradition.
In the collection *Sur la route*, he expressed his hostility toward

those who invaded the streets with their cries of "Down with the law!" Against them, a country voice responded that "my son will have his plow, like me"; that he would go forth to defend his country, hearth, and faith, "like me"; and that finally he would die as a landowner, "like me." Bruant was a countryman himself, and, in 1901, rich from his fifteen years of cabaret ownership, the sale of his paper and books as well as beer, and his tours through France, he went back to his native village of Courtenay. There he lived in a château, surrounded by dogs and servants, and spent his time hunting and fishing.[32]

Bruant's populism always contained a strong element of posturing. In the years when he kept his cabaret on Montmartre, he lived in a rural setting, and had a servant who was instructed never to call him *monsieur* but only *chansonnier populaire: "Chansonnier populaire*, come along, the roast will be overdone."[33] His lower-class themes and argot were always packaged for bourgeois consumption, and his manner of packaging them was precisely the one Goudeau had set up in the original Hydropathe society. The paper and the café each served as an advertisement for the other. But the system of commercialized Bohemia invented by Goudeau was pushed one step further: not only the spirit of *fumisme* and *blague*, but also the allure of social and political protest, now served as the material of self-advertisement. Bruant in a certain way repeated Courbet's discovery that radicalism could be exploited as a source of notoriety, but in an atmosphere at once more self-conscious and less permeable to real conviction.

The Montmartre world represented by the Chat Noir and Le Mirliton drew its clients with a remarkable mixture of elements: sensual abandon, metaphysical anxiety, political passions difficult to define. Perhaps what the patrons of these establishments were seeking was, more often than not, what all three experiences had in common: the release of feelings and emotions that were repressed or restricted in everyday bourgeois life. Here, as before, Bohemia was a realm of liberated fantasy, a space where—as in the unconscious Freud would begin to explore at the end of the century—

wishes and anxieties associated with sexual passion, death, and violence eddied in and out of each other. Simply to enter the Chat Noir was to experience the permeability of these boundaries. Inside was a theater of exaggerated respect only narrowly removed from the raillery and *blague* from which it had sprung. To enter that stage, one had to pass through the aura of mystery and uncertainty that surrounded the lowlife of Montmartre. The mixture of excitement and danger was still more heady at Le Mirliton, where the aggression acted out in Bruant's rituals of denunciation challenged the power of humor to contain it. As the Chat Noir and Le Mirliton came to be surrounded by imitators, the styles of fantasy experience available multiplied. One cabaret dubbed itself "Heaven," placing its visitors among clouds, angels, and harps. Its opposite, the Cabaret de l'Enfer, draped itself in the trappings of hell, its waiters dressed in devil costumes. Clients entered its doors through the gaping mouth of a monster, cut into a facade whose misshapen windows were set off by what seemed a kind of solidified primal ooze, within which the nude bodies of sinners were suspended. Another neighbor styled itself the Cabaret des Truands. Here, customers were confronted by costumed bandits and criminals—not unlike those who had been dramatized as *Les bohémiens de Paris* in the popular play of 1843. That sexual experiences, perhaps of an irregular sort, were also available at some of these places—as they certainly were elsewhere in Montmartre—seems likely, even if direct evidence about them is lacking.[34]

The Montmartre cabarets that descended from the Chat Noir were a new departure in the history of Bohemia. Rather than a *Bohème* either true or amateur in Murger's terms, this was a Bohemia for the bourgeoisie, a place where the increasingly organized and regulated life of the modern city could be left behind for an evening by those unable to escape it for longer. Here non-Bohemians might seek release from ordinary social boundaries, take part in the play of breaking conventions and violating tabus. That Bohemia had such a relationship to bourgeois life was suggested in 1895 by a newspaper writer commenting on Murger's bust in the Luxembourg Gardens. The typical bourgeois had, he said, "deep in his heart, a perverse attraction for Bohemia. He experiences a lively desire to live there subjectively"—as long as he had the means to guarantee his return.[35] It was just such a desire that the cabarets of the *fin de siècle* both exploited and fulfilled.

CHAPTER 9

Compulsion
and Disorganization

IN 1878, A GERMAN WRITER published an account of his visit to
Paris. He was Max Nordau, later to become famous for popularizing the notion of degeneration, and his Parisian sketches included a
section on *die Bohème*. What seemed remarkable to him as a
foreigner was the widespread acceptance Bohemians found in Parisian society. Other cities had their quantity of *déclassés*, eccentrics,
and irregulars. But only in Paris were they treated with so much
consideration. Immediately recognizable by their outlandish dress
or unkempt hair, Bohemians were to be found in the boulevard
cafés and even in bourgeois homes and respectable salons. In Paris,
people took care of Bohemians, gave them free meals and drinks,
and found sinecures for them when the threat of advancing age and
its consequences began to dog their steps.

Why were Parisians so indulgent toward Bohemia? Nordau
thought the answer could be found in the role Bohemianism had
played in modern French culture. The great age of Bohemia had
been the time of Romanticism, the years around 1830, when the
government and its official institutions had denied recognition to
some of the great talents later hailed as national heroes. That former difficulty of gaining recognition no longer obtained. The Paris
of the 1870s was a city constantly in search of new sensations; if
Zola or the Impressionist painters were rejected by the official culture, they still had no trouble finding private individuals ready and
able to pay them handsomely for their talent and work. "But so
strong is the aftereffect of a great period, that Bohemia can still

242

sponge off the pretext of representing an officially opposed new tendency," just as certain swindlers posed as Poles exiled by uprisings against the czar.[1]

It is hard to be sure exactly whom Nordau was thinking about. There was, however, one famous—and notorious—case that illustrated Parisian solicitude toward Bohemians. Nordau could hardly have had Paul Verlaine in mind in 1878, because he was absent from Paris then and did not return until 1882, but Verlaine was probably the most popular poet of the *fin de siècle*, and the one best known as a Bohemian.

Verlaine's identification with Bohemia was strikingly illustrated when he died in early 1896. His many obituaries described him as living "a truly Bohemian life," falling into "the most obscure Bohemia," "launched in a life of Bohemia and poverty," living out his Bohemian existence "through to the end." These images of Verlaine arose especially out of his last decade, when he camped among whores and pimps in one of the worst corners of the Latin Quarter, scrounging for money, in and out of the hospital, yet known as a poet of great talent and the inspiration of many younger ones. This was the period during which the poet and illustrator F. A. Cazals sketched Verlaine hobbling through the streets, dressed in a pastiche of worn and floppy garments, his shuffling gait and costume both proclaiming his uncertain and problematic relationship to society (see figure 8). The Verlaine of this period was sheltered and protected even beyond what Nordau had in mind in 1878. The Paris police commissioner gave orders to his officers that Verlaine was never to be arrested, no matter what he did. Two separate groups organized subscriptions to support him, and the Ministry of Education provided several large payments as well. To be sure, it was to the poet Verlaine, not the Bohemian, that these aids were addressed, but in his case the two identities had become deeply tangled. For some who clustered around him in his last years his nature as a poet was hardly separable from the Bohemian character that made him unable to survive without his protectors.[2]

Together with his friends Arthur Rimbaud and Stéphane Mallarmé (both greater writers than he), Verlaine was one of the main architects of French poetry's late-nineteenth-century reconstruction. By their efforts and example, a specifically modernist poetry now arose out of the remnants of Romanticism and, especially, the legacy of Baudelaire. To use Verlaine's term, the new poetry was "absolute": not the expression of ideas or feelings that arose outside it, but the visionary exploration and cultivation of an autonomous poetic universe. We shall have something to say about Rimbaud in what follows; were this a book about literary history, Mallarmé would have to receive at least equal treatment with the others. But Mallarmé's ties to Bohemia were limited to his friendship—mostly distant—with Verlaine. He spent his life as a respectable lycée English teacher, living first in the provinces, and then, after 1871, in Paris. His attempt to recast poetic language, suffusing it with the experience of dream life and freeing it from the prose syntax of realist description, was carried out wholly within himself. He never sounded the depths of external disorder. With Verlaine and Rimbaud, it was different.

Their story puts us in the presence of a phenomenon that was coming to occupy a larger space in cultural history during their lifetimes: homosexuality. Earlier figures were certainly fascinated by homosexuals; both Baudelaire and Courbet had used the theme of Lesbianism to evoke human potentialities only discoverable outside the conventional boundaries of society and nature. Some readers have also found overtones of male homosexuality in Baudelaire's poetry. But Verlaine and Rimbaud announce the major role that real homosexual experiences, both admitted and denied, would play in modern art and literature. Their liaison was destined to end in disaster, given the unremitting condemnation of homosexual practice in their time and the conflicted feelings both experienced in regard to it. Verlaine's impulses were strongly divided between heterosexuality and homosexuality. The Verlaine-Rimbaud affair broke up the marriage Verlaine had made in 1870, from which a son was born in October 1871. In 1873, the affair ended in Belgium, with Verlaine shooting Rimbaud in the wrist. Verlaine spent two years in a Belgian jail as a result, where he underwent the religious conversion that made him a mystical Catholic for the rest of his life.

8. Cazals, two views of Paul Verlaine walking in the Latin Quarter.

Meanwhile, the experience helped nudge Rimbaud toward his famous abandonment of poetry, for a life as a commercial agent in co-
lonial North Africa.

Verlaine's personality was one of the most troubled and troubling in the history of poetry, and of Bohemia. As Maurice Barrès
observed, he was not a *révolté* but a *distrait*, an innocent, childlike
figure whose estrangement usually took the form of withdrawal
from a world he could not bear. He would have preferred, and several times sought, a stable, regular life. His fervent if unorthodox
Catholicism was one form of submission, but mysticism was also an
escape from ordinary reality. Alongside it, his withdrawal from the
pain of existence often took place through drink, and sometimes alcohol induced uncontrollably violent rages in him, episodes of real
savagery and destructiveness. Shooting Rimbaud was a mild out-
burst compared with those he directed against his mother and wife.

His biographers have sought the origins of Verlaine's complex
character in both heredity and environment. Heavy drinking and
explosive tempers ran in his father's family, piety and a love of
order in his mother's. The family was well off: his father was a military officer, his mother the daughter of a successful sugar refiner.
Élisa Verlaine suffered three miscarriages before Paul's birth in
1844; she preserved the fetuses in jars. When Paul came along, he
received the obsessive and indulgent mothering that such behavior
portended; in some way, his childhood put his father's martial independence out of reach as a model for his own life. Placed in a
boarding school at the age of nine, young Verlaine ran away, an
evasion in which A. E. Carter has seen the model for a life of repeated attempts at flight. At times, those escapes were toward ref-
uges of order and purity—his marriage, his religious conversion. At
others, they led through drink to the violence that was Verlaine's
only way of appropriating his father's military legacy. The drinking
and aggressiveness began in his teens, somehow tied up with guilt
and despair about the awakening of a sexuality that drew him powerfully toward both women—at first prostitutes—and men.[3]

Verlaine was a precocious poet, publishing his first two collections, *Poèmes saturniens* and *Fêtes galantes* in 1866 and 1869. But

his personal life in the same period guaranteed that his literary career would not follow a straight path. In the summer and fall of 1869, Verlaine made at least two violent attacks on his mother, threatening to kill her (how genuinely remains unclear), and on one occasion breaking the glass jars in which the three dead fetuses were kept. These episodes seem to have been tied up with guilt about Verlaine's homosexual passion for his friend Lucien Viotti. In June of that year, however, he had met Mathilde Mauté, half-sister of another friend, Charles de Sivry, a sixteen-year-old girl who seems to have represented an innocence and stability that Verlaine clutched at as a source of protection from the dangers of his own inner nature. Marriage was a flight from the threatening reality of his life. The dream could not survive the awakenings that followed: Viotti's death in the Franco-Prussian War; Verlaine's discovery of his own cowardice during the final episodes of the Commune, which he supported; the birth of his and Mathilde's son; and the arrival in Paris of Arthur Rimbaud in September 1871.

By early November, Verlaine was deep in drink, and appearing publicly with Rimbaud in ways that made the nature of their attachment all too clear. He made violent scenes with his wife, culminating on the night of January 13, 1872, when he threw their son against a wall (the baby was unhurt) and attempted to strangle Mathilde. That was the beginning of the end of their marriage; he tried to set her hair on fire in May, and chased her around a table with a knife in June. In July, Mathilde went to Belgium, where Verlaine was living with Rimbaud, in an attempt to bring him back and resume their life. Her failure marked the last time they saw each other.

The story of Verlaine's liaison with Rimbaud led from Paris to Belgium to London and back to Belgium again, before ending with the pistol attack that landed Verlaine in jail. No amount of twentieth-century willingness to accept homosexuality as normal behavior can liberate this particular relationship of its sordidness. The undercurrent of violence was visible in Paris, where Rimbaud wounded Verlaine with a knife. The suppressed hostility came out in quarrels and insults. The confusion and self-delusion were manifest in the contrast between Rimbaud's attempt to portray the relationship as a source of emancipation ("Only with me can you be free," he wrote after Verlaine fled from him in London) and the reality of Verlaine's weakness and subservience. Rimbaud recognized in his friend's desire to humble himself the spring of a religious conversion, even before it occurred.[4]

It was not only the shooting and his imprisonment that led Verlaine to mystical religiosity, but also the news that Mathilde had obtained a legal separation from him. (Later, after divorce was established in France in 1884, she divorced him and married a building contractor.) He made his confession, received Communion, and wrote the first of the religious and mystical poems that would later appear in *Sagesse*. Released from jail in 1875, he spent two weeks with Rimbaud in Germany, their last time together. He may have wavered in his religious conviction, but faith now won out—not moving him away from homosexuality, but temporarily calming the volcanic temper of his life. From 1875 to 1877, Verlaine lived mostly in England, where he taught in a series of schools. In the fall of 1877, he returned to France to teach at a Catholic school in Rethel, near Reims. It seemed an ideal situation. But there he met a young peasant lad who was to play a central role in the next period of his life, Lucien Létinois.

Létinois was in part a substitute for Verlaine's own son (whom he visited occasionally in these years), but he also seems to have reminded him of Rimbaud, and on one level the attraction between them was sexual. Whether it was ever consummated is uncertain, with the latest opinion coming down on the negative side. But the involvement scotched any possibilities of Verlaine's achieving continuing stability in his life. He was drinking again, and the consequences of this (perhaps combined with suspicions about his relations with Létinois) cost him his job. Lucien meanwhile had failed his examinations. Verlaine got them both posts teaching in England, but Létinois was so bad at it that he was fired after a few months. Back in France, Verlaine convinced his mother (who still retained a fair part of her once considerable capital) to buy the Létinois family a farm, which they ran until it failed in 1882. Verlaine meanwhile (alongside occasional puffing efforts to work in the fields himself) was attempting to reestablish ties in Paris. He found a Catholic publisher for *Sagesse*, and brought out other new poems in small reviews and papers. He also tried to recover the small administrative job in the Hôtel de Ville he had held at the time of his marriage but had lost after the Commune. Despite recommendations from some established friends, the request was denied when the records of his Belgian trial and imprisonment (with their reports of physical examinations proving homosexual practices) arrived. Then, at the beginning of 1883, Lucien Létinois caught typhoid fever and died.[5]

Verlaine now fell into almost total dissolution. Living with his mother in a small village where she owned a farm, he drank and made violent scenes (he still wrote and looked for publishers, however), creating a scandal in the area. Early in 1885, he made a series of attacks on his mother, culminating with a violent scene in the house of some neighbors where she had gone to escape him. He was arrested, fined, and sentenced to jail, where he stayed for a month. Released, he attempted to settle financial affairs arising from the Létinois family farm fiasco, but then entered into several weeks of utter vagabondism, wandering the roads, sleeping where he could, unwashed, badly fed, seeming to care about nothing.[6]

Yet, by the middle of June 1885, he was back in Paris, there to begin the last period of his life, the famous Bohemian existence in the Latin Quarter. One thing that helped make this possible was the support of his mother, who through it all had never abandoned him, even despite—perhaps because of—his violent attacks on her. She joined him in Paris, bringing the last twenty thousand francs that remained of her fortune, now stuffed into a mattress. What Verlaine might have done with it, we shall never know. She died early in 1886, and Mathilde, informed of the death because Verlaine was in the hospital and someone was needed to represent the family at the funeral, quickly acted to seize whatever wealth Élisa Verlaine might have left behind. Verlaine had never paid a sou of the support he had legally owed Mathilde since their first separation in 1874. Left without resources, in and out of the hospital, he now began the series of liaisons with down-and-out prostitutes that continued, through quarrels, reversals, and deluded projects of marriage, to the end of his life. Meanwhile, his homosexual passions were still alive, especially aroused by his young friend Cazals, who calmly but firmly rejected the proposals. In 1887, Verlaine seems to have been near death by starvation. But the sympathy of doctors, his growing reputation as a poet, and the support of younger writers turned the threat of complete collapse into the often sordid and painful but survivable marginal life that would be his until death came in 1896.[7]

Verlaine's early verse, written under the influence of the school called the Parnassians (Lecomte de Lisle the chief figure), shared their aspiration to classical harmony, their cultivation of a marble impassivity, to replace the Romantics' overblown sentimentality and subjectivism. To Verlaine, Parnassianism represented a stability and calm that he also sought in marriage and religion. Yet even in this early work, especially the poems of *Fêtes galantes*, Verlaine used the classical and rococo subjects favored by the Parnassians as vessels for the moonlit transformations of reality into dreaminess, the explorations of poetic nuance, musical moodiness, and indefinable states of feeling that were his real hallmark. The closeness of his imaginative flights to sheer sentiment was shown in the often soupy verse he wrote for Mathilde at the time of their courtship, the overdone sweetness of *La bonne chanson*. Much of that flavor survived in the work associated directly with the Rimbaud episode, published in 1873 as *Romances sans paroles*. In this collection, poems about Rimbaud and about Mathilde existed side by side. Here, however, the sweetness and innocence were disturbed by the suggestion of more troubling and uncertain feelings underneath. This whole mood then gave way to the confessional humility and mystical transports of Verlaine's religious verse. The amorous and erotic impulses survived, however, and in 1889 Verlaine insistently displayed the continuing force of his sensual side in *Parallèlement*.

The title meant just what it seemed to imply: that Verlaine's poetry, like his life, would find expression on the two perpetually separate levels of transcendent spirituality and unrestrained eroticism. Here we find enthusiastic evocations of his adventure with Rimbaud, as well as other frankly homoerotic verse.

Verlaine never subscribed to any aesthetic theory. The naïve, impulsive nature that gave immediacy and vividness to his best verse made him suspicious of formulas. But, on one occasion, he did put some general ideas about poetry on paper—appropriately, in a poem, and one that contributed greatly to his fame when it was published in 1882. In "Art poétique," Verlaine spoke in terms that were later extended and systematized by the Symbolists: musicality above all; liquidity in sound joined to a language that prized suggestion over direct statement; nuance rather than sharpness; no more servility to rules. His taste for populist unrestraint fired his explosive recommendation that poets "take eloquence and wring its neck." Poetry meant openness to adventure and freshness of response, and "all the rest is literature," pointless formality, and debilitating subservience to the past.[8]

The question of Bohemia was never central to Verlaine's writing, but images and references to it appeared often enough to show that the many associations made between Verlaine and *la Bohème* by others were not simply imposed from outside. In the last months of his life, he took the trouble to deny that Rimbaud had been a Bohemian: "He had neither the disheveled mores [*moeurs débraillés*], nor the laziness, nor any of the faults generally attributed to that caste, vague enough and ill-defined up to our time." Perhaps he meant the denial for himself as well. Only a few months before, however, Verlaine had responded positively to Cazals's request that he participate in a banquet honoring Henry Murger. In connection with the unveiling of Murger's bust in the Luxembourg Gardens, an official banquet had been announced, to be held at the Café Voltaire and costing six francs; Cazals and others organized a counterbanquet at the Café Procope, for two francs, and invited Verlaine to come. Confined to the hospital, Verlaine declined, but he wrote a letter of support to the organizers, and published an article about Murger in the paper *Les Beaux-Arts*, in which he defended Murger against attacks on his literary defects. Murger was no great writer, but he had charm and *esprit*, and a combination of fantasy, gaiety, and melancholy that fit his subject. As for the question of whether he was "really" a Bohemian—the old debate, aired in 1861 and now alive again—Verlaine didn't care. It was good to multiply the celebrations in his memory, and especially to have one at the Café Procope, "always frequented by Bohemia and especially—uniquely—by the Bohemia that works." There was, then, after all, a Bohemia characterized by work rather than by laziness, and with which Verlaine could associate himself.[9]

Verlaine also acknowledged his connection to the Bohemian milieu in his memoirs. One section was called "Un bon coin": the nice spot was a cheap café, a refuge, where the owner could be counted on to be sober (more or less) and honest (or almost), and where the waiters made jokes with the customers. The latter consisted of poets, some long-haired, others (Verlaine himself) too bald, as well as "former magistrates proud of their poverty," and ex–army officers whom it was better not to insult. In a manuscript apparently intended for the same memoirs, Verlaine described another café, probably the Voltaire. Here he seems to have included himself again, under one or perhaps two disguises, Chose and Machin—both slang equivalents for "what-do-you-call-it." Chose was "a Frenchman from the north [Verlaine was born in Metz, but his family had many ties to the north], a bit Bohemian and very familial, a good guy underneath, even if he thinks himself nicer than he doubtless is." Machin was "an errant who is not a knight, who has even ceased to be an errant, but who could call himself Don Quixote." Verlaine's association of himself with Don Quixote was an old one, and also had Bohemian overtones. It went back to one of his earliest poems, written while he was a lycée student. The poem addressed the champion of illusions as "old paladin, *grand bohème.*" The lonely knight's death was a martyrdom, his life a poem; he beckoned poets to assault the heights of fantasy and promised poetry's victory over inept reason. Here Bohemia stood for the liberation of dream life and the abolition of boundaries, especially that between imagination and reality.[10]

Bohemia had similar associations, more strongly developed, in the poem of *Parallèlement* that gave the fullest account of the Rimbaud affair. The occasion of "Laeti et Errabundi," which means "happy and on-the-loose," was the arrival of a (false) report that Rimbaud had died in Africa, which Verlaine refused to believe. To credit the report would have meant death to the miraculous and philosophical poem they had lived together and to *"ma patrie et ma Bohème."* Instead, Rimbaud was alive in Verlaine's life: "Tu vis ma vie!"

Verlaine's coupling of *"ma patrie et ma Bohème"* evoked the parallelism of stability and disorder of which his whole existence was composed. Bohemia stood for the side of his life that could not be contained within definite boundaries; without it, the other side—*patrie*—seemed meaningless, too. One dimension of the Rimbaud adventure had been the attempt to escape the limits of ordinary material existence—a vision Verlaine also attached to homosexuality elsewhere—into a kind of disembodied transcendence of nature. The young men were like "two happy specters, lightly floating in the subtle air." But that image quickly turns into one of simple escape from restraint: leaving women "and the last prejudice" behind, they can do anything "because once the boundary is crossed, there is no longer any limit." They drink until the spirit rises and the body sinks; then travel over land and sea. Censured by green-eyed envy, "We dined on public condemnation and ate the same for supper." Pursued by poverty, they find refuge in joy and potatoes. Through it all, they were content, knowing that they were "freer than the freest of the earth."[11]

"Laeti et Errabundi" contained a remarkable catalogue of Bohemian themes, of which poverty and the willingness to accept the moral disapproval of society in the search for liberation were the most obvious. The clear association of *"ma Bohème"* with the dissolution of moral and material boundaries led to the final image of personal fusion: "Tu vis ma vie!" Here Bohemia stood for the penetration of every social and personal limit to individual existence. It was as close as the unphilosophical Verlaine could come to the Baudelairean vision that associated Bohemia with "the vaporization of the self."

The appeal Verlaine made to the generation emerging in the 1880s and 1890s was closely bound up with his Bohemian features. One figure who made this clear was the novelist and rightist politician Maurice Barrès, who organized a subscription to provide Verlaine with a regular income in 1894 and wrote an obituary. Verlaine had his faults, Barrès admitted, but they were the other side of his strong attraction to life, a force so powerful that it made him act destructively. His rejection of convention had been essential to his effect: "Paul Verlaine was our rallying point, for all of us who sought a free space, outside of the academies, outside of success, outside society itself." His liberation of poetic form was part of a broader impulse to freedom. He gave heart to "an immense army of intellectual proletarians." The young would accompany him to the grave. "When they lower him into the trench, more than one will think (like that Murger, of whom, with all his art Verlaine had something of the sentimentality), 'Adieu, ma jeunesse!' "[12]

Two books published later also identified Verlaine with Bohemia. Lucien Aressy, author of one, had been a student in the Latin Quarter in the 1890s. He called his collection of memoirs *The Last Bohemia: Verlaine and His Milieu*. Most of the companions he named have been forgotten by now, together with the groups they founded—Synadelphes, Argonautes, Latiniens. "There false artists rubbed elbows with true ones; to be consecrated as an artist, it sufficed to have long hair, a disheveled [*débraillé*] mien, or to display a profound disdain for everything that was bourgeois." Aressy told about Verlaine's life and his relations with some of these people, notably Cazals, but that story was told more completely by Cazals himself in a book he published with Gustave Le Rouge (there was a preface by Barrès). Called *The Last Days of Paul Verlaine*, the book had chapters on his hospital stays, his mistresses, his friends, his cafés, his death.[13]

The chapter on café life was particularly extensive. Although Verlaine did not write in cafés, he spent much time in them, drinking and having long conversations with his friends. Among these were both figures of his own generation and the younger writers who would become the Symbolists. Sometimes they emptied Verlaine's glass under the table when he wasn't looking, so that he was surprised to discover he had drunk so much and been so little affected. Nonetheless, alcohol was for him, as Baudelaire said of Poe, "a magic conveyance that transported him to the enchanted spaces of the unreal." His drinking was one reason why he slept little, the explanation in turn for why he could be found walking around the Latin Quarter at practically any hour. He was known everywhere, frequenting an unending series of cafés, some literary haunts, others much more ordinary places. Occasionally, he went to Montmartre, visiting the Chat Noir, where his ex–brother-in-law Charles de Sivry was one of the pianists. On at least one occasion he went to Bruant's Mirliton. The rhythm of Verlaine's life alternated famine and feast in a way that (although Cazals did not say so) echoed Murger's tales. Once, together with some friends in one of their favorite locales, Verlaine was without money. It was a melancholy occasion until Cazals began to take from his pocket a series of coins, first small, but then of increasing value. By the time he got to a ten-franc piece, "the enthusiasm became delirious," and the *patron* was sent to find good wine from his personal stock.[14]

One other traditional feature of Bohemia emerges from Cazals's account of Verlaine's last days: its mixture of disheveled and dandyish characters. Verlaine drew to himself people who shared his own *débraillé* style and others who were at the opposite pole. Among the latter was Barrès, always careful and elegant in his dress. We shall see later that he converted Charles Maurras from what the latter called a penchant for "Bohemian brutalism," and that he worked out a peculiar and original relationship between Bohemianism and austere elegance. Cazals described another dandy, Maurice Du Plessys, as "a veritable Brummell of literature," passionately concerned about his appearance, and just as elegant in his manners. "He dreamed of an aesthetic renovation of our morose modern costume, which he wanted to be sumptuous, as in the time of the Italian Renaissance." But next to Du Plessys was Paterne Berrichon, hairy and dark, and "just as rude in his language and as bitter and vehement in his imprecations as Du Plessys was pleasant and courteous." Berrichon (his real name was Dufour) was a radical who often argued against the conservative and royalist opinions Verlaine had adopted at the time of his religious conversion. Later, he married Rimbaud's sister, and devoted his career to popularizing and defending his brother-in-law's work.[15]

But Verlaine's Bohemia was not Murger's. Emerging in the era Émile Goudeau described, it was characterized by the new practices and activities familiar from the Chat Noir cabaret. Verlaine actually published a poem in the newspaper *Le Chat Noir* (he also wrote a brief tribute to Rodolphe Salis), and it was important in his relations with younger writers. Appearing in May 1883, "Langueur" began: "Je suis l'Empire à la fin de la décadence" ("I am the Empire at the end of its decadence"). The term "decadence" had been appearing from time to time in French literature for many years, often associated with Baudelaire and his legacy, but now it became the rallying cry for young poets, many of whom would begin to call themselves Symbolists after 1886. Two journals, *Le Décadent* and *La Décadence*, were founded. The movement owed a great deal to J.-K. Huysmans's novel *À rebours* (*Against Nature*) of 1884, in which Verlaine, together with Mallarmé, was praised as the fountain of a new aesthetic attitude. In Huysmans's heady terms, the taste for decadence led to a withdrawal from the hard light of everyday reality into an inner state. There, through a twilight murkiness, one could penetrate by suggestion to the hidden depths of the soul, a realm of dark secrets where the mind experienced "*langueurs* enlivened by the mystery of the breath more guessed at than felt."[16]

The aesthetic theory of decadence underlined its adherents' willingness to see the public world decline, if the powers of the inner world could thereby be released; they plumbed the psychological depths in ways that remind us we are in the age of Freud. But the counterpart of this search for private truths was a remarkable sensitivity to the importance of publicity. Verlaine himself showed that sensitivity. In 1883, he began to publish a series of essays about recent poets, collected in book form the next year, of whom Mallarmé, Rimbaud, and himself (under the anagram Pauvre Lelian) were the main ones. Verlaine included new and unpublished poems by both Mallarmé and Rimbaud in *Les poètes maudits*, and, as he later wrote: "The little work had all the success wished for, and a certain uproar followed." Mallarmé and Rimbaud, who had previously been known only to a small elite circle, began to take hold in the public mind and "caught the ear of the press." The notion of the *poète maudit*, accursed poet, was a deliberate challenge, intended to cause just the uproar Verlaine said he welcomed. He later viewed the term "decadent" in the same light. Responding to a newspaper interviewer (another aspect of the *fin-de-siècle* world of publicity), Verlaine said: "People were throwing it at us as an insult, that epithet; I took it up as a war cry."[17]

The same spirit of public challenge was alive in the paper *Le Décadent*, edited by Anatole Baju, to which Verlaine contributed during 1896. The paper was full of attacks and provocations, a spirit of combativeness and bravura that made it a visible center of controversy. For Baju and his collaborators, the idea of decadence served some of the same function of self-advertisement that the undertone of explosive violence in the social depths did for Bruant. That this was understood at the time is apparent in an article the literary magazine *La Plume* published in 1890. *La Plume* equated the decadents with the political movement of Boulangism. Both, the article observed, issued from the same widespread discontent with the official establishment—poetic or parliamentary—of the day, and both achieved rapid success "thanks to the American technique of publicity."[18]

Literary publicity was an important aspect of the Symbolist movement, too. Symbolists and decadents were in many cases the same people, changing labels after the term "Symbolism" was popularized in a series of manifestos during 1886. There was some infighting, however. Verlaine rejected the term as too literary, and the Symbolists' penchant for obscurity and for theoretical statements at times made the difference between the two terms simply a contrast between followers of Mallarmé and of Verlaine. But that contrast receded only a year later, and Verlaine was a frequent visitor at the literary evenings the young Symbolists organized under the sponsorship of *La Plume* at a café called Le Soleil d'Or, where young poets came together to hear each other's verse read aloud. The occasions were self-consciously serious, and one of the participants, the poet Adolphe Retté (greatly admired in the 1890s, forgotten since), insisted on their contrast with what went on at the Chat Noir. The *soirées* of *La Plume* were organized for purely literary purposes, in contrast to the "hype [*pufisme*] and parody" of art at Salis's cabaret. But that disclaimer was required precisely because of the resemblances and personal ties between the two milieux. Jean Moréas, who wrote an important Symbolist manifesto, and Gustave Kahn, who edited one of the movement's major reviews, had both moved in the same circles as Goudeau in the 1870s, and together with other future Symbolists participated in the early activities of the Hydropathe society. (*La Plume* included a sympathetic article about Goudeau in its first issue, during April 1889.) The magazine's *soirées* were, as one writer said at the time, avant-garde but eclectic, providing mutual encouragement and support within which young writers could "feel themselves rise together." *La Plume* was itself served by publicity posters all over Paris (Retté saw one in a railway station when he arrived in the city for the first time), and like the Chat Noir it organized exhibitions of art in its offices, including lithographs of Toulouse-Lautrec.[19]

Verlaine's Latin Quarter life therefore had many similarities with the more organized and more self-conscious Bohemia we encountered in Goudeau's career and his memoirs. His Bohemia was not that of Murger's impecunious young would-be artists and rebellious amateurs. His last years were not devoted to the conscious search for experience Baudelaire defined as the cult of multiplied sensation, nor was he drawn by the radical social and political visions of a Vallès. He saw his poetic career as fully compatible with the aspirations to bourgeois stability represented by his marriage, and he sought a similar refuge in religion. What made both attachments partial and impermanent was the deeper psychological necessity of his nature, an uncontrollable physical need that sometimes issued in savage acts of violence. Bohemia was an irresistible fatality for him, imposed by a near-biological compulsion, deserving comparison with the Darwinian nature Goudeau symbolized in the deformity of Tignassou.

These qualities helped to make Verlaine the archetypical Bohemian for the *fin de siècle*, as Murger and Privat had been for the generation brought up on Romanticism. Bohemia was still the counterpart of bourgeois life, and the key term is Verlaine's own: *parallèlement.* Like Murger, but more radically, he was both a convert to bourgeois respectability and a reprobate unable to renounce the transgressions that put him outside society. He stood both for a more demanding mode of reconciliation—Catholicism—and for a deeper and more permanent estrangement. His friends knew that (as Cazals put it) "he detested, deep down, the café life, to which he would have preferred a calm, happy existence, obscure and above all well ordered." In the Parnassian aesthetic of impassivity, he sought a refuge against what he called "the *Débraillé* that had to be fought off." Everywhere he saw the alternative between uprightness and dissolution, even in his nostalgia for the suspenders he once wore in London, which he believed gave firmness to both his body and his mind. "In them you feel held-up, held-back, held-in," whereas to wear a belt was "a sign of moral disorder." But the result was only that he could never reconcile his two natures. Speaking of some of Rimbaud's early choleric and anticlerical poetry, he had to judge it "a masterpiece in my opinion as an artist, often very reprehensible to my Catholic mind."[20]

That such parallels coexisted without ever meeting in his life was part of his appeal. It is partially correct to say, with A. E. Carter, that Verlaine was popular because—by contrast with Baudelaire—there was nothing unpleasant or difficult about his verse. But much in it was ambivalent and unresolved, and those who needed their religion and morality straight and unsullied did not usually like it. Many orthodox Catholics were suspicious of Verlaine, and questioned whether his conversion was genuine. The people he appealed to were those who, like himself, mixed loyalty to social stability with openness to forces that might threaten to undermine it. Such a person was Rachilde, who was introduced to Verlaine by Cazals. She later credited Verlaine with freeing her from "some ridiculous bourgeois prejudices," but she was also touched by his own bourgeois impulses—his love for the silk scarves that put a layer of distance between himself and the shirts he often could not get washed, and his desire to excuse his own drinking as the unavoidable consequence of giving hospitality to his friends.[21]

Such people, too, were the Mautés, the family that gave their daughter to Verlaine in marriage. Verlaine after the breakup tried to paint the Mautés as typical bourgeois, stiff, conventional, and materialistic. They were bourgeois in many ways. Mathilde's father was a notary, cautious about money and sharp-eyed about status, and the whole family had a penchant for flaunting their rather tenuous connections with the aristocracy. But they were bourgeois whose milieu overlapped with artistic and political radicalism. Mathilde's mother was a music teacher who once gave lessons to Debussy, and Charles de Sivry, Mathilde's half-brother, was a pianist who had many ties to avant-garde circles and played at the Chat Noir. Both he and his sister attended the unconventional salon of Nina de Callias (also called Nina de Villard), gathering place for many young artists and writers. It was there that she saw Verlaine for the first time; before they met, she had read a good deal of his early published verse. That Charles de Sivry, like Verlaine at the time, was a Communard (he was imprisoned for several months after the defeat in May) was not out of harmony with his family's orientations. One of their friends was Louise Michel, the radical anarchist "incendiary" thought to be responsible for some of the fires set by the Communards in the Tuileries and other public buildings during the last week of the struggle. In the late 1860s, she had been a schoolteacher in the Montmartre district where Mathilde's father was one of the inspectors. Charles de Sivry had also taught with her in a Montmartre school for young working women. Mathilde exaggerated in her later claim that M. Mauté had been Louise Michel's only correspondent after her deportation to New Caledonia in 1871, but he was one of a very small group. Moreover, Mathilde seems not to have known that her father had sent a letter to the military authorities defending and praising Louise Michel after her capture. At a time when few respectable Parisians were willing to admit they had any positive associations with the Communards, it was an act of real courage. The family into which Verlaine married was one in which the stability Mathilde represented to him coexisted with an ability to recognize values outside the boundaries of strict bourgeois order.[22]

That same openness, on a larger scale, contributed to the relationship between Bohemia and bourgeois society that Max Nordau remarked in 1878. Parisian society protected and sheltered a Bohemian like Verlaine partly out of nostalgia for a simpler age, as Nordau understood. But, in addition, Verlaine could appeal to those bourgeois who somehow recognized in themselves, consciously or unconsciously, impulses whose destabilizing potential they needed to reconcile with their commitment to social integration. Verlaine was fatally unable to understand the incompatibility between the instincts that drew him toward the order he longed for, and those that carried him into the disorder he feared. For people able to make that distinction, protecting him was a way of both acknowledging their own potentially disruptive instincts, and limiting their destructive power. Edmond Lepelletier, whom Verlaine chose to write his biography because he combined loyalty with respectability, saw a deeper purpose to Verlaine's Bohemianism than the old desire to shock the bourgeois. Verlaine, he believed, had plumbed the depths in search of personal knowledge, undergone dissolution in order to explore the deeper eddies of the self, examined his own capacity for vice like a "Saint Augustine of the beer halls." It was the same Lepelletier who wrote, when Murger's bust was set up in 1895, that many bourgeois harbored a desire to live "subjectively" in Bohemia. Verlaine's parallels provided tracks along which that desire could be fulfilled.[23]

As a poet and as a person, Arthur Rimbaud had none of the naïve, childlike quality people often remarked in Verlaine. In contrast to the dreamy sentimentality that linked his friend's poetry to Romanticism, Rimbaud's displays a hard-edged antilyrical modernism. In the terms he once used, it is not subjective poetry but objective, the expression of a vision beyond the ordinary limits of personal existence. His is a poetic universe liberated from ordinary experience, tossed rudderless on the sea and caught up in a fluid medium between earth and sky—like the "Drunken Boat" he once chose as its emblem. To twentieth-century writers, Rimbaud's work has often seemed to embody the escape from nineteenth-century romantic humanism sought by the modernist avant-garde.

Personally, too, Rimbaud seems far removed from the weakness and dependency so often displayed by Verlaine. He was beset by deep and powerful inner conflicts, to be sure, but instead of finding himself unwillingly in their grasp, Rimbaud called them up from the depths, like a sorcerer doing battle with the powers of darkness. The image we have of his personality is partially distorted by the circumstance that most of what we know about him comes from his adolescence: he was seventeen when he and Verlaine met in Paris, and hardly twenty-four when he left Europe for Africa. His poetry, for all its brilliant originality, is the spiritual metamorphosis of an adolescent crisis, as Yves Bonnefoy has observed. Much of his behavior in the period when he was a writer should be seen in the same light. Nonetheless, Rimbaud's uncompromising harshness, his near-savage violence, gave a special quality to his antisocial features. Verlaine's explosions appear to have surprised him and they still somehow surprise us. With Rimbaud, the aggression and hostility seem more in character.[24]

Several contemporaries thought it worthwhile to deny that Rimbaud was a Bohemian. As we have seen, Verlaine insisted that his friend had neither Bohemia's *moeurs débraillés* nor its laziness. But Verlaine understood that the connection came easily into people's minds; so did others. A writer in *La Plume* in 1890 declared that Rimbaud should not be counted a Bohemian despite his bizarre appearance, his distance from the ordinary rules of life, and his haughty disdain for all received customs. The same point was made by a young poet, Rodolphe Dargens. All these denials emphasized Rimbaud's seriousness and importance as a poet, qualities that made him "neither a Bohemian nor a dilettante," as Dargens put it. Such protestations pointed to important features of Rimbaud's career, including his own sense that the traditional Bohemian identity belonged to a world he wanted to leave behind; but it clung to him all the same.[25]

One of Rimbaud's early poems, "Ma Bohème," depicts himself as a vagabond poet, wandering freely under the stars, hands in his worn-out pockets, trousers torn, wearing a coat "that was becoming ideal," making music out of the tatters of his costume. The setting was rural, close to Rimbaud's real wanderings in the neighborhood of his native town of Charleville. The life he led on his visits to Paris, both before and after he met Verlaine there in 1871, was closer to the classic image of urban Bohemia. Arriving in the city without money, Rimbaud slept in doorways, to be arrested and sent back home as a vagrant. When he later stayed for a time in the Mautés' house, where Verlaine and his wife were living, he did everything to make his antisocial feelings apparent; once Verlaine returned to find him sleeping outside on the pavement. Verlaine moved him out before Mathilde's father, who had been out of town, returned, and he then found shelter with a succession of Verlaine's literary friends. Rimbaud made his refusal of ordinary life apparent with them, too, departing one place to sleep with tramps, throwing his dirty laundry out the window of another. Verlaine and Rimbaud at this time belonged to a group that called itself the "Cercle Zutique," which provided a gathering place for poets and published an *Album* of scabrous and often pornographic poems, many satirizing well-known literary figures. Both friends contributed to it. In November 1871, Edmond Lepelletier, upset by the pair's behavior in public, mentioned in a newspaper that he had seen Verlaine with "Mademoiselle Rimbaud" on his arm. At a dinner hosted by Lepelletier as a peace offering, Rimbaud attacked him with a knife. A few months later, a second violent incident occurred. During a dinner at the poetic circle Les Vilains Bonhommes (The Lowlife Goodfellows), Rimbaud, half drunk, punctuated the reading of a poem he disliked with a series of declarations: "Merde." Thrown out of the room by the artist and photographer Étienne Carjat, Rimbaud waited outside and attacked Carjat with a sword-cane. The damage was slight, but the uproar considerable.[26]

For Rimbaud, the adventure with Verlaine in England and Belgium was one stage along the way that led to the end of his associations with the Parisian literary world and, eventually, with literature. By 1875, if not earlier, he had ceased to write; in 1878, he left for Africa. This was the beginning of what many writers have called Rimbaud's *embourgeoisement*. His aim as a commercial agent was quite simply to make his fortune. Many of his dealings were in coffee and animal hides. He seems not, as some have thought, to have participated directly in the slave trade that still existed in Africa, but he did sell guns to Africans who did. He made and lost a moderate capital, then spent nearly two years recovering it. In 1891, at the age of thirty-seven, he returned to France, and died of a tumor in a Marseilles hospital.

On the surface, the story has all the markings of a classic trajectory from Bohemian youth to bourgeois manhood. Some elements of Rimbaud's writing support this view. The long autobiographical prose poem *A Season in Hell* speaks of a childhood where all hearts were open and "every wine flowed." The writer's rebellion against beauty and justice ends this paradise, and gives rise to the infernal season of the title. How and when will it end? The hope that charity might be the key that would return Rimbaud to the old feast of life is declared a mere dream from the start. Yet he is now estranged from a form of life in which "I ended up considering the disorder of my mind sacred." In the last section, Rimbaud speaks of a return to the soil, to the rugged reality of country life. At the end of his wanderings and experiments, he arrives at the state in which "it will be permitted to me to possess truth in one soul and one body." That conclusion seems a clear recognition of the need to accept something like the boundaries and limitations of ordinary existence.[27]

Even if it works on one level, however, that reading of Rimbaud's life and writing does not capture their real quality. The common pattern seems in his case a kind of false front, behind which a different structure of experience prevailed. To begin with, Rimbaud's life in Africa was no simple *embourgeoisement*, for it dramatized his continuing distance from ordinary life. In 1883, he wrote to his family that he thought his sister should marry if the right opportunity came along. "As for me, I regret not being married and having a family. But at present I am condemned to wander, tethered to a distant business, and each day I lose my taste for the climate, the way of life, and even the language of Europe." In 1884, he said he would be like a foreigner if he came back to France. The next year, he thought that people who had lived a few years in North Africa could no longer bear European winters; they would die if they returned. In 1888, tired, ill, and in financial trouble, he imagined that his existence was tumbling to its end, but he still could not return to Europe: "I would die in the winter, and I am too much accustomed to a wandering and gratuitous life." Bored and depressed, lonely, disgusted with the Africans, whose condition he would have liked to improve, he feared becoming an animal: only illness and death made him return to France. As Robert Klein has written, Rimbaud "undertook his embourgeoisement like a saint his mortification. Which is to say, he was not 'converted' to Order, but rather chose Order as the last phase, the logical self-transcendence, of his position outside the law."[28]

The novelty of Rimbaud's form of personal resistance appears if we compare him to another provincial and rebel against order, Courbet. Both were intent on showing the Parisians that the remarkable talent each was sure he possessed did not require urban polish to show its value. But Courbet, like others of his generation, was in search of what he called "an independent sense of my own individuality." He wanted to use art to win his intellectual liberty. Rimbaud in 1871 had put such notions clearly behind him. It was not some personal uniqueness that he sought in poetry, but something external or foreign that would speak through him. In the now famous pair of letters he wrote to a former teacher and a friend in mid-May 1871, he made the astonishing declaration, "Je est un autre"—I is someone else. A piece of wood found itself a violin, a hunk of brass woke up as a trumpet: both were the vessels of a power that expressed itself through them. Similarly for the poet or the thinking man. "I am present at the bursting out of my thoughts,

I watch it, I listen to it," but it came from another source. Some interpreters suggest that this idea of Rimbaud's derived from mystical writers who would later affect the decadent and Symbolist poets, and they see the *autre* as a universal spiritual power that speaks through individuals. But the sense of the "I" being used by forces outside itself is compatible with a wider range of late-nineteenth-century intellectual currents. Rimbaud may have known neither Schopenhauer nor Darwin, but his thinking belongs to the same dissolution of faith in the integrity of the individual person that made their ideas so popular and forceful in these years. Émile Goudeau associated the impact of Bismarckian power politics and Darwinian materialism in his generation with the very "Zutist" flaunting of skepticism and raillery against tradition that Verlaine and Rimbaud joined.

Rimbaud was no skeptic in 1871, at least not about the future of poetry. But his way of asserting its power makes his distance from the Romantic conception of the poet as a rounded and organically whole personality unmistakable. The poet had to know and cultivate himself, but "in the manner of a man implanting and cultivating warts on his face. The Poet makes himself a *visionary* [*voyant*] by a long, immense, and methodical disorganization of all the senses." The personality that served for participation in everyday life had to be taken apart. The instruments of its dismantling were "all the forms of love, of suffering, of madness." The poet sought the depths of his being by exhausting within himself "all the poisons, so as to retain only their quintessences." Great in his illness, his criminality, his accursedness, he would be the supreme savant, the explorer of the unknown.

Rimbaud's vision of the poet certainly had roots in earlier writers, and above all in Baudelaire, whom he recognized as "the first *voyant*, king of poets, a real god." The formula of a sustained and methodical disorganization of the senses recalls Baudelaire's image of "the vaporization of the self." The two projects shared a whole series of instruments: erotic excitement and experimentation, drugs, alcohol, humiliation, flirting with madness. But the Baudelairean legacy was here invested in an enterprise of a sharply different kind. Baudelaire's vision of vaporization was accompanied by its necessary opposite, concentration, in which the poetic personality was distilled and purified, so that experience could be subjected to the power of form. But to Rimbaud, this cult of form was small-minded, *mesquine.* Rimbaud's poet had no such commitment: "If what he brings back from over-there has form, he gives form; if it is formless, he gives formlessness." Rimbaud's radical departure from the classical ideal of art and literature still alive in Baudelaire anticipated the revolt against art itself that would drive him away from writing and make him a patron saint of the twentieth-century avant-garde.

For Rimbaud, the quest undertaken in the name of literature had writing only partially as its object. Its larger purpose was to transform the world. Few writers have been so determined as Rimbaud to make the world begin over again from their entry into it. Even "love has to be re-invented." The poet was the Promethean "thief of fire," the discoverer of a new language able to express all the soul's powers, the awakener of the unknown. He would make enormity the norm, become a "multiplier of progress," stand in advance of society. Rimbaud did not expect to see such poets right away; for the moment, it was enough to cultivate the visionary project. But "these poets will exist!"[29]

To renounce writing poetry was to abandon this exalted vision. There seems hardly to have been a moment when Rimbaud did not harbor doubts about it. Even the first poems that sought to embody the project, like "The Drunken Boat," begin with wild exaltation only to end, as Yves Bonnefoy remarks, "as the victory of lucidity over an initial swell of hope." That lucidity appears often in *A Season in Hell.* "Does he perhaps have secrets for *changing life?*" the Verlaine figure in the poem asks. "No, he is only searching for them." What Rimbaud called "The Alchemy of the Word" turns out to be not a transformative science but mere illusion. "I habituated myself to simple hallucination: I very sincerely saw a mosque where there was a factory, a school of drummers made up of angels, carriages on the roads of heaven." Substituting hallucination —sometimes through drugs—for the vaunted power of vision to transform reality, Rimbaud "ended up finding the disorder of my mind sacred."[30] His isolation and sense of abandonment in North Africa were the reflexes of the impossible tasks set by his idea of the poet as agent of visionary transformation.

But the poems remained. Those who recognized the aesthetic revolution they represented were right to insist on Rimbaud's difference from what had traditionally been understood as Bohemianism. Rimbaud himself denounced *les bohèmes* in the letter of 1871 that has come to be known as the *lettre du voyant*. They were part of the banal schoolboy Romanticism of Musset and his imitators, which visionary poetry had to reject. Presumably, Rimbaud's own earlier fantasy, "Ma Bohème," was to be left behind for the same reasons. The rejection of Bohemia was part of a campaign against the whole Romantic sensibility that had helped produce it. Nonetheless, something in Rimbaud's career made people associate him with Bohemia, and made the denials by Verlaine and others necessary. Rimbaud affirmed on principle what Baudelaire had only accepted with reluctance: that the poetic expression adequate to modern existence had to rest on a real experience of personal disorganization. No merely imagined voyage into the unknown, and no dandified observation from a distance, would suffice. Rimbaud reveled in personal degradation. His notion of poetry made the visionary flight into the unknown depend on a life not just of freedom or irregularity, but of personal decomposition and willful disorder. He participated in the transformation of Bohemianism after 1870 visible in the Montmartre cabarets and in Verlaine's career, replacing the earlier search for a rounded and autonomous individuality with a more driven and artificial consciousness. To make poetry depend on so uncompromising a flight from ordinary existence gave a much more radical and desperate turn to the Bohemian equation of art with the life lived in its name.

CHAPTER 10

Cults of the Self

A SWISS FROM NEUCHÂTEL who had lived in Paris from 1869 through the mid-1870s published a fictionalized memoir of his life in 1879. Looking back on his time in Paris from the safe perspective of distance, Georges Jeanneret told a story of near disaster. He had evidently come within a hairbreadth of falling permanently into the social depths, yet he saw his personal history as corresponding to the needs, even the unconscious desires, that had led him to Paris in the first place. As a young foreigner in the great capital, he had gone in search of new impressions, opening himself up to the unknown. He was "hungry for famines and privations." His model had been the Romantic Bohemia of Murger, Gilbert, and Hégésippe Moreau. His tale had many Murgerian echoes—relationships (both physical and sentimental) with working-class girls, seasons of cold and hunger, trips to the pawnshop, and myriad ruses for obtaining money. But like many others, Jeanneret had discovered that Bohemia could be harsh and dangerous. He (or, in the book, his autobiographical hero) had slipped into vagrancy, ending up with no place to live, eating irregularly, living and sleeping out of doors. Devoid of will and initiative, he was in a state of near dissolution not unlike that of the Goncourts' Anatole Bazoche. But Jeanneret was saved from Bazoche's fate by a kind of *deus ex machina*, a letter with a job offer from his Swiss homeland.

Jeanneret's book was sentimental and weak, but it gave an unusually clear statement of what Bohemia had meant to him. Paris, he said, was "the natural cradle of my stormy and obscure career. There I was at home to curse the world, to conspire and hope against it, together with the poor, the artist, the *déclassé*." Bohemia had been a kind of salvation through descent. "Oppressed as I was by social necessities, that state, which comes only once and belongs only to one age, permitted me to live and saved me from becoming an outright brute. Thanks to Bohemia, my future was not lost. Thanks to Paris, Bohemia was permitted to me. Paris is the great refuge, the consolation of the unhappy." Jeanneret saw Bohemia as a space in which to live out his rebellion at a time when he was psychologically unable to meet the demands of membership in society. It was a respite from the demands of maturation, what Erik Erikson has called a moratorium.[1]

Earlier writers had certainly been aware that adolescent rebellion and withdrawal were one element in the compound of Bohemian life, but Jeanneret may have been the first to isolate it. In the Romantic era, the aspirations of the young were commonly tied up with broader hopes for change and rebirth in society as a whole. Literary and political movements took names like Les Jeunes-France and Young Europe. By contrast, the youth cultures of the *fin de siècle* were often movements of secession; the special needs of adolescents were identified and pursued in isolation, no longer finding an echo in the larger social whole, whose large-scale, bureaucratized structures appeared rigid and unresponsive.[2]

The salvation Jeanneret's Bohemia offered was purely personal. That he was an outsider is one reason this was so: even though he lived through the Commune, the broader social and cultural resonances of marginal life in Paris meant little to him as a foreigner. (Many later foreigners experienced Paris in similar, psychologically rich but socially impoverished terms.) But some of the conditions that made Bohemia a purely personal experience for him also altered its relation to youth and personal development for natives. We can see this in the linked careers of Jean Richepin and Paul Bourget.

*   *   *

That Richepin and Bourget constituted two poles in the field of Bohemian life during the 1870s was first suggested by Émile Goudeau, who paired them in both *La vache enragée* and *Ten Years of
Bohemia*. Goudeau reported that he often saw them together at the
Latin Quarter cafés. Their association was based on a union of contrasts, however, for Bourget always sought elegance, striving to
imitate the great master of dandyism Barbey d'Aurevilly, while
Richepin by contrast was a Bohemian of the pure stripe, owning
only one suit of clothes, got up in a bizarre fashion with rings and
bracelets, and affecting the manners of the beggars and down-and-
outers about whom he wrote in his poetry. Together with a third
young writer, Raoul Ponchon, they formed a group called the *vivants*. Ponchon's literary orientation is well represented by the title
of the collection of poems he succeeded in publishing only much
later: *La muse au cabaret*.[3]

Bourget and Richepin wrote about their experience of Bohemia
in ways that were as different as their constrasting styles of dress.
Bourget's short-lived association with Bohemia had certainly ended
by 1878, at which time he was becoming a well-known journalist
and a regular frequenter of elegant salons in the aristocratic faubourg Saint-Germain. There, he hobnobbed with famous dandies
like the count Robert de Montesquiou, and met Charles Haas, the
original of Proust's Swann. Even when Goudeau regarded him as a
Latin Quarter fixture, his style of life and work was hardly Bohemian. Supporting himself as a private tutor, he regularly went to
bed early and arose at 3:00 A.M., so as to have several hours for
writing before his day of lessons began. At times, he made himself
ill from overwork. Already he had begun to acquire the love of elegant surroundings that stayed with him all his life.[4]

In his early poem *Edel*, Bourget shows both his intense desire to
escape the Latin Quarter café milieu in which Goudeau met him and
the reasons for his link to it. He describes it as a dull and trivial
world of tired-out ex-students with blank eyes, seeking forgetfulness in absinthe. Coming back to this world from a visit to the Louvre, in the company of a young girl too puzzled by his poetic

anxieties to return his love, Bourget finds himself on the edge of tears. The café was "the symbol, visible only to me, of the life that would seize me, the day that my soul, carried off into a blue paradise of supernatural love, would fall back down, flat on its face, into the real world." Bohemia was a reminder of the consequences of failure. Closeness to Bohemia served Bourget as a spur to the difficult work he knew success required; at the same time, it provided an objective embodiment of his fears of inadequacy. His hostility to Bohemia was formed out of an awareness of how close he was to it.[5]

The closeness to Bohemia served Bourget in other ways. One was as a contact with segments of life and experience foreign both to his own provincial origins, and to the Parnassian school of literature to which he was first attached. The Parnassian aesthetic of classical elegance and formal perfection appealed to Bourget in ways aligned with his aspirations to a personal life of luxury and beauty. But from the mid-1870s, it was clear that such an orientation was inadequate as a preparation for the kind of literature he wanted to write. He saw himself in the tradition of self-consciously modern literature, devoted to encompassing the experience of contemporary life. *Edel* would provide, next to elegant scenes of aristocratic Paris, contrasting evocations of the modern city, with its impersonal streets, its buses, its asphalt, and its turbulent crowds. His desire, he said, was "to wring from that life whatever sweat of beauty it possesses." By freeing him from the restrictions imposed by the Parnassian ideal of literature, Bourget's contacts with Bohemia helped widen his literary compass to include a whole range of specifically modern experiences the Parnassian vision excluded. His passion for *le moderne* encouraged a Zolaesque naturalism, reinforced by the scientific culture of the day. Soon that passion turned him toward the project that distinguished his mature work of the 1880s and made him one of the best-known writers of his day: the literary exploration of modern states of mind, what he called *la psychologie contemporaine.*[6]

For Bourget, Bohemia also provided entry into another element of modernity: the nihilistic loss of faith in traditional values. Not for Bourget's generation the transformation of religious commitments into secular forms, so often practiced by the Romantics. The old collective faiths were dead, political regimes arose and crumbled, there was no form of evil the new generation had not already experienced in its youth. "Last bastards of an enraged century, we young men see all that once was, dissolve." For a writer determined to explore the moral and personal consequences of this modern skepticism, Bohemia was the ideal laboratory. "Blowing cigar smoke in the faces of the fallen gods"—the life of *blague*, of selfish pleasures and refusal to take responsibility for the world or oneself—was precisely the way to experience the moral atmosphere of modern nihilism. Bohemia was the locale in which to taste and touch the modern loss of faith.[7]

In contrast to Bourget, Jean Richepin's connections to Bohemia lasted throughout his life. He first became well known with a collection of poetry called *The Beggars' Song* (*La chanson des gueux*) in 1876; the raucous and insistent populism of the lyrics led the government to prosecute the author, and Richepin spent several months in jail. Inspired in part by Verlaine (who disliked them, however), Richepin's verses provided models for the songs of Aristide Bruant. The poems depicted not only Parisian street people, but also the poor of the countryside and, in a final section, *"nous autres gueux,"* Richepin and his literary friends in the Latin Quarter.[8]

Richepin chose to write about beggars because they stood for something he felt about himself, but beggars were only one of several symbols with direct Bohemian associations he employed. In 1872, he made his literary debut with a book on a different kind of Bohemian subject—Jules Vallès. Richepin's essay on Vallès, written when he was not yet twenty-two (a serial version appeared in a newspaper during 1871), was a remarkable demonstration of literary precocity, and remains one of the most interesting analyses of Vallès's career down to the time of the Commune. Richepin took Bohemia as the framework for understanding what he called in the title *The Stages of a Réfractaire*, and the book shows the tortuous attraction-repulsion Richepin felt toward Bohemia even in his early twenties. Murger had described "this Bohemian life, created by modern society," in terms that made it appear too bright and attractive. Vallès provided "the true portrait, heartbreaking and cruel, of this miserable existence." The book was dedicated "to the *réfractaires* and their friends."[9]

Describing the intellectual leaders of the Commune as *déclassés* ex-bourgeois, Richepin included—apart from Vallès—Courbet, Pyat, Vermersch, Rigault, and half a dozen others. All were talented people, impatient, proud, and unwilling to submit to the common yoke. Their likes would be driven outside the normal paths of society "as long as our social order contains the inextricable prejudices that stand in the way of free movement." Yet Richepin's account of Bohemian *déclassés* like Vallès contained an undertone of suspicion. Vallès had exhibited his pride, desire for glory, and spirit of revolt even in his youth, before he discovered the injustices of modern society, and his inability to achieve a stable place was the fault not of prejudice or exclusion, but of his own indiscipline. "A man who will have the courage to throw himself into adventures, to take life wherever he can find it and to fight with it, even unto death, ought to be able to find in himself the ordinary courage for a regular job." Instead, the compound of ambition and embitterment drove him in contradictory ways. He might hope for revolt, but while waiting for it, "he made use of his *réfractaires* only to open up the path of notoriety and ease. By painting them, he earned what he needed to leave them behind."

The fall of the Second Empire brought Vallès's inner turmoil to the surface. "He found himself in his element, disorder, where he could forge a weapon—insurrection—to arrive at his goal—power." Yet the actual establishment of the Commune faced him with a new and unsuspected turning: he wanted the regime set up in March to last, and the only way to make it stable was to rally the bourgeoisie to the Commune. Now Vallès worked for social harmony. He grasped at his moment of happiness as at a branch breaking from its own weight, crying for peace just as loudly as he had called for struggle. "But the torrent for which he had helped to break the dike was stronger than he, and it carried him panting and furious into its unchecked whirlpool." Seized again with a desire for vengeance, Vallès contributed to the violence of the Commune's last days, seeing the destruction of Paris as his final duty.[10] The impulses that led Richepin both to identify with Vallès and to ferret out his inner contradictions were manifest, in an inverted form, in his own career. Following his imprisonment, Richepin lived a restless life for a time, going to sea, traveling with a band of gypsies according to one story, joining up with a circus according to another. But in the same period, he was making contacts with established writers, including Barbey and François Coppée. In 1879 he married, and in 1881 engaged briefly in a debate with Vallès over the latter's attempt to claim André Gill's mental breakdown as the consequence of insufficient political commitment. In 1883, he reappeared as the *enfant terrible* he had seemed in 1876, publishing a book of poems called *Blasphèmes*, full of invective, obscenities, and frank nihilism. The book was condemned by several reviewers, including Barbey, and Léon Bloy writing in *Le Chat Noir*. But in 1886, Richepin's voice grew calmer, even dreamy and almost mystical in the manner of the Symbolists. His new book, *The Sea*, contained some verses that recalled the cynicism of his earlier work, but also sentimental scenes of parting, nights under the stars, and even the quiet musings of retired sailors.

Richepin preserved Bohemian themes and images in many of these writings, and also in his most popular work, the play *The Vagabond (Le chemineau)* of 1897, to which he owed much of his reputation as a leading writer of the time. Its chief character, the *chemineau* of the title, is a tramp of a special sort. His quality as an artist is made apparent by his power to enchant others with his songs. At harvesttime on the farm where the action takes place, he makes others work beyond their own abilities, and without fatigue, by the power of his singing, and his magical skills cure animals and people of illnesses. He never ages, is not subject to domination by social hierarchies or conventions, and his presence overcomes the social distances between characters. In short, Richepin's *chemineau* is a miracle-working artist; his lack of stable social position expresses the separation from society attributed to poets throughout the nineteenth century. (The real drama of the piece is the *chemin-eau*'s temptation—resisted—to end that separation and settle down with an old love.) These Bohemian theses were hardly original, recalling George Sand's *La dernière Aldini*: the tramp's decision to go back to his wandering life—"Chemineau, che-mine!"—echoed the cry of Sand's itinerant artist, *vive la Bohème!*[11]

By 1897, Richepin's employment of Bohemian images had lost its aggressive and hostile edge. His sense of distance was softened by sentimentality; his inability to live an ordinary life became a matter of sadness, not revolt. In fact, as his book on Vallès already suggested, there had always been uncertainty and hesitation in his identification with outcasts and beggars. No doubt Richepin felt genuine sympathy for the down-and-outers, pimps and *truands*, about whom he wrote. But just as he understood, as early as 1871, that writing about *réfractaires* had been a way of achieving notoriety and recognition for Jules Vallès, so did he understand the possibility of following a similar path, more self-consciously and pragmatically, himself.

Several of his more astute readers recognized this from the start. Verlaine condemned *The Beggars' Song* as artificial and false; and Zola complained that Richepin's details of lowlife were pasted up for effect, while other, more friendly, critics suggested that Riche-pin's lyrics had something about them of school exercises. French lycée students were taught to write correct classical style by imitating eminent models. Richepin, one critic said, had simply stood the pedagogical technique on its head, making speakers of argot into literary exemplars, replacing the rhetorical *gradus ad Parnassum* with a *gradus ad guillotinam*. *The Beggars' Song*—the same critic concluded—was a pistol shot in the streets of literary Paris, a loud demand for recognition. Maurice Barrès later voiced a similar opinion.[12]

These comments seem close to the mark. Throughout his life, Richepin was nothing if not theatrical. His dress and behavior in the Latin Quarter cafés of the 1870s were calculated to make an effect. One English observer who saw him in those days thought he seemed like a figure from a comic opera. The actress Sarah Bernhardt, with whom Richepin had a brief affair in the early 1880s, appreciated him for just these qualities. Once, in public, she flung open his coat to reveal the scarlet-and-gold vest underneath, crying out: "He is even more fantastic and ham-actorish [*cabotin*] than I am—that's why I love him." More than one contemporary remarked that Richepin seemed to be a succession of different personalities, each one living a different life.

Adolphe Brisson, a writer who admired Richepin and wrote about him in the early 1890s, provided a striking detail in this regard. Richepin had collected photos of himself at various ages, representing the stages of his career, and Brisson thought that two pictures Richepin hung side by side summed up his development especially well. One, from the early or mid-1870s, showed Richepin with Bourget and Ponchon; in it, he appeared in a broad-brimmed hat, long-haired and bearded, his clothes "of a primitive cut." With his burning eyes, he looked, Brisson thought, like a young faun. The second picture showed the former Bohemian some fifteen years later as a quiet and respectable man of the world, the proprietor of the surroundings in which he appeared, everything about him declaring: "Here I am at home." Brisson recognized that some of Richepin's "former comrades . . . failed Parnassians and collapsing old Bohemians," held the change in style against him, but Brisson defended Richepin's life as an exemplary "masterwork of harmony and prudence." He had started out as a poor young poet, full of imagination, needing his cleverness to survive, and fond of show. "And, finally, like all his generation, he had read the books of Henry Murger. He took Bohemian life seriously and sincerely believed that a self-consistent poet could not bend himself to an ordinary existence without losing something. He set himself to playing the role of Schaunard, an Asiatic Schaunard, truculent and sumptuous."

There was real spontaneous feeling in all this, Brisson thought, but at the same time a modern spirit of straightforward careerism that separated him and his generation from Murger and the earlier Bohemians. Modern painters and writers, like doctors, "from the time of their adolescence, look the problem of the struggle for life right in the face. They work to amass a capital and to draw some advantage out of it." The spontaneity of Richepin's youth could not be separated from the self-conscious, careerist posing. The successive stages of his life shown in his collection of photos corresponded to a plan of development that, on some level, the poet of beggars and thieves had possessed from the start.[13]

Brisson and others who knew Richepin recognized that for him Bohemia served much the same function as it did for his café companion Émile Goudeau: a form of advertising. Perhaps Max Nordau understood something of this when he spoke of Bohemia in 1878 as exploiting the memories of Romanticism to gain acceptance in a Paris no longer so confident about its right to resist artistic and literary innovation. Bohemia might remain in the *fin de siècle* as a way of gaining experience, of living on a small income, of dramatizing ambivalence toward bourgeois life. But it was also now a prime way of advertising oneself as a writer. Bourget, Goudeau, and Richepin all followed diverse paths, reflecting the differences in their personalities. But they found that in building their careers, they had to employ the same elements of skeptical pragmatism, self-conscious posturing, and frank materialism that were transforming *la vie de Bohème* at the end of the nineteenth century.

These elements were nowhere more fully appropriated than by the writer who provided them with the most novel configuration during the 1880s and 1890s, Maurice Barrès. Barrès focused on many of the problems of modern individuality that appear in Bourget and Richepin. But he placed them in the context of modern politics, which the other two usually avoided. Barrès was not only one of the best-known novelists of the *fin de siècle*, but also an important political publicist. His meditation on Bohemia took shape at the same intersection of cultural practice, personal development, and political involvement where Courbet and Vallès had located Bohemia. But the signposts he discovered at the crossroads led in quite different directions.

One can say of French politics in the 1880s and 1890s what Carl Schorske has said about Vienna's: it was being played in a new key.[14] The Third Republic was a regime of liberal parliamentarianism based on universal male suffrage. For the first time, France enjoyed a democratic franchise that was genuinely the foundation of political authority, by contrast with the plebiscitarian facades of the two Bonapartist empires. But the Republic faced many enemies from the start; and they developed new political styles in order to appeal to the voters. The clericals and monarchists defeated by Gambetta in 1877–78 searched for a new base from which to challenge republicanism, while workers began to organize in unions and parties, asserting with increasing insistence that the conservative policies of the middle-class Republic did not represent their interests. The actions and behavior of the elected deputies to the National Assembly provided plenty of fuel for critics. The provincial lawyers and notaries who represented their districts in Paris used influence and patronage to aid their constituents and to advance and enrich themselves; coalitions in the diverse and unstable assembly were sometimes cemented by gifts and favors. Complaints that the parliamentary regime was the preserve of self-serving and corrupt parvenus received public confirmation in a series of political scandals, of which one involving Panama Canal shares in 1892–93 was the worst.

In this atmosphere, antiparliamentary forces challenged the regime in two major crises, associated with the names of Boulanger in the late 1880s and Dreyfus at the end of the 1890s. Supporters of Boulanger and opponents of Dreyfus shared a nostalgia for a world in which national life was not organized around the abstract structures of the market and the representative assembly. They preferred symbols around which an aroused nation could recover its organic unity and free itself from the stigmata of defeat and corruption. Military glory, a return to tradition, and anti-Semitism were their rallying cries. Supporting these movements was a patchwork of those whom the world of modern industry and politics, with its orientation toward individualism and progress, had left behind: aristocrats and notables; clerical conservatives; threatened artisans and—at least in the Boulanger crisis—some workers; and, increasingly, the lower-middle class of small property owners and shopkeepers who were challenged by new forms of commercial and economic life like the department stores.

Maurice Barrès was an important publicist for the new style of antiparliamentary politics in both the Boulanger and Dreyfus affairs. His opposition to the political forms and spirit of the Third Republic was structured around a nationalism that drew on earlier French traditions, including Jacobinism and Bonapartism, but infused these traditions with the post-Darwinian biological theories of racial and national existence that were so characteristic of the time. His Boulangist speeches and writings combined a vision of heroic national regeneration with anticapitalistic themes in a way that placed him uncertainly between Left and Right, in an attempt to rally working-class and socialist supporters of General Boulanger as well as those who aimed at some kind of conservative restoration. By the time of Dreyfus, his politics had moved more frankly to the Right. Although, like Édouard Drumont, Barrès hoped his anti-Semitic slogans would find sympathy in the working class, he saw that this was less likely at the end of the 1890s than it had been a decade earlier. Organized working-class political forces saw their own enemies in the anti-Semites, and the latter recognized that their appeal had to be to the lower-middle class of property owners and shopkeepers. Barrès regarded anti-Semitism as a way of unifying a profoundly divided country, not only against republicanism but also against socialism.[15]

Barrès presented the dilemmas of modern individualism accompanying these political activities in two series of novels, one at the time of each political crisis. The trilogy published in the years of Boulanger's notoriety was *Le culte du moi*, the cult of the self. The series that appeared in the years of controversy over Dreyfus was *Le roman de l'énergie nationale*, the novel of national energy. Much in these books was autobiographical, reflecting Barrès's experiences as a child in Lorraine, as a young writer and critic in the Latin Quarter, and as a politician.

Barrès was considered by many to be a leader of French youth at the end of the 1880s, and there are many testimonies to the power of his personal presence and style. One was given in an incident that Charles Maurras, later the leader of the royalist Action Française, remembered from his early friendship with Barrès. Maurras sought out Barrès soon after reading one of his novels. Maurras was then, he said, passing through a crisis attributable in part to the effect of Paris, with its free and exhilarating life; contacts with students and artists had drawn him into "some bad ways of speech and dress, an untidy and Bohemian brutalism that promised to free me from the entanglements of my upbringing." Barrès cured Maurras of all this at a stroke when, as the two were walking together, he gave up the sidewalk to a quite ordinary and undistinguished-looking woman. This politeness, with its pride, delicacy, and good taste, immediately appeared superior to Maurras's opposite style.[16]

Maurras's story jibes with many other accounts of Barrès's polished and elegant demeanor. But Barrès was seldom hostile to Bohemia. In 1888, he published a short book about the Latin Quarter, the daily life of students and their neighbors, and the cafés there. Many people were then suspicious of the so-called *brasseries des femmes*, beer halls in which young women served as waitresses, encouraging their largely student clientele to consume food and drink. Sometimes the women were for sale, too, and the establishments were often criticized as dangerous and corrupt. But Barrès treated the *brasseries* with considerable sympathy and indulgence, regarding them as scenes for flirting and the kinds of sentimental fantasies appropriate to young students away from home. The atmosphere was restrained, he thought, resembling salons more than the anterooms of the *maisons tolérées*. Liaisons were sometimes begun there, but they were the modern counterparts of the loves of Mimi and Musette. In this atmosphere, the students prepared themselves not for ruin but for the dyspepsias and gastritises that "around the age of 40 would give them a distinguished physiognomy." Nor did Barrès think that the cafés bred Bohemian politicians of the sort respectable people believed to be responsible for the Commune, like Vallès or Gambetta. To be sure, one could still see specimens of the old type, raucous and besotted, talking through the night, vomiting up guttural insults. But such people were not to be feared. Born too late, they grew timid in the daylight, where they deserved only pity. Any young people who envied or admired them would quickly see the ridiculous side of their lives. "And, besides, it takes so much money to be a Bohemian today."[17]

Barrès expressed a similar indulgence toward Bohemianism many years later, when in 1909 he welcomed Jean Richepin to membership in the French Academy. Richepin's Bohemia had not been all poetry and singing, Barrès insisted: "It is always extremely difficult for adolescents drunk on pure thought to adapt themselves to the ordinary conditions of an existence that, inevitably, disappoints their first dreams." But Richepin had never been an enemy of society. Even his evocations of Vallès had been intended to light a fire only in his own imagination. Barrès admitted that he, too, had been drawn to some of the same literary and personal exemplars— not only Baudelaire, but even Vallès, whose funeral he had attended in a spirit of homage in 1885. (As we have seen, Barrès expressed his sympathy with Bohemian traditions in connection with another funeral, that of Paul Verlaine, whom he compared to Murger.[18])

It was Baudelaire who showed Barrès the deeper meaning and importance of Bohemianism. Barrès wrote an enthusiastic essay when a collection of Baudelaire's letters and diaries appeared in 1887. One of the striking things about Baudelaire's life, he noted, was the contrast between the elegant politeness he cultivated as part of his ideal life of poetic calm and repose, and his beer-hall existence among down-and-outers. Barrès explained this contradiction partly as an effect of Baudelaire's "sick nerves," and partly as an expression of his need for "light, conversation, noise." But the poet's attraction for Bohemia had a further significance, revealed in Baudelaire's formula, "To glorify wandering and that which may be called Bohemianism: the cult of multiplied sensation." This was, Barrès believed, the expression of Baudelaire's passion "to see clearly, whatever may come of it." Barrès had been struck by this passage as early as 1885, when he wrote: "Nothing passionate exists in the world without Bohemianism. Thus Baudelaire . . . told us to glorify Bohemianism."[19]

To understand how Barrès developed these Baudelairean ideas and images we need to turn to the first of his trilogies of novels. The parts of *Le culte du moi, Sous l'oeil des barbares* (*Under the Gaze of the Barbarians*), *Un homme libre* (*A Free Man*), and *Le jardin de Bérénice* (*Berenice's Garden*) dealt with the questions of how the individual in search of freedom should respond to the demands and conditions of the external world; with the nature of the self, particularly the modern self; and with the relationship of these problems to politics. By the end of the trilogy, the narrator, Philip, has become politically active, in apparent contrast with his insistence in the first volume that he must concentrate wholly on his own inner development, doing nothing that might subject him to the will of others. But there was no contradiction. Philip's evolution mirrored a development Barrès himself had completed by the time the first book appeared in 1889, when Barrès was a Boulangist candidate for the National Assembly. The right kind of politics was a form of self-cultivation.

Barrès's autobiographical narrator begins with a radical need for independence. His enemies, as Barrès later insisted, are not merely the bourgeois: the barbarians whose gaze he wishes to elude include anyone whose nature differs from his own. Every stage of personal history confirms his impulse to escape into an ivory tower of protected interiority. Writing about Barrès in 1891, Anatole France described him as a person who could reverse a well-known saying of Gautier and declare: "I am a man for whom the outside world does not exist." Yet, this was not the whole story. Even though fear and hatred of the barbarians throws the Barrèsian narrator continually back on himself, he cannot remain there. Each successive attempt at a fully self-contained existence leads to discouragement, loss of spirit, and a cold sense of isolation. Total independence is barren. The young man in search of himself has always to look for something exterior to nurture and warm him. He needs an outside spur to rescue him from the potential immobility of his unattached personality, and tries out philosophy, ambition, mysticism, sensuality, literature, and finally his home region of Lorraine. To begin with, each of these has to be rejected, throwing the narrator back on his self, for each threatens to subject him to something that is not wholly his own, something that would assimilate him to the barbarians. How can he escape dependence and isolation?[20]

Barrès's solution to this dilemma appears at the end of the second novel, *A Free Man*. What made the problem of living independently in the world seem insoluble was a false notion of the self's integrity; the conviction that the individual can be free only if his being is unified and self-consistent leads to a rejection of every exterior form of life that threatens to alter or dilute him. Barrès's narrator abandons this conviction. The separate elements in a multiform personality can form their own attachments without corrupting the whole. "I have found a way that allows me to bear it without bitterness when parts of myself reach for vulgar things. I have partitioned myself into a great number of souls. None of them is defiant; all give themselves to whatever feelings pass over them." The paladin of autonomy who recoiled from every exterior involvement because it threatened his independence now allows himself every indulgence.[21]

Barrès's image of the personality recalls both Rimbaud's project of disorganization and Verlaine's experience of parallel exaltation and degradation. But there is no doubt that it was the most cynical of all the *fin-de-siècle* positions we have considered. That part of him was drawn to religion and another to prostitution did not bother him; what had been fatality for Verlaine became a source of pleasure. "I do not hate the fact that some parts of my soul lower themselves sometimes; there is a mystical pleasure in contemplating, from the depths of humiliation, the virtue that one is worthy of achieving; moreover, a truly adorned spirit should not be distracted from its preoccupations to weigh the villainies that he commits at the same moment." Barrès described the philosophy of his *culte du moi* as appropriate for "a generation disgusted with many things, perhaps with everything."[22]

Barrès saw this morality of the self as a combination of Bohemianism and dandyism. The *culte du moi* novels are filled with descriptions of dandyish behavior; the personal style of the narrator was clearly that of Barrès himself. But they also contained references to the Bohemian spirit of passionate sensation-seeking that Barrès invoked elsewhere in the same years. For the narrator, to trace the course of his life is to "abandon himself to the Bohemia of his mind and his heart." How the two styles fit together was a question Barrès answered most directly in an essay published in 1892, "The Wonderful Secret." Here he described a mixture of dandyish containment and Bohemian abandon that made independence and respectability the framework for a special kind of indulgence. The virtue of a highly polished personal surface, smooth and redolent of cultivated self-control, was that it "covered up and allowed all the fantasies." Sensuality flourished best in secret. Barrès recounted a story from the seventeenth-century memoirs of Saint-Simon. A bishop was intimate with a duchess and received her in his house every day. Afterward, they would walk together in his garden while servants followed behind, raking the paths smooth to erase the marks of their footsteps. To Barrès, the rakes symbolized the culture of truly civilized societies, in which superior individuals could by a double existence gather all the fruits life offered. It was "Bohemianism in the soul, austerity on the outside." This double life, with its secrets and its freedom to be what no one suspected, was the highest form of pleasure. "How sharp must be the thrill of those adventurous souls who, in the act of accommodating to their ordinary environment, taste and realize the pleasures of two or three different and contradictory moral lives."[23]

Thus did Barrès recast Baudelaire's combination of dandyism with the Bohemian cult of multiplied sensation. The Barrèsian individual willingly took on the trappings of an ordinary respectable existence. All the same, he persevered in the Bohemian refusal to take a number in life and accept the demands of social discipline. Those who knew him in his everyday appearance only saw a shadow; his real life was elsewhere. As the narrator Philip would say in the third *culte du moi* novel, *Berenice's Garden*: "You have to show people a smooth surface, give them only the appearance of yourself, be absent."[24]

Barrès's combination of surface polish with inner abandon is not easy to interpret. Sometimes it seems to imply a real life of indulgence behind the facade of order (as in the case of Saint-Simon's bishop); at others, the "Bohemianism in the soul" appears to refer only to a life of inner liberation, suggesting an identification of what matters in human life with the psychological depths. It also calls to mind those engines for the liberation of fantasy that were the cafés and cabarets of Montmartre, most of whose patrons lived eminently respectable lives. But the adventure Barrès yearned for was to be pursued not merely in the imagination. To see what Barrès thought might be the practical consequences of his reorientation of Bohemianism toward the secrets of inner life, we must turn to his politics.

The connection between politics and the cult of the self appears in *Berenice's Garden*. It is an oddly fascinating book, more readable than the first two because it contains more of traditional novelistic narrative, but still bathed in a heated atmosphere of mystical sensuality, cynicism, and psychological ambiguity. On one level the story is an allegory, showing the collapse and promise of Boulangist politics. The Boulangist narrator, Philip, is opposed by Charles Martin, who stands for the impersonal and rationalistic political culture of the Third Republic. They compete not only in an election, but also for Berenice, a young girl who embodies the soul of the people— seemingly innocent, sensual, anxious, manipulable, and full of energy. Charles Martin can no more understand the real needs of the impulsive Berenice than he can appreciate the natural contours of a landscape. Philip becomes the girl's spiritual guide and confessor. But the two are never lovers, and in the end Philip abandons her, recognizing that she was of interest to him only in her unhappiness. Berenice therefore marries Charles: Boulangism being powerful only as a movement of opposition, the nation is delivered over to its parliamentary masters. Unable to survive her marriage to the rationalist, Berenice dies, but we are left with the expectation that she may be resuscitated by a miracle worker in the future, just as the Boulangists hoped for a new hero whose antiparliamentary energies would bring the nation back to life.

As an image of the common people's simplicity, innocence, and need for guidance, Berenice is a figure with many roots in French literature, but she has none of the uncomplicated beneficence of the Romantic image of the *peuple*. Her sensuality cannot be contained within the bounds of convention: in addition to her many affairs with men, she has a Lesbian relationship with a shadowy character who lives in her house. Earlier she worked as a performer in a Parisian "Eden"—a place where girls of nine or ten perform lascivious dances. There she acquired the explicitly sexual nickname by which the narrator remembers her, *petite secousse*, for the "little shake" of her hips that made customers come to see her. It is just this release of instinct, this "little shake," that French politics needs to arouse a heroic and mysterious nation against the parliamentary system.

Berenice's role is to give her little shake not only to the public world of politics, but also to the private world of the narrator. Politics is one of his modes of self-cultivation, a way to invest his cool, stale sensibility with warmth and life. Boulangism is the only movement that can accomplish this, because it alone recognizes the people as at once a mass to be dominated and a source of instinctual energy. Berenice gives the narrator "a revelation of the unconscious." Her ability to inject dynamism into a personality in danger of becoming limp and slack paralleled that of Boulanger himself. In a dream, Philip compares himself to Lazarus, brought back to life by a redeemer. "The marvelous agitator resuscitated you." This temporary revival, like Barrès's ability to believe in Boulangism, provides an example of how to keep the self alive.[25]

Barrès understood this descent into the world of popular life, action, and instinct as a form of Bohemianism. The meaning of Berenice becomes clear to Philip when he visits a shrine of Saint Sara, "the patron of the *bohémiens*." Her mystery is contained in her "voluntary humiliation," a formula that returns Philip's thoughts to Berenice, the "petite bohème" who, with all her degradations, seems called on to bring him "the good doctrine." That message is the revelation that unconscious, instinctual forces exist both within himself and in the masses, and that the individual who understands them can use them for his purposes. Bohemian "voluntary humiliation" is a plunge into social and psychological depths;

lowering himself to the world of the common people, the narrator puts himself in touch with their sources of energy, appropriating them both to develop himself and to dominate others.[26]

Barrès did not think he was the first to associate Bohemian voluntary descent with the liberation of instinctual powers repressed by modern civilization. In 1909, he used his speech welcoming Jean Richepin into the French Academy as an opportunity to talk about Jules Vallès. Vallès's revolt against the world of education and culture he wanted to enter had been the reaction of a powerful animal against the heavy weight of the cultural burdens piled on its back. His life was testimony to the potential for rebellion created by the modern attempt to impose intellectual culture on a nation of peasants. Barrès was fascinated by Vallès in part because he helped him to recognize the instinctual, animal sources of his own hatred of discipline, and of ordinary parliamentary politics. But Barrès's response to the primitive and repressed forces in his own personality had none of the direct spontaneity of Vallès. He called them up in order to direct them for a purpose. "I have spontaneous feelings," Philip says in *Berenice's Garden*, "but I also cultivate them with a method." The method was just as self-consciously worked out as that of his rationalist opponents. The return to the popular and primitive that had been a personal necessity for Vallès became in Barrès's version a matter of pragmatic and self-conscious manipulation.[27]

Barrès is an important figure in the history of politics because he was one of the first to seek symbols that could arouse psychic energies on a national scale. His politics of dominating the masses by self-consciously participating in their confused instinctual desires marks him as a precursor of fascism. But he also represents the intensified psychological consciousness that spread through society and culture as the larger-scale, more distant and bureaucratized, institutions of the *fin de siècle* turned individuals more deeply inward in the search for instruments of personal development. Pragmatic self-consciousness marks his meditations on Bohemianism as a product of the age of Goudeau, Richepin, and Bourget. Individual liberation was still a goal, but it had to be sought in more devious, more complex, and sometimes more desperate ways.

The bust of Henry Murger set up and dedicated in the Luxembourg Gardens in June 1895 was financed by a campaign organized by well-known figures in journalism and literature. Who originated the idea remains obscure—François Coppée, who helped to publicize and organize it, spoke only of "some students"—but once it was under way, it seems to have garnered broad support.

Articles about Murger and Bohemia produced for the occasion covered a broad spectrum of attitudes. Coppée, praising Murger as a poet of youth and love, took the occasion to retract some carping comments about Murger's literary value he and other Parnassian poets had made earlier. At the other extreme was Georges Rodenbach, writing in *Le Figaro*, who rehearsed every standard anti-Bohemian theme: Murger and all those who spoke well of Bohemia were literarily and morally suspect; they lived in a world beclouded by pipe smoke, and all their intelligence found expression in *blagues d'atelier*; dissipated and undisciplined, they wasted their energies in talking endlessly about work they would never complete.[28]

But the passions Bohemia could arouse in the 1890s were better revealed in the celebrations that accompanied the bust's unveiling. The organizing committee arranged a ceremony—complete with an address by the minister of education (later president of the Republic), Raymond Poincaré—followed by a banquet. But these plans did not go unchallenged. A group calling itself the True Bohemia organized its own ceremony to unveil the bust a day early, so that the official delegation with its "gentlemen of the literary and learned bourgeoisie will find on Friday a monument only half-virgin and already inaugurated by *la Bohème* itself." This countergroup, among whom was F.-A. Cazals, also organized the alternative banquet to which Verlaine sent a message of encouragement. Then a third group emerged with plans for an "intransigent" banquet.

Held at the Cabaret de la Bohème, it featured a meal that cost only seventy centimes (the official banquet cost six francs, Cazals's two). At the ceremony unveiling the statue, one member of this group shouted: "Down with the pedantic and pseudo-literary bourgeoisie" as he tossed his bouquet. In the evening, they dined on sausage and fried potatoes, with only a toothpick for dessert.[29]

That two separate movements of protest against the official celebration of Bohemia were required was characteristic of the heated atmosphere, in the years just before the public storm of the Dreyfus Affair. But it would have been difficult to predict what actually occurred: the Murger celebration, caught up in the student protests and demonstrations that were part of the anti-Semitic Right's assault on the Third Republic, ended up in a riot.

This turn of events was brought about by a writer already known for his provocative and unrestrained sallies against the political establishment. Laurent Tailhade, a year earlier, had commented on an anarchist bombing with the never-to-be-forgotten *mot*: "What do vague humanitarian sentiments matter, so long as the action is beautiful [*pourvu que le geste soit beau*]." Tailhade's anarchism was more literary than political, but it was full of punch. What he called "the apotheosis of Murger" filled him with disdain. It was one of several recent events in the Latin Quarter that he decried, the others being a memorial for Sadi Carnot, the president of the Republic assassinated a year before, and the mystical enthusiasms of the Catholic student organizations. In his eyes, French students were selfish and hypocritical, devoted to no cause more exalted than assuring their own future as respectable bourgeois. Tailhade's special target was the anti-Semitic students of the Catholic associations, but he lumped them together with the celebrants of Murger in an article that helped to ignite an already volatile situation: diplomatic maneuvering had led the government to make a conciliatory gesture toward Germany, sending a delegation to help celebrate the opening of a new canal at Kiel, and angering French revanchists. Student demonstrations had been going on for a week when the article appeared on June 26; it provoked outbreaks that turned into riots lasting for two days.

Several committees, including two set up to defend Murger and Bohemia, came together to organize processions to the offices of Tailhade's paper, *L'Écho de Paris*. The police intervened to keep the students from getting across the city, and fighting broke out. At least one paper, *Le Journal*, said that the police acted brutally, beating up students and journalists and conducting themselves "like real savages." Apparently, some of the students succeeded in reaching the *Écho de Paris* offices on the second day, from which they then went on to Édouard Drumont's paper *La Libre Parole* to cheer him. The commotion seems to have receded after that. But through the rest of the 1890s (if not later), groups of students in the Latin Quarter came together to mark the anniversary of the bust's unveiling with banquets in honor of Murger and Bohemia. The police, remembering what had taken place in 1895, sent secret agents to attend the celebrations and report on what occurred.[30]

The association these events created between Bohemia and the antirepublican, anti-Semitic Right was accidental and temporary. Édouard Drumont himself did not welcome it, having greeted the Murger bust with a condemnation of Bohemia as a sentimental veil woven around the bourgeoisie's exploitation of other elements in French life. As often before, Bohemia's political indeterminacy was clearly demonstrated: it released energies that were available for political ends but it could not define their direction; it was contested as a symbol of opposition to establishment culture at one moment, falling in with anti-Semitic activists but rejected by their leader the next. As before, Bohemia was a locus of ambivalence and a means for exploring and testing the boundaries of bourgeois life. But the period since 1871 had brought new boundaries to explore, and new modes of contestation.

PART III

FROM BOHEMIA TO THE AVANT-GARDE

CHAPTER 11

Temperament, Narcissism, and Provocation

WHILE THE IMAGE AND EXPERIENCE of Bohemia were being transformed, new styles and movements in art and literature were creating what has come to be known as the modernist avant-garde. The avant-garde and Bohemia were not the same, and should not be confused. The separation between genuine art and Bohemia, insisted on by Baudelaire, Flaubert, the Goncourt brothers, and even Rimbaud, would have been reaffirmed by many later modernists. As vanguard movements developed, however, they took over themes and activities that were rooted in Bohemia, identifying art as much with the life of the artist as with the production of special objects, and transforming artistic practice in ways that made the dramatization of a personal relationship to society ever more central to it. By the 1920s, many Bohemian features had been absorbed into the avant-garde.

Impressionism was in many respects the first example of an avant-garde movement in art. The Impressionists' self-conscious experimentalism, their exploration of the conditions and implications of artistic production in a modern market setting, and their sense that they bore the burden of an unavoidable opposition between innovation in art and society's hostile incomprehension—all made their experience paradigmatic. Here we cannot attempt to analyze the technical innovations and practices that underlay Impressionism as a painting style. Suffice it to say that when the first works by artists who came to constitute the school began to appear during the 1860s, they were notable for their specifically modern subjects, the frequent attempts to replace studio conditions with direct, natural lighting, and generally their lightened palette of pure colors. Later, these features developed into the qualities now usually considered to define Impressionism in the strict sense: the attempt to render a pure, momentary experience rather than to create a formal and finished composition; and the use of painting to analyze how light and color were perceived, so as to reconstruct and extend visual experience itself.[1]

The aesthetic goals of the Impressionists had little to do with specifically Bohemian themes or practices; nonetheless, there were occasional congruences, among them the shared association with Parisian café life. Before the Impressionist group began to give its independent exhibitions during the 1870s, it had already achieved considerable unity of spirit and purpose through informal meetings first at the Café Guerbois and later at the Café de la Nouvelle Athènes. The Guerbois was in the Batignolles district, where Édouard Manet had his studio, and it was he who drew the others there to pass evenings together. Although Manet painted few if any Impressionist pictures in the strict sense, his insistence on painting modern life free of the veils of tradition or idealization, and the notoriety this gained for his early canvases, made the slightly younger Impressionists look to him for guidance and affirmation. The one member of the group usually ready to dispute his leadership was Edgar Degas, like Manet an educated and articulate upper bourgeois. The Café Guerbois was the scene of many debates between them. Apart from Manet and Degas, the painters Renoir, Monet, Bazille, and several writers interested in art—Émile Zola, Zacharie Astruc, and Edmond Duranty—came regularly to the Guerbois. Pissarro and Cézanne attended less regularly, since neither lived in Paris. Cézanne was also distinguished from the rest by his rough, sometimes ragged exterior, as was the radical anarchist Pissarro by virtue of being the only one with strong political convictions. Despite all the personal contrasts and differences, a strong sense of unity drew the group together around a shared desire to evolve a new painting outside the boundaries of official art. For a time after 1870, they met less regularly; the disruption caused by war, the

Commune, and the travels of several of the painters to England temporarily lessened their cohesion. By the mid-1870s, however, they were reassembled in a new locale, not far from the first, the Café de la Nouvelle Athènes.

The Guerbois and the Nouvelle Athènes served the Impressionists and their supporters in ways that were by then familiar in Parisian cultural life—not only as places of meeting and escape from the struggle and isolation of daily artistic work, but as a substitute society. Here, the negative opinions of the outside world were overborne by the group's shared confidence in the rightness of what its members were undertaking. Monet later remembered the evening talks as an important source of reassurance and confidence, at a time when most outside reactions were still hostile. "From them we emerged with a firmer will, with our thoughts clearer and more distinct." Courbet's Brasserie Andler had served a similar purpose for his generation. It was something very close to this creation of a substitute society that the Goncourt brothers had in mind when they referred to Bohemia as "a freemasonry of publicity."

The tone of the Impressionists' cafés differed from that of the Brasserie Andler. Manet and Degas cultivated elegance and refinement, and Degas's social ideas in particular have sometimes been compared to those of the Goncourts. In contrast with them, however, Cézanne's habits and behavior sometimes recalled Courbet's, as a countryman's dramatization of distance from Parisian ways. On one occasion, he reportedly refused to shake hands with the carefully turned-out Manet, excusing himself because he had not washed in a week.[2]

Nor was Cézanne the only one noted for his raggedness. One of the most assiduous participants in the evenings at both cafés was a painter now mostly forgotten, Marcellin Desboutin. (Some accounts suggest it was Desboutin's dislike for the Guerbois that convinced the others to move to the Nouvelle Athènes.) Desboutin had spent some years in Italy, where he owned a villa near Florence, but his carelessness and extravagance eventually did away with what seems to have been a comfortable fortune; during the early 1870s, he had to sell his villa and move back to Paris. There he lived from selling his pictures, but poorly. He participated in the second Impressionist exhibition, of 1876, and later he achieved considerable public recognition, but in the mid-'70s, his life was still tattered and irregular enough to be generally regarded as Bohemian. He himself attributed his artistic failures to what he called "my woeful Bohemian habits." When his entries for the Salon of 1874 were refused, he wrote to a friend: "This is once again the result of the eccentric life, outside of every social convention, within which I have closed myself up in my artist's individuality for years. It makes me, I know, impossible, and very often shocking to the milieu of respectable people, living a regular and sociable life."[3]

Manet depicted Desboutin in a canvas called simply *The Artist*, where his features and costume recall the extravagance and exoticism of the 1830s, in contrast to Manet's own more elegant and respectable manner (see figure 9). Degas made Desboutin the central figure in the most famous image of the Nouvelle Athènes, *The Absinthe*, where he appears seated at a café table with a woman (the model was a well-known pantomime actress, Ellen Andrée; see figure 10). Desboutin's presence in the picture underlines its imagery of social decline; the woman—sometimes interpreted as a prostitute between clients—drinks absinthe, and seems to be lost in a fog of reverie induced by the drink. Desboutin himself drinks beer, his mien more independent and clearheaded than his companion's, though he seems to be staring off into space. The complete lack of interaction between the two figures, their sense of being united only by a common experience of isolation, aptly illustrates what Paul Bourget, in the same years, meant by the state of social decadence: the progressive weakening of social cohesion, leading society to dissolve into its separate component parts.[4]

Whether this was Degas's own reading of his picture must remain a matter of conjecture, since no clear evidence in regard to it seems to exist. But Degas's identification with the comfortable upper classes may well have led him to feel critical about an artist so different from himself as the acknowledged Bohemian Desboutin. Other participants in the meetings at the Guerbois and the Nouvelle Athènes definitely came to feel uneasy about some of the potential for antisocial attitudes the group seemed to nurture, and identified that potential with Impressionism's closeness to Bohemia. The clearest example was Émile Zola.

Zola first defended the new painting against the association with Bohemia others claimed to perceive in it; later, he insisted on that link himself. His ties to Impressionism were both personal and professional. He and Cézanne had been childhood friends in Provence, and the two were in regular touch during the early 1860s in Paris. Discussions with Cézanne provided one source for Zola's ideas about painting. But when Zola took up art criticism he wrote especially about Manet. Manet's pictures were the subject of widespread attention, most of it hostile, in the mid-1860s. In championing Manet, Zola defended the importance of individual vision and temperament, rejecting the academic allegiance to an absolute and unchanging form of classical beauty. Good art saw the world through the screen of a temperament. Reality was fixed, but the "various temperaments are the creative elements that have given differing characters to the works." Every great artist provided "a new and personal translation of nature." The search for beauty in art was therefore equivalent to the search for humanity, for the power human beings possessed to respond to and interpret reality in ever-changing and renewed ways.[5]

In the face of Manet's critics—and his own unsympathetic readers—Zola insisted that the painter's innovations constituted no abandonment of artistic seriousness or respectability. Temperament provided coherence and unity in an artistic work, replacing the idealization on which classical composition had been founded. Manet himself was a wholly reassuring figure, a refined, polite, distinguished man, a lover of elegance, a hard worker and a person whose homelife embodied "the calm joys of the modern bourgeoisie." His pictures had the same qualities of solidity and elegance. Zola found it necessary to insist on this, because Manet's opponents were presenting him in other ways. Contemporary cartoonists and satirists, Zola complained, had "turned Édouard Manet into a sort of Bohemian, a child of the streets, a ridiculous boogeyman."[6]

Zola's denial that Manet was any kind of Bohemian was fully

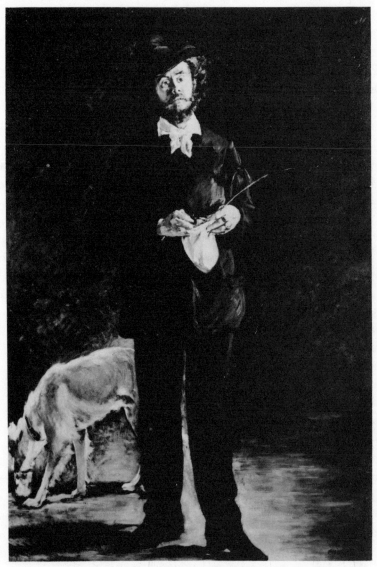

9. Manet, *The Artist*, a portrait of Marcellin Desboutin.

10. Degas, *The Absinthe, Portrait of Marcellin Desboutin*.

supported by the painter's personal manner and style. Yet there were several reasons why the charge might be made. Manet early set himself the task of painting contemporary life, including some of the lowlife Parisian figures dear to Baudelaire and Privat d'Anglemont. These interests brought him into touch with the group around Courbet, still meeting at the Brasserie Andler, where Manet sometimes also went. He seems never to have gotten on with Courbet, each finding the other's personal style—Courbet's beery populism and Manet's self-conscious elegance—unpalatable. But several other Impressionists were close to Courbet during the 1860s, and a common early term for the new school was Realist. Manet's associations in this period included other members of the original Bohemian circles of the 1840s. He is reported to have known Murger around 1860, and he became friendly with Baudelaire. Both men were driven by a fascination with the underside of modern urban life, combined with a dandyish determination to preserve their distance from it. In Manet's case as in Baudelaire's, however, the barriers erected did not always hold up. When Manet submitted his picture of a ragged street-dweller, called *The Absinthe Drinker*, to the Salon in 1859, his former teacher Thomas Couture declared that there was only one absinthe drinker made visible by the work, Manet himself. His portrait of Desboutin provoked similar reactions.[7]

Zola believed that the association of Manet with Bohemianism and disorder had another source: his individuality. "Originality, that is the great horror. We are all more or less, unawares, creatures of routine . . . every new route scares us. As soon as a personality appears, defiance and fright take hold of us." A similar view appeared in the catalogue of Manet's private exhibition of 1867, written probably by Zola or Manet himself. "It is the effect of sincerity to give to the works a character that makes them resemble a protest, whereas the painter only wished to render his impression. M. Manet never wanted to make a protest." The image of Manet (or other painters whom Zola supported, specifically Cézanne and Monet) as a rebel arose, he believed, from the public's failure to distinguish the originality on which all progress depended from the revolt that set some individuals outside social life itself. Zola found that he himself was now identified in similar terms. Dedicating his Salon criticism to Cézanne, he expressed surprise on behalf of both that the ideas they had explored together turned Zola into a revolutionary in the eyes of the public.[8]

Zola's confidence that the aesthetic of temperamental individualism could be a principle of coherence and stability, both in art and in life, was the foundation of his early championing of the new painting. But that view changed as time went by. Partly Zola was influenced by the recurring crises of self-criticism and despair he observed in his childhood friend Cézanne; partly by the contrast between his own increasing success and acceptance during the 1870s and 1880s, and the persisting pariah status of the Impressionists; perhaps, too, he came to see in the Impressionist painters certain antisocial elements that he needed to put at bay because he recognized them, with anxiety, in himself. The image of the new school of painting he gave in the 1860s was in many ways inverted by his novelistic portrayal of 1886, *The Masterpiece (L'oeuvre)*.[9]

The hero of that book, the painter Claude Lantier, is a composite figure, his chief traits taken from Manet and Cézanne. Cézanne's visionary transports, his crises of self-doubt, predominate, but elements of Manet's character and career are also present—the hostile public reaction to his early pictures, with their subjects bound to shock the bourgeoisie, and his surprise and hurt when he was not accepted by them. The painter Zola presents as embodying the talents and aspirations of the new art is a man so devoted to his own visions and dreams that he is destined to lose himself in a world of fantasy. His character is summed up in his ending: suicide in front of a picture that he cannot finish. His work is the ground where his inner vision battles the external reality that refuses to embody it. The theme was not a new one in the nineteenth century; Zola was reworking a story by Balzac, "The Unknown Masterpiece," about the derangement lurking in the Romantic attempt to impose dream and imagination on reality. Taking Balzac as a model underlined Zola's point: the malady that affected the Claude Lantiers of the world was an aftereffect of Romanticism. They had failed to learn the lesson that modern culture had to learn if it was to be healthy and vigorous—the lesson of science.[10]

In Zola's view, the artist who could not shake off Romanticism was also mired in Bohemianism. Claude Lantier's story was a tale of falling backward into Bohemia instead of emerging from it. Drawn down into poverty, he and his wife live in one room "like regular Bohemians." At the painter's funeral, his childhood friend, the writer Sandoz—Zola himself in fictional dress—weeps Murgerian tears: "He felt he was burying his own youth," the best part of himself, "the illusions and enthusiasms." Burying those illusions was a task Zola had described before, in his very first published novel, *The Confession of Claude.* There, in a story that explicitly invokes images of Latin Quarter life inherited from Murger and Musset, Zola tells of his own susceptibility to, and abandonment of, Bohemian illusions. That the heroes of this early novel and of *The Masterpiece* were both called "Claude" (the name Zola also used as a pseudonym for his Salon criticism of 1867–68) underlined his sense that he was writing about himself, as well as about Cézanne, in his later novel, too. But Sandoz is a person liberated from his youthful fantasies, living an ever more regular life as he feels himself to be part of existing society. The history of the new painting, as he gives it in *The Masterpiece,* goes in the opposite direction. Hostile to external reality because it resists his visionary transformations, Claude Lantier is reduced to isolation, impotence, and finally death.[11]

The Masterpiece amounted to a recognition that the aesthetic formula of "reality seen through a temperament" contained more pitfalls than Zola's early art criticism had been willing to acknowledge. His anxieties about the Impressionists in this regard followed lines that had been suggested as early as 1874 by another critic with experience of both Romanticism and Realism, Jules Castagnary. Writing about the first Impressionist exhibit (and specifically about Manet), he worried that only some subjects lent themselves to the new approach and that the school would split between those most interested in the representation of contemporary life, and the others, devoted above all to their own personal perceptions. These, he feared, would pass "from idealization to that degree of unbridled Romanticism where nature is nothing but a pretext for reveries, and where the imagination becomes impotent to formulate anything other than personal, subjective fantasies, without echo in generally shared thinking [*la raison générale*] because they are devoid of possible checking or verification for their truth."[12] The sources of Castagnary's worries were precisely Manet's paintings of the 1860s, where he saw a potential for explosive subjectivity in Manet's concern for the purely painterly aspects of art, the play of colors and forms: to make such abstract elements central to painting was to cut art off from any moorings in the shared external world that was its ostensible subject, he believed. To Zola in 1867, the same interest in producing beautiful arrangements of tones and surfaces had indicated that Manet was devoted to scientific objectivity, that he wished to put clear, definite relationships between shapes and colors at the foundation of his art. By the time of *The Masterpiece*, however, he was describing Claude Lantier's search for pure color and form in terms that substituted Castagnary's judgment about their significance for his own earlier one. The Impressionist interest in color was encouraged by the discovery—correct in itself—that the color of objects changed with changing atmospheric and temporal conditions. But for a Claude Lantier, this led to the conclusion "that things have no fixed color, that their color depends upon circumstances and environment." The original scientific observation, Zola explained, made a buzz in the painter's brain, leading him toward the madness of "overthrowing all the accepted habits of the eye and producing purple flesh-tints and tricolor skies." Zola now associated the aesthetic of temperamental individualism with the refusal to accept the limits of ordinary existence from which he had sought to distinguish it before. It was this refusal that left a Claude Lantier stuck in the Bohemian isolation from which Zola believed he himself had escaped.[13]

It may not be easy to sympathize with the volte-face that made Zola so unsympathetic to Cézanne in the 1880s, but it is important to try to understand it. His reaction was also in part bound up with new relations then developing between artists and their audience.

When Zola championed Manet in 1867, he tried to demonstrate his seriousness by a willingness to put his money—had he had any—where his convictions were. "I am so certain that M. Manet will be one of the masters of tomorrow that I believe I could make a good speculation, if I had any wealth, by buying up all his canvases today. In fifty years, they will be sold for fifteen or twenty times as much." The then impoverished Zola was unable to test the force of such predictions, but there were others who did, notably the pioneering art dealer Paul Durand-Ruel. When he succeeded his father as head of their family business in 1865, Durand-Ruel first championed the so-called Barbizon school of landscapists, who had preceded and influenced the Impressionists through painting nature by direct observation outside of the studio, *en plein air.* By the early 1870s, he had turned to the artists still known only as the Batignolles Group, and in 1872 did just what Zola had spoken of doing, buying up everything Manet had—twenty-three canvases, for which he paid the then very large sum of thirty-five thousand francs. Following the same practice with other members of the school, Durand-Ruel assured their survival while at the same time preparing enormous profits for himself. Although his own and his artists' incomes varied with economic conditions, by 1880 the major Impressionist painters had yearly receipts nearly on a level with those of high state functionaries.[14]

Durand-Ruel's practice created a wholly new relationship between artists and picture merchants. Dealers in fashionable painting had long existed, selling work by artists sanctioned through the Academy and the Salon. And speculative and often shady art merchants were willing to explore the studios of obscure artists, either to order cheap work or to purchase what seemed promising to them and look for buyers for it. But Durand-Ruel established a relationship of a different sort with the painters he favored. It allowed them to paint as they wished, based on the expectation that they would come to be recognized and appreciated as individuals, despite their distance from official institutions and practices. Durand-Ruel believed this recognition would eventually come, but he worked to hasten and further it, holding exhibitions and sponsoring art journals devoted to publicizing the new styles. From this time, the picture dealer assumed a part in the diffusion and commercialization of new aesthetic forms, in the education of a new audience, rather than simply satisfying the tastes of an already existing market.

That this process would have to take place outside the official Salons was recognized in the independence of the Impressionists' exhibitions. In fact, neither the Impressionist artists nor their supporters understood this altogether at the start. The critic Théodore Duret even advised Pissarro against participating in the 1874 exhibit on the grounds that the Salon was the only way for an artist to become publicly known and accepted by dealers and art lovers. Manet and Degas were of the same opinion, as was Renoir, who wrote to Durand-Ruel as late as 1881 that there were at best "in Paris scarcely fifteen art-lovers capable of liking a painter without Salon approval." The independent exhibitions seemed at first to be only a stage on the way to the Salon, not a substitute for it. Nonetheless, the real importance of the independent exhibitions was caught by the critic Armand Silvestre, who wrote the catalogue for the first of them. The painters were submitting their work, he said, "directly to the public, to the public that makes reputations even when it seems only to submit to them, and which will not fail to turn away, someday, from those who are content to follow its taste toward those who make an effort to guide it." Silvestre's view shared much with the notion being developed at the same time by Émile Goudeau and Rodolphe Salis of how literature would find its market. Both had roots in the earlier appreciation of publicity shown in the 1850s by Nadar's series of "Panthéons." It was Nadar who provided space for the first Impressionist exhibition in 1874, lending the studio he was just moving out of on a corner of the boulevard des Capucines.[15]

Though they were slow to develop, the new commercial arrangements, together with the Impressionists' stylistic innovations, transformed the relations between modern art and its audience. Whereas that relationship had once been based on shared assumptions and expectations between artists and their patrons, it now comprised simultaneous but opposing attitudes of incomprehension and "overcomprehension" (the latter term was coined by Max Ernst). Beholders of every new avant-garde style experienced discomfort and distance in the presence of new work, but at least some part of the audience—or some part of each viewer—was aware that these initial reactions would evolve into acceptance and appreciation, both aesthetic and economic. Painting became an object at once of derision and of speculation. This situation was immediately comprehended by some observers: Zola was one; another, more critical and introspective, was the Romantic poet and critic Théophile Gautier.

> Faced with all the paradoxes posed by this sort of painting, it seems that one is afraid, if one does not accept it, to pass for a Philistine or a bourgeois. . . . One feels one's pulse in something of a panic, one puts one's hand on one's belly and on one's head to reassure oneself that one hasn't become stout or bald, incapable of understanding the courage and daring of youth. . . . And one is reminded of the horror which, some thirty years ago, was inspired by the first pictures of Delacroix, Decamps, Boulanger, Scheffer, Corot and Rousseau, who were kept out of the Salon for so long. . . . And the more conscientious, when faced with such striking instances, ask themselves whether it is in fact possible to understand any art other than that with which one is contemporary, that is to say the art with which one shared one's twentieth birthday. . . . It is probable that the pictures of Courbet, Manet, Monet and *tutti quanti* do conceal beauties which are invisible to us old Romantics, whose hair is now laced with silver.

Gautier, a member of the original Romantic generation of the 1830s, had identified the struggles of his own youth with the emergence of an aesthetic style and attitude appropriate to modern life, liberated from traditional restraints and open to color and movement. To find the experience repeated made him see the possibility—fulfilled many times since—that every generation would have to undergo the same experience anew. Modernity could not be encompassed in a single style, but engendered a continuing progression of them. Knowing this in advance only made the uncomfortable complex of incomprehension and overcomprehension more pointed and inescapable.[16]

Gautier's comments were prescient, but other observers thought the Impressionists' relationship to their audience might be problematic for reasons that went beyond the Romantic comparison. The Impressionist emphasis on art as a means to alter and expand perception itself made surprise and disorientation necessary features of the beholder's experience. New art could not be immediately understood, because it had to proceed through the disorganization of the viewer's expectations. The critic Jules Laforgue, defending the Impressionists in 1883, argued that while "the language of the palette with respect to reality" was "a conventional tongue susceptible to new seasoning," and the Impressionist spice was lively and fecund, the new painting posed a sharp challenge to existing ways of perceiving the world. "The haste of these Impressionistic notes taken in the heat of sensory intoxication" would bewilder and exasperate some viewers, and others would "cry out against willful eccentricity."[17] History has generally upheld Laforgue's judgment that the latter were blind to art's real needs. Nonetheless, as Gautier suggested and as Leo Steinberg has reminded us, discomfort in the face of new styles is by no means limited to philistines; it has sometimes been the experience of the best artists themselves. Modern art asks us "to discard visual habits which have been acquired in the contemplation of real masterpieces." The sacrifice of expectations it demands can produce "a feeling that one's accumulated culture or experience is hopelessly devalued, leaving one exposed to spiritual destitution."[18] It was just such a feeling of impoverishment that Laforgue feared some beholders of Impressionist pictures would experience.

Zola went beyond these aesthetic questions. His deepest anxiety was that the new painting represented a form of cultural practice that was self-destructively entangled in its own opposition to existing life. Pushed to its limit, the aesthetic of temperamental individualism devalued reality in ways that would, as Castagnary also feared, place the artist in permanent rebellion against the world from which he had to draw his sustenance. Zola's finding this con-

dition in Claude Lantier now seems neither charitable nor perceptive, given the remarkable new vision that the real Cézanne was
able to create out of his inner torment. Nonetheless, Zola's sense
that the avant-garde would have to pay a price for the Bohemian refusal to accept the limitations of ordinary existence—including the
limits of art itself—that partially powered it highlights some elements of modernism that more celebratory descriptions often fail to
recognize. These features were especially prominent in the career
of Alfred Jarry.

Jarry's history was one of unremitting challenge to convention and
tradition. He was perhaps the first figure to make direct confrontation with his audience a generating principle of his work. All the
twentieth-century movements that make action and provocation
central to artistic practice were foreshadowed by him. Equally cor-
rosive of the traditional notion of art and the artist was Jarry's ability to collapse the distinction between art and life. André Breton
later declared that "beginning with Jarry, much more than with
Wilde, the differentiation long held to be necessary between art and
life has been challenged, to wind up annihilated in its principle."
With Jarry, the old Bohemian fusion of art and life—celebrated by
Murger, decried by Baudelaire and the Goncourts, put to new uses
in the Montmartre cabarets—began to appear as the substance of
artistic activity itself.[19]
   When Jarry arrived in Paris from Brittany in 1891, many of the
movements and developments we have been discussing were already in full swing. Jarry was influenced by the spirit of *fumisme*
enshrined in the Chat Noir and its imitators (which he sometimes
visited), and upheld the new principles of Impressionist painting,
but his sense of how art and life were related was especially shaped
by Symbolism in poetry and anarchism in politics.
   Anarchism, then emerging as an important presence in French
life, was nurtured by many intellectual influences, including Proudhon and the Russian prince Peter Kropotkin. Workers were drawn

to it when their traditional antiauthoritarian attitudes made them suspicious of the often complex, hierarchical organization of the socialist movement; disillusionment with the Third Republic, as demonstrated by the Boulangist crisis, swelled these anarchist currents, too. The movement's potential for radical action was demonstrated in the spring of 1892, in a succession of terrorist bombings.

A number of prominent young Symbolists were sympathetic to, or actually involved in, the growth of anarchism. Among the most committed were Adolphe Retté and Bernard Lazare. Paul Adam, Gustave Kahn, and Laurent Tailhade all had anarchist phases, too. Many writers and visual artists contributed to anarchist publications, especially those associated with the ex-shoemaker Jean Grave. The two groups shared a commitment to liberation from external rules and restraints, and awareness of this connection was at its height in the early 1890s. Remy de Gourmont, the most prominent Symbolist critic, coupled the two movements on the basis of their shared insistence that every individual was a bearer of visions and ideals that no external force had the right to restrain. "One individual is one world, a hundred individuals make a hundred worlds, each as legitimate as the others." The radical Symbolist poet Pierre Quillard described art as itself an engine of social liberation, whether its subject matter was politically oriented or not: "Whoever communicates to his brothers in suffering the secret splendor of his dreams acts upon the surrounding society in the manner of a solvent, and makes of all those who understand him, often without their realization, outlaws and rebels." Just such an aesthetically grounded individualism, so intense that it turned interiority into confrontation, was the basis for Jarry's unique and uncompromising revolt against the ordinary conditions of existence.[20]

In the mid-1880s, when Jarry was at school, the French educational system was infused with the faith in science and progress on which the militant secularism of the Third Republic rested. Against this positivist celebration of science, Jarry directed his schoolboy skepticism and irreverence. He later referred to himself as a *potache*, a word that conveys mixed exasperation and admiration for the maddening, clever antics of spirited schoolboys. He excelled in studies, but was known for wild escapades. It was an identity that he never outgrew.[21]

His schoolmates' jokes and pranks were especially inspired by one of their instructors, the physics professor Félix Hébert. Unbeknownst to his classes, Hébert had done serious work on meteorology. But to them, his attempts to expound "my science of physics" appeared merely ludicrous. He was one of those teachers totally unable to control a class. When taunted by his students for his odd appearance, dress, and manner, he could be counted on to respond ineffectually with tears and supplications. If, instead, he retaliated, it was most often against the wrong pupils. A whole mythology grew up around him, with fantastic stories about his origins, his past, his exploits.[22] The figure of Hébert seems to have taught Jarry the important lesson that scientific ideas that claim to provide an objective and solid truth about the world cannot but be shaped or, rather, deformed by the personalities and idiosyncrasies of their holders.

This intuition about the fundamental subjectivity of science led him to transform Hébert's teaching into what he called the science of "'pataphysics." 'Pataphysics was the revenge of individual spontaneity on positivistic science. As Jarry defined it later, it "will be, above all, the science of the particular, despite the common opinion that the only science is that of the general." It provided knowledge about a "supplementary universe" made up entirely of exceptions; it vindicated originality against the perpetual sameness of physical laws. As "the science of imaginary solutions," 'pataphysics was the liberation of the imagination from the chains of physical determinism. It was the revenge of art, accomplished in the name of science. How close 'pataphysics came to the ideas upheld by radical Symbolists can be seen in a dialogue the poet Pierre Quillard wrote to defend the terrorist Ravachol. Quillard's rejection of law extended to every field of human experience. Between two actions, "there can never exist any common standard of measurement, because two identical acts have never been accomplished, and no one will ever know how to foresee the uncountable multiplicity of characters and circumstances."[23]

Hébert gave Jarry not only the inspiration for the science of 'pataphysics, but also the first model for the character who made Jarry notorious, Père Ubu. Presented to the Parisian public in the play *Ubu roi (King Ubu)* in 1896, Père Ubu was the distillation of the mythology that had grown up around Hébert at the lycée in Rennes. Much of the play Jarry owed to two of his schoolmates (a circumstance he acknowledged at the time, but that led to his being accused of plagiarism). Ubu is, as Jarry said in an introductory speech, "a puppet-figure, a *potache's* deformation of one of his teachers, who represented for him everything grotesque in the world." Ubu is a puppet in the sense of having no clear sense of inner direction, but once his passions are aroused—his desires for power and money, and his aggressive impulses—nothing can restrain his violent, if often bumbling, pursuit of them. He becomes king of Poland by treachery and murder, squeezes money out of peasants, betrays those who help him, and is eventually deposed. It is often hard to see the outlines of poor Hébert in Ubu, save as a man too self-involved to adjust to the world. But he mirrors the arbitrariness of external authority and of accepted conventions and limitations.[24]

In *Ubu roi*, Jarry turned theater into outright confrontation with the audience. An elaborate publicity campaign assured that the house was full for the first production at A.-F. Lugné-Poë's Théâtre de l'Oeuvre, known for its connections with Symbolism and anarchism (Jarry was then Lugné-Poë's secretary). Some critics knew the text beforehand, but few in the audience were prepared for the first word spoken by Père Ubu: *"Merdre!"* (the closest English equivalent, it has been suggested, would be "shite"), whereupon an uproar broke out that delayed the proceedings for fifteen minutes. The rest of the play—hilarious and unrestrained, full of slapstick, irreverence, and outrage—fully preserved the spirit of the opening. Jarry was famous, forever after to be identified with the art of provocation and insult.

Ubu was also one focus for Jarry's abolition of the boundary between art and life. He cultivated the character in many ways, adding new chapters to his history and preparing a series of Ubu *Alma-*

nacks. He even came to be known as Ubu himself, using the royal "we," and signing letters "Père Ubu." Jarry also "spoke Ubu," a style consisting of a staccato series of uninflected and unaccented syllables, which André Gide once compared to the speech one might expect from a nutcracker.[25]

Yet the relationship between Jarry and his character was more complicated than the usual description of it as "literary mimesis"—Jarry's conscious imitation of his own creation—suggests. The speech known as *parler Ubu* had been Jarry's before the play existed: the actor, uncertain how his character ought to talk, took over the suggestion that he imitate Jarry's peculiar diction. But Jarry never resembled other features of Ubu. No one who knew him thought of him as a bumbling, aggressive puppet-figure who carried his conscience (as Ubu did in a later installment) in a suitcase. He had a violent streak, but it came out in very different ways. And though he was extremely unconventional, his style was usually one of exaggerated politeness, within which his verbal provocations and eccentricities made him seem mysterious and unreal.[26]

To try to grasp the relationship between Jarry and Ubu is to come upon the contradictions inherent in both. If Ubu was Jarry, he was also others. Jarry himself identified Ubu with the audience, "presented with its own image on the stage" and upset by seeing its reflection. Jarry used the word *mufle* to describe the viewer— "clod" might be the best English equivalent. But elsewhere he wrote that Ubu "is not exactly Monsieur Thiers or the bourgeois, or the *mufle*. Rather, he would be the perfect anarchist, together with that which prevents *us* from ever becoming the perfect anarchist, which is that he is a man, from which cowardice, dirtiness, ugliness, et cetera." His soul, Jarry added, was lodged wholly in his gullet. Did this description also fit Jarry? Was he a near bourgeois, an almost *mufle*, a would-be perfect anarchist, held down by the earthly limits of his material nature? Jarry's comments on Ubu suggest that he, too, shared features with the cloddish bourgeois from whom he struggled to separate himself. Anarchist individualism and bourgeois egotism were cousins, after all. We cannot understand

Jarry—or what the avant-garde drew from him—unless we see how dark were the depths he was plumbing.[27]

What Jarry sought to overcome in his life and art was nothing less than material existence itself. His deep need for that escape made itself felt in his personal relationships, and especially in his tortuous attitude toward love and sex. Jarry had a certain number of friends but very few intimate personal relations. No one has ever been able to document any heterosexual affair. His one close female friend, the novelist Rachilde (whom we met earlier in the circle of Verlaine), was never his mistress. There is a lot of heterosexual comedy in Jarry's writings, but the only serious treatment of sex appears in a homosexual work, *Haldernablou*, which portrayed Jarry's relations with a known bisexual, the poet Léon-Paul Fargue. Whether he and Jarry were actually lovers is still disputed, although the message of *Haldernablou* was that they were—the title comes from the coupling of the names that stood for each, Haldern for Jarry and Ablou for Fargue. The play describes both the temptation homosexuality held for Jarry and his conviction that its consequences were—or would have been—disastrous. Haldern is in search of a love outside of sex, a partner who is "neither man nor woman nor monster at all, a devoted slave and one who could speak without breaking the harmony of his sublime thoughts"—in other words, a lover who is an extension of himself. The androgynous Ablou seems to fit the description. From the start, however, Haldern sees that a physical relationship will end their connection: once the "sleeping panther" of sexuality arises between them, Haldern's thoughts of Ablou become murderous. "I despise him as impure and venal . . . for, according to good theology, you have to destroy the beast with which you have fornicated."[28]

The impossibility of loving another person because the relationship cannot withstand the physical experience of sexuality is a theme that appears elsewhere in Jarry's writing. The novel *Exploits and Opinions of Doctor Faustroll, 'Pataphysician*, contains the following passage on the temptations and dangers of love: "The soul is wheedled by Love who looks exactly like an iridescent veil and assumes the masked face of a chrysalis. It walks upon inverted skulls.

Behind the wall where it hides, claws brandish weapons. It is bap-
tized with poison. Ancient monsters, the wall's substance, laugh
into their green beards. The heart remains red and blue, violet in
the artificial absence of the iridescent veil that it is weaving."[29]
Jarry's images of love move between narcissism and violence—a
pattern underlying his relationship to everything that could not be
assimilated to his own will and consciousness. His need to live in the
world of material things—of bodies, limitations, physical laws—
threatened his personal existence so deeply that he could react to it
only with violence.

This is the key to Jarry's identification with the violent and aggressive Ubu. The points at which he himself could not escape the
materiality of existence, the life of the bourgeois or the *mufle*, were
the places in his self where his own violent nature showed through.
The violence of Ubu was partly Jarry's attempt to overcome the external world of material existence, and partly the acknowledgment
of his own inevitable participation in it. Jarry did not imitate Ubu so
much as see within him his own deepest conflicts and ambivalences,
his membership in the world that both promised and denied him liberation. Jarry's attraction for anarchism was, as he fully understood, the position of a man who, like Ubu, would be king or be
nothing, a person unable to live in a world that did not reflect his
own selfhood back to him. In several of his works, Jarry presented
creatures he called Palotins. These, he said, were "rubberized servants . . . perfect for anyone who wishes his will to be sovereign
law." Their own will was the exact parallel of their master's. They
were, Jarry explained, an advance over the bomb thrower Ravachol,
because they were able to "make themselves explode by a mere act
of will." Their death was compassed in the following dialogue:

External coercion: We arrest you.
Palotin: No, sirrah!
          (Terrible explosion, with twin effects.)[30]

The intimate relationship between Jarry's 'pataphysical imagination and his attraction to violence appears best in his "neoscientific

novel" *The Exploits and Opinions of Doctor Faustroll, 'Pataphysi-cian.* This mysterious work, often on the edge of incomprehensi-bility, full of private allusions and extravagant jokes, contains Jarry's clearest account of 'pataphysics as well as some of his most lyrical prose writing (including the daunting admonition against love quoted earlier). There are many references to contemporary literary and artistic figures, some admired by Jarry, others hated, all encountered—disguised—on a mythical voyage around Paris. But *Faustroll* is something more in addition: a fantasy of destruction and self-destruction.

In the novel, Faustroll is aided by a servant, a grotesque dog-faced baboon called Bosse-de-Nage, an extension of Faustroll's will, a kind of Palotin without the ability to make himself explode. Faus-troll can both kill him and bring him back to life, and he carries out the doctor's destructive wishes, "befouling and ravaging everything indiscriminately." What is the source of this aggressiveness? Bosse-de-Nage speaks only two words in response to any stimulus: "Ha-Ha." This was not only the vocabulary of Jarry's refusal to take the world seriously, but also (as he made clear in a philosophi-cal chapter) an exposition of the principle of identity in duality: the discontinuity between the self and the world was to be overcome in the unity of the imagination. Bosse-de-Nage knows only his self; he has no notion of anything or any person that can not be encom-passed in the formula of unity-in-duality. His perpetual "Ha-Ha" makes the world identical with himself. The formula fails, however, when brought up against reality. Faustroll is an artistic alchemist, the possessor, he says, of the philosopher's stone with which "I could easily transmute all things." But that imaginative transmuta-tion is to no avail, for "I have found by experiment that the benefit extends only to those whose brain is that selfsame stone"—in other words, only those who transmute reality in the same way as he. And that number is null, since, as we are finally told, "Faustroll defined the universe as *that which is the exception to oneself.*" 'Pataphy-sics, then, the science of exceptions, was a recipe for isolation; it showed that the only real formula for identity was to be found in violence, against the world or the self. In Jarry's novel, the 'pataphysician Faustroll finally destroys Paris—all its buildings and, in particular, all its paintings—and then commits suicide.

Jarry's life has often been seen as a suicide, too. The critic Roger Shattuck calls his ending "suicide by hallucination." Rachilde, who knew Jarry perhaps as well as anyone could, said that he was the victim of a cruel mirage in his brain, the desire to fit his existence to his literary program. He refused "to take the road of real life." What he wanted to put in its place was something less conscious than literature, however, the world of dreams. "All my hours the same, dreaming or awake," he wrote in an early text. The Jarry-like figure in the novel *Days and Nights*, called Sengle, believes that he controls things with his thoughts. "He made no distinction whatever between his thoughts and his actions, or between his dream and his waking." The need to live in a world where fantasy was not hemmed in by material existence made the ordinary world uninhabitable for Jarry. No normal living place would do for him. His early years in Paris were passed in an apartment decorated with religious objects and shared with owls. Jarry called it the "Dead Man's Calvary," affixing bloody handprints along the stairwell. After he spent his inheritance, Jarry found an even more remarkable lodging place. It was in a building whose floors had been horizontally divided in order to provide more space for apartments and more rent for the owner. Jarry was short enough to stand upright, but many visitors had to stoop. He called the rooms "our great *chasublerie*"—priestly vestment shop—after the seller of religious objects on the ground floor. Pinning a label that suggested largeness to a world reduced in size must have appealed to his 'pataphysical imagination. (In one episode of *Faustroll*, the doctor reduces himself to tiny dimensions.) Jarry kept an outsize plaster phallus on his mantelpiece, and when a female visitor once asked if it was a cast, he replied, "No, madame, it is a reduction."[31]

Jarry's manner, with its eccentricity and detachment, allowed him to keep his aggressive urges close to the surface. The stories about him are legion. Many of them included the revolver he seems to have carried regularly. Once, annoyed by a diner's pipe in a café, Jarry stood up, revolver in his hand, calmly aimed at the pipe, and fired. He missed, hitting instead a glass at the rear of the café. Sitting calmly down, he turned to his companion and said, "Now that the *glace* [both "glass" and "ice" in French] is broken, let's talk." Another time, when Jarry was doing target practice with bottles at the country house owned by Rachilde and her husband, Alfred Vallette, a neighbor objected, fearing that one of her children might be hit by a stray bullet. If that happened, Jarry remarked calmly to the woman, "we would make some others with you." Apollinaire told of walking around Paris with Jarry late at night. When an unknown passerby asked for directions, Jarry pulled out his gun and made the man stand six feet away before giving them.[32]

Jarry's outrageous public behavior recalls some stories about Baudelaire, but in a harsher mode. Baudelaire had been known for sometimes dyeing his hair green. Jarry went further, painting his hands and face green. He once turned up at a theater with a bow tie painted on his shirtfront. Having no shoes to wear to Mallarmé's funeral, he borrowed yellow high-heeled ones from Rachilde (they wore the same size). On the same occasion, Jarry's pants were so dirty that his friend Octave Mirbeau couldn't help looking suspiciously at them. "I have a dirtier pair at home," Jarry assured him. His contempt for social conventions and logical consistency was evoked by Rachilde when she described Jarry living in his half-sized apartment "like a recluse, sleeping in the day after having passed his nights with drinking and with dizzying his comrades with the most contradictory stories, mixing up, as if in his own glass, concoctions the least constructed to harmonize with themselves." He pushed his mystification "to the point of mystifying himself."[33]

To have become the victim of his own unrestrained imagination was a fate earlier writers had attributed to Privat d'Anglemont. Jarry shared with him a fascination for the ability of Paris itself to inspire such confusions. In 1903, he published an article called "A Klondike in Paris—What One Does with Old Paving Stones." Its subject was a certain M. Donzé, who had been Jarry's concierge some years before. According to Jarry, he once found Donzé in his room surrounded by paving stones on one side and an apparatus used by counterfeiters on the other. Donzé was looking for gold.

Having read that the Seine contained minute quantities of the precious metal, he had concluded that it must have washed off the stones that paved the city's streets. Grinding them up, he did find gold in them. But unlike Privat's, Jarry's *métier inconnu* offered no prospect of worldly success or profit. The stones cost thirty centimes each and the value of the gold extracted from each was only fifteen centimes. The Klondike—Jarry might have concluded—was in Donzé's mind.[34]

Jarry seems never to have used the term "Bohemian" about himself. Perhaps—rather like Rimbaud—he found the images associated with Murger and Romanticism too tame and sentimental to encompass his more intense and hard-edged ambivalence. Others were less circumspect. To Rachilde, Jarry was an "incorrigible Bohemian." His dress, style of life, attitude toward work and money, all demonstrated it. The Jarry who often had no money to feed himself or keep warm by the end of his life was poor "because, quite incapable of repressing his caprices or his passions, he had eaten up his inheritance from the first year of his liberation from school and from the control of his parents." For some time in Paris Jarry had lived in a pretty little apartment in the boulevard Saint-Germain, "furnished with old family furniture that still gave off the scent of a former life that was very bourgeois and very ordered. Then, having eaten, or drunk, his inheritance, Jarry descended the staircase of his dangerous fantasies down to the cellar of the worst poverty." It was a story that recalled Paul Verlaine's.[35]

Certainly Jarry resembled Verlaine in seeking flight from reality in drink. If Rachilde can be believed (and Jarry always regarded her as a genuine friend), he would often drink from morning to night—white wine at breakfast, absinthe in the morning, red wine with lunch, liqueurs mixed in coffee during the afternoon, more wine at dinner. Rachilde claimed that she never saw him genuinely drunk, but she also recognized that his free-floating, unrestrained verbal aggressiveness owed some of its quality to a constant mild intoxication. Jarry sought release from ordinary experience not only in stimulants but also in the disorientation caused by the speed of machines: "Fueling one's mind with crushed, confused fragments relieves the memory's secret dungeons of their destructive work, and after such an assimilation the mind can more readily re-create entirely original forms and colors."[36]

Roger Shattuck has suggested that we see Jarry's drinking as Baudelaire saw Poe's—a mnemonic entry into realms of imagination excluded from ordinary states of consciousness. That seems right on one level, but it misses the important point where Jarry departs from Baudelaire. The older poet had always carefully distinguished between the artificial paradises of drink and drugs and the, to him, only genuine realm of transcendence, the poetic imagination. Jarry abandoned that distinction. "We do not know how to create out of nothingness," he admitted, "but are capable of doing so out of chaos." In this, Jarry was less the heir of Baudelaire than the double of Rimbaud, like him seeking access to vision through the methodical disorganization of the senses, and willing to count form or formlessness as equal products of the visionary flight. For Baudelaire, the escape into drugs had been important, but only as a sign of the human need for a transcendence that only art could offer under modern conditions. For Jarry, art and mysticism were one, and drink and drugs another available escape from the unbearable weight of ordinary life.[37]

Here we return to André Breton's observation that it was Jarry who first abolished the principle of a distinction between art and life. Those who quote Breton often fail to notice that he went on to identify Jarry's merging of art and life with his opening up of ordinary experience to transformation by the unconscious, the Freudian id. Breton had good reason: Jarry's visionary departures from waking life often remind us of Freud's exploration of the unconscious through dreams, most notably in Jarry's repeated insistence on abolishing the principle of noncontradiction. The oppositions of night and day, reason and madness, evil and good, self and other, even of life and death, were all to be done away with in his world. Behind Jarry's annihilation of the distinction between life and art was a longing for individual annihilation. His fascination with guns, with fencing, even with bicycling (which he loved both for its speed and for its assimilation of man to a machine), all suggest his perpetual flirting with self-destruction. Jarry never turned any of those instruments on himself, but, as Rachilde put it, "He savored the joy of martyrdom when he drank absinthe, knowing perfectly well that he was killing himself." Unable to work steadily, too poor to feed himself or keep warm, Jarry descended into illness. He sought out medical help at the end—more, it seems, as a way of confirming his approaching demise than of preventing it. A month before his actual death, he wrote Rachilde a letter not only announcing his end but welcoming it. Père Ubu, Jarry said, "believes that the brain, in its decomposition, functions beyond death and that it is *his dreams* that are paradise."[38]

But this annihilation of life was far from the triumph of literature that some have seen in it. Literature—here Jarry set the tone for many avant-garde figures who followed him—was deprived of its independence, too. The world of art was but the augury of a visionary transformation that remained incomplete as long as it did not remake life. Literature was coming to consist in a confrontation with life. Jarry stood at the transition point between the older, Bohemian identification of art with the life of art, in which art retained its traditional forms and definitions, and the coming avant-garde version of their unification, in which the very notion of art itself was questioned and transformed. The artist in Jarry's mold was the person who lived most integrally in a world of pure possibility, displacing actual existence to the margins where it had banished challenges to everyday reality before. It was more than Murger had bargained for when he described the Bohemian world that made art possible for him as turning everyday life into a work of genius.

Another kind of assimilation of Bohemian elements to the emerging avant-garde was being carried out in the same years by a figure whose ties to Bohemia were more explicit than Jarry's, the composer Erik Satie. Satie's music was just as determinedly revolutionary and just as deeply personal as Jarry's poetry, but its directness and simple humor make it accessible in ways that Jarry's writing seldom is. Satie wanted to do for music what others were doing for literature and the visual arts, specifically setting out to find musical equivalents for the means of representation and expression developed by the Impressionists in painting. His liberation of music from the overblown gestures and metaphysical aspirations of post-Wagnerian Romanticism made him an exemplary figure for younger modernist composers in the years before and after World War I—Milhaud, Poulenc, Honegger, and the others who constituted "The Six." Closely involved with other avant-garde art forms, he was associated at various times with Cubism, Dada, and Surrealism; his collaborators included Picasso, Diaghilev, Cocteau, Picabia, and Marcel Duchamp.[39]

Satie shared many characteristics with his contemporary Jarry. (He was seven years older, but began to make his impact only after 1900, and he outlived Jarry by eighteen years.) Friends and acquaintances found both of them alternately charming and difficult; both were known for odd dress and habits, and had unusual sex lives that suggested fear of intimacy. Jarry's unaccented, staccato-like speech was matched by a similar rhythm in Satie's prose and, often, his music. Both were drawn to medieval images and disguises, finding in them postures in which spiritualist withdrawal and personal aggression concealed and supported each other. Both lived in small rooms to which they gave grand labels, Jarry's *grand chasublerie* matched by Satie's *Abbatiale*, headquarters of an elaborately organized "Metropolitan Art Church of Jesus the Conductor," in which Satie was the only real one among some ten million fancied members. Satie hid his timidity and fear of public exposure behind a facade of boldness and exhibitionism, creating a thick veil of eccentricity beneath which his enormous need for privacy and his powerful impulse for fantasy were given free rein.

Satie's life was a self-conscious prolongation of youth. Never a *potache*, like Jarry, Satie was instead a withdrawn, daydreaming *distrait*, living on the same plane as other people only where his separate universe happened to intersect with theirs. Debussy, dedicating some songs to Satie, described him as a medieval musician who had accidentally strayed into the nineteenth century. Satie's motto for himself, attached to a series of self-caricatures, was "I came into the world very young, at a very old time." Throughout his youth, Satie wrote in 1920, people told him that he would "see" once he was fifty years old. "I am fifty years old. I haven't seen anything." When he was nearly forty, he went back to school to study counterpoint, as if to dramatize his continually postponed maturity. Even after success and recognition came, Satie resisted being one who had "arrived," lest his journey seem to be over. "In art there must not be any servitude. I have always tried to throw followers off the track, in form and content, with each new work. It is the only way for an artist to avoid becoming the head of a school, which means being a tutor for schoolboys [*pion*]."[40]

Satie's music bore the imprint of all these qualities—charm and distraction, intimacy and eccentricity, timidity and boldness, directness and evasiveness. It was marked by a cleanliness and precision that excluded all romantic gestures, and by a self-restriction and miniaturism that sometimes veiled its originality. The eternal child in Satie made his work an unending series of jokes, contained sometimes in the music itself and sometimes in its titles: *Three Flaccid Pieces (for a Dog); Desiccated Embryos; Next-to-Last Thoughts; Bureaucratic Sonata; Three Pieces in the Form of a Pear; Five Grimaces.* Satie seemed to come upon everything in music as if, like a child, for the first time; he made extremely simple, even trite, material interesting by acting as if it had never been discovered before, and was able to treat with complete seriousness things that a more "grown-up" sensibility would have relegated to the realm of mere play. As Rollo Myers has suggested, Satie approached even bizarre material with matter-of-factness, thereby (like the Surrealists who followed him) bringing his listeners into a universe decidedly, if mysteriously, at variance with the ordinary one. He was "a classically minded musician on the one hand, and an inveterate *blagueur* on the other."[41]

A Norman by birth, Satie had sailors in his family tree, a Scotswoman for a mother, and an unsettled and irrepressibly undisciplined paternal uncle on whom he seems to have modeled himself. His interest in music started in boyhood, but began to take its characteristic turn after his widowed father married a piano teacher with a very academic spirit. Confirmed in his rejection of all academic discipline, Satie seems to have passed nearly unscathed through the Paris Conservatory, where he studied both piano and composition. He ended his military service quickly, catching bronchitis by going shirtless on a winter night. (Jarry had made his military uselessness apparent simply by being himself.) His early passions, next to music, were exotic literature (Flaubert's *Salammbô* was a favorite) and gothic reverie. For a time, he became involved with the then popular Rosicrucians, for whom he would write a musical play before breaking away in 1892 to start his own aforementioned "Metropolitan Art Church of Jesus the Conductor." In these same years of fascination with mystical spirituality, Satie was also found in a different kind of milieu—the cabarets of Montmartre. It is not known what led Satie to them (perhaps he was introduced by one of Salis's regulars, Alphonse Allais, who like Satie came from Honfleur), but by the end of the 1880s, he was spending many evenings in those surroundings. He took an apartment in the rue Cortot, not far from the Chat Noir. He even worked there for a time, but after falling out with Salis moved to one of the Chat Noir's neighbors, the Auberge du Clou. There he played the piano and produced a mystical ballet, *Uspud.*

By the early 1890s, Satie had entered into a period of self-conscious Bohemianism. According to his friend Contamine de Latour, Satie "sowed his wild oats": he did away with his bourgeois clothes, let his hair grow, and made his opposition to respectable manners and opinions known in every way he could. In 1893, Satie had a brief affair with one of the most remarkable inhabitants of Montmartre, the model and later painter—of considerable talent— Suzanne Valadon, already the mother of Maurice Utrillo. Earlier, in 1891, the Spanish painter and friend of Picasso Ramón Casas did a portrait of Satie in Montmartre that he entitled simply *The Bohemian* (see figure 11). It should not surprise us that Satie's period as a cabaret fixture coincided with his mystical involvements and enthusiasms. Similar combinations were effected by his contemporaries, notably Léon Bloy and Maurice Rollinat.[42]

Then, in 1898, Satie left Montmartre, moved to the rather gray

11. Ramón Casas, *The Bohemian*, a portrait of Erik Satie.

and mostly petit-bourgeois suburb of Arcueil on the outskirts of Paris, and changed his ways, returning to respectable clothes and a kempt appearance. After a decade or so, he became active in local civic affairs in Arcueil, where he was known as "the velvet gentleman." He still traveled to Montmartre to work, but in 1905 he began to study counterpoint at Vincent d'Indy's Schola Cantorum, where his teacher was Albert Roussel. When, around 1910, his music was taken up and praised by younger composers, Satie's career entered its final, most public phase.

The change in Satie's life after 1898 was striking, but he did not become less eccentric or more ordinary. Instead, he seems to have discovered (perhaps like Barrès) that he could hide just as well behind a bourgeois facade as behind a Bohemian one. He became increasingly mysterious. No one knows whether he had any relations with women. There were no visitors to his room—literally no one entered it until Satie died in 1925. In the meantime, dust and dirt accumulated, the curtains and furniture deteriorated. At his death, several manuscripts Satie believed he had lost on a trolley were found behind the piano.

Much of the spirit of Satie in those years can be seen in two of his famous writings, "The Musician's Day," and "What I Am." Intended to be parts of a collection, *An Amnesiac's Memoirs*, both mixed mystification with pure *blague*. "The artist must regulate his life," Satie began the first. His own exact schedule included arising at 7:18, receiving inspiration from 10:23 to 11:47, meals and horseback riding "deep in my park" at similarly designated times, "another inspiration" from 3:12 to 4:07 in the afternoon, various occupations afterward, and dinner from 7:16 to 7:20. The musician ate only white foods, cooked his wine and drank it cold with fuchsia juice, never spoke while eating "for fear of strangling myself," breathed carefully a little at a time, while talking held his sides and looked fixedly behind himself. He slept with one eye open on a round bed with a hole for his head. "Once an hour a servant takes my temperature and gives me another one [temperature]." Satie began "What I Am" by declaring, "Everyone will tell you I am not a musician. That is correct." Instead, he had always been a phonometrographer, a recorder of sound measurements. All his works were to be classed as phonometrography. No musical idea had given birth to any of them: "it is scientific thought that dominates." His phonometer in hand, Satie worked with joy and assurance. "The first time I used a phonoscope, I examined a B-flat of medium size. I assure you I have never seen anything more repugnant. I called my servant to show it to him." Phonology was superior to music, more varied and more financially rewarding. "I owe my fortune to it." His apparatus allowed him to notate many more sounds in a given time than any other musician; this explained why Satie had been able to produce so much.[43]

These writings, with their outrageous invocations of wealth and servants, their mock-serious description of things Satie never did, show the composer in one of his favorite postures: hiding behind pretended self-revelations. Many of his earlier positions seem to have served the same function of concealment. The "Metropolitan Art Church of Jesus the Conductor" was a decorative structure whose pretended range and size sheltered both Satie's unadmitted fantasies of recognition, and his isolation. The same entangled impulse toward self-revelation and concealment seems visible in the curious title he gave to an early set of piano pieces, *Gymnopédies.* The literal translation of the Greek elements in this title is "Nude Children." Satie knew the etymology and quoted a passage from Cicero that referred to it. The pieces have the apparent innocence and directness of children, but Satie's progeny were only nude to those who saw them at a distance. Each piece was labeled with a definite feeling—pained, sad, solemn. In fact, however, as Anne Rey points out, their texture and design do not call forth such clear emotions. "Their atmosphere is, rather, refined, and their charm ambiguous." That same formula, ambiguity hiding behind apparent transparency, appears over and over again in Satie's career. Satie called himself "gymnopedist" for a time, hiding his serious musical claims behind an image of innocent self-exposure. Roger Shattuck points out that he was both timid and exhibitionistic, and that even drinking was, for him, a way of "exposing certain parts of himself and hiding others."[44]

It is not usually noticed how deeply and almost obsessively the theme of publicity and his own relationship to it ran through Satie's career. Satie wrote for newspapers, both during his Montmartre period and again, later on, in Arcueil. At both times, he made clear his fascination with publicity, satirizing it but in ways that rose out of involvement as much as distance. In 1888–89, he signed a series of newspaper columns in the Montmartre cabaret paper *La Lanterne Japonaise* with the pseudonym Virginie Lebeau. One of the first columns reported that the writer had received "from all sides letters asking us where one can find the complete works of Erik Satie." The definitive edition was not yet in the works, he explained, but the *Troisième Gymnopédie* could be purchased for very little at an address in the boulevard Magenta. A short time later, the same columnist published a letter supposedly received by Satie. The writer was a woman who had been cured of a whole range of afflictions— liver troubles, rheumatism, and a polyp on the nose—by listening to his music. "One hearing of your *Ogives* produced a noticeable improvement in my state; four or five applications of your *Troisième Gymnopédie* cured me altogether." Here as everywhere Satie made himself into a joke, but the humor called attention to himself and his work in the very act of poking fun at it. The paper Satie wrote for was a frank imitator of Goudeau and Salis's *Chat Noir*. He seems to have understood the nature of the Goudeau-Salis "system," finding his own way of participating in it.[45]

Some years later, in 1900, Satie wrote part of a *Guide to Montmartre for Foreigners*, for which Émile Goudeau wrote the preface. One of Satie's contributions to the life of Arcueil was to write notices advertising local civic activities and organizations for the town newspaper. These began with announcements about meetings of the volunteer firemen and of various social clubs, but went on to include free advertising for dance classes and a movie theater. In the Arcueil period, Satie also amused himself by drawing up calligraphic advertisements for imaginary objects. They include a series advertising medieval castles for sale or rent, particularly to magicians or sorcerers, some for fantastic weapons, others for toy soldiers with magical properties, and even some more mundane notices about clothing, groceries, inns, and department stores.[46]

Perhaps most remarkable were Satie's musical advertisements. Some seemed to suggest a kind of imaginary musical carnival, with attractions that included a two-headed cellist, "the thinnest flutist in the world," pianos in odd shapes, paper violins, and drums made of crocodile skins. Satie also imagined a kind of musical department store, offering 100,000 quartets, microscopic steel double-basses, and "used intervals," including transparent fourths and augmented fifths (fifty centimes extra). Other features were arrangements of requiems and masses for dances, harmonic "repairs" and musical transformations, including "serious music rendered gay," and difficult pieces arranged for one finger. These operations put "subtlety within reach of everyone . . . Our music is guaranteed playable." Satie went on to imagine dialogues between customers and salespeople. "A symphony? Here you are, madame." "It doesn't look very amusing." "We can give it to you arranged as a waltz, and with thirteen words. It is played in all the cafés." All this was pointedly intended to be critical of those who made music an item of commerce. The various musical transformations were made without concern for the approval of composers, one of whom Satie pictured as asking a merchant: "What do you like more—music or delicatessen?"[47]

Yet Satie's attitude toward turning music into an object of commercial utility was not simply hostile. All through his life, Satie was drawn to popular music, not just for its simplicity but also for its ties to a broad audience. For some years, he made much of his meager living as an accompanist for the fashionable *chansonnier* Vincent Hyspa. From this association and other popular music he heard in Montmartre cabarets, Satie absorbed material that he incorporated into many of his own compositions. His complex relationship to music as a commercial object finally issued in 1920 in a project with important implications for the avant-garde as a whole. It was called "furniture music," *musique d'ameublement.*

The idea of furniture music was to integrate music into everyday life, eliminating it as performance so that it became simply an object that facilitated other activities. It has been seen as a model both for the canned music now so pervasive, and for moving-picture music. Satie once told Fernand Léger that he looked to furniture music to soften both street sounds and the clicking of knives and forks in restaurants, filling up empty spaces in conversations, and making recourse to banalities unnecessary. In his notebooks, Satie described the new kind of music as "fundamentally industrial." Its purpose was to satisfy utilitarian needs to which art had not so far contributed. It was to "create vibration," filling the same role as "light, heat, and all the forms of comfort." Satie wrote model advertisements for it: "Ask for furniture music." "Furniture music for notaries, bankers, etc. . . . No wedding without furniture music." In cooperation with Milhaud, Satie tried to demonstrate *musique d'ameublement* during the intermission of a play in 1920, hoping that the audience would circulate and talk while it was being played; the attempt failed, however, the members of the audience returning to their seats as soon as the musicians began to play.[48]

The whole project was, like everything Satie did, steeped in irony, but it was serious, too. Satie really did want to produce furniture music. Turned into an object of pure utility, music became what a wholly commercial society seemed to require of it. But it also fulfilled Satie's different intent to undermine the barrier between life and art. On one level, furniture music looks like a kind of proto-Muzak, a reassuring lubricant for other activities; but it was equally the opposite, an attack on the inherited hierarchies that consigned art to a separate sphere, outside of everyday experience. Such a challenge to the familiar produced discomfort, not reassurance, which was why the first audiences refused to accept furniture music. The project fused Satie's long fascination with publicity and commerce with his campaign to displace music from its traditional roles and attachments.

Satie drew on more than the usual quantity of nonmusical sources as inspiration for his work. His early compositions evoked the atmosphere of the Romantic writers he read and his fascination with medieval spiritualism and the half-light of Gothic buildings. For a time, he worked within a system of composition based on mystical number theory. Another early aesthetic impulse was to find a musical equivalent for the directness and colorism of Impressionist painting. Roger Shattuck has observed that "it is both the quality and the shortcoming of Satie's music that for long periods he subjected himself almost exclusively to nonmusical influences." Perhaps his return to the study of counterpoint after 1905 was a kind of repentance for this. But when Satie began to be recognized and celebrated by younger composers in the years before World War I, it was his early works that were praised. The result was—as he intimated in an ironic letter to his brother—that his original musical "ignorance" turned out to be the right foundation for his work after all.[49]

It is hard to think of any composer before Satie who made so much of the extramusical packaging and description of his work. When in 1903 Debussy suggested that Satie's works needed more form, he responded with *Three Pieces in the Form of a Pear*. But there was little new music in the "new" work: most of the parts— and there were seven—had been composed much earlier. Often Satie refused to let his music speak for itself. His 1914 piano work *Sports and Diversions (Sports et divertissements)* was meant not only to be played but also to be appreciated for the visual qualities of the score. It was published in a giant format, reproducing the author's careful and florid handwriting, and using both red and black ink. In one of the pieces, "The Water-Slide," the series of descending notes give a visual as well as a musical image of the fall; over the first two staves, Satie wrote a text telling his performers—or readers—that the water-slide would not make them too sick if they had strong hearts, but it would be like tumbling from a scaffold, he warned: watch out! Other works included similar commentaries, some of them more distant from the music. These included whole—quite outlandish and confusing—stories, like the *Heures séculaires et instantanées* of 1913. Performers have often not known what to do about these texts, some trying to read them aloud as they play the music. But Satie made clear that this was not his intention, warning in a preface that whoever did so would incur his indignation. The prose therefore seems to have had two other purposes: to establish that the scores were to be read as well as performed—that they were not merely musical notation but a combined art form in which Satie's humor and poetry had roles; the other was to mystify the performers. That Satie intended to upset the expectations of his performers is shown also by another characteristic of his later works: the use of unnecessarily complicated, often outlandish, notation. Simple scales and chords were disguised behind harmonically unnecessary sharps and flats—sometimes double sharps and flats.[50]

The same was true, even more strongly, of Satie's relationship to his audience. To listen to Satie's music is to be charmed, amused, and touched, but it is also to be mystified and upset. Even the seemingly simplest pieces are punctuated by surprises, sudden stops or unexpected juxtapositions. Satie's music demands to be noticed, while apparently blushing in its unblemished simplicity. It is music at once very well mannered and very eccentric, calling attention to itself while forgoing any large gesture that might make its claims for recognition too visible. Sometimes a single phrase is repeated over and over again, so often that Satie's repetitions led John Cage to conclude that repetition, if continued long enough, ceases to be boring and arouses new interest. With Satie, the composer's desire to challenge his listeners' assumptions, to expand and alter their consciousness by undermining the system of expectations they bring to the act of listening, became a principle of composition itself. Music served as a stage on which to dramatize the composer's relationship to his audience.

Jarry and Satie reveal both the general features of late-nineteenth-century cultural life that were helping to shape the modernist avant-garde, and some of the alternatives that could emerge in response to them. In these years, art was often identified with an integral subjectivity, a form of existence that resisted being shaped by the external world, even while it drew sustenance from it. Such a view inspired the decadent and Symbolist writers, the aesthetic politics of Maurice Barrès, and the Impressionist attempt to preserve a fleeting moment of personal experience. This intensified subjectivity was the end toward which Zola's aesthetic of temperamental individualism tended, and which Breton, looking back to Jarry, defined as the abolition of the division between art and life. For if the artist was recognized by his subjective integrity, then his identity had to be tested in his life as much as his work.

For Jarry, preserving that integrity meant creating a persona on which the external world's purchase was so much reduced that living itself came to be problematic, and eventually impossible. Satie discovered a different solution. Part of his genius lay in finding ways to fulfill his need for privacy and withdrawal through the very structures of publicity that were emerging around cultural life. He played with publicity throughout his career, using it to hide behind, just as he used Bohemianism in the 1890s and the trappings of bourgeois respectability later on.

Satie brought to light the unstated presuppositions behind Émile Goudeau's transformation of Bohemian *fumisme* into a system of public relations. If art was both identified with an integral subjectivity, and inserted into a system of market relationships, then the features that defined an artist's distance from ordinary bourgeois life were inseparable from the gestures best calculated to serve as self-advertisement. This was the hidden spring that made Goudeau's system work, and Satie was one of the first to draw out its potential. Writings like "The Musician's Day" and "What I Am" were brilliant examples of self-advertising through eccentricity: the peculiarities they flaunted were signs of some different content hidden underneath, which the reader was challenged to discover if he could. The same challenge sounded in Satie's music. Satie's advertisements for himself also provided energy for his campaign against the traditional limits of musical composition. Through them, even the claims of a commercial society to remake art along utilitarian lines (the claims he took on in the project of furniture music) could be manipulated to serve a different kind of attack on the traditional division between art and life. Those who have regarded commercialization as a fate that has deprived the avant-garde of some presumed potential to transcend bourgeois social relationships fail to recognize how much early figures like Satie were attuned to absorbing and exploiting commercial relations. Commercial society was a fundamental framework of avant-garde practice from the start. Separately and together, Jarry and Satie show how the Bohemian dramatization of ambivalence, both in its original Romantic version and in the transposed form it was taking on in the *fin de siècle*, shaped the configurations of avant-garde culture. Their alternative responses to the dilemmas of individuality and sociability, their contrasting modes of fusing art and life, would reappear in others.

CHAPTER 12

Art and Life
in Montmartre

IN THE DECADE before the outbreak of World War I, Bohemian Paris and the modernist avant-garde occupied a common territory—the streets and squares of Montmartre. The legacy of the Chat Noir (the original cabaret closed in 1897) was only one of several reasons for this convergence. That the name of Montmartre now seems nearly synonymous with the heroic age of twentieth-century art owes much—but not all—to the fact that Picasso settled there when he moved to France in the years just after 1900. His friends and companions then included not only other artists like Georges Braque and Juan Gris, but also André Salmon, Max Jacob, and Guillaume Apollinaire, all important figures in the history of contemporary poetry. Other notable Montmartrois included Maurice Utrillo, himself a child of Montmartre (and the only notable twentieth-century painter to make it his major subject), and Modigliani, who settled there before World War I. But the quarter's artistic importance was not a novelty; its picturesque quality had attracted artists throughout the nineteenth century, including Delacroix and the illustrator Gavarni. The cafés favored by the Impressionists were nearby; Cézanne and Renoir spent long stretches of time there, as did many other, lesser-known, even totally forgotten, artists. The apprentice painters, *rapins*, surrounded by their hangers-on—models, *amateurs*, picture dealers—gave Montmartre its oft-remarked exoticism.

Those who have written the quarter's history remind us, quite properly, that there were in fact two Montmartres. The Montmartre of cheap artists' living quarters was on the "Butte," the summit of the little hill that had long made the region famous for its pure air and its quaint old windmills. But the more easily accessible and developed quarter just below was one where Parisians had long come for entertainment and cheap wine (bistros outside the official city customs walls were free of excise tax). In the boulevard Rochechouart, the boulevard de Clichy, and (somewhat later) the place Pigalle could be found bars, *café-concerts*, and popular dancing establishments that drew a colorful and socially mixed population on weekends and holidays. The most notable of these, the Moulin de la Galette, a favorite subject for the Impressionists, still functioned in the years before 1914, and Picasso painted it in 1900. By then, however, the more recent Moulin Rouge, opened in 1889 and made famous by Toulouse-Lautrec, had taken over much of its clientele. This lower region of Montmartre was already the home of the Chat Noir, Bruant's Le Mirliton, and many other cafés and cabarets. The Medrano Circus also drew crowds and provided subjects for the artists with studios near the place Pigalle. Other magnetic attractions and dangers could be found in the side streets stretching up the hill from these squares and boulevards—prostitutes, brothels, marginal street people, pimps, pickpockets, con men, and armed thieves.[1]

The appearance and character of the "Butte" were very different. In many ways, it was still a village before 1914, complete with animals, gardens, pasture, quaint old buildings, and a population that still looked and behaved like villagers. One important activity that gave character to the Butte was religion. The new—and often much resented—Sacré-Coeur, begun after the Commune, would be completed only in 1911, but the older abbey church Saint-Pierre de Montmartre recalled the region's history as a place of pilgrimage. (One explanation for the name Montmartre derives it from "hill of martyrs.") Both artists and visitors frequented the cheap restaurants clustered around the place du Tertre, now the center of Montmartre's artistic tourism.

By the 1890s, the population of artists was large and noticeable. They were colorful, enthusiastic participants in the series of costume dances begun in the late 1880s under the sponsorship of the popular newspaper the *Courrier Français*. The spirit of these dances—extravagant, sensual, sometimes wild—was continued in the next decade in the annual Bal des Quatz' Arts, which drew artists, students, and many others from all parts of Paris to the Moulin Rouge. It was in the mid-1890s that the young artists and *rapins* of the Butte also put on parades in the name of the *vache enragée*, declaring their obeisance to the life of hunger and poverty. The parades were elaborately prepared, with floats representing the cow herself, *"la Belle Étoile"* (to sleep *à la belle étoile* was to be without shelter), the muse, free song, the barricades, liberty, and a dozen other themes. Meant to be annual, the parade took place only twice, partly, it seems, because its organizers were demoralized when poor planning and a damaging rainstorm made a disaster out of the second one. Other humorous festivals remembered later by participants and observers included the annual wedding of the cartoonist Francisque Poulbot. For several years he and his companion Leona would put on a mock country wedding, complete with friends costumed as a priest, a shepherd, and a wet nurse (the latter identified by large cardboard breasts).[2]

Writers of Montmartre memoirs like André Warnod and Roland Dorgelès later looked back on these festivals as the products of an age still innocent of the commercialism they saw beginning to invade the quarter after the Great War. Certainly, they suggest a subculture of artists and hangers-on who were highly conscious of their separation from the rest of society, and given to dramatizing the imaginative, irregular aspects of their lives. The unconventionality, visibility, self-consciousness, and theatricality of this Montmartre life at the turn of the century led many to speak of it as "Bohemian"—the word appears regularly in accounts written both before 1914 and later; in Gustave Charpentier's popular light opera about the love between a young poet and a working-class girl, *Louise*, first produced in 1900, all the poets and artists of the quarter are referred to as *bohèmes*. But the desire of Warnod and others to see this Bohemia as free from the later taint of commercialism gave it an innocence it hardly possessed. The separation between the two Montmartres was never complete; the extravagant gestures associated with the costume balls and the parades owed much to the world of the boulevards. Commerce and publicity were important elements in the dances from the start, creating a relationship between papers like the *Courrier Français* and establishments like the Moulin Rouge that recalls the Chat Noir's mixture of commercial journalism and artistic entertainment. The parades were both spontaneous social theater and publicity stunts; the Moulin Rouge certainly had a float (other establishments may have had them as well), and some of the others were designed by artists with long experience in advertising, like Willette, Jules-Alexandre Grün, and their friend Roedel.[3]

The persisting power of the Chat Noir spirit appears best in the operation of the cabaret most closely associated with Picasso and his friends, the Lapin Agile. The Lapin was located on the Butte, not in the boulevards, in an out-of-the-way, almost rural setting where there had long been a local bar. In the years after 1900, it became popular with many groups—local artists and writers, a fringe of shady Montmartre characters (including pimps, eccentrics, and simple down-and-outers), students visiting the Butte from the Latin Quarter, and a sprinkling of well-heeled bourgeois out on a lark. The proprietor Frédéric Gérard, known to all as Frédé, was a colorful ex-fishmonger who knew how to exploit his popular origins and manner. He kept as a mascot the donkey that had once served him to transport fish, played the guitar (badly, according to some), and gave meals and drink to young artists and poets who had no way to make ends meet.

The popularity of his establishment was not due to Frédé alone, however, despite what many of his patrons thought. The association of the Lapin Agile with art and letters had begun in the early 1880s when André Gill, the cartoonist and poet who had once been a friend of Jules Vallès, took the bar over. Gill had been associated with Goudeau's Hydropathes in the late 1870s, and his management of the cabaret owed much to the Chat Noir. He christened it Cabaret des Assassins, decorating the locale with prints and memoirs of a famous Second Empire criminal. (He also painted a sign for it, a rabbit jumping into a pot, known later as "Gill's Rabbit," *le lapin à Gill*, then transformed into the "agile rabbit.") There Gill declaimed his own poetry, much of it radical in inspiration, but he had only a minor success, perhaps because he made no effort to rid the place of its all-too-shady clientele. Then, from 1886 to 1903, the café was run by a former boulevard dancer called Adèle, the companion of another original Hydropathe and Chat Noir fixture, Jules Jouy, who often performed there. When Adèle went on to open a more conventional restaurant in 1903, she sold the Lapin Agile—as she had rechristened it—to no other than Aristide Bruant. Bruant wanted it simply for an investment and hired Frédé to run it for him, eventually letting him take it over altogether. Frédé had by then acquired experience as a *cabaretier*, having set up a place called Zut partway down the hill (in the square now named for Émile Goudeau), frequented by Picasso and his Spanish friends as well as by a contingent of local anarchists. Both groups became clients of the Lapin Agile when Frédé moved there after 1903, in the years when Picasso's friends were becoming increasingly French rather than Spanish.[4]

The Lapin Agile was much smaller than the Chat Noir, of course, simply one room with a terrace. But its popularity was based on the familiar combination of traditional bar and artistic cabaret. The performers included nearby residents and Latin Quarter visitors, all hoping to further their careers, or at least to get free food and drink in exchange for a poem or a song. The most serious poets among Picasso's friends—Apollinaire, Pierre Reverdy, André Salmon, and Max Jacob—never performed there, but a circle of younger, less self-confident writers did, including Roland Dorgelès, Francis Carco, and Pierre MacOrlan. Local artists, notably Picasso himself, provided decorations. Although the Lapin Agile never had a newspaper like the ones associated with the Chat Noir and other Montmartre cabarets, it used similar forms of publicity to attract customers. Francis Carco told how he had read about it in a Montmartre paper while he was still living in the provinces, and responded to the offer of a coupon good for a free drink at the Lapin in return for a year's subscription—a gimmick entirely in the spirit of Bruant.[5]

One of the Lapin's regular performers whose activities help fill in the picture of what the place was like was a famous Montmartre character, Jules Depaquit, especially well known after the war as the spirit behind what he called "The Free Commune of Montmartre." The secession of Montmartre from the French state expressed Depaquit's anarchist politics, but it was also a publicity campaign, complete with a traveling road show that spread the folklore of Montmartre throughout France. The show, which included music, dancers, and a banquet with speeches, the participants costumed as *sans-culottes* of the Great Revolution, represented the kind of commercialization of popular traditions that has been the fate of much folklore in the twentieth century. The idea of Montmartre as an independent unit did not originate with Depaquit, however, but with Goudeau and Salis during the 1880s; Depaquit had performed at the Chat Noir, and his style was a radicalized version of the one in vogue there. Politics was often his instrument of self-dramatization; during the 1890s, he claimed to be responsible for a terrorist bombing in fact committed by the anarchist Ravachol. Sexual themes and parodies of traditional literature were also prominent in his work, and the unrestrained, sometimes seemingly unhinged character of his performances caused the Dadaists to claim him as a predecessor.[6]

Even those enthusiasts for the simple charm of the Butte for whom it represented a world of premodern innocence always admitted that its state of special grace was precarious at best. André Warnod's portrait *Le vieux Montmartre*, published in 1911, gave an idyllic image of free and uncorrupted gaiety, but he acknowledged that the Montmartre he was sketching was already disappearing before the assault of commercialization. When he returned to the subject during the 1920s, it was with a different lens, which brought the sordid and dangerous features of the district's life, even before 1914, into sharper focus. There was, he still remembered, a backward-looking and sentimental quality to the Bohemia of the Lapin Agile before the war, a spirit of nostalgia that contrasted with the determined modernity of the art produced by its patrons. But next to the bands of young *rapins* who constituted "the last representatives of a Bohemia imitated from Murger," there was a world of equivocal and sometimes dangerous figures whose different Bohemia was as brutal as it was colorful. That the violence of this second world could invade the dreaminess of the first was illustrated in 1911, when Frédé's son was shot dead in the cabaret. The criminal underworld, present on the Butte itself, combined with the many temptations of the more commercial boulevards below to produce a *"Bohème peu galante."*[7]

The most sustained and perceptive dissections of Montmartre life before the war were from the pen of Francis Carco, a poet and novelist who arrived there around 1907, when he was twenty-one. His first writings, collected in *Instincts* in 1911, mixed sensuality, drink, and violence with a strong dose of sentimentalism, much in the spirit of the more famous Montmartrois Guillaume Apollinaire. Later, Carco would describe the milieu of prostitution—in all its varieties—in a novel *Jésus-la-Caille.* Next to these fictionalized portraits, Carco produced a long string of memoirs, beginning in 1919 and continuing down into the early 1940s. The spirit and attitude of Carco's memoirs, even those produced at considerable distance from the world they described, remained remarkably consistent throughout. It was a point of view at once affectionate, nostalgic, and disillusioned. Carco's Bohemia contained many familiar features alongside characteristics that marked it as peculiarly modern.

Two comments Carco made in introducing a series of recollections of the Lapin Agile in 1919 set the tone for his writings. "Living was the great thing," he said, "and literature often a last resort." He knew, he went on, that the Bohemians who spent their time drinking on credit in Montmartre bars were sacrificing their talents "in order to maintain a legend opposed to common sense within the bourgeois imagination." Bohemia was a form of social theater, then, for which its ostensibly hostile audience felt an obscure need. Bohemian life often led to nothing, Carco believed, because its flow was "a perpetual dispersion." New possibilities, new temptations, confronted its denizens at every moment. Their minds were beset by contradictory goals and attractions, rendered more persuasive by idleness, boredom, and poverty. Like Baudelaire, Carco believed that the only effective escape from this Bohemian evaporation of the self was to give oneself over to work. The inner demands of a project—in his case, a novel—had to impose their own discipline. But this prescription would not work for everyone. Some, who had been the early companions of talented artists or writers but who were fated to remain obscure themselves, would spend their lives fruitlessly pursuing the chimeras of their youth. Between the two wars, Carco found that Cubism had left behind a human debris that reminded him of the earlier ex-companions of Toulouse-Lautrec: "these endings of generations are horrifying."

The atmosphere of Bohemia also bred illusions more dangerous than the mere hope that youth and innocence were equivalent to talent. Those who yearned to live the legend of artistic life were prey to desires that slackened reality's hold on their minds. Carco told of meeting people in Bohemian haunts who said they still knew Verlaine and the Symbolist poet Jean Moréas, long after both were dead. "On certain rainy days the boundary between the real and the possible, the present and the past, is such that one no longer knows which of the two prevails, or deserves our attachment." Such ambiguous states of mind were known to all poets, who often—in poverty, idleness, and drink—exploited the dizzying visions that came from upsetting the conditions of normal perception. But true artists knew that reality had its own limits, which were not those of the imagination; the Bohemian danger was to forget this distinction. That the members of his own generation seemed particularly susceptible to such confusions was a circumstance Carco attributed in part to the weight of the nineteenth-century literary tradition that culminated in the decadents. Nothing could be taken at face value any more, life became a continual testing of how far one could go on pure imagination. "Everything became a subject for experiment. We did not live, we imagined ourselves to be living; we chose our form of life and led it against nature. That was what it was to be an artist."[8]

Yet modern literature and poetry owed a great deal to the willingness to experiment with life in these potentially dangerous ways.

Since the days of Romanticism, writers responded to the require-
ment that poetry bear a meaning at once highly personal and shared
by the writer and his audience. For the moderns there had to exist
"a secret, inexplicable correspondence between the writer and the
reader, that kind of *aura* that rises up out of the depths of the creative sensibility, and for which the classical writers hardly ever felt
the need." It was this situation that gave Bohemia its special relationship to modern art. Bohemians felt a peculiar anguish, a sense
for the precariousness of life, pushed sometimes to the extremes of
despair. Their willingness to explore these depths made their lives
exemplary enactments of the human condition for others, even
those hostile to their style and behavior. This quality of Bohemian
existence, Carco believed, made Montmartre the setting for the
most original and influential developments in contemporary art.[9]

In his own case, Carco saw the significance of Bohemian life in
psychological terms that mark his account as a twentieth-century
one. The son of a moralistic and often physically cruel father, Carco
recognized that within the ties that bound him to his family was a
secret need to afflict and torment his parents. As a youth, he imagined losing himself in the woods, knowing the anguish his family
would feel, and desiring to cause it. His father, devoted to productivity and respectability (he hated at once "the actor, the gambler,
and the cop,"), saw in the son's ambition to write a desire to "share
the promiscuities of the artistic life." But Carco found some features of that life repugnant from the start, notably its exhibitionism.
He believed he would not have remained in Bohemia as long as he
did had his father not tried so hard to keep him out of it. The "spirit
of contradiction" this provoked made him willing to bear the misery
and suffering of life in Montmartre. His complex relationship to his
family bred in him an unconscious desire for self-punishment that
drew him toward the sordid depths and real dangers of Montmartre
life.[10]

Carco knew that the attraction to danger and corruption was not
his alone. Around 1910–12 (Frédé's son was murdered in 1911),
the artistic milieu of Montmartre lived in such close proximity to
the lowlife and criminal contingent of the quarter that, in his view,

the two were sometimes indistinguishable. (Their common commerce with prostitutes formed the closest link.) Carco has been criticized for this claim; probably he exaggerated. But his view of the psychic interaction between Bohemia and criminality is still worth attending to. He believed that other Bohemians were, like him, drawn to corruption and vice by "the secret and cruel obsession" to live at the bottom of their despair. This psychic condition attracted Carco to the most tormented and fragile of all the Montmartre personalities of the era, Maurice Utrillo.[11]

The son of the model and artist Suzanne Valadon, and of a still-uncertain father, Utrillo grew up in an atmosphere of shifting liaisons and instability. Given strong drink as a child to make him more tractable, by the age of fifteen he was already taking a cure for alcoholism. Painting seems to have served him first of all as a therapy, but it never wholly worked. He paid for his drinks with pictures. In the years around 1907, when he was beginning the famous white-toned Montmartre scenes, he was often drunk and unkempt, sometimes going on binges that included breaking streetlamps with rocks. He first began to base his paintings on postcard views of Montmartre because he feared the children who taunted him in the streets. Later, that technique came to be more important after his mother began to lock him indoors.[12]

Carco believed that the cultural situation that made Montmartre the cradle of the avant-garde also made Utrillo one of its natural representatives. The innate melancholy of his pictures echoed the sense of personal fragility others were seeking to explore on the Butte. It was important that in Utrillo's case the sadness was linked to a refusal of all discipline. His genius was easily recognized in "a period where one wanted no more schools or academies. Whoever came along, from wherever he came, sought the 'new thrill.' Each one formed himself alone." But Utrillo's career also illustrated the counterpart of that situation: when art was an exploration of—or, in Utrillo's case, an escape from—threats hidden in the depths of the psyche, the line between artistic expression and self-dramatization was especially hard to draw. Faced with all the examples of *poètes maudits*, it became difficult to remember that genius was not interchangeable with the direct reproduction of an eccentric or maimed existence. People talked a great deal about the personal eccentricities and failures of an Utrillo or a Modigliani. These qualities seemed to be what made such artists objects of attention. Only with an effort could people remember that they were "not too badly gifted." Carco's conclusion was resigned: "That's the fate of Bohemians." He meant it was the fate of all those whose path to artistic work led through the exploration of those marginal and extreme states that Montmartre life allowed and encouraged.[13]

So naturally did people in Montmartre associate art with eccentricity, even with derangement, that some who knew Utrillo made little distinction between his apparently haphazard way of putting paint on canvas and the techniques of his untalented imitators. It was only necessary to "get the stroke" *(piger le coup)*, as the ex-police sergeant who looked after Utrillo in his periods of mental breakdown liked to say. The sergeant himself did not hesitate to try his hand at painting, with results that the bemused Utrillo was willing to praise and—as the demand for works in Utrillo's style grew—others to put up for sale. Real artistic products were still distinguishable from ones that merely imitated their surface gestures and features, Carco thought, but he feared the day when the boundary between the two would disappear.[14]

The situation Carco described had parallels in other contemporary activities. The most famous example was a project organized by Roland Dorgelès, to have Frédé's donkey paint a picture. This enormously successful stunt made clear that the line between acceptance of avant-garde styles and hostility to them ran through Montmartre and not around it. Dorgelès, with the cooperation of his friend André Warnod and of a notary as witness, placed a canvas under the donkey's tail, to which he tied a succession of brushes dipped in various colors. The resulting "painting," attributed to an imaginary Italian Futurist, Boronali, was exhibited in the Salon des Indépendants. There it received commentary not unlike that of other modernist works and was sold for a good price. Dorgelès had even prepared the picture's appearance by drafting a manifesto of a new, dissident Futurist school, Excessivism, in Boronali's name.[15]

Dorgelès disliked abstract painting, believing that once artists stopped trying to reproduce the objective world in some recognizable form, no way to judge art was left. For him, the content of Cubist and Futurist work was identical to the surface gestures that created their styles and manifestos. To reproduce the appearance was to produce the object. Without benefit of Max Ernst's notion of overcomprehension, he understood that the unwillingness of public and critics to trust their initial reactions to a new work would make the *blague* work.

Dorgelès's joke was Bohemian and philistine at the same time. It was an example of *fumisme*, but one inspired by a belief that artistic practices that allowed states of mind to substitute for the objective depiction of reality could not distinguish themselves from *fumisme*. The prank fulfilled Baudelaire's fears: to identify art with the unconstricted subjectivity of those who lived in the name of it made the genuine article indistinguishable from its imitations.

The Montmartre figure who best combined a devotion to modernism with participation in the quarter's self-conscious Bohemianism was the poet Guillaume Apollinaire. Like Baudelaire and Zola, Apollinaire was a writer who devoted much energy to publicizing and justifying the newest styles in the visual arts. Like them, too, he was deeply aware that the search for new forms of poetic and artistic vision derived from the characteristically modern need to explore the dilemmas of personal identity in a world devoid of stable models and attachments.

Apollinaire was the first important literary publicist for Cubism, as well as an early supporter of Matisse, Fauvism, and the Italian Futurists. He was also one of the first to use the word "Surrealism," though he did not mean by the term what André Breton and others would. His own aesthetic was rooted in Symbolism, and in some ways he always remained a Symbolist poet, reorienting that aesthetic in a more modernist direction. He was an enthusiast for Alfred Jarry, in whom he recognized a similar refocusing of Symbolist energies. He worked at various forms of journalism, and his review *Les Soirées de Paris*, published in 1912–13, was a major organ of prewar modernism. Earlier, he was the animating spirit behind a series of lesser-known publications that united and sustained modernist literary and philosophical currents between 1903 and 1905: *Le Festin d'Ésope, La Revue Immoraliste*, and *Les Lettres Modernes*.[16]

But Apollinaire's passions were not wholly for what was new. He was a temperamental eclectic, sympathetic to many contrasting styles and attitudes. His identification with high culture did not keep him from being a writer of pornography. At the same time, he was fascinated by medieval symbolism and the mystical spirituality it called up. In one of his most innovative and experimental poems, "Zone," he would declare that

> Religion alone has remained wholly new religion
> Has remained simple like the hangars of the airport.

Only Christianity was not antiquated, the poet added; the most modern European was the pope. In a later poem, Apollinaire described his personal task as judging the "long-standing contest between tradition and innovation, between order and adventure."

This heady mix of modernism, sensuality, and religion was of course not unique in either Bohemia or the avant-garde. (The poet Max Jacob, one of Apollinaire's Montmartre friends, known for his sometimes orgiastic binges, was a mystical visionary who ended his life as a monk.) What made Apollinaire's case especially interesting was his awareness that his own identity sometimes disappeared within the many and contrasting elements out of which he tried to construct it. In the poem "Cortège," he viewed the world as a procession of all the people and interests that populated his universe but within which he could not find himself.

> One day I waited for myself
> I said to myself Guillaume it is time that you came
> So that I may know at last the person who I am
> I who know the others.

The roots of this personal need are not hard to uncover. The illegitimate son of a flamboyant and pleasure-loving Polish-Italian

woman whose family contained high Catholic officials, Apollinaire
was long believed to be the son of a Roman dignitary, even, some
suspected, the pope. His probable father belonged to a distinguished line of Italian soldiers and adventurers who had often
served the Church. Known first by his mother's name, Kos-
trowitsky, Apollinaire took his more poetic name from his maternal
grandfather. Brought up in Monaco (he also attended school in
Nice and Cannes), he was French by education, but officially
remained a foreigner. Life in his mother's household was comfortable, even elegant, but its aura was mysterious and its underpin-
nings precarious. In 1899 (Guillaume was then nineteen), her
relationship with a wealthy Jew named Weil brought about the family's move to Paris, but two years later financial difficulties forced
them to leave for Belgium. There, Guillaume and his brother were
left to spend several months in a hotel, where they made a very favorable impression until the day their mother telegraphed, ordering
them back to Paris, but providing no money to pay the bill. The two
successfully crept away in the night and joined their mother. Apollinaire, however, became subject to a criminal charge he would later
have to answer in Paris.[17]

From the beginning, then, Apollinaire's was a life of expedients,
sometimes shady associations, and intense but often unsatisfying
emotional entanglements. A charming and outgoing person who
made friends easily, Apollinaire had an intense need for the com-
panionship and reassurance he found in Parisian literary and artistic circles. His early sources of income included ghostwriting stories
for a seedy journalist, and acting as secretary to a suspect stock-
market operator. Lack of success in his first serious sentimental attachment encouraged him to take work as a tutor in a family about
to spend some time in the Rhineland. There he began to know
something of German life and fell in love with the family's young
British governess, Annie Playden, whose rejection he was to memo-
rialize in a famous early poem, "La chanson du mal-aimé." Back in
Paris, Apollinaire worked in a bank, began to publish in literary
magazines, and became a regular participant in the *soirées* organized by *La Plume*. The series of reviews that would appear under

Apollinaire's leadership began toward the end of 1903 with *Le Festin d'Ésope*. At this time he began his associations with André Salmon, Jarry, and an anarchist who was a well-known café figure, Mecislas Golberg. In 1904 or early 1905, Apollinaire met Picasso and Max Jacob, friendships central to his career until his death in 1918.

The variety of Apollinaire's interests and attachments, his readiness to engage in practically any project, respectable or shady, his simultaneous enthusiasm for causes and people who seemed incompatible to others, his air of mystification, have puzzled his biographers. André Billy, a friend for many years, wrote in an apostrophe after his death: "You were full of mystery and surprises; you knew your aim quite well, but liked to pretend to wander and to be lost." But Marcel Adéma, Apollinaire's biographer, found in his nature a pliability that was both his strength and his weakness. He followed many roads but none to the end. "His aim was to have no aim."[18]

Apollinaire was attracted to what Carco called the "perpetual dispersion" of Bohemian life because his inability to find a solid interior center led him to grasp at nearly every external attachment that offered itself. In the poem "Cortège" he represents himself as *oiseau qui nidifie en l'air*, a bird that builds its nest in air, seeking to find a home in the element of insubstantiality. The cortège compensated for his inability to find a solid resting place: its participants brought, bit by bit, the elements out of which his identity was constructed.

> The procession passed along and I sought my body there
> All those who went by and were not myself
> Brought one by one the pieces of myself
> They built me bit by bit as one erects a tower
> The peoples heaped themselves up and I myself appeared
> Whom all bodies and all human things had formed

This self-image was, on one level, an emblem of the poet, formed out of all his subjects through his ability to assume the shapes and absorb the contents of the world around him. But on a more personal plane, it tells us about some of the deep internal needs that lay behind Apollinaire's remarkable sociability, his seemingly unending need for friends and companions. He sometimes described himself as a kind of chameleon, referring in one letter to "that mobility which continually modifies my face." Others, too, reported that he uncannily seemed to take on the characteristics of whomever he talked with. Apollinaire drew strength as a poet from his remarkable receptivity to outside experience.[19] In a late "calligram," he depicted himself inside a mirror of words, declaring himself to be enclosed within it, "living and true as one imagines angels and not as reflections are."

```
                    DANS
             FLETS       CE
          RE                MI
         LES                  ROIR
        SONT                    JE
        ME                      SUIS
        COM     Guillaume       EN
        NON                     CLOS
        ET      Apollinaire     VI
        GES                     VANT
         AN                     ET
         LES                   VRAI
          NE                  COM
           GI             ME
             MA       ON
                  I
```

But did the mirror reflect himself or the world? Some of his friends perceived a moral debility in the impulse of his personality to reflect whatever was around it, believing, as one reported, that "he is weak and would let himself be drawn into anything."[20]

Apollinaire's romantic attachments, exemplary of all his others, were central to his poetic personality: "People used to believe that a cat's eyes grew and diminished with the waxing and waning of the moon: in the same way the poetic faculties are always at the level of the poet's passions." Apollinaire once said that all his poems commemorated events in his life; many of these were romantic. Annie

Playden, Marie Laurencin, Madeleine Pagès, and Jacqueline Kolb ("la jolie rousse") were each responsible for important sections of his poetic *oeuvre*. Literary critics may object to the comparison of Apollinaire with Murger, but despite their different levels of talent and imagination, the two had in common an inability to write in the absence of some direct emotional stimulus.[21] Apollinaire's romantic life was stormy in part because he made great demands on his mistresses, ones that frightened some away—like Annie Playden—or that in Apollinaire's view they could not fulfill. In one poem he wrote of himself:

> I really believed I could have all your beauty
> and I only had your body
> the body alas is not eternity.

The passion with which he wooed Annie Playden was of a very direct and physical sort that seems to have startled and upset the very properly brought-up Victorian girl she was. The history of this affair raises the suspicion that Apollinaire on some level needed the failure it ended with, a precondition for transmuting his somewhat brutal passions into the material of poetic idealization. This pattern of intense need and repeated rupture was what Apollinaire meant when he described himself as *le mal-aimé*, the ill loved.

The Bohemian elements in Apollinaire's personality and his work were both explicit and implied. The editorial program of the last of Apollinaire's early literary reviews, *Les Lettres Modernes* of 1905, placed its activities explicitly within Bohemia. "These pages," the editorial committee declared, "will not be published with great regularity, first of all because to act any other way would be disloyal to the Bohemianism we are calling for; it means less to us to appear on fixed dates than to try to find new thrills, and since that quest is uncertain and capricious, we prefer to subordinate the secondary desideratum to the primary one."[22] The Bohemian rejection of regularity in the name of the search for experience reappeared at many levels in Apollinaire's work—in the form of his verse, which pushed the original Symbolist insistence on freer verse toward the elimination of punctuation, and into new typographic experiments;

and in its content, which introduced the whole range of objects and experiences encountered in modern urban life—electric lights, automobiles, airplanes, buses, sirens. This dedication to the unpredictable, unexpected quality of modern life, this loyalty to *le hasard*, made the Surrealists see Apollinaire as their predecessor. Apollinaire did not always carry out this program under the sign of Bohemia, but one finds in his work a highly developed and consciously justified example of what Barbey d'Aurevilly fifty years earlier had defined as the Bohemian literary consciousness, the writer who "lived intellectually by the random occurrence of his thought, his feelings, or his dreams."

More than any other notable Montmartre figure in the period before the war, Apollinaire's personal history bore the marks of the closeness between the milieu of Bohemia and criminality on which writers like Francis Carco and André Warnod insisted. In 1911, a sensational theft occurred: the *Mona Lisa* was stolen from the Louvre. The person arrested and accused was Guillaume Apollinaire. He spent two days in solitary confinement before the efforts of his friends and the good sense of a judge produced his release. Apollinaire had nothing to do with the crime, but in the preceding few years he had been friendly with a mysterious Belgian, Géry Pieret, who on several occasions stole statues from the Louvre; in 1911, Apollinaire even employed him as his secretary. Pieret saw in the *Mona Lisa* affair a chance to make money: he took one of "his" statues to a newspaper, which then publicized the lax security at the museum. The uproar that followed soon exposed Apollinaire's ties to Pieret and led to his arrest. The incident—extremely painful to Apollinaire, who had had brushes with the law before and feared expulsion from France—was a piece of very bad luck, but it arose out of the attachment to Montmartre lowlife that was one part of his search for thrills and adventures.

Other features of his literary personality also recall the Bohemianism consciously put forward in the program for *Les Lettres Modernes*. He wrote irregularly: periods of inactivity were interspersed with bursts of inspiration during which whole works were produced in a single sitting. In his poetry, he consciously sought the appearance of such spontaneity, and may have worked to produce it artificially. Some of his prose writings, however, read as if they had simply never been subjected to editorial revision and correction. Apollinaire was also a champion *fumiste* and *mystificateur*, often living in a world called forth by his imagination. He wrote serious reviews of imaginary books. In 1913, he published an account of Walt Whitman's funeral in the *Mercure de France*, despite the fact that he did not attend it. Earlier, he invented a woman critic, Louise Lalanne, out of whole cloth, as a screen for his authorship of a series of reviews about literature by women writers. He claimed to have discovered new techniques for understanding the world around him, including *la capnomancie*, the art of judging people by the smoke of their cooking.[23]

Apollinaire's participation in the famous banquet held in Picasso's studio to honor the primitivist painter Henri Rousseau in 1908 was also steeped in *fumisme*. The purpose of the banquet—a hilarious, disorderly, and sentimental affair—has been disputed. It appears that Picasso genuinely admired Rousseau's painting, but it is far less clear that Apollinaire ever did; he sometimes criticized it, and he seems to have kept in a cellar the portrait Rousseau did of him with Marie Laurencin. It may be that the general atmosphere of joking and provocation that surrounded the evening made some of the participants uncertain about whether others were serious in their desire to celebrate Rousseau or not. What is certain is that Apollinaire made up myths about Rousseau that still circulate: that he was a *douanier*, or customs official (he was a town revenue collector); and that he had been to Mexico during the 1860s (he never went there).[24]

Apollinaire's writings, including his defense of Cubism, express a deep tension between all these modes of Bohemian openness to each new moment of experience on the one hand, and his search for a source of stable and independent inner identity on the other. In the poem "Cortège," the bird who builds its nest in the air is dazzled by the sight of sun and earth. Apollinaire tells him—himself— to close his eyes (in the poem his "second eye"), so that the inner light of memory may shine forth. This image of illumination from within, opposing and replacing the mirroring of external things, appears in many of Apollinaire's discussions of art. "Every divinity creates in his own image, and that is true of painters," he wrote in 1908. "Only photographers make reproductions of nature." On this basis, Apollinaire sought to establish the superiority of Georges Braque's pictures over those of the Impressionists. The earlier school had been "a furious storm of more or less noble temperaments attempting to express feverishly, hastily, and unreasonably their astonishment before nature." (Apollinaire admitted this was not true of its best products.) The new art, represented by Braque, was free of such primitive spontaneity. "Seeking within himself for the elements of the synthetic motifs he depicts, he has become a creator. He no longer owes anything to his surroundings. His mind has purposely induced the twilight of reality, and suddenly a universal rebirth is taking place within him and outside him." In such work, art could achieve a vision that distinguished it from every other activity: "Each work becomes a new universe with its own laws." Matisse possessed the same virtues. He was "one of the rare artists who have completely freed themselves from Impressionism. He strives not to imitate nature, but to express what he sees and what he feels through the very materials of painting." Picasso's achievement could be described in the same language. "The great revolution of the arts which he achieved almost unaided, was to make the world his new representation of it."[25]

These aesthetic aspirations were also Apollinaire's own, and in his poetry he tried not only to express an intensely personal vision, but also to develop poetic counterparts of the Cubist techniques, which he read as declarations of independence from external reality. But when one knows anything of Apollinaire himself, one cannot fail to see that the artistic character he attributed to Impressionism, and that he praised the new painting for overcoming, described his own personality. It was precisely Apollinaire's passionate, sometimes primitive openness to the world around him, his seeking after stimuli, his openmouthed fascination for the world of real life, that defined the special quality of his poetry. Marcel Raymond has written that "nearly every one of his poems gives the impression of having been written by a different poet." Apollinaire's eclecticism was part of the same configuration, making him open to all the new currents flowing through the world he inhabited, but also robbing his own stance of firmness and stability.[26]

This alternative between reflecting the world outside and expressing a vision formed within was particularly sharp in Apollinaire's art criticism, perhaps because he saw in the new art one answer to his inner conflicts. Many writers—beginning in Apollinaire's own time—have been aware that his real understanding for the problems and achievements of the new painting was limited. He knew very little about painting as a medium or about its history. But he quickly saw in Fauvism and Cubism certain meanings and possibilities of great significance to himself. Here was an art immune to his own impulsiveness and pliability in the face of experience, and it was the art of his own time. By associating himself with it, Apollinaire was able to identify himself both as the person he was and as the person he yearned to be, to accept his own character as mirror of the life that went on around him, but to show in the glass an artistic personality that glowed with its own inner light. Becoming the champion of abstract art provided an anchor against Apollinaire's own mobility of identity.

From the beginning, an important part of Apollinaire's relationship to Cubism was his friendship with Picasso. Lasting until the poet's death in 1918, the relationship survived at least one great disappointment, Picasso's refusal to come to his aid—even to admit that he knew him—at the time of the *Mona Lisa* affair in 1911. When they met, Picasso was painting the working-class figures and traveling circus performers of his "blue" and "rose" periods, and Apollinaire immediately recognized him as an artist who shared some of his own qualities. In his first article in behalf of Picasso, published in *La Revue Immoraliste* in 1905, he denied that Picasso's melancholy was a mark of disillusionment. "Everything enchants him, and his undeniable talent seems to me to serve an imagination in which the delightful and the horrible, the low and the delicate, are proportionately mingled." Picasso showed a frank sensuality (for instance in his willingness to paint pubic hair) that likewise Apollinaire shared (though later on he emphasized the chasteness of Picasso's Cubist neoclassicism), as well as a "naturalistic love of precision" combined with a penchant for religious mysticism. Apollinaire did not point out that both used their art as an instrument for directly dramatizing and working through their personal dilemmas. Picasso's early pictures refer—unmistakably if sometimes mysteriously—to the inner, sometimes sexual, anxieties of himself and his friends, and throughout his life his successive amorous relationships provided both energy and content for his paintings and drawings. Even some of his more abstract works, like the famous *Guernica*, are full of private symbols. Indeed, it is hard to think of any modern painter before Picasso who made his painting such a direct mirror of his personal development, with the exception of another non-Parisian, Gustave Courbet.[27]

But, in contrast to Apollinaire, the clarity of Picasso's identity was never in doubt. Apollinaire was especially struck by the independence of his vision. His powerful line gave a stable aspect to the world, one "unaltered by the light which modifies its form by changing its colors."[28] Here, in 1905, Apollinaire was already preparing the distinction he would later draw between Cubist autonomy and Impressionism's more passive and dependent qualities. For Apollinaire, Picasso was an artist able to impose himself on the world instead of being subject to it. That Picasso's strength had personal as well as aesthetic importance to Apollinaire is suggested by the fact that the Spaniard found for his friend the woman who was to be his companion for longer than any other, Marie Laurencin. The painter saw her one day in 1907, at her job in an art gallery, thought she and Apollinaire would suit each other, and sent him to meet her. Their often stormy liaison lasted until 1914. This ability to judge the personalities of other people was something Apollinaire often claimed to possess himself, but to which many of his personal attachments—the example of Géry Pieret is sufficient—gave the lie.

Apollinaire's celebration of the Cubist autonomy in regard to nature never overcame his deep need to make himself a reflector of the world around him. His last critical writing, a brief essay, "The

New Spirit and the Poets" (written after he received a serious head wound during the war, and perhaps showing some of its effect), reads very differently from his essays on the new painting. Much of it revolved around the notion that poetry could not "ignore the magnificent exuberance of life which the activities of men are adding to nature." Even mechanization was a source of wonders to which poets had to be sensitive. Included were such technological advances as airplanes and X rays. These marvelous new phenomena threatened to surpass the products of poetic imagination. Modern life embodied a spirit of constant and renewed surprise; its products undermined and weakened commonly held beliefs, making real things that had once existed only in imagination and myth. These modernist themes here took on a form that identified Apollinaire with the enthusiastic fascination before nature and experience that he had once rejected under the sign of Impressionism.[29]

This recognition of his own reliance on external experience makes it appropriate that Apollinaire should have summed up his attitude toward the avant-garde and his presence within it in a poem dedicated to the last of the women to serve as stimulus for his work, Jacqueline Kolb, "La jolie rousse." In the poem, the woman's beauty took form as that combination of passion and reason (*la raison ardente*) that the poet sought to achieve. The "pretty redhead" of the title appeared in Apollinaire's life, he declared, at a time when his youth was past and he was full of experience. Her presence made him see himself as judge between tradition and innovation, between order and adventure. Apollinaire knew that he stood for the second term in each of these oppositions, but he addressed the following plea to those who represented the first:

Be indulgent when you compare us
To those who were the perfection of order
We who seek everywhere after adventure

We are not your enemies
We want to give to you vast and strange realms
Where flowering mystery offers itself to whoever wants to gather it
There are new fires there colors never seen

A thousand imponderable phantasms
To which reality must be given
We want to explore goodness enormous country where all is still
There also is time which one can send away or bring back
Pity for us who always fight at the frontiers
Of the limitless and of the future
Pity for our errors pity for our sins

Apollinaire's image of the artist on the frontier of adventure was no portrait of a rebel against ordinary life. The explorers of fantasy realms were pioneers, opening up new forms of experience for those unwilling and afraid to cross established boundaries themselves. Apollinaire here spoke the language of stability in the name of innovation, recognizing that the life of art and adventure was marred by error and sin. The vocation of modernism was to energize and enrich the world of everyday existence, not to corrode it. It was a fitting summing-up for a figure whose position in the avant-garde revealed much of the territory it shared with Bohemianism. Carco's view that willingness to endure the precariousness and uncertainty of modern life was what made Bohemia a breeding ground for modern art and literature describes Apollinaire's career very well. That the impulse behind Parisian modernism was less often revolt against modern life than the need to explore its dilemmas, together with those of the art that participated in them, appears also when we turn to a production sometimes taken to signify the opposite, the ballet *Parade.*

Parade was first produced at the Châtelet Theatre in 1917, the year of Apollinaire's poem "La jolie rousse." Apollinaire himself wrote program notes for the first performance, a task assigned him by Picasso, who designed the scenery and the costumes. The choreography was by Léonid Massine, one of the major figures in Diaghilev's Ballets Russes, which mounted the production. Erik Satie wrote the music, and the scenario was by the young poet Jean Cocteau. All the participants had considerable reputations by the time they collaborated: Satie had been gaining recognition since about 1910; Picasso was selling paintings for high prices and five years before had abandoned Montmartre for the more comfortable surroundings of Montparnasse; the Ballets Russes had been drawing large crowds for years. Nonetheless, *Parade* seems to have given a heightened recognition to the avant-garde as a movement. The premiere was not quite the scandal some have since alleged, since the performance was applauded by at least a large part of the audience. But the critical reaction was mostly hostile, and Satie sent an insulting postcard to one critic, who sued him in response.[30]

Parade was conceived by Cocteau at the premiere, also given by Diaghilev, of Stravinsky's ballet *The Rite of Spring* on May 29, 1913. That evening, there had indeed been a scandal, comparable to the outbursts that greeted Hugo's *Hernani* in 1830 and Jarry's *Ubu roi* in 1896. Stravinsky's music was inspired by a biological and naturalistic conception of spring far from the expectations of popular sentimental romanticism, and the orchestration embodied experiments and novelties for which much of its audience was altogether unprepared. Alongside the fashionable public who had come to be entertained, Diaghilev had placed enough invited supporters of his experiments to assure that the confrontation would be direct and—as it turned out—even violent. Stravinsky said he was astounded that the conductor could keep the performance going to the end. Later, Cocteau reported that Diaghilev and the dancer Vaslav Nijinsky were dejected, but Stravinsky thought that Diaghilev, although angry, was also pleased, having understood ever since his first encounter with the score that the ballet would have enormous publicity value.[31]

Whatever the truth, Cocteau was struck by the reaction of many in the audience against what they took to be an attempt by avant-garde artists to mystify and mock them. When he set down the theme of *Parade* in 1915, he saw it as a response to that kind of audience reaction. To understand Cocteau's idea, we must remember that the French word *parade* does not mean "parade" in English, but (to quote the dictionary definition Cocteau wrote out for Satie) "a comic act, put on at the entrance to a traveling theatre, to attract a crowd." It was a sideshow, a come-on. The scenario is brief enough to be quoted in full:

> The scene represents houses at Paris on a Sunday. Traveling theater. Three music-hall numbers serve as *parade*.
>
>
>
> Chinese Musician
> Acrobats
> Little American Girl
>
>
>
> Three managers organize the publicity. They communicate to each other in their terrible language that the crowd is taking the *parade* for the show inside [*le spectacle intérieur*] and grossly try to make them understand. No one goes in.
>
> After the last number of the *parade* the worn-out managers collapse on top of each other.
>
> The Chinese, the acrobats, and the little girl come out of the empty theatre. Seeing the managers' extreme effort and their fall, they try in turn to explain that the show takes place inside [*que le spectacle se donne à l'intérieur*].[32]

The relation of this scene to what Cocteau believed had happened at the premiere of *The Rite of Spring* does not need to be underlined. The audience had confused the outward show, the surface spectacle of the performance, with its inner content. They had never gotten beyond the exterior; therefore, they had been unable to experience the real nature of the work or to know whether it might have spoken to them. In the preface to one of his own plays written a few years later, Cocteau made clear that this was indeed the meaning *Parade* bore and that the problem it pinpointed was especially important to modernism: "Every living work includes its own *parade*. Those who do not enter see only that *parade*. But the surface of an original work shocks, intrigues, irritates the spectator too much for him to enter. He is repelled from the soul by the face, by the novel expression which distracts him like a clown's grimace at the door." In another work, Cocteau declared that "the hate against the creator is the hate against the person who changes the rules of the game." Zola had responded similarly to an earlier audience's rejection of Manet's painting: "Originality, that is the great horror."[33]

But the situation he symbolized in *Parade* contained another level of meaning for Cocteau. The imagery appealed to him because it was an emblem for the condition of avant-garde art itself. The modern age, Cocteau observed, deserved to be called the age of misunderstanding. One cause was the abundance of books and forms of publicity. The need to make oneself noticed among the crowd of writers and the ease of appearing in public meant that "everybody speaks, expresses himself, complicates the game, overloads Arthur Rimbaud and Stéphane Mallarmé, embalms old anarchies." Young artists and writers thought that to prove themselves, it was necessary to be rejected by regular society. The desire to assume the pose of *poète maudit* made the person who seemed to suffer from society's malediction a privileged figure: "today the place of the accursed poet is sought after." Artists developed a taste for *tics*, thinking that a plenitude of odd mannerisms was the equivalent of a style. The old situation in which artists without imagination, *pompiers*, were simply those who followed conventional academic styles had turned into its opposite. The avant-garde now had its own traditions and conventions, derived from its great heroes. These latter were in danger of being turned into *pompiers*, "and very soon, we ourselves."[34]

It was not only the audience that could not distinguish the *parade* from the *spectacle intérieur*, therefore. It was the representatives of the avant-garde itself. The *tics*, repeated, left permanent lines, etched into the person of the actor who had thought to produce and eliminate them at will. Modern art movements characteristically acquired labels, often as the result of some *boutade* or witty sally. "The *boutade* succeeds, to the point where the artists adopt it and where it would be dangerous to deny it afterward." Artists were condemned to identify themselves permanently with the surface eccentricities they had thought were merely temporary expedients, ways of declaring their independence and making themselves known.[35]

The subject of *Parade*, then, was the confusion that had grown up between art and the life that parodied it, the entanglement of modernism with Bohemia. No one had lived more deeply within that knotted skein than the composer to whom Cocteau turned for music. Cocteau understood how much Satie owed to his attraction for places where, as he said, "life swarms." He was no mere improviser but knew how to "profit from a temperature." In the score of *Parade*, Cocteau believed, Satie had "discovered an unknown dimension, thanks to which one hears simultaneously the *parade* and the *spectacle intérieur.*" It was a comment that captured a constant and essential feature of Satie's style, his pervasive fascination with facades and what could simultaneously be hidden and revealed behind them.[36]

Cocteau's relations to the problem he symbolized in *Parade* were different. From a wealthy and cultured family, Cocteau had an easy entry into Parisian artistic and literary circles. His striking good looks and charm, together with a precocious and acrobatic verbal faculty, made him a popular salon figure even in his mid-teens. By the same age, he was already writing a stream of polished, if somewhat facile and imitative, verse. A public reading arranged by some friends in 1906, when Cocteau was only seventeen, created a great stir; it was followed by five years of glittering literary life. The crisis came in 1912, when a stinging review of his poems appeared in the *Nouvelle Revue Française*, warning that too early success was ruining the young writer's real talent. Cocteau responded by withdrawing into himself, in search of a different style, one that would not be exhausted in the highly polished surfaces he so easily brought forth.

Whether Cocteau's work ever came to embody the deeper level of significance he now sought, or remained graceful and charming but superficial, is an issue still debated. But in the years leading up to *Parade*, he was much concerned about the question. His too easy path had led him to stagnation, he later said. It was better for talented young people to develop in some evil milieu, make their mistakes freely, flout their indiscipline and bad taste, than to make easy progress on comfortable routes. They would then be prepared for the solitude and independence that artistic innovation required. Cocteau after 1912 seems to have tried to make up for the lack of these experiences in his life earlier. He did not become a libertine, but withdrew from society, and for a time from Paris. The work he now produced, *Le Potomak*, was woven together out of dream states, distorted forms of existence, suspensions of normal logic, and erratic, discontinuous actions. Cocteau's homosexuality, with which he was then coming to terms, was one dimension of the world of mystery and perversion he sought to explore.[37]

The problem of confusing art with its surface appearances and gestures was therefore one Cocteau knew from personal experience. But by comparison with Satie, his knowledge was closer to that of the dandy than the Bohemian. Cocteau's facade was not composed of *boutades* and imitations of Rimbaud, but of the social polish and verbal glitter appropriate to salon life. His association with the opposite style expanded before and during the war, as he became more involved with avant-garde figures like Picasso, Satie, and Apollinaire. It seems that Cocteau was both drawn by their ability to shock and offend the public whose too early adulation had deluded him, and put off by the potentiality for pretense and disorder that their form of life contained. His combination of loyalty to artistic innovation—what he called "the artistic Left"—with suspicion about *tics* and *l'attitude maudite* was the expression of this ambivalence. His involvement in both modernist cultural experimentation and in the salon society that was offended by it led him to become at once an unconditional supporter of innovation and a critic of actions and gestures that merely wore the mask of originality.[38]

In production, *Parade* failed to convey the message that inspired it. Part of the reason was that Picasso and Massine objected to Cocteau's original notion of having the managers shout "Le spectacle se donne à l'intérieur" through megaphones, and Cocteau agreed that this would have given the ballet an undesirable quality of imbalance and shock. So deeply did the message recede that few who have seen or written about the work since seem to understand what it was to have been about. The specifically Cubist features of the ballet made the greatest impact—the outsize costumes, the artificial noises inserted into the music (meant as a parallel to the newspapers and other objects then being included in Cubist pictures).

Those aspects of the performance shocked part of the audience and critics: a confirmation of Cocteau's observations about how easily the meaning of modern works got lost behind the labels used to identify artistic movements. In the end, *Parade* took its place within the tense and ambivalent field created between modern artists and their audiences by the complex of publicity, alienation, and self-advertisement, which Cocteau identified as responsible for the modern "age of misunderstanding" in art. But at the same time, *Parade* gave added notoriety to the figures associated with it, and became an important milestone in the popularization of the avant-garde. It thus demonstrated the related truth Satie had intuited earlier, that the dramatization of distance from bourgeois life was modern art's best form of self-advertisement.[39]

Cocteau's scenario and its realization show what was happening to the project once so dear to Baudelaire, the attempt to preserve real art from confusion with the surface features of the life lived in the name of it. Cocteau still felt the need to distinguish the external qualities of modern art works from their inner significance, and to separate the postures and gestures of the artistic life from the products that were its aim and justification. But that border was much more difficult to chart and defend now than it had been in Baudelaire's day. The world war, in the midst of which *Parade* was first produced, made preserving such a distinction still more questionable. Already, new tendencies had appeared, identifying the future task of modern art with its entire abolition.

CHAPTER 13

Dissolving the
Boundaries

THE UNEXAMPLED SLAUGHTER on the battlefields of World War I, combined with the success of revolution in Russia after 1917, gave rise to a potent mix of revulsion against existing society and—for some—faith in the possibility of its transformation. The resulting mood had parallels with the period of the 1840s. For many people, the pessimism of the *fin de siècle* was dissolved by the possibility of new forms of action. Cultural innovation and revolutionary politics were drawn together more powerfully than at any time since the demise of Romanticism. The Dada movement, born in Zurich in 1916, most fully embodied the spirit of unbridled revolt, dramatizing the new animosity toward bourgeois society and culture. Some of that spirit was welcomed into France after the hostilities ended, when the leading Dada figure, Tristan Tzara, arrived in Paris. But the power of Dada in France ebbed by 1922, as many of those who had supported Tzara declared their independence from the movement's undiluted negativism. These French writers, led by André Breton, gathered under the banner of Surrealism.

Neither Dada nor Surrealism was properly a Bohemian movement. Neither one explicitly invoked Bohemia as an antecedent; members of both would have found reasons to object to the connection. Yet, they belong at the end of our history, for they represented in their time a relationship between cultural innovation and Bohemianism similar to the one Baudelaire had embodied in his: the attempt to define the task of art under modern conditions led them to share ground with Bohemia whether they wanted to or not. Like

366

Baudelaire and Rimbaud, they brought a cult of multiplied sensation into the center of artistic practice. In their activities, the artist's work as a producer of objects was fused with—in part dissolved within—a life devoted to marking off distance from conventional society.

As it happens, the moment of transition between Dada and Surrealism in Paris corresponded with the hundredth anniversary of Murger's birth, in 1922. The Dadaists and Surrealists did not notice, but ceremonies were held both at Murger's tomb in Montmartre cemetery, and at his bust in the Luxembourg Gardens; articles appeared in several newspapers—some devoted to aspects of Murger's life, some supplying new documents. One theme predominated: that Bohemia was at an end. Modern life had become too serious, too demanding, too much invaded by what one writer, Lucien Descaves, called the worm of politics, to allow for the old lightheartedness and spontaneity. Murger's own abandonment of Bohemia had become his most imitated example. Perhaps the young were still tempted by the old vision of a free life, Descaves suspected, but society as a whole offered little scope for it.[1]

The Murger centennial was followed by a wave of valedictory nostalgia. Two books about Paul Verlaine appeared in 1923, one a new edition of Cazals's memoir about Verlaine's last years (first published in 1911), the other Lucien Aressy's *The Last Bohemia*; Francis Carco edited a series of books under the general rubric *La vie de Bohème* during the next few years, including Rachilde's biography of Jarry. As before, the conviction that Bohemia could be assigned to the past was premature, but it reflected some important shifts in Bohemia's meaning.

Some of these changes are suggested by glancing for a moment at the one group in Paris who would have stoutly denied that Bohemia was finished in the early 1920s: the American "exiles" who flocked there in the years after the war. To that famous generation, chronicled by Matthew Josephson and Peggy Guggenheim, the cafés and boulevards of Montparnasse seemed full of Bohemians. Fleeing New York or the Middle West, these Americans gave a powerful stimulus to the myth of Paris as a center of Bohemia, swarming with people who lived sexually free and economically shaky lives in the name of art or literature. Not since Puccini's opera *La Bohème* in the 1890s had any foreigners done so much to popularize the image of Bohemian Paris. These Americans were separated from their French hosts by many contrasts and barriers, however. They were able to survive—in some cases, to live well—in Paris on what seemed to them relatively little money, because of the favorable exchange rate. They knew little of French life; most of them (Josephson was one exception) spent their time among other Americans. These Yankee Parisians exemplified one of the most favorable conditions for the continued vitality in the twentieth century of something like the original Romantic Bohemia: expatriation. Americans in Paris were natural Bohemians: free of ties to the surrounding society and culture, ready to devote their lives to their own self-development, able to participate in the city's pleasures while acting out their independence from tradition and convention, and predisposed to a life of liberated fantasy by virtue of having left their everyday identities, with their attendant restrictions, on the other side of the Atlantic.[2]

Paris still had its stock of traditional Bohemian types, of course: young artists, students, eccentrics, down-and-outers, marginal people of many kinds. But to interpret their own lives in Bohemian terms could no longer carry the significance it had for a Charles Pradier, a Privat, an Aimé Cournet, a Goudeau, or even a Francis Carco, formed in the atmosphere of Montmartre before the war. One reason was the "worm of politics" Lucien Descaves mentioned in his article on the Murger centenary. Young bourgeois who felt estranged or excluded from their own surroundings and destinies had to confront the issues raised by the war and the Russian Revolution, and the hard question of political commitment made the softer, more ambivalent postures native to Bohemia less meaningful. Some people had experienced a similar displacement of Bohemia at earlier moments of political crisis—notably Jules Vallès after 1871. By the end of the war, feelings of estrangement or ambivalence that had once received expression in Bohemian terms were finding other outlets.

*   *   *

The Surrealists claimed many sources and ancestors. Among them were Rimbaud, Apollinaire, Jarry, Picasso—in fact, the whole constellation of luminaries who created the avant-garde in France. But two different names bespeak the special character of Surrealist modernism, as well as their rejection of the usual boundaries of artistic practice—Freud and Marx. When Breton sought to define the movement in the first *Surrealist Manifesto* of 1924, it was around the discovery of the unconscious and the secrets of dream life that he structured its program. During the next three years, he led his followers—still carrying their Freudian baggage—toward Marxism and membership in the French Communist Party. Depth psychology and political activism would continue to be central reference points for the Surrealists. But they always rallied to them in their own way. Breton and his followers were never interested in Freudian psychology as a therapy, but as a visionary testimony to the existence of mental powers that seemed to promise a transformation of life. The idea of revolution appealed to them in a similar way, equally abstracted from its proletarian and Leninist attachments. The relations between Surrealists and Communists were never smooth, leading through many disputes to a major rupture in the mid-1930s. The Surrealist appeal to Marx and Freud was one of the first to treat those two thinkers less in terms of definite intellectual commitments than as figures in a kind of mythology of modern life, gods of those who looked to modernity as a constellation of transformative forces. To invoke them was to demand that society renounce its claims to stability, that individuals learn to live, as Breton put it, by starting over every day from the beginning.[3]

Breton insisted on the absolute radicalism of the Surrealist stance, yet there was much in his posture that presupposed and required the stable external reality he so loudly contested. He had a strong vein of moral seriousness that contrasted with the *fumisterie* of some who became his friends and associates. And from each pull toward nihilism and personal dissolution he would draw back into an ambivalent but never wholly negative position. As a self-conscious Freudian, he must have understood that some of his rebellion was a protest against the narrow and rigid values of his family, exemplified by his mother's declaration in 1920 that André's giving up the study of medicine was a worse misfortune than if he had been killed in the war. But his revolt was always clothed in a staid and righteous casing that bespoke his family origins.

Even as a child, Breton sought a literary escape from the cold atmosphere created by his unloving mother, first in tales of adventure, then, in his teens, in aestheticism. He was an enthusiast for Maurice Barrès, as well as for Baudelaire, the Symbolists, and Mallarmé. At seventeen, in 1913, he associated his love of poetry with its ability "to undermine the walls of the real that enclose us." Drawn toward escapism on one side, Breton was attracted by the spirit of revolt on the other. One of his childhood memories was of disgust at all the sentimental inscriptions seen in a cemetery, among which only one appealed to him, Blanqui's forthright protest: "Neither God nor master." In the years before 1914, Breton was a reader of the anarchist press, including a review that called itself *L'Action d'Art*. The paper declared in its program for 1913: "We are individualists and *réfractaires*. . . . For us revolt is the action of art and each one will demonstrate it according to his temperament." Later on, Breton would point to anarchism as one of the seeds of Surrealism.[4]

The experience of the war did not disrupt the aesthetic attitude Breton had been developing before its outbreak, but, rather, confirmed and intensified it. Discovering Rimbaud in 1914, Breton found in the horrors of war the experiences of shock and disorganization, the "school of good brutalizing works" that Rimbaud saw as preparation for the visionary state. Yet, Breton was never—now or later—really tempted by the extreme program of personal dissolution that the young Rimbaud had undertaken. He quickly discovered Rimbaud's second thoughts, his drawing back from the state where he had made a fetish out of mental and spiritual disorder. Trying to preserve the visionary energy of Rimbaud's poetry without having to confront the personal dangers his project created, Breton was led to a less radical exemplar of modernism, Apollinaire. In Apollinaire's attempt to free poetry from traditional restraints by tying it to the constantly changing experiences and stimulations of modern life, Breton found an aesthetic liberation that was not subject to the perils of Rimbaud's sensory disorganization. This Apollinairean openness of poetry to chance, to the surprise occurrences and shocking juxtapositions of modern life, is visible in many of Breton's later positions.[5]

Breton met and befriended Apollinaire during the war years, but the person whose example affected him most deeply at that time was a more obscure and much more mysterious figure, Jacques Vaché. The two met in the Nantes hospital where Vaché was a patient and Breton a medical orderly in 1916. Their friendship lasted until Vaché's death—probably by suicide—in 1919. Part of a literary group in Nantes that had published short-lived reviews before the war, Vaché was a remarkable combination of Baudelairean dandyism, Privatian *blague*, and Jarryesque refusal to let his identity be defined by any conditions external to himself. He affected English clothes and an extreme, exaggerated elegance of manner. One of his favorite poses was that of the English tourist, unable to speak French. Sometimes Vaché would disguise himself in a costume and refuse to acknowledge his friends. After the war, he worked as a longshoreman in Nantes, unloading coal barges, passing afternoons in cheap waterfront bars, from which he would depart in the evenings to go from café to café, from cinema to cinema, spending outlandishly and telling outrageous stories, creating what Breton called "an atmosphere at once dramatic and full of vitality." His sexual life was part of the mystery, leading those who knew him to wonder whether he was a libertine, a homosexual, or chaste.[6]

For Vaché, this histrionic life was a self-conscious substitute for writing poetry. In his letters and conversation, he insisted that to attempt art in a degraded and self-destructive world was to set oneself up for failure; those who persisted were either too stupid or too self-important to understand. Toward Breton's desire to become a writer, Vaché expressed his disdain for the *"pohète,"* the aesthete mired in the past, "who had not benefited enough from the lesson of the epoch." In place of art, Vaché put what he called *umore*, the determination to find in life nothing more exalted than amusement, and to live out his detachment through eccentricities and mystifications. These he carried—or so Breton was convinced—even to the extreme of suicide. Whether his death from an overdose of drugs was actually intentional remains uncertain, but Breton had no doubt it was self-induced. It was Vaché's declaration of independence from life, his last *fourberie drôle*.[7]

Vaché made a deep impact on those who knew him. Louis Aragon later explained his power by his total unpredictability. No one ever knew what he would do next; he embodied the quality of surprise and shock that Apollinaire had identified as the spirit of modern life. Breton said Vaché had taught him to identify "whatever can be *finished* in the domain of mind" with "the worst servility or the most complete bad faith." He inspired Breton and the others with a determination to hold out against any fixation of their activity, any commitment to an existing social identity, including that of artist or poet. The title they gave to their review of 1919, *Littérature*, bristled with irony. Echoing Paul Verlaine's "Art poétique," it proclaimed their rejection of any effort to raise literature above life.[8]

It was partly the example of Vaché that led Breton at this time to conceive art in a surprising way—as *réclame*, advertising. He meant the equation of art with publicity in a special sense, as he wrote in letters to his friends Aragon and Théodore Frankel in 1919: the sense in which Christianity was a form of publicity for heaven. In other words, art was a way of life and a system of convictions that embodied the yearning for a transcendent form of being within the limitations of the present. Its purpose was to draw people out of the here and now, and into that better life. This formula inverted the Romantic notion that a certain sort of life was appropriate for an artist because it provided inspiration or allowed him to do work; the claim to be a poet or an artist was now justified only because it contributed to a life beyond art.[9]

That Breton had begun to think in these terms by the end of the war prepared him to hail the similar aims of Dada. The movement had several sources, but its first clear appearance took place in Zurich at the Cabaret Voltaire, in 1916. Echoes of the old Chat Noir were present in activities organized there by Hugo Ball and Tristan Tzara. The Cabaret Voltaire combined music, poetry, dance, and the visual arts, and newspaper publicity was an important element. But the program was one of cultural revolution rather than entertainment and integration. In an atmosphere influenced by the presence of antiwar activists and Bolshevik exiles (several of the early Dada figures recalled seeing Lenin), all the modernist tendencies that challenged artistic practice with provocation, spontaneity, and primitive instinct were focused together. The result was a revolutionary equation of artistic innovation with the subversion of reason and the rejection of external limitations. The Dada figures made poems of random words clipped from newspapers or from series of animal sounds. They said or did whatever came to mind at any moment. Consistency and coherence were abandoned in order to recover the vital power present in primitive artistic practices and to search out elementary forms at the base of reality. Energies earlier devoted to a renewal of artistic practice were turned toward the destruction of art as a productive activity. What Vaché had undertaken by example and with the intensity of self-absorption, the Dadaists pursued through manifestos, public theatricality, and provocations of every sort. By the time Tzara arrived in Paris at the beginning of 1920, his activities were organized around challenge and outrage for their own sake, a pleasure in violence and vulgarity, in contradiction and even self-contradiction that knew no boundaries because its principled intention was to destroy them all. This included the boundary between Dadaists and their audience. "I am an idiot, I am a farceur, I am a *fumiste*. . . . I am like all of you."[10]

Once in Paris, the Dadaists acknowledged their similarity to some figures with Bohemian roots—praising Jarry, working with Satie, and finding their principles foreshadowed in the cabaret performances of Jules Depaquit at the Lapin Agile. On one level, Dada was the ultimate development of the spirit of *fumisme* that had animated the original Chat Noir.

Between 1920 and early 1922, Breton and his friends were

largely absorbed in the Dada movement. Breton seems to have seen Tzara as a kind of second Jacques Vaché, a person emancipated from the suffocating desire to have a social identity, notably that of poet. Some students of modernism still see the whole Surrealist group as an offshoot of Dada, becoming independent only because Breton lost out to Tzara in a struggle for leadership. Certainly, the attraction that existed between them was marked by tensions and the clash of strong egos, but the conflict was not simply over power. From the start, the two groups were on different tracks. Breton's revolt had its roots outside Dada, and he was constitutionally out of tune with its spirit of unbridled destructiveness. He had already fended off the temptation to equate art with disorganization once, in his encounter with Rimbaud. For all his desire to upset tradition, Breton was a person in search of ideas and convictions; nonsense for its own sake never had the positive value for him that the Dadaists were willing to assign to it.[11]

The differences began to appear in public when the Dadaists staged a mock trial of Maurice Barrès during 1921. Breton, like Tzara (and Cocteau at that time), admired the young Barrès of the *culte du moi* novels and essays while he deplored the role Barrès had played during the war as a patriot and defender of traditional French culture. The trial was largely Breton's idea, with Tzara and the others joining in. The disagreement came on the question of how to avoid Barrès's path from enemy of the laws to their advocate. To Tzara, the best defense was to renounce moral conviction itself, dedicate oneself to confrontation and contradiction for their own sakes. Breton contested this, insisting that such a moral void offered no resistance against being enlisted whenever some momentary enthusiasm tempted the person who experienced it. To guarantee oneself against following Barrès's track required opposing modern society with principles that promised to transform it. The Dada movement had cut its ties not only with outworn traditions, but with the very figures—Rimbaud, Jarry, Picasso—who provided example and encouragement for those who hoped for the transformation of art. By 1924, Breton had come to seek that renewal under the rubric of Surrealism.[12]

* * *

The term "sur-real," coined by Apollinaire, was used with some regularity in the years after the war. In an article of 1920, Breton invoked it in support of the Dadaist cult of spontaneous and arbitrary expression. Such license allowed the mind to produce images ("coral lips" was one example) whose very power to become clichés proved that they possessed a mysterious superiority over mere reality. This notion of the surreal was, from the start, tied up with asserting the higher claims and powers of the imagination. But the term could also denote an actual or potential order of reality, a sense developed by Breton when he adopted it as a banner in 1924. Dream life was real, revealing essential truths about the human world that were veiled whenever realism was limited to reproducing external conditions. "I believe in the future resolution of these two states, in appearance so contradictory, that are the dream and reality, into a sort of absolute reality, of sur-reality, if one may speak that way." The human world was partly the creation of mind, and was continually being reshaped by it. Surrealism highlighted this aspect of reality by expressing "the way thought really works." It rested "on belief in the superior reality of certain forms of association that have been neglected until now."[13]

This attempt to make the notion of reality include the dream underlay the prominence given to Freud in the first *Surrealist Manifesto*. Breton was no orthodox Freudian. For him, the unconscious life represented in dreams was what it had been for many poets: an ever-renewed reservoir of imagination, a guarantee that the possible expressions of human life could never be exhausted or limited by the daylight reality of everyday. Freud provided a scientific account of dream life, of the mental forces and processes out of which dreams were constructed. He therefore offered support for the project of bringing the dream back into the compass of reality. No longer imprisoned in the confines of logic, the mind would regain access to its buried powers. "Cannot the dream also be applied to the resolution of some of life's fundamental questions?"[14]

The means by which the real workings of the mind were to be revealed and become the basis for works of art was "psychic automatism." By this, Breton meant a free expression of unconscious mental processes, unchecked by reason, morality, or aesthetic traditions. The notion owed much to Freudian free association; it also had close ties with Dadaist practices. By giving unhindered expression to momentary states of mind, the Dadas had also intended to bring hidden mental powers into view. But in place of the Dadaist desire to substitute these expressions for traditional works of art, Breton proposed to use psychic automatism to extend the range of poetic imagination. Bringing unconscious processes to the surface was not a replacement for creating works of art, but the point from which their construction was to begin.

Breton was first struck by the notion of automatism during the war, when he read Freud and worked in the army mental hospital at Nantes. Soon after, he became fascinated by the apparently irrational, but often strangely powerful, phrases and images that came to mind in states of daydreaming, or at the moment between wakefulness and sleep. In 1919 he and Philippe Soupault set about creating such states of mind intentionally, noting down as poetic material the images they experienced. Their book of 1920, *Magnetic Fields*, contained the prose and verse that resulted. Later, Breton's friends René Crevel and Robert Desnos experimented with hypnotism, spiritualism, and trance states. Many of the techniques of Surrealism were born in these experiments. Here as elsewhere, Surrealism involved a flirting with the unknown and the irrational that recalls Rimbaud and the Symbolists. Breton was conscious that there were dangers in such procedures (he had experimented with free association among mental patients at the Nantes hospital), and did not want to descend too far into the depths. His early letters to his friend Frankel spoke both of the promise and the peril of exploring the irrational. He feared the possibility of real derangement. When he began to experiment with automatic writing, one reason he took on Soupault as a partner was the fear of confronting such states alone.[15]

By 1924, Breton had concluded that such Surrealist images could be achieved in wider, less threatening ways. What made an image Surrealistic was its juxtaposition of two distant realities.

Brought into proximity, they produced a kind of spark, an explosion of light that was the more beautiful and powerful as the distance between the two components was greater. Phrases such as Lautréamont's "champagne ruby," or his own "The cat-headed dew rocked itself on the bridge," were examples of Surrealist images. Such figures, Breton believed, arose out of spontaneous mental activity. But he no longer limited that activity to such psychic experiments as he and Soupault had conducted in 1919, or to the spiritualist activities of Crevel and Desnos. The chance juxtaposition of different phrases from a newspaper could produce them. Other techniques might be found in the future.[16]

In fact, the human world was full of traces left by man's constant and repressed desire to remake reality along the lines of dream. Whatever embodied this "irremediable human inquietude" could nurture the determination not to give in to everyday reality. Ruins had served as such repositories of unconscious forces for the Romantics. The department-store mannequin was one equivalent in Breton's own time. Such objects provided a foretaste of that resolution of dream and reality that defined the surreal. In his work of 1926, *Paris Peasant*, Breton's friend Louis Aragon hoped to construct a new mythology of modern life, a storehouse of real images that, like medieval churches, would seed everyday life with the promise of transcendence. Gasoline pumps, with their brash colors, their mysterious dials, their words in foreign languages, were metallic phantoms that sometimes gave off an allure like that of primitive divinities, those of ancient Egypt or of cannibal tribes. "O Texaco motor oil, Eco, Shell, great inscriptions of human potentiality."[17] Aragon set most of his book in a shopping arcade, the passage de l'Opéra, finding in the life there—the objects and vices for sale, the hotels, the coming and going of people—an incitement to reverie and an invitation to pass beyond the ordinary limits of his personality. The arcade provided "a method to free myself from certain constraints, a means to get beyond my own forces and into a still-forbidden realm." The chance encounters of modern life, the surprising juxtapositions, gave such a place the quality of a passage into dream life. Its ephemeral nature introduced its denizens to the experience of living outside of stability and permanence. "The ephemeral is a divinity as polymorphous as its name."[18]

In *Paris Peasant*, the "fever of phantasmagoria" that made the modern world hospitable to Aragon's attempt to live in the passage between the present and the future, between waking life and the dream, included advertisements, shop signs, and menus. Breton, too, created poems and images out of newspaper advertisements and stories, both in his 1919 book *The Pawn Shop (Mont de piété)* and in the 1924 *Manifesto*. The Surrealists' fascination with advertising was part of their cultivation of the fantasies aroused by contemplating any desired object or activity before it was experienced. "I would like to know what longings, what poetic crystallizations, what castles in Spain, what structures of *langueur* and hope, rise up in the head of an apprentice, at the moment in the beginning of his career when he decides to become a hairdresser, and begins to care for his hands."[19]

Having the renewal of art as their goal separated the Surrealists from the Dadaist love of contradiction and provocation for their own sakes. Nonetheless, the distinctions between Dada and Surrealism were never wholly clear and stable. Within Dada, too, there were those who felt the tension between the ideology of antiart and their own desire to go on producing paintings or poems. And the Surrealist attitude toward art as a productive activity remained similarly ambivalent. Part of Breton's path to Surrealism was traversed by throwing off the example of Jacques Vaché, for whom *umore* and even suicide were the only coherent responses to the impossibility of artistic productivity in modern life. The 1924 *Manifesto* concluded that "the imaginary solutions are either to live or to cease to live. Existence is elsewhere." But the example of Vaché's preference for personal drama over art never lost its power. Breton's opposition to finished work, his love for the incomplete in life as in art, were its residues. Following a line of thought opened up by Paul Valéry, Breton regarded artistic works as valuable not for themselves but for their ability to embody a moment of creative activity. They were signs of the human power to impose imagination on the world, to render an exterior object "adequate to desire." Picasso's pictures were exemplary because they demonstrated the artist's power to make reality conform to an inner vision. Although Breton and his friends did continue to produce objects, they insisted on their hostility to traditional art and literature. The works they approved had to be justified as going "beyond Art."[20]

Producing objects was only one part of a life equally devoted to acts of public confrontation and challenge. The Surrealists reveled in eccentricity. Soupault was especially valued for his histrionics. He would ask concierges if they knew where Philippe Soupault lived, address waiters with his own name, stop a bus late at night by putting a chain in its path, enter it, and ask all the passengers the date of their birth. The group disrupted public events, and a banquet they organized in 1925 to honor the Symbolist poet Saint-Pol Roux led to antipatriotic outbursts that produced a near riot. That evening, Soupault ended up swinging from the chandeliers, kicking over dishes and bottles on the tables. Fistfights erupted and the police had to be called. In 1928, the Surrealists celebrated the fiftieth anniversary of Charcot's researches on hysteria, greeting the condition as "in every respect a supreme means of expression." The second *Manifesto* contained Breton's famous *boutade*: "The simplest Surrealist act consists in going out into the street, revolver in hand, and shooting at random, as much as one can, into the crowd."[21]

The themes that lie behind the ballet *Parade* were significant for the Surrealists, too, but in an inverted form: their project was to eliminate the distinction between the surface and the interior, to make the inner meaning of an artist's work fuse with the features that proved it alien to the activities of everyday life. The effect of a Surrealist image did not depend on any particular content. Breton believed that "every act carries its justification within itself." Far from regretting, as Cocteau had, the air of mystification that surrounded the avant-garde's activity, the Surrealists reveled in it. In 1919, the group's collective purpose had been to "avoid satisfying the appetites of other people, to become unusable [*infréquentable*] for them, scoundrels, suspects." Ten years later, Breton described public approval as the thing to be avoided above all. "It is absolutely necessary to prevent the public from *entering* if one wants to avoid confusion. I add that it is necessary to hold them at the door, exasperated by a system of challenges and provocations." The image was precisely the one Cocteau had conceived for *Parade*, but with all the signs reversed.[22]

Whereas many earlier figures specified what attracted or repelled them in Bohemia, the Surrealists seem never to have done so. We therefore cannot define their relationship to Bohemianism in terms they provide themselves, as we could for Baudelaire. Nonetheless, their project of abolishing the distinction between art and life was in many ways the end point of a development that began under the sign of Bohemianism. Michel Sanouillet, an authority on Parisian Dada, has observed that Dada-Surrealism, while the vehicle of important discoveries for some, was "for many others a break which gave them a literary life rather cheaply." Similar views of the movement were sometimes expressed by contemporaries. As early as 1923, Jacques Rivière, editor of the *Nouvelle Revue Française*, cautioned Louis Aragon against growing old without softening his attitude of revolt. He ran the risk of becoming only the chief of "the café literati, the clan of failures."[23]

There are several reasons why Breton and his friends were not interested in such continuities, among them distance and the pressing issues of how avant-garde culture was to reorient itself in the face of war and revolution. The Surrealist absorption of Bohemian traditions mostly took place at a remove, through figures for whom Bohemia had already become a negative identity, like Rimbaud, or whose connections they may not have noticed, like Apollinaire. Aragon, in his first novel, *Anicet* (1921), declared that his generation was no longer attracted either to Rimbaud's kind of adventurous life, or to the traditional ideal of literary poverty, still embraced by Apollinaire's and Picasso's friend Max Jacob. Other elements in Bohemianism—its playfulness, indulgence, and susceptibility to *embourgeoisement*—made it an unserviceable point of orientation for them.

In some ways, however, it was the Surrealists' closeness to bourgeois life, rather than their distance from it, that separated them from Bohemia. Breton's withdrawal from Dada corresponded with his meeting and marrying Simone Kahn, a woman whose wealth allowed him to live in considerable comfort. In 1920, he characterized their relationship's meaning for him by asking her: "How is it that I, in appearance a misanthrope, in reality have a taste only for that which has the effect of attaching me to life?" In 1922, Matthew Josephson visited the couple in their comfortable apartment, decorated with canvases by Picasso, Braque, and others (some of them lent by the man who employed Breton for a time as secretary, Jacques Doucet). Breton shared with most of his followers a surprising ability to feel at home in the world. Photographs testify that their dress was seldom eccentric and their surroundings matched those of other cultured bourgeois. There were, it is true, two suicides, Jacques Rigaut and René Crevel. But Breton seems to have spoken for the others when he presented the movement as a rejection of Jacques Vaché's example. Despite Breton's celebration of Jarry, the Surrealist manner of abolishing the distinction between art and life did not share Père Ubu's need to create a special personal environment that mirrored his own inner state. Modern life, for them, was rich enough in invitations to live out fantasies without that. From the start, they had many supporters in established social and literary circles, which may help to explain the intensity of their fears that public approbation and acceptance might weaken their movement's force.[24]

In fact, the Surrealists took over many long-standing Bohemian postures without needing to acknowledge them. Their identity rested on the rejection of all existing occupations. Aragon apostrophized an audience in 1925: "Ah, bankers, students, workers, officials, servants, you are the fellators of the useful, the masturbators of necessity. I shall never work; my hands are pure." Breton had complained earlier: "One can't make a place in the sun without suffocating under some animal hide." Like Murger's Bohemians, the

Surrealists insisted on their right to remain constantly open, available for every new experience, unattached to any stable position in society.[25]

The novelty in the Surrealist manner of holding out was its inclusion of poetic and artistic identities among those rejected. Bohemia had been built around the claim to live life for art's sake, a claim Breton insistently abandoned. Yet it is here, just where Surrealism seems furthest from Bohemia, that their parentage is closest. The essential equivocation in the Bohemian claim to live in the name of art had been pointed out often since the 1830s, beginning with Félix Pyat's original diagnosis of *artistisme*. In reality, Bohemians had always appropriated the life lived in the name of art for another purpose, as a stage to dramatize ambivalence toward the bourgeois life they could never wholly escape. Dada and Surrealism made Bohemia's spontaneous appropriation of art as social theater into a self-conscious principle. Soupault's antics and the group's various public confrontations lay somewhere between the Murgerian transformation of everyday life into a work of genius, and the later twentieth-century artistic "happening." Breton's rejection of finished work as servile and an evidence of bad faith validated the behavior and experience of generations of Bohemians.

The aesthetics of Surrealism completed a line of development whose coordinates had been plotted during the nineteenth century. Writing of Poe as "King of Bohemians" during the 1850s, Barbey d'Aurevilly identified the Bohemian writer as the typical intellectual product of the modern world, devoid of stable values and attachments. Living mentally for the moment, he made his work out of whatever happened to enter his mind. Such intellectual existence *au hasard de son esprit* was raised to a principle by the Surrealists. Aragon said that Jacques Vaché's fascination derived from his unpredictability; no one knew what he would do in the next instant. Francis Picabia wanted to be an intellectual nomad, "to traverse ideas the way one traverses countries and towns." Philippe Soupault's high degree of psychic mobility was the reason that André Breton chose him as his partner for the experiments in automatic writing. Even more than Apollinaire—whom they admired on these grounds—the Surrealists pursued liberation by plunging into the chance happenings, the fortuitous comings and goings, the psychic shocks and surprises of modern urban life. They did not, like Apollinaire, link this principled irregularity explicitly with Bohemianism, but Barbey d'Aurevilly would have had no trouble in identifying them as exemplars of those aspects of modern culture that made Bohemianism its representative product.[26]

The Surrealists' notion of the relationship between art and life has other similarities with classical Bohemianism. Murger said that Rodolphe stayed in Bohemia because only there could he continue in the heightened state of arousal that made writing possible for him. Literature had to be an immediate reflection of experience; to be an artist meant living a life exalted by the power of erotic excitement, devoted to adventure, and open to the unexpected. It was a world where the power of fantasy was recognized and exploited: Musette defined love as the exchange of reciprocal illusions, and Rodolphe urged Jacques D. to stir up his imagination by kissing his dead love on the lips of another woman; the enticing displays in Parisian shops were encouragements to fantasy, spurs to making everyday life a work of genius. The Surrealists modernized the Bohemian unification of art and life by their explicitly Freudian identification of the psychic depths as the real source of the energy earlier sought in a free life. Their aesthetic demanded a cultivated passivity, an openness to those repositories of unconscious psychic power located in individuals and in the larger cosmos of modern urban life. For them, too, art was a slice of the life that liberated fantasy.

In the 1880s and 1890s, Maurice Barrès had sought to combine the often juxtaposed identities of dandy and Bohemian. Accepting the need to conform to social conventions in appearance, he proposed to preserve a personal space of liberated fantasy by dividing his life into separate spheres, one public, one secret: "Bohemianism in the soul, austerity on the outside." Breton admired Barrès from his youth, citing the book in which this image appeared as his favorite work. In the first *Manifesto*, Breton formulated the Surrealist ideal of life in terms of the child's sense of unchecked possibility, the "perspective of several lives lived at once," paraphrasing Barrès's appeal to "the pleasures of two or three different and contradictory moral lives." Both formulas were transformations of the Bohemian cult of multiplied sensation, inherited from Baudelaire.[27]

Baudelaire had rejected the Romantic equation of poetry with spontaneous feeling, because he thought it made poetic expression indistinguishable from the passions of everyday life. Surrealism confirmed his fears, contributing to the much discussed contemporary crisis of the object, "the eclipse of the work of art." One can trace the origins of this crisis, back to Romanticism's fascination for the ugly or grotesque, to the Impressionists' attempt to use painting as a form of visual experimentation, or to Rimbaud's willingness to let poetry be formless. It emerged full-blown in Marcel Duchamp's famous 1913 project of turning bicycle wheels (later hat racks and urinals) into art objects—"ready-mades."

By exhibiting industrial objects to which he had signed his name, Duchamp asserted that any human product could be art, once it was removed from its normal context and associated with an artist's personality. Artistic creativity was an arbitrary restriction of the wider human power to construct a world. Dada and Surrealism raised this devaluation of the art object to a level of principle. In doing so, they completed the process, begun during the nineteenth century, by which premodern hierarchies of aesthetic value were dismantled. If there existed no transcendent values, independent of human action in the present, then there was no longer any point to making objects that stood apart from life by virtue of their claim to embody or represent such values. The vocation of art was, instead, to call men to a freer and more fulfilling existence by releasing the transformative energy present in life itself, and directing that energy against the resistances and barriers that repressed or impeded it. Such a scenario, using art to turn the promise of modern life against its own limitations, had been enacted, since the 1840s, by generations of known and anonymous Bohemians and *réfractaires*.[28]

Surrealism embodied the legacy of Bohemianism not only in its cultural program, but also in its relationship to politics. From his teens, Breton had been attracted to anarchist politics of a kind that echoed the attitudes and even the language of the Vallèsian *réfractaire*. The mixture of political and cultural rebellion found in the Surrealists had one of its clearest anticipations in Vallès. Even his style at times foreshadowed the Surrealist attempt to use language as a vehicle to jolt readers out of their everyday frame of mind, putting them into contact with deeper psychic currents. Consider the image of Jacques Vingtras "grinding my teeth when memories of humiliation made my flesh crawl over my bones like the meat of a cutlet as the blood pours out under the knife." Here passionate revulsion led to an aesthetic of shock that was exemplified in Surrealist literature, painting, and cinema.[29]

Anarchist themes were often prominent in their activities, with religion, the law, and family life providing favorite targets. "Open the prisons, disband the army!" declared the first number of *La Révolution Surréaliste* in 1924. The anarchist impulse remained visible even through the period of cooperation with—and then adherence to—the French Communist party in the late 1920s and early 1930s, keeping tension between Surrealists and Communists high. Breton and his group persisted in asserting their independence, and did not hesitate to describe the inner revolution promoted by Surrealism as deeper and more radical than the mere changing of material conditions aimed at by Marxism.

Given the differences, what made the Surrealists decide to become Communists at all? The answer seems to be that they became convinced it was the only way to demonstrate the moral seriousness of their proclaimed commitment to revolution. In 1926, the Surrealist Pierre Naville wrote a pamphlet arguing that the vast majority of people in the world could not even begin to participate in the process of mental liberation the Surrealists called for until their material circumstances were altered. If the Surrealists were serious about their own aims, they had no choice but to devote themselves to the real revolution whose possibility had been demonstrated in Russia. Naville's challenge provoked a defense of Surrealism by Breton, but it also led to the inner questioning that brought him and his four closest followers to join the Communist party in 1927. The cooperation between Surrealists and Marxist sympathizers that began earlier had already been partly responsible for the separation of Soupault, Antonin Artaud, and Roger Vitrac. The increasing politicization of the movement continued the process of desertions, expulsions, and denunciations that characterized its history in the 1920s and 1930s. Later, the break with the Communists left Louis Aragon—probably the movement's most talented writer—permanently in the Marxist camp.[30]

The Surrealist project to unite dream and reality brought its representatives to support the Communist revolution, Breton wrote in the second *Manifesto* in 1930, but it aimed at a deeper transformation. The campaign for surreality would continue in any foreseeable form of social life: it had no serious chance of reaching an end "as long as man succeeds in distinguishing an animal from a flame or a stone." Nor did Breton count strictly on the proletariat to work for this revolution. He addressed his message to young people of all sorts—in lycées, seminaries, streets, and prisons, as well as workshops (factories were not mentioned)—tied together not by class but by a common refusal to bend to society's demands. The work of the Surrealists had nothing to do with the creation of a proletarian culture (in whose present possibility Breton did not believe); instead, it had to be addressed to the bourgeoisie it was attempting to overthrow, the class "to which we belong in spite of ourselves, and which we will not be able to contribute to abolishing outside ourselves before we have succeeded in abolishing it within ourselves."[31]

Breton's awareness that his project would always remain an attack on the bourgeoisie from within defines the nature of his rebellion. Like those of earlier bourgeois radicals—Proudhon, Courbet, and Vallès come to mind—his efforts to link himself with the working class arose out of the desire to realize potentialities simultaneously created and frustrated within the bourgeoisie itself. The Surrealist vision of modern urban life—especially the life of technology, commodity relations, and advertising—as containing vessels in which the power of fantasy was stored, and where the instruments of psychic liberation could be charged up, demonstrates their necessary attachment to the world they claimed to reject. Like that of Vallès's *réfractaires*, their rebellion arose from a dedication to the principle of individual, subjective liberation, so intense that it dissolved any social framework that resisted it.

Underlying the Surrealists' history of political involvement and withdrawal, of fragmentation and denunciation, was a peculiar dialectic between the project of individual liberation and the matrix of collective life. From the start, it was important to Breton and the others that Surrealism was a movement, a social grouping that gathered its individualities around a common purpose. In the first *Manifesto*, Breton presented a fantasy vision of himself and his Surrealist friends (twenty-two of them, plus Picasso hunting nearby) living together in a restored medieval castle not far from Paris. The image was a "poetic lie," but it could be made real by the will to impose imagination on the world. "We really do live inside our fantasy, *when we are there*." Most of the same people appeared in a group portrait by Max Ernst of 1922, *The Friends' Meeting* (*Au rendez-vous des amis;* see figure 12). But Ernst's group portrait in fact shows a collection of separate individuals, each one looking his or her own way (there was one woman), no two minds focused on the same thing. Such a vision perfectly matched Breton's notion of what sociability really was, and where it led. The possibility for genuine communication between any two people—the first *Manifesto* insisted—was no greater than that between a sane person and a madman. One of the aims of Surrealism was to reestablish this truth about the nature of human dialogue, hitherto hidden by social obligation and the force of habit. Relieved of the conventions of politeness, each of the participants in a Surrealist dialogue "simply pursues his soliloquy." The real purpose of Surrealist community was to provide a field within which each member's separate individuality was energized by the tension of his relations to all the others.[32]

This conception of society and individuality led the Surrealists to establish a position between literature and revolution, where social theater could put itself forward as a substitute for both. The aims of poetry and political action converged in a practice that dramatized the individual's attempt to draw the energy of his liberation out of

12. Max Ernst, *Au rendez-vous des amis*.

the tension between inner and outer life. In politics as in art, Surrealism's project was to tap the energy set free by the complex of achievement and frustration within modern existence, turning that power against the limits and barriers that society erected to contain it. Central to Surrealism was a message that had been enshrined in *la Bohème* from the start: the promise of liberation bourgeois society contained was a call for the continual testing of its own limits.

The fusion of art and life proclaimed by vanguard artists in the early twentieth century had deep roots in Bohemia. It was not the imitation of life by art in the traditional sense of holding up a mirror to nature. Nor was it the simple inversion of this relationship posited, for instance, by Oscar Wilde when he asserted that London fogs were coming to look like Impressionist paintings. The vanguard union of art and life was a substitution of actions and gestures that dramatized a self-conscious separation from existing life for the activity that fashioned objects. In Dada and (less uncompromisingly) Surrealism, the artistic object was rejected in principle, even where it partially survived in practice. The theater of *fumisme* replaced, at least in part, the poems and paintings it had once advertised. This exchange reached perhaps its highest point in the career of Marcel Duchamp. His substitution of "ready-mades" for traditional art objects led finally to an abandonment of painting and sculpture after 1923. Ceasing to be a practicing artist became a central action in defining Duchamp's career as a paradigmatic avant-garde figure: the very gesture of abandoning art was now able to claim and be accorded artistic significance.

Duchamp's career summed up the evolution of art we have been observing, replacing the production of objects with the self-dramatization of the artist, as the representative figure of a society unable to set clear limits for the identities and activities of its members. It is here that the Bohemian theater of ambivalence proved to be prophetic of the shape artistic practice itself would assume in the twentieth century. The traditional figure of the artist as a maker of texts or images was absorbed in a new role, as explorer of marginal states of being and consciousness. The avant-garde took over from Bohemia the redefinition of the artistic vocation as challenging the limits of individual and social existence, distilling and concentrating the task that modern society in principle sets for all its members, even while it gives only a few the tools and the leisure to pursue it.

Not all vanguard artists followed Tristan Tzara in equating this task with social dissolution. Many felt estranged from society, but sometimes the *boutades* of aggression covered an effort to explore deep layers of personal ambivalence and anxiety—as the cases of Jarry, Satie, and Apollinaire all reveal. Some avant-garde activities that seemed devoted to challenge and provocation of their audience contained attempts to question the practice of artists, too, as we saw both in Roland Dorgelès's trick of having Frédé's donkey paint a picture, and in Cocteau's project for the ballet *Parade*. The avant-garde shared with Bohemia not only its challenge to existing life, but also its practice of self-examination and—more often than has been recognized in both cases—self-criticism.

The Surrealists placed limits on how far their rebellion extended, fearing the possibility of personal dissolution that was opened up by their descent into the unconscious. This inward limit was matched by an external one: the sense that the world outside art was the source of energies that artists could tap nowhere else. Apollinaire's fascination for the vital powers being released in modern life was characteristic of much modernist practice. For Satie and the Surrealists, even advertising was a realm that could be colonized in the service of their transformative project. Jules Vallès, too, had seen the commercial world as a reservoir of energy that attracted him when the traditional aspirations of literature seemed hollow; he described the activities of the stock exchange as the sacred poetry of modern life.

As I have suggested, by 1900 it had become very difficult to separate the gestures best calculated to advertise artists from those that set them apart from the everyday world of commerce and utility. What made art magnetic and fascinating—in a time when it no longer offered reassurance or support for what were once shared communal values—was its identification with those spheres of experience that a highly organized and (as Max Weber put it) disenchanted society made difficult of access. Edmond Lepelletier's observation that many good bourgeois desired to live subjectively in Bohemia was one contemporary recognition of this, seconded by Carco's understanding that the thrill of danger had a power of attraction, drawing people from respectable backgrounds like his to the threatening yet liberating depths of Montmartre. More recently, André Chastel has suggested that the phenomenon of the *artiste maudit* has served an important function for society as a whole, providing a kind of sacred and sacrificial figure who performs for others both the extravagant celebrations of life, and the ritual subjection to destructive and irrational feelings that in primitive cultures were the subject of periodic rites of carnival, magic, and exorcism.[33]

All these considerations suggest that the avant-garde, like Bohemianism, was seldom simply a rejection of the bourgeois world it declared to be its enemy. Renato Poggioli has resorted to paradox in describing the relation between modern society and the art it produces. The art of a bourgeois society, he proposes, seems to be necessarily antibourgeois, defining itself through hostility to its own matrix and audience.[34] The relations between the avant-garde and Bohemianism suggest that this was often an opposition from within; the energy modernists drew on to mount their attacks flowed at least as much from the ground they, sometimes unconsciously, shared with other members of society, as it did from their ability to inhabit different regions.

Such an image of how modern art is related to society contrasts with two visions of cultural history that have many followers among historians and critics of our own time. Both neoconservatives and critical Marxists share a notion of modernist art as fundamentally out of tune with the society around it. According to the first, perhaps best represented by the sociologist Daniel Bell, "a culture which is concerned with the enhancement and fulfillment of the self and the 'whole' person" contradicts modern society's basic organization around roles and specializations justified by some kind of functional utility. Social needs and cultural forms "lead people in contrary directions." Bell believes that modern culture, triumphing over society, has produced a destructive hubris exemplified in "the refusal to accept limits, the insistence on continually reaching out" for the nonexistent.[35]

That Bohemia and the avant-garde were both concerned with values beyond the reach of specialization and utility, as well as with the questioning of established limits, is a point often confirmed in these pages. But those concerns were not so far from the needs and meanings posited by underlying social relationships as Bell's view suggests. Modern society has required that individuals accept a limited role defined by functional needs, but it has also claimed that by opening careers to individual merit and ability, its economic organization allows for levels of personal development and satisfaction not possible in earlier and more traditional social forms. If there were—and are—contradictions between the demand for discipline and work and the promise of satisfaction, they arise from within society, and not from a supposedly separate realm of culture. As Jürgen Habermas has observed, Bell's formulation "shifts onto cultural modernism the uncomfortable burdens of a more or less successful capitalist modernization of the economy and society."[36] Both culture and the economy were, at different moments, sources of social integration and of dissolution. To portray activities contributing directly to the economy one-sidedly, as pure sources of stability, and to attribute disorder and instability to artists and Bohemians, was already a well-developed tactic of conservatives in the nineteenth century. Then as now, they refused to recognize how much the forms of culture they rejected perform vitally necessary tasks of resolution and reconciliation for a society whose sponsorship of self-development for the sake of economic individualism creates constant moral dilemmas for its members.

By drawing them into the open, cultural practice sought to resolve such tensions as often as it aimed to make them more explosive. Baudelaire's admitted hatred for utility certainly separated him from the values many good bourgeois proclaimed. But his rejection of spontaneity in favor of hard work and his attempt to locate his aesthetic practice between *jouissance* and *travail* tied him much more closely to many of those same bourgeois than either he or they wanted to recognize. From the beginning in the days of Murger's Water-Drinkers, Bohemia contained a current of stoic or puritanical discipline and self-denial, often in opposition to the spirit of indulgence and the search for quick satisfactions present in society at large. Privat's portraits of the *métiers inconnus* depicted a world much more in harmony with the dominant ideals of work and utility than conservatives of the period suspected; the combination of imagination with discipline and determination to succeed helped make the underside of Paris a place where Privat could pursue his need for personal self-discovery. Even Verlaine pointed to the link between Bohemia and hard work, a connection in which Francis Carco saw a remedy for the dangers he knew lurked in Bohemia. Apollinaire's image of the new painting as an antidote to the diffusion of personal boundaries he feared brought the Baudelairean determination to counter *vaporisation* with *centralisation* into the era of Cubism.

The Marxist view presents the discord between modern society and modernist culture similarly, but regards it in a different light. Culture is the bearer of values that repeatedly call dominant social practices into question, but it is unable to effect their transformation. Modernist art and literature seesaw back and forth between revolutionary challenges to existing life, and their subsequent reabsorption or recapturing, submitting to the power of commerce or weakened by the contradictory attitudes of artists themselves. This pattern conforms to the larger Marxist vision of modern history as shaped by social conflicts whose normal outcome would be revolutionary change, but whose potential for deep transformation has somehow been denied or defeated. To place the history of Bohemia and the avant-garde in this frame is to associate their critical thrust with energies that, if fully liberated, would lead to a different form of social order. The failure to carry the critical project through to the end appears as an abandonment of the revolutionary possibilities inherent in it, or a sign that the identification with them was never wholehearted or complete. The avant-garde thus turns out—much as in the neoconservative view—to have promoted a practice that was inauthentic, essentially empty, or purely negative and destructive. These images derive from some formidable figures—not only Marx himself, but the members of the Frankfurt School that came out of Weimar Germany, Walter Benjamin, Theodor Adorno, Herbert Marcuse, and their many followers.[37]

This view of where the energies that power Bohemia and the avant-garde come from, and what they signify, needs to be challenged, too. To regard modernist visions as portents of a radical social transformation is to mistake a tension whose presence has been a source of renewal in modern society for an impulse to undermine or overcome it. Many artists have been irritated by the power of sheer wealth in the modern world, but we have seen how self-consciously figures like Courbet, Satie, Breton, and Aragon were able to turn the forms of commerce and publicity into materials for constructing their own projects. The Surrealists sought to draw energy from the reservoirs of psychic tension they found all around them; their ties to existing life included recognizing their own membership in the bourgeoisie and seeking to exploit collective experience to release individual mental powers.

The neo-Marxist view reminds us that hopes for a better social world beyond the bourgeois order still survive, even in the absence of a revolutionary actor to replace Marx's vision of the proletariat. That modern life creates such aspirations, through its puzzling and disorienting combination of injustice and oppression with the promise of liberation, is a truth that has been present throughout our story, from the generation of 1848 who first experienced it down to the Surrealists. But alongside the strength of those expectations has been the reality of their continual disappointment. There may be little reason to applaud that outcome, yet perhaps it has not been without its compensations. The form of life we may call bourgeois today would hardly be recognized by those who defended it a century ago. If we still yearn for a different kind of existence, we can no longer be so confident that we know what the limits of bourgeois experience are, much less that they have already been reached. Bohemia has been one, but not the only, force operating against the assumption that bourgeois social relations can create new possibilities only by preparing their own destruction. Marx himself had others in mind when he acknowledged, ten years after the failure of the Revolution he hoped would put an end to the bourgeois world, that "no social order ever perishes before all the productive forces for which there is room in it have developed."[38]

In the end, Bohemia cannot fulfill the promise of utopia for which it alternately served as foretaste and substitute. But if its history has anything to teach us, it is that individuals in modern society can explore forms of action and experience, enter new territories of personal and social life, without the cataclysm of revolution. Whether we wish to inhabit those territories or not, we are often enriched by their discovery. It was this that Apollinaire—who knew the anxieties and disappointments of Bohemia as well as he knew its joys—pointed to when he insisted that the seekers after adventure were not the enemies of order. Their pioneering exploration of new worlds aimed to enlarge and enhance the old one, bringing back to it

> . . . new fires . . . colors never seen
> A thousand imponderable phantasms
> To which reality must be given.

Bohemia has not remained within the confines of the country that gave it birth, spreading quickly outward from Paris to colonize other places. London, Milan, Munich, and Greenwich Village all became theaters of Bohemian life before the end of the nineteenth century. The new Bohemias took on the characteristics of their locales, but they also followed larger patterns by now familiar to us—nurturing themselves on the mixture of art and life, merging rebellion with ambition, simultaneously sponsoring real artistic vocations and appropriating the artist's image to dramatize ambivalence toward the beckoning destinies of ordinary social existence. Nor did Bohemia's history end with Surrealism in the 1920s. As recently as the 1960s, one could still discern an element of Bohemian politics within the mix of radicalism spurred by the antiwar movement on both sides of the Atlantic. For many in those days—Yippies and Situationists come easily to mind—political action was part of a drama of individual liberation so intense that solidarity with a cause and withdrawal into indifference or isolation seemed to issue from the same impulse. Meanwhile, new avant-gardes—pop art, action painting, minimalism—have discovered their own ways to identify art with the liberated spontaneity of those who live in the name of it. *Blague* and *fumisme* have remained part of their practice.

Yet the distance from Bohemia already visible in Surrealism has grown greater in those more recent movements. In some ways, the ground of Bohemian life seems to have slipped away. Barrès's observation about how much money Bohemian life requires has become ever more true. The free spaces—both real and metaphorical—once occupied by Bohemia have become narrower and harder to find. Politicization has taken on new forms, shaped first by the Cold War polarization after World War II, and more recently by a politics that challenges individuals to define themselves in relation to collective causes like feminism, ethnicity, or homosexuality. The very success of the campaign in our day against rigid social and moral standards has made some traditional challenges to bourgeois limits less relevant. Gestures and practices once commonly linked with Bohemia have by now broken out of the marginal spaces that once confined them. Unusual styles of hair or dress, drug usage or experimentation, unconventional sexual behavior, are becoming features of ordinary life. This may be occurring most rapidly in the United States, where the weight of convention and tradition is lighter than across the Atlantic. But its effects are visible in European countries as well. These developments seem to reduce both the scope and the need for the Bohemian dramatization of ambivalence.

The fact that Bohemia's history has not been ended by these changes suggests that what has declined since the 1920s is only one particular form of it. We may now call it the classic Bohemia, corresponding to the classic phase in the history of modern bourgeois society that extended between the French Revolution and the First World War. In that period, the new social forms linked to modern industrial capitalism and liberal democratic politics spread into more and more areas of life. But they were seldom unopposed; forces of tradition and resistance—institutions, people, values— still offered serious and dogged opposition. In the twentieth century, those forces inherited from the Old Regime have more fully succumbed to the fate often predicted for them. The result has been, as François Furet points out, that many of the issues placed at the center of political and social controversy by the French Revolution, and which continued to dominate public debate into our own century, have begun to lose their power.[39] With them, the tensions between Bohemia and the rest of society have diminished, too, permitting the migration of once Bohemian practices toward the center of social life. More recently, the classic modernist tension between art and society may have relaxed, too, with the growing recognition that modernism belongs to our culture much in the way earlier styles belonged to theirs, the appearance of forms and movements that are self-consciously postmodernist, and the accompanying proclamation of the end of the avant-garde.

In this perspective, the classic Bohemia seems a phenomenon of the past. Yet, if its spaces become less inhabitable and its gestures no longer serve the same needs, its lineage is not extinct. New spaces have been discovered and new styles appropriated or invented. The need to reconcile individuality with social membership is still a source of tension, as new layers of subjectivity are liberated, but in a society that continues to make rigid demands on its members. The obituary of Bohemia has often been written, but so far at least always too soon. When it is finally required, it will not be enough to say with Murger's Rodolphe, "O ma jeunesse! c'est vous qu'on enterre!" A whole form of life will have passed away.

DOCUMENTATION

A NOTE ON HISTORIES OF BOHEMIA

Because I have not carried on arguments with other historians in the text of this book, unwary readers may get the impression that Bohemia's history has never been written before. That is not the case. Among existing accounts, the most serious and important is by a German sociologist: Helmut Kreuzer, *Die Bohème, Beiträge zu ihrer Beschreibung* (Stuttgart, 1968). Kreuzer's book is wide-ranging and packed with information. In contrast to my treatment, his strides across many national cultures and contexts, and attempts to deal with the phenomenon down to the 1960s. Defining Bohemia as the subculture of nonbourgeois or antibourgeois intellectuals in modern industrial societies, Kreuzer provides an enormous catalogue of the expressions, attitudes, and practices found within this group. But the entries in the catalogue are sometimes only lists. Like other examples of sociological inquiry from the 1960s, Kreuzer's treatment is unhistorical in several senses: there is too little attention to particular contexts; no sense of development from the early Romantic Bohemia through the *fin de siècle* toward the present; no attempt to distinguish Bohemia from the general literary and artistic subculture; and no place for the individual histories that allow Bohemia to emerge as real, concrete experience. Bohemia's complex, ambivalent relationship to bourgeois life as a whole remains unclarified. Kreuzer understands Bohemia only one-sidedly, in terms of its distance from the bourgeoisie; he is unable to integrate that side of Bohemianism with its underlying attraction for bourgeois life.

His book is nonetheless on an altogether different level from that of James Miller, *Bohemia: The Protoculture Then and Now* (Chicago, 1977). Whereas Kreuzer came to the subject in the age of the Beat Generation and with an eye on the European marginal groups of the 1920s and 1930s, Miller wrote out of the interests created by

the counterculture of the Vietnam war era. There is much sympathy
in his account, and again the range is wide. But the result is superficial and slight. By contrast, one other attempt to approach Bohemia in the light of a history of youth also inspired by the experience
of the late 1960s remains helpful: John R. Gillis, *Youth and History*
(New York and London, 1974), 89–92. Gillis deals only with the
early Bohemia of the 1830s, approaching it solely within the context of bourgeois youth in that era. But within those limits, his
treatment is illuminating.

Two books by British scholars cover much of the ground explored in the present one. The first is by Joanna Richardson, *The
Bohemians: La vie de Bohème in Paris, 1830–1914* (London,
1969). Richardson provides a great deal of information (and a very
helpful bibliography), but her general stance toward Bohemia is
that of the superior British gentleperson, looking down her nose at
the morally suspect French. From this perspective, the real significance of Bohemia simply remains invisible. Closer to genuine cultural history is Malcolm Easton, *Artists and Writers in Paris: The
Bohemian Idea, 1803–1867* (New York, 1964). Easton's treatment of individuals, Murger among them, is sensitive and acute.
But apart from the restricted chronology, and an unfortunate tendency to end up with a perspective similar to Richardson's, Easton's
history is limited by his idea that Bohemia arose out of the growing
esteem in which visual artists were held during the nineteenth century, and their consequently greater commerce with writers. The
result was a demand for freedom, combined with an experience of
insecurity that Easton sees as the formula for Bohemia. It is a narrow framework, with no scope for politics, and does not point toward the issues that made Murger, Vallès, and even Courbet central
figures in the history of Bohemianism.

Both Easton and Richardson belong largely to the most common
tendency in approaches to Bohemia: to treat it as a subject in the
sociology of art and literature. One further example of this way of
thinking about Bohemia is Cesar Graña, *Bohemian vs. Bourgeois:
French Society and the French Man of Letters in the Nineteenth
Century* (New York and London, 1964). Graña understands the

opposition in his title wholly in terms of the economic and social position of literary men during the nineteenth century, the system of market relations that created a field of tension between society and writers. The result is an excellent essay on the sociology of literature. But Graña's work is not really about Bohemia: the issue of Bohemian consciousness never arises; Murger appears only casually, Privat and Vallès not at all; the treatment of Baudelaire does not focus on the matters that made Bohemia explicitly interesting to him. Stendhal and Flaubert, to whom Graña devotes considerable attention, were too distant from Bohemia to make them revelatory points of entry into the subject.

A somewhat similar starting point is found in a now old but still influential book: Albert Cassagne, *La théorie de l'art pour l'art en France* (1906). Cassagne deals with Bohemia only as part of his larger subject, but his views have often been repeated, especially in France. To him, Romanticism was a genuine revolt against the commercial society emerging in the nineteenth century, but Bohemia was merely a pale echo of it. Those who built the image of Bohemia self-consciously recalled the Romantics of the 1830s, but in terms that transformed the real Romantic estrangement into an idealization of bourgeois youth. Cassagne's account fits some representatives of the *école de bon sens*, like Émile Augier, whom he discusses. But to view Bohemia as the watered-down version of a revolt that was genuine only when it issued from writers more serious than Murger is to confuse literary history with the broader issues of social and cultural history that made Bohemia so powerful a symbol in the nineteenth century.

The most intelligent and provocative recent attempt to deal with Bohemia is that of T. J. Clark, *Image of the People: Gustave Courbet and the 1848 Revolution* (London, 1973). Seeking to place Courbet in the Bohemian milieu that was so important to him, Clark understands the inner links between Bohemian styles and aspirations and those of the bourgeoisie from which they arose. But Clark's attempt to enlist Bohemia in his project of radical cultural criticism leads him to a distorted view of it. To him, bourgeois society's association with liberty was only part of the revolutionary myth of 1789. In this Marxist schema, the boundaries of bourgeois experience are known in advance; uncertainty, ambivalence, and the testing of limits disappear. Those who drew apart to seek liberty with more coherence than regular social life allowed necessarily divided into two parts: a genuine Bohemia, which abandoned bourgeois existence and fought with the insurrection in June of 1848 (like Baudelaire); and a false or merely sentimentalized Bohemia—Murger's—that sought privatization as a path back into bourgeois life. Influenced by Cassagne, whom he cites, Clark thus tries to identify Murger with an already corrupted form of Bohemianism, opposing his stance to a genuine Bohemia whose natural expression was in rebellion. Such a view mistakes a division that existed within individuals, and which was often shifting and uncertain, for a firm distinction between one group and others. The notion that there was a Bohemia fighting with the rebels in June 1848 rests on a casual remark by Remi Gossez, a French historian of the workers' movement. There is no real evidence for it. Baudelaire's actions in June did not represent any general group of Bohemians, and probably should not be taken to stand for anyone beyond himself. Clark attempts to find a population for his radical Bohemia by way of an unfortunate misquotation from Champfleury (*Image of the People*, 65; see below, note 24 to Chapter 3). Even if the author of *Les excentriques* had believed that his visionaries constituted "*the* true Bohemians" (he only claimed that they were "true Bohemians"), this would hardly provide a reason for regarding their form of membership in *la Bohème* as more genuine than Murger's. That the attempt to break the two sides of Bohemian ambivalence apart into definite stances of rejection and acceptance of bourgeois life leads to such misreadings of the record is a sign that the nature and significance of Bohemianism cannot be grasped from such a viewpoint. Understanding Bohemia's role in cultural history requires—the present book has argued—that Bohemia be separated from the sociology of art and literature to take its place as part of the history of a developing bourgeois consciousness and experience; and that the nature of bourgeois life be freed of the narrowing perspective that a Marxist approach like Clark's imposes on it.

NOTES

The place of publication for all French titles is Paris unless otherwise noted.

CHAPTER 1

1. Henry Murger, *Scènes de la vie de Bohème* (*Scenes of Bohemian Life*) (1851; cited here in the edition published by Juillard, 1964), 26; Théodore Barrière and Henry Murger, *La vie de Bohème* (*Bohemian Life*) (1849), 14.

2. Honoré de Balzac, "Un prince de la Bohème" (*Scènes de la vie parisienne*), *Oeuvres complètes de Balzac*, 24 vols. (Club de l'Honnête Homme, 1956), XI, 294–95.

3. Adolphe D'Ennery and [Eugène] Grangé, *Les bohémiens de Paris* (1843), 8–9.

4. Henri Monnier, *Physiologie du bourgeois* (*Bourgeois Physiology*) (n.d. 1841?).

5. Adeline Daumard, *La bourgeoisie parisienne de 1815 à 1848* (1963); George Dupeux, *French Society, 1789–1970*, trans. Peter Wait (London and New York, 1976).

6. Patrick-Bernard Higonnet, "La composition de la Chambre des Députés de 1827 à 1831," *Revue Historique* 239 (1968), 351–77; David H. Pinkney, *The French Revolution of 1830* (Princeton, 1972); André-Jean Tudesq, *Les grands notables en France (1840–1849)* (1964).

7. G. W. F. Hegel, *The Philosophy of Right*, trans. T. M. Knox (Oxford, 1952), 84, 280; see also 109, 123–24, 133.

8. The quotation is from the preface to Balzac's *La peau de chagrin* by his friend Philarète Chasles, written in 1831.

9. Clifford Geertz, "Deep Play: Notes on the Balinese Cockfight," in Geertz, *The Interpretation of Cultures* (New York, 1973), 453.

10. For an analysis of these changes, see Cesar Graña, *Bohemian vs.*

Bourgeois: French Society and the French Man of Letters in the Nineteenth Century (New York and London, 1964), Chaps. 4 and 5.

11. John and Muriel Lough, *An Introduction to Nineteenth-Century France* (London, 1978), Chap. 4. Édouard Montague, *Histoire de la Société des Gens de Lettres* (1889).

12. See the letter signed "Un Artiste," in *L'Artiste* IV, 7 (1832), 81; also Théodore Muret, "Un artiste au Moyen Âge," *L'Artiste* II, 9 (1831), 90–91. Similar themes were developed by Sainte-Beuve, "De la littérature industrielle," *Revue des Deux Mondes* 19 (1839), 675–91.

13. Saint-C. [Alexandre de Saint-Cheron], "De la position sociale des artistes," *L'Artiste* IV, 5 (1832), 53.

14. Alfred de Vigny, *Chatterton*, ed. François Germain (1968), 25–34. The expansion of the poetic identity is entirely missed in most commentaries: e.g., Graña, *Bohemian vs. Bourgeois*, 40–41.

15. Félix Pyat, "Les artistes," *Nouveau tableau de Paris au XIXme siècle*, Vol. IV (1834), 1–21 (p. 9 for the term *bohémien*). For a similar indication of the expansion of the term "artist" see *L'Artiste* I, 1 (1831), and, somewhat later, "Sylvius," *Physiologie du poète* (1842).

16. George Sand, *La dernière Aldini* (1882 ed.), 6, 77, 172, 200, 201.

17. John R. Gillis, *Youth and History* (New York and London, 1974), Chap. 2.

18. Louis Mazoyer, "Catégories d'âge et groupes sociaux: Les jeunes générations françaises de 1830," *Annales d'Histoire Économique et Sociale* X (1938), 385–419, and Gillis.

19. For some of the national contrasts, see Lillian Furst, *Romanticism in Perspective* (London, 1969).

20. Louis Chevalier, *Laboring Classes and Dangerous Classes in Paris During the First Half of the Nineteenth Century*, trans. Frank Jellinek (Princeton, 1981).

21. For the earlier history of these matters, see Bronislaw Geremek, *Les marginaux parisiens aux XIVe et XVe siècles*, trans. Daniel Veauvois (1976); and Roger Chartier, "La 'Monarchie d'argot' entre le mythe et l'histoire," in *Les marginaux et les exclus dans l'histoire*, Cahiers Jussieu Numéro 5, Université Paris 7 (1979).

22. Charles Nodier, *Histoire du roi de Bohême et de ses sept châteaux (History of the King of Bohemia and His Seven Castles)* (1829). Review of Eugène Sue, *Plik et Plok*, in *Le Figaro*, January 28, 1831.

23. "Bohémiens," *Magasin Pittoresque* XIX (1851), 593–94.

24. Robert C. Darnton, *The Literary Underground of the Old Regime* (Cambridge, Massachusetts, and London, 1982). George Levitine, *The Dawn of Bohemianism: The Barbu Rebellion and Primitivism in Neoclassical France* (University Park, Pennsylvania, and London, 1978). The quote is from Watelet's *Dictionnaire;* see p. 16.

25. *Le Figaro* published series of articles on both the Jeunes-France (beginning August 30, 1831) and the Bousingots (beginning February 3, 1832). See Francis Dumont, *Nerval et les Bousingots* (1958). On the *petit cénacle,* see also Benn Sowerby, *The Disinherited: The Life of Gérard de Nerval* (New York, 1974); also Graña, *Bohemian vs. Bourgeois,* 73ff.

26. *La Liberté, Journal des Arts* (1832). For Borel and O'Neddy, see Pierre Labracherie, *La vie quotidienne de la Bohème littéraire au XIXe siècle* (1967).

27. Gautier's review of Murger's play in *La Presse,* November 26, 1849. See also his comment in *Revue des Deux Mondes* for July 1, 1848, cited in P. Citron, *La poésie de Paris dans la littérature française* (1961), II, 311–12. Arsène Houssaye, *Les confessions, souvenirs d'un demi-siècle, 1830–80* (1881?), 289ff. Gérard de Nerval, *Petits châteaux de Bohème,* ed. Jules Marsan (1926), 6–7.

28. In 1844, Gautier used the term in regard to Liszt, in an article about a concert of solo piano pieces. Gautier saw Liszt's Bohemian appearance as an important part of his appeal. See *La Presse,* April 22, 1844.

29. On the *physiologies,* see Andrée Lhéritier, "Les physiologies," in *Études de Presse,* n. s. IX (1957), 1–51; Claude Pichois, "Le succès des Physiologies," *ibid.,* 59–66; and Antoinette Huon, "Charles Philipon et la Maison Aubert (1829–62)," *ibid.,* 67–76. The works cited in the text are Louis Huart, *Physiologie de l'étudiant* (1841); "Sylvius," *Physiologie du poète* (1842); Édouard Ourliac, *Physiologie de l'écolier* (1841?), esp. 106ff.

30. Anon. [According to a pencil notation in the Bibliothèque Nationale copy, the authors were Delord, Fremy, and Texier], *Paris-Bohème* (1854); Henry Murger, Pierre Dupont, G. Mathieu, A. Delvau, et al., *Chants et chansons de la Bohème* (1853); Champfleury, *Les excentriques* (1852); *id., Les aventures de Mademoiselle Mariette* (1854); Charles Reybaud, "La dernière bohémienne," *Revue des Deux Mondes* (1853); Arnould Fremy, *Confessions d'un bohémien* (1857); Alphonse de Calonne, *Voyage au pays de Bohème* (1852). Many other appearances of the term will show up in the following chapters.

CHAPTER 2

1. *Histoire de Murger, pour servir à l'histoire de la vraie Bohème, par Trois Buveurs d'Eau* [by Adrien Lelioux, Léon Noël, and Nadar (Félix Tournachon)] (1862), 22.

2. Pierre Dufay, "Des Buveurs d'Eau à la 'Vie de Bohème,' " *Mercure de France* CLV (1922), 59–60.

3. The best account of Murger's life is Robert Baldick, *The First Bohemian: The Life of Henry Murger* (London, 1961). Where the source of details is not given, they come from his book. See also Georges Montorgueil, *Henri Murger, romancier de la Bohème* (1929).

4. For Murger's links to politics, see the following chapter. On Pottier and his milieu, Edward Berenson, *Populist Religion and Left-Wing Politics in France, 1830–52* (Princeton, 1984), 52ff.

5. Baldick, Chap. 2.

6. The best source for the history of the Water-Drinkers is Murger's correspondence, substantial excerpts from which are printed in the *Histoire de Murger . . . par Trois Buveurs d'Eau*. See also Dufay, "Des Buveurs d'Eau."

7. In addition to the works already cited, see A. Schanne, *Souvenirs de Schaunard* (1886), and Champfleury (Jules Fleury), *Souvenirs et portraits de jeunesse* (1872). Also Charles Monselet, *Petites mémoires littéraires* (1885).

8. The photograph is reproduced in Nigel Gosling, *Nadar* (New York, 1976), 69.

9. Louis-Sébastien Mercier, *Tableau de Paris,* new ed. (Amsterdam, 1782), VIII, 133–37. Paul de Kock, "Les grisettes," *Nouveau tableau de Paris au XIXme siècle* (1834), I, 169–79; Théodore Muret, "Le Quartier Latin," *ibid.,* IV, 188–89.

10. Alfred de Musset, "Mimi Pinson" (1845), in *Oeuvres complètes* (Geneva, 1969), VII, 211–39.

11. Joan W. Scott and Louise A. Tilly, *Women, Work and Family* (New York, 1978).

12. Murger, *Scènes de la vie de Bohème,* 306. Alfred Delvau, *Grandeur et décadence des grisettes* (1848).

13. See the letters in *Histoire de Murger . . . par Trois Buveurs d'Eau,* 141, 145, 169–70.

14. The subtitle appeared with "Le cap des tempêtes," July 9, 1846.

15. *Le Corsaire-Satan,* October 5, 1845, February 21, 1846 (for

the two stories of Champfleury), and September 24, 1846, for E. Plouvier, "Fragment des mémoires d'un Bohémien: L'Héritage de Job-le-
rêveur." On the editor's liking for such stories, see Champfleury, *Les
aventures de Mademoiselle Mariette* (1856 ed.), 54. The Murger tale
was called "La maîtresse aux mains rouges," *Le Corsaire-Satan*, July 1,
1846.

16. Gustave Simon, "Henry Murger: Lettres inédites à Victor
Hugo," in *Le Temps*, April 18, 1922.

17. Barrière and Murger, *La vie de Bohème* (1849); on the controversy over the ending, see the discussion in Chap. 6.

18. *Scènes de la vie de Bohème* (hereafter *Scènes*), 370.

19. *Scènes*, 26ff.

20. Lemercier de Neuville, *Souvenirs d'un montreur de marionettes*
(1911), 164; *Histoire de Murger*, part one and part three.

21. Armand de Pontmartin, "Un jeune écrivain, étude morale:
Henry Murger et ses oeuvres," *Revue des Deux Mondes*, 2d ser., XXXV
(1861), 711. Edmond and Jules de Goncourt, *Journal, mémoires de la
vie littéraire*, ed. Robert Ricatte, 22 vols. (Monaco, 1956–58), II, 163.
More on the Goncourt brothers below.

22. Champfleury, *Les aventures de Mademoiselle Mariette*, 54.
There is a great deal of information about Murger's personal and financial situation during this period in the manuscript collection Autographes
Nadar, Bibliothèque Nationale, Paris, Nouv. Acq. Fr. 24279. I have not
made a close study of these documents, but several of them suggest
(e.g., numbers 6945 and 6946) that the often repeated assertion that
Murger was underpaid and exploited by his publishers, especially Michel
Lévy, needs to be considerably revised. He seems to have received signif-
icantly more than he was owed in 1851–52, and his overall payments
from Lévy amounted to 5,690 francs.

23. *Scènes*, 115, 304–7, and *passim*.

24. *Scènes*, 211ff.

25. *Scènes*, 210, 291–92.

26. Murger's letter of September 22, 1842, in *Histoire de Murger*,
141–42. *Scènes*, 357.

27. *Scènes*, 31–32.

28. Pontmartin, "Un jeune écrivain," 715. Théodore Pelloquet,
Henry Murger (1861), 19–20.

29. *Scènes*, 296ff.

30. See, for instance, *Scènes*, 123ff.

31. *Scènes*, Chap. 18, "Le manchon de Francine."

32. Murger, *Les Buveurs d'Eau* (1853).

33. *Ibid.*, 80.

34. On bourgeois values in this period, see Adeline Daumard, *La bourgeosie parisienne de 1815 à 1848* (1963).

35. See the various well-known works of Erik H. Erikson: *Childhood and Society* (New York, 1950); *Young Man Luther* (New York, 1958); *Identity: Youth and Crisis* (New York, 1968). See also Kenneth Keniston, *Young Radicals* (New York, 1968).

36. *Scènes*, 285.

CHAPTER 3

1. For the commentary on the size of the audiences and the box office, see, for instance, *Le National*, December 4 and 13, 1849. There were two exceptions to the reviews' beginning with a definition of Bohemia. Both in *Le Corsaire*, successor to the paper where Murger's sketches had first appeared, and in *Le Charivari*, which prided itself on standing outside established attitudes and opinions, the reviewers declared that their readers would already know what the term meant. Jules Janin, writing in the *Journal des Débats*, explained the term's meaning and listed the writers who had written about Bohemia in the *Corsaire-Satan* as Murger's predecessors. See *Le Corsaire*, November 26, 1849; *Le Charivari, November 26, 1849; Journal des Débats*, November 26, 1849. The reviewer for the more prominent and widely read *Le Siècle* (same date) began: "Do you know what Bohemians are?"

2. *Journal des Débats*, November 26, 1849, and December 31, 1849.

3. *La Réforme*, December 3, 1849. Armand de Pontmartin, writing in the *Revue des Deux Mondes* (n.s. IV [1849], 911), also said that the play had been received with indulgence because its carefree spirit soothed "our minds, tired out by agitation and sadness."

4. *Corsaire-Satan*, June 12, 1846, and January 7, 1845.

5. *Ibid.*, January 7, 1845, December 1845 *(passim)*; on Jean Journet, April 8 and 18, 1846.

6. Champfleury, *Souvenirs et portraits de jeunesse* (1872), Chap. 16, "Silhouettes de rapins d'un autre époque." *Histoire de Murger . . . par Trois Buveurs d'Eau*, Part III. The Balzac story is cited in Chap. 1, n. 2.

7. Murger's letters in *Histoire de Murger*: September 18, 1841,

99; July 30, 1844, 164–65. Champfleury, *Souvenirs,* Chap. 18, "Murger"; Nadar in *Histoire de Murger,* 234.

8. See Ch. de Ricault d'Héricault, *Murger et son coin, souvenirs très vagabonds et très personnels* (1896), for a recollection of Murger in the spring of 1848.

9. *Scènes de la vie de Bohème,* 146, 157, 163, 181.

10. The story is published as an appendix in the Juillard edition from which we have cited Murger's work.

11. On Jean Wallon, see the notice in *Polybiblion, Revue Bibliographique Universelle,* 2d ser., 16 (1882), 74–75. Still sympathetic to democracy in 1848, he feared it as leading to socialism by 1849. See his various works: *Le bonhomme Richard* (1848); *Les partageux: Dialogues à la portée de tous* (1849); *La presse en 1848, ou revue critique des journaux* (1849); *Du pouvoir en France* (1852).

12. See the various references to Hussonet in Gustave Flaubert, *Sentimental Education,* trans. Robert Baldick (Penguin Classics ed., 1964), 43–44, 57, 145, 212, 359, 416.

13. Karl Marx, *The Eighteenth Brumaire of Louis Bonaparte,* in Marx and Frederick Engels, *Selected Works in One Volume* (New York, International Publishers, 1968), 138, 145.

14. A. Chenu, *Les conspirateurs . . . Les sociétés secrètes, la préfecture de police sous Caussidière* (1850). Lucien de la Hodde, *Histoire des sociétés secrètes et du parti républicain de 1830 à 1848* (1850). See Marx's review from the *Neue Rheinische Zeitung-Revue* in Karl Marx and Friedrich Engels, *Gesamtausgabe (MEGA)* I, x (Berlin, 1977), 275–89.

15. For a somewhat similar view of some 1848 republicans and social democrats, but without including the Bohemian label, see Alexis de Tocqueville, *Souvenirs,* new ed., ed. Luc Monnier (1942), 86, 107.

16. De la Hodde, 16.

17. On Caussidière, see Maurice Agulhon, *1848, ou l'apprentissage de la République, 1848–52* (1973), 24, 33, 47, 50, 64, 65, 76. Also, the notice in Jean Maitron, *Dictionnaire biographique du mouvement ouvrier français* I (1964), 365–66.

18. See Caussidière, *À ses concitoyens* (1848), and *Mémoires,* 2 vols. (1849).

19. Both articles appeared on May 17. *La Presse* on the same day said that Caussidière had friends among the conspirators and demanded his removal.

20. Chenu, *Conspirateurs,* 110–11: "Il dût bien regretter alors la vie de Bohème qu'il avait menée jadis." De la Hodde, 345, 357–58, 50.

21. Tocqueville, *Souvenirs,* 82–83, in English in *The Recollections of Alexis de Tocqueville,* trans. A. T. de Mattos, ed. J. P. Mayer (London, 1948), 82–83. Louis Reybaud, *Jérôme Paturot à la recherche de la meilleure des républiques* (1849), 77. Daniel Stern [Comtesse d'Agoult], *Histoire de la révolution de 1848,* 2 vols. (1850), II, 174–75. *L'Illustration, journal universel,* April 8, 1848, "Lettres d'un flâneur: Les affiches de Paris." See also Peter Amann, "The Paris Club Movement in 1848," in *Revolution and Reaction: 1848 and the Second French Republic,* ed. Roger Price (New York and London, 1975), 122, for a *Club démocratique des hommes de lettres sans emploi.*

22. *Le Corsaire,* December 19, 1850. See also the same paper for August 7, 1850.

23. Champfleury, *Les excentriques* (1852).

24. Champfleury's sketches have been discussed as exemplary expressions of what Bohemia meant around 1848 by T. J. Clark, *Image of the People: Gustave Courbet and the 1848 Revolution* (London, 1973). Clark attempts to use Champfleury's work as evidence for his claim that the genuine Bohemia stood for an authentic, radical rejection of bourgeois life, in opposition to something he calls the avant-garde and to Murger's merely romanticized Bohemia, which were ready for integration. In making this argument, Clark fails to notice that Champfleury used the term "Bohemians" about his eccentrics only in his preface; earlier, he had preferred to reserve it for artists and writers. More important, Clark badly misquotes Champfleury, who never said that *excentriques* were *les bohèmes véritables,* as if others were less genuine, but only *bohèmes véritables,* worthy of belonging to the category. Clark, 65; Champfleury, 8.

25. *L'Illustration,* April 14, 1848. On *Le Bohémien de Paris,* see the list of journals in *Le Croque-Mort de la Presse,* number 1, December 1848 (this survey is available in the microfilm collection *Journaux éphémères de 1848).*

26. For Courbet's biography, see Jack Lindsay, *Gustave Courbet: His Life and Art* (New York, 1973), and Petra Ten-Doesschate Chu, ed., *Courbet in Perspective* (Englewood Cliffs, New Jersey, 1977). Many of the sources for Courbet's life are printed in [Pierre Courthion, ed.] *Courbet raconté par lui-même et par ses amis,* 2 vols. (Geneva, 1948). Recent studies of great interest are Clark, *Image of the People;* James Henry Rubin, *Realism and Social Vision in Courbet and Proudhon*

(Princeton, 1980); and Linda Nochlin, *Gustave Courbet* (New York, 1976).

27. Lindsay, Chap. 5.

28. On Courbet's realism, see Klaus Berger, "Courbet in His Century," *Gazette des Beaux-Arts* XXIV (1943), and in Chu, ed., *Courbet in Perspective,* 34–42. The last quote in the text is from an article by L. Peisse, in *Le Constitutionnel,* June 8, 1851.

29. The classic discussion of this subject is Meyer Schapiro, "Courbet and Popular Imagery: An Essay on Realism and Naïveté," *Journal of the Warburg and Courtauld Institutes* (1941), 164–91, reprinted in Schapiro's collection *Modern Art* (New York, 1978), 47–85. See also Clark, *Image of the People.*

30. Lindsay, 40–44; Clark, 29–30.

31. On lower-middle-class taste, see Schapiro, "Courbet and Popular Imagery." The letter of 1854 (to Alfred Bruyas) in *Courbet raconté par lui-même et par ses amis,* 78–79. On Courbet and Trapadoux, see Clark, 51–52, 71, and 165 for the letter to Champfleury, mentioning Trapadoux and the priesthood.

32. Théophile Gautier in *La Presse,* February 5, 1851. Courbet to *Le Messager,* November 19, 1851, quoted in *Gustave Courbet (1819–1877),* Catalogue of the Exhibit Held at the Grand Palais, Paris, September 30, 1977–January 2, 1978 (1977), 29, 36.

33. Rubin, 106–7. *Courbet raconté par lui-même,* 81–82.

34. Lindsay, 26. The self-portraits are reproduced and discussed by Hélène Toussaint in *Gustave Courbet (1819–1877);* see numbers 3, 13, 16, 19 (cited below as *1977 Catalogue*).

35. *1977 Catalogue,* 97; letter to Bruyas cited by Alan Bowness, "The Painter's Studio," in Chu, 133, Courbet to his family, March 15, 1846, in *Courbet raconté par lui-même,* 73.

36. Lindsay, 59; *Courbet raconté par lui-même,* 78.

37. See Lindsay, 75ff.

38. The letter to Bruyas in Rubin, 105–9. See also *1977 Catalogue,* 31–32. Lindsay, Chap. 8.

39. Jean Prinet and Antoinette Dilasser, *Nadar* (1966).

40. On the links between Nadar's *Panthéon* and *The Studio,* see Benedict Nicolson, *Courbet: The Studio of the Painter* (New York, 1973), 65–66.

41. Max Buchon, "Annonce," in *Le Peuple,* June 7, 1850, trans. in Chu, ed., *Courbet in Perspective,* 60–63. For this view in a different form, Clark, *Image of the People* (the quote in the text appears there on

p. 141). My discussion of the *Burial* owes a great deal to Clark's probing analysis, even though I dissent from most of his implications and conclusions.

42. See Rubin, *Realism and Social Vision*, on Proudhon's theory of art. Also, for a modern view, Hélène Toussaint, in *1977 Catalogue*, 98–105.

43. Champfleury, "In Defense of the *Funeral at Ornans*," in Chu, ed., *Courbet in Perspective*, 71, 73.

44. Alfred Delvau, *Histoire de la Révolution de Février* (*History of the February Revolution*) (1850), 88–91. P. J. Proudhon, *Selected Writings*, trans. Elizabeth Fraser, ed. Stewart Edwards (London, 1969), 176.

45. For the politics of 1848 in the countryside, see Maurice Agulhon, *1848, ou l'apprentissage de la république* (1973); and most recently, Edward Berenson, *Populist Religion and Left-Wing Politics in France, 1830–1852* (Princeton, 1984). The quotation in the text is in Clark, 141.

46. Lindsay, 66.

CHAPTER 4

1. For Baudelaire's life, see Enid Starkie, *Baudelaire* (London, 1957; Penguin ed., 1971). For Baudelaire's contemporary links with Bohemia, see Charles Asselineau, *Charles Baudelaire, sa vie et son oeuvre* (1869), and Charles Dornier, "Un témoin de la Bohème littéraire," in *La Revue de France*, March–April 1925, 68–69. The poem, "L'Héautontimorouménos," can be found in *Les Fleurs du mal*.

2. For the quotes, "The Painter of Modern Life," in Baudelaire, *Selected Writings on Art and Artists*, trans. P. E. Charvet (Penguin, 1972), 419; and *Mon coeur mis à nu*, ed. Beatrice Dedier (Le livre de poche, 1972), 114.

3. Ellen Moers, *The Dandy: Brummell to Beerbohm* (Lincoln, Nebraska, 1978), Chap. 1.

4. Moers, 17.

5. Jules Barbey d'Aurevilly, *Du Dandysme et de G. Brummell* (1887 ed., in *Oeuvres de Jules Barbey d'Aurevilly*), 40.

6. Barbey, *Du Dandysme*, 59, 62, for the quotes. On Brummell's decline see Moers, 28ff.

7. See, in addition to Moers, Elizabeth Creed, *Le Dandysme de*

Jules Barbey d'Aurevilly (1938), and P. J. Yarrow, *La pensée politique et religieuse de Barbey d'Aurevilly* (1961).

8. Creed, 26–34.

9. Creed, 71, 105. For Barbey's later evolution, see Yarrow.

10. For a contemporary account of Roger de Beauvoir's life, see H. de Villemessant, *Mémoires d'un journaliste*, new ed. (Paris, 1884), I, 161–206. Also Jules Marsan, *Bohème romantique* (1929).

11. Charles Monselet, *Petites mémoires littéraires* (1885), 2–3; Alfred Delvau, *Les dessous de Paris* (1860), 266–67; Philibert Audebrand, *Un café de journalistes sous Napoléon III* (1888), 91–92.

12. Baudelaire, "The Painter of Modern Life" (hereafter, PML), 425–27, 420; *Mon coeur mis à nu*, 113.

13. PML, 421–22. "Théophile Gautier," in *Selected Writings on Art and Artists*, 260. French text in Baudelaire, *L'art romantique*, ed. L. J. Austin (Flammarion, 1968), 240.

14. Jules Mouquet and W. T. Bandy, *Baudelaire en 1848* (1946), 44.

15. *Mon coeur mis à nu*, 62, 64.

16. Mouquet and Bandy, 45–47.

17. PML, 399.

18. PML, 399 (I have altered the translation); *Paris Spleen*, trans. Louise Varese (1947), 108. *Mon coeur mis à nu*, 127. So far as I know, this was the first use of the term "Bohemianism."

19. Baudelaire, *Lettres à sa mère* (1932), 22–24, 34–35, 50–51, 77, 81–83.

20. Champfleury, *Souvenirs et portraits de jeunesse*, Chap. 22, "Rencontre de Baudelaire."

21. "Edgar Poe, sa vie et ses oeuvres," and "Notes nouvelles sur Edgar Poe," *L'art romantique*, 151–92.

22. *Ibid.*, 168–70.

23. J. Barbey d'Aurevilly, "Le roi des Bohèmes, ou Edgar Poe," *Le Réveil*, May 15, 1858, 231–33.

24. On Baudelaire's friendship with Barbey, see the letters in Baudelaire, *Correspondance*, ed. Claude Pichois (Pleiade, 1973), I, 494, 503, 524–25, 552–54. Barbey's letter to Baudelaire in *Lettres à Charles Baudelaire*, ed. Claude Pichois with the collaboration of Vincinette Pichois (Neuchâtel, 1973), 54. See also J. Ballery, "Marginalia inédits de Baudelaire," *Revue des Sciences Humaines*, n.s., LXXIII (1954), 49–56.

25. *Mon coeur mis à nu,* 111.

26. *Ibid.,* 45.

27. PML, 400. *Paris Spleen,* 3.

28. *Paris Spleen,* 74; Charles Baudelaire, *Les paradis artificiels,* ed. Claude Pichois (Gallimard, 1961), 92, 100, 121.

29. PML, 408.

30. "The Life and Work of Eugène Delacroix," *Selected Writings on Art,* 372; *Mon coeur mis à nu,* 115, 122.

31. *Mon coeur mis à nu,* 141. *Les paradis artificiels,* 144–45, 93.

32. *Paris Spleen,* 20; "The Life and Work of Eugène Delacroix," 379.

33. Léon Cladel, *Les martyrs ridicules* (1862).

34. From the reprint of the preface, in *L'art romantique,* 362.

35. *L'art romantique,* 354–55.

36. *Selected Writings on Art and Artists,* 109; *L'art romantique,* 246–51.

37. *L'art romantique,* 249, 189–90, 186–87.

38. Baudelaire to Narcisse Ancelle, February 18, 1866. Baudelaire, *Correspondance,* ed. Claude Pichois, with Jean Ziegler (1973), II, 610.

39. *Mon coeur mis à nu,* 140, 141, 143, 144, 147, 148, 150. Baudelaire knew Franklin's *Autobiography* and was probably aware of how close he came to Poor Richard in these maxims. See his project for a play, *La fin de Don Juan,* in *Oeuvres* (Pleiade), 1243.

40. "L'art philosophique," in *L'art romantique,* ed. Jacques Crépet (*Oeuvres complètes de Charles Baudelaire*—not the volume of the same title cited earlier—1925), 119.

CHAPTER 5

1. *Scènes de la vie de Bohème,* 19. *Histoire de Murger,* 204–5.

2. *Journal des Débats,* December 1, 1849. *Gazette des Tribunaux* (hereafter *GT*), November 29, 1849, and December 13, 1849.

3. Alexandre Privat d'Anglemont, *Paris inconnu* (1875 ed.), 40.

4. T. J. Clark, *The Absolute Bourgeois* (London, 1973), 119ff. on *saltimbanques* and the law.

5. *GT,* August 5, 1843.

6. *GT,* September 20, 1843, and July 15, 1846.

7. *GT,* November 22, 1846.

8. *GT,* August 14, 1849, and September 12, 1850.

9. *GT,* July 15, 1846.

10. *Scènes,* 149ff, 31; *GT,* September 28, 1849.

11. Théodore de Banville, *Les pauvres saltimbanques* (1853), 13.

12. Louis Jourdan in *Le Siècle,* March 29, 1855; *Le Bohème, journal non politique,* April 1, 1855; V. S. Fournel, "Les artistes nomades," *Revue de Paris,* April 1 and October 1, 1854 (the reference to Pradier is in the second part, pp. 107–8); Firmin Maillard, *Histoire anecdotique et critique de 159 journaux parus en l'an de grâce 1856* (1857), 47–48.

13. *Le Bohème,* April 1, 1855.

14. *Ibid.,* April 22 and May 6, 1855.

15. Paul Saulnier, "Du roman en général et du romancier moderne en particulier," *ibid.,* April 29, 1855.

16. *Le Bohème,* May 6, 1855.

17. Pradier, "Pères et fils," *ibid.,* April 29, 1855.

18. Jules Vallès, "Les irréguliers de Paris," in *Les réfractaires* (*Oeuvres complètes de Jules Vallès,* ed. Lucien Scheler, 1955), 52–77.

19. *Le Sans le Sou, journal hebdomidaire artistique et littéraire,* November 19–20, 1854.

20. *Ibid.,* December 3–10, 1854; April 22–29, 1855; and April 29–May 6, 1855.

21. *Le Figaro,* August 9, 1859. See also the obituary by Alfred Delvau in *Le Siècle,* July 22. *Le Corsaire* published several stories about him during August, September, and October of 1849.

22. Jean-Léo, "Paris-Bohème: Alexandre Privat d'Anglemont," offprint from *Synthèses* (Brussels, 1949).

23. Jean Ziegler, "Essai biographique sur Privat," *Études Baudelairiennes* VIII (1976), 219–52.

24. Théodore de Banville, *Mes souvenirs* (1883), 63–72. For more on Privat's *blagues,* see *Le Corsaire,* October 23, 1849.

25. Pierre Citron, "Quatre lettres d'Alexandre Privat d'Anglemont à Eugène Sue," *Revue des Sciences Humaines,* n.s., CIII (1961), 393–416.

26. Walter Benjamin, "Die Bohème," in *Charles Baudelaire, ein Lyriker im Zeitalter des Hochkapitalismus,* ed. Rolf Tiedemann (Suhrkamp, 1974), 9–32. See also Jean-Paul Bouillon, *Félix Bracquemond, les années d'apprentissage (1849–59): La genèse d'un réalisme positiviste,* thesis, Université de Paris, I (1979), esp. 390ff. That Privat's claim to have written forty volumes published under other people's names was a rodomontade is the sensible conclusion of Pierre Citron in the article cited above.

27. See the letter in Citron, "Quatres lettres," 398–99.

28. Privat, *Paris anecdoté* (1885 ed.), 58. Also quoted by Pierre Citron, *La poésie de Paris* (1961), II, 314.

29. Privat, *Paris anecdoté, passim.*

30. *GT*, October 3, 1852; Murger, *Scènes,* 19.

31. Privat, *Paris anecdoté,* 163–64, 105, 132.

32. *Ibid.,* 180ff.

33. Privat, *Paris inconnu* (1875 ed.), 64ff.

34. Privat, *Paris anecdoté,* 27.

35. Frédéric Soulié, "Les existences problématiques," *Nouveau tableau de Paris,* V, 32–37.

36. Gabriel Guillemot, *Le bohème* (1868).

37. Philibert Audebrand, "La grande Bohème," *Le Figaro,* July 26, 1859. Audebrand attributed the idea to the editor of the *Revue des Deux Mondes,* François Buloz. Henri de Rochefort, *La grande Bohème* (1867). *La Bohème Financière,* 1880–82. Ch.-M. Flor, *La Bohème bourgeoise* (1890). For a later survival of Privat's kind of research, done in the positivistic spirit of the 1880s, see J. Barbaret, *La Bohème du travail* (1889).

38. *Physiologie du bourgeois (Bourgeois Physiology),* 44–45. For some related comments on the term *état,* see William H. Sewell, Jr., *Work and Revolution in France: The Language of Labor from the Old Regime to 1848* (Cambridge, England, 1980, 24, 190–91).

39. *GT*, August 5, 1843; September 20, 1843; July 15, 1846.

40. Baudelaire, *Paris Spleen,* trans. Louise Varese (New York, 1947), 77. Alfred Delvau, *Les dessous de Paris* (1860), esp. 229ff.

41. W. H. Pellow, "Alexandre Privat d'Anglemont: Les singes de dieu et les hommes du diable," *Études Baudelairiennes* VIII (1976), 253–71. See also the comments of Pierre Citron in his article "Quatres lettres" on Privat's inability to embody his quest in literary work.

CHAPTER 6

1. *Le Figaro,* January 31; February 3, 7, 10, 14.

2. *Journal des Débats,* February 4, 1861; Armand de Pontmartin, "Un jeune écrivain, étude morale: Henry Murger et ses oeuvres," *Revue des Deux Mondes,* 2d ser., XXV (October 1, 1861), 708–18; Charles Coligny, "Henry Murger et la Bohème," *L'Artiste* n.s., XI (February 15, 1861), 74ff.

3. *L'Opinion Nationale,* February 3, 1861. Veuillot's article was reprinted in his collection, *Les odeurs de Paris* (1868), 84–91.

4. Théodore Pelloquet, *Henry Murger* (1861), esp. 17ff. Lemercier de Neuville, *Souvenirs d'un montreur de marionettes* (1911), 119.

5. On Nadar and the Water-Drinkers, see Georges Grimmer, *Cinq essais nadariens* (1956), 36ff. Grimmer's belief that Nadar had little to do with the book seems to me unacceptable, however, since it was he who had asked Murger to remove the chapter "His Excellency, Gustave Colline" from the second edition, and the author of the third part identified himself as the person who made that request. Alfred Delvau, who would certainly have known, identified Nadar as the author of Part III in his own biography of Murger, discussed later in the text.

6. *Histoire de Murger . . . par Trois Buveurs d'Eau,* Parts I and III.

7. Alfred Delvau, "Les mangeurs de bourgeois," *Le Figaro,* February 17, 1861.

8. Alfred Delvau, *Henry Murger et la Bohème* (1866).

9. "Les premières heures de 1867: Conversion d'un bohème," *Le Figaro,* January 6, 1867.

10. On the Goncourt brothers, see André Billy, *Les frères Goncourt* (1954); Robert Ricatte, *La création romanesque chez les Goncourt* (1953). On their links to Art Nouveau and their interest in eighteenth-century art, see Debora L. Silverman, *Nature, Nobility and Neurology: The Ideological Origins of Art Nouveau in France, 1889–1900,* 2 vols. (thesis, Princeton University, 1983).

11. Edmond and Jules de Goncourt, *Journal, mémoires de la vie littéraire,* ed. Robert Ricatte, 22 vols. (Monaco, 1956–58), I, 51, 87, 202–3; II, 59; III, 93–95.

12. *Ibid.,* II, 129.

13. E. and J. de Goncourt, *La révolution dans les moeurs* (1854), 25–26; *Journal,* II, 43.

14. *Journal,* I, 242.

15. *Ibid.,* I, 246–47; II, 60–61, 111–12.

16. *Ibid.,* II, 107–8, 163ff.

17. *Ibid.,* I, 81, 88, 203, 236, 244; II, 163, 184–85.

18. *Ibid.,* IV, 154ff.

19. *Ibid.,* II, 110–11.

20. Edmond and Jules de Goncourt, *Les hommes de lettres* (*The Men of Letters*) (1860), 89.

21. *Ibid.,* 68.

22. *Ibid.*, 20–23.

23. On the models for the characters, see Ricatte, *La création romanesque chez les Goncourt.* For the quotes, *Les hommes de lettres,* 116ff.

24. *Les hommes de lettres,* 88.

25. *Ibid.*, 251ff. On the sources of these ideas in nineteenth-century psychiatric medicine, see Ricatte, 144ff.

26. For the intended contrast, see the brothers' essay *La femme au dix-huitième siècle* (1862).

27. *Journal,* x, 80. See Ricatte, esp. 142.

28. Ricatte, 312ff.

29. On Chenavard see, in addition to Ricatte, Joseph C. Sloane, *Paul Marc Chenavard: Artist of 1848* (Chapel Hill, 1962). For the quotes, *Manette Salomon* (1889 ed.), 62, 122–23.

30. *Manette Salomon* (1889 ed.), 18, 28–30, 55–56.

31. *Ibid.*, 137–38, 161.

32. *Ibid.*, 323–24.

33. *Ibid.*, 353–54.

34. *Ibid.*, 368–71.

35. *Ibid.*, 443–44.

36. Quoted by Roger L. Williams, *The Horror of Life* (Chicago, 1980), 66.

37. For these differences, see Ricatte, 47–51; for the last quote, Billy, 45–46.

38. Quoted by Billy, 46.

39. See Edmond's remarks, quoted in *ibid.*, 409–10.

40. *Journal,* II, 117, and III, 93–95, for the passage with the later addition by Edmond.

41. E. Drumont, "Le monde de Murger," *La Libre Parole,* June 26, 1895.

CHAPTER 7

1. E. Caro, "La fin de la Bohème: Les influences littéraires dans les derniers événemens," *Revue des Deux Mondes,* XCIV (July 15, 1871), 241–67. On Caro, see *Dictionnaire de biographie française,* ed. M. Prévost et Roman d'Amat (1956), Vol. VII, cols. 1190–91. Also Claude Digeon, *La crise allemande de la pensée française* (1959), 158ff.

2. Jules Clère, *Les hommes de la Commune* (1871). Jules Forni, *Raoul Rigault, Procureur de la Commune* (1871).

3. *Le Prolétaire*, May 10, 1871. On Lecomte de Lisle, see P. Lidsky, *Les écrivains contre la Commune* (1970), 58. *Enquête parlementaire sur l'insurrection du 18 Mars, vol. II: Dépositions des témoins* (Versailles, 1872), 207. "Les grands hommes d'Estaminet," *Le Gaulois*, September 2, 1872 (clipping in Archives de la Préfecture de Police, Paris [hereafter PPo], Bᵃ24).

4. Gabriel Guillemot, *Le bohème* (1868). Philibert Audebrand, "La grande Bohème," *Le Figaro*, July 26, 1859; Henri de Rochefort, *La grande Bohème* (1867). On the pamphlet by "Jacques Bonhomme," see J. M. Roberts, *The Paris Commune from the Right, English Historical Review* Supplement 6 (1973), 34–35. The pamphlet's title was "Qu'est Paris en France? Absolument tout. Que doit-il [sic] être? Infiniment moins." Karl Marx, *The Civil War in France*, in Karl Marx and Frederick Engels, *Selected Works in One Volume* (New York, 1968), 295, 300.

5. "La Rive Gauche," in *La Rive Gauche, Journal Littéraire et Philosophique*, November 20, 1864. The article was signed by one of the editors, Robert Luzarche.

6. Aimé Cournet, "La Bohème: À propos d'un cours de M. Deschanel," *La Rive Gauche*, December 18, 1864.

7. "Notre premier mot," *Le Critique, Journal Littéraire et Scientifique*, July 1, 1866.

8. Paul Lafargue, "Aimé Cournet," *La Rive Gauche*, July 1, 1866. Cf. Albert Ferré, "Aimé Cournet," *Le Courrier Français*, June 24, 1866.

9. Eugène Vermersch, *Lettres à Mimi, sur le Quartier Latin (Letters to Mimi about the Latin Quarter)* (1866); see also *Le Latium moderne, lettres à un étudiant en droit* (1864); *Le lanterne en vers de Bohème* (1868). During 1860, there had been a kind of pamphlet war over the issue of whether the old traditions of the Latin Quarter were still to be found in modern student life. Many of these writings are bound together at the Bibliothèque Nationale under the catalogue number 8°Z Le Senne 6038.

10. Maxime Vuillaume, *Mes cahiers rouges au temps de la commune* (1909; republished 1971), 155, 184, 212.

11. Eugène Vermersch, *Opuscules révolutionnaires* (London, n.d.). There were six brochures, five of which are bound together in the copy in the Bibliothèque Nationale.

12. The basic data on Rigault can be found in Jean Maitron, *Dictionnaire biographique du mouvement ouvrier français*. Many more de-

tails are given in the biography by Jules Forni already referred to. The Rigault dossier in PPo B^{a}892 contains two anonymous manuscript biographies, which, however, seem to draw largely on Forni, as well as a number of newspaper clippings. Many writings of the 1860s can be found in *Le Critique* and *Le Candide*, two anticlerical papers with strong Blanquist sympathies. See also Vuillaume, *Mes cahiers rouges*. For a good account of his career during the Commune, in a Blanquist framework, see Patrick H. Hutton, *The Cult of the Revolutionary Tradition: The Blanquists in French Politics, 1869–1893* (Berkeley and Los Angeles, 1981).

13. Forni, 5, 10.

14. Stewart Edwards, *The Paris Commune, 1871* (London, 1971), 211, 212. See also the article from *Le Gaulois,* March 28, 1871, in PPo B^{a}892. For a harsh view of Rigault from a writer generally sympathetic to the Commune, see Charles Proles, *Raoul Rigault* (1898). For one famous incident, see Maurice Choury, *La Commune au Quartier Latin* (1976), 274–75. Edwards is mistaken that Rigault advocated sexual promiscuity during the Commune—the writing he refers to (291) was from several years earlier. Nonetheless, the moral puritanism of the Commune should not be exaggerated, as it has been by Édith Thomas, *Les pétroleuses* (1963).

15. See the discussion of Caussidière in Chap. 3.

16. See the article of September 8, 1870, reprinted in Louis-Auguste Blanqui, *La patrie en danger* (reprint of 1871 ed.), 33–34.

17. Treatments of Vallès that stress this difference include Helmut Kreuzer, *Die Bohème, Beiträge zu ihrer Beschreibung* (Stuttgart, 1968), and T. J. Clark, *Image of the People: Gustave Courbet and the 1848 Revolution* (London, 1973), 33. A much earlier view of Vallès that similarly recognizes his differences from Murger is the sympathetic and sensitive treatment by Jean Richepin, *Les étapes d'un réfractaire: Jules Vallès* (1872). See also, Arno Munster, *Das Thema der Revolte im Werke von Jules Vallès* (Munich, 1974). The basic biography is Gaston Gilles, *Jules Vallès, 1832–1885* (1941).

18. Jules Vallès, *Le bachelier* (Le livre de poche, 1964), 432.

19. Vallès, *L'insurgé* (Garnier, 1970), 69; for the English ed., *The Insurrectionist*, trans. Sandy Petrey (Englewood Cliffs, New Jersey, 1971), 13–14; *Le bachelier*, 445.

20. *L'insurgé*, 76; *The Insurrectionist*, 18–20.

21. There is an excellent account of Vallès in these years: Roger

Bellet, *Jules Vallès, journaliste du Second Empire, de la Commune de Paris et de la IIIe République* (1977). I draw greatly on Bellet for what follows. On the connection commonly drawn between Gustave Planche and Bohemianism, see the popular pamphlet biography by Eugène de Mirecourt, *Gustave Planche* (3d ed., 1869), where he is described as "the king of literary Bohemians."

22. Bellet, 24ff. Vallès, *L'argent*, in *Oeuvres*, ed. Roger Bellet (Pleiade ed., 1975), I, 3–37.

23. Vallès, "Lettre à Monsieur Jules Mirès," *Oeuvres*, 3–10. For the review by Victor Chauvin in *La Revue de l'Instruction Publique*, see R. Bellet's notes in the same volume, 1164.

24. In addition to the sensitive account by Roger Bellet, there is an interesting, if less sympathetic, description of Vallès's relations to the journalistic establishment by the editor of *Le Figaro*: H. de Villemessant, *Mémoires d'un journaliste*, 4th ser. (1875), 208ff.

25. Vallès, "Les morts," in *Les réfractaires* (*Oeuvres complètes de Jules Vallès*, ed. Lucien Scheler), with a preface by René Lacôte and notes by Lucien Scheler (1955), 117.

26. Vallès, "Les réfractaires," in *ibid.*, 23–47.

27. Vallès, "Les victimes du livre," in *ibid.*, 163–86.

28. Vallès, "Culte de l'antiquité et culte jacobin," *Le Progrès de Lyon*, September 1864; in Vallès, *Littérature et révolution*, preface and notes by Roger Bellet (1969), 110. "Les Francs-parleurs," from *Le Courrier Français*, August, 1866, in *ibid.*, 283. The comment on Proudhon appeared in Vallès's paper *La Rue*, from which it is reprinted in Marie-Claire Banquart, *Jules Vallès* (1971), 110.

29. Vallès, *Oeuvres*, I, 1044–45.

30. Beyond my own reading of Vallès, this analysis draws greatly on two contributions to the University of Lyon *Colloque Jules Vallès 1975* (Lyon, 1976): Claude Burgelin, "Éléments psychanalytiques dans *L'enfant*," and Roger Bellet, "Du journal au roman: Trois images vallèsiennes d'une enfance." For the typicality of Jean-Louis Vallez's experience, Paul Gerbod, *La condition universitaire en France au XIXe siècle* (1965).

31. Vallès, "À propos d'un poème des champs," *Le Progrès de Lyon*, September 12, 1864, quoted by Jean-François Tetu, "Aspects de l'idéologie de la révolte chez J. Vallès," *Colloque Jules Vallès 1975*, 97.

32. Article in *L'Événement*, March 11, 1866, reprinted in *Littéra-*

ture et révolution, ed. Bellet, 259–62. The ties between Proudhon, Vallès, and Courbet recall the important observations on the rural origins of French radicalism by Maurice Agulhon, John Merriman, and others.

33. Vallès, "Un chapitre inédit de l'histoire du 2 Decembre," *Courrier de l'Intérieur,* September 8, 1868, quoted in Arno Munster, *Das Thema der Revolte im Werke von Jules Vallès,* 58–59; also in *Oeuvres,* I, 1976. On this period, the account in Bellet remains indispensable.

34. Bellet, esp. 142–43 and 363ff.

35. The best work on the Commune in English is the book by Stewart Edwards, cited above. The literature is immense and need not be listed here. A recent and extremely useful account by one of the best French students of the movement is Jacques Rougerie, *Paris libre 1871* (1971).

36. Reprinted in Vallès, *Le Cri du Peuple,* with preface and notes by Lucien Scheler (1953). Also in *L'insurgé,* 233; *The Insurrectionist,* 166–67.

37. *L'insurgé,* 237ff., 247–49.

38. "Paris, ville libre," *Le Cri du Peuple,* 98–99.

39. "Décidez-vous," *Le Cri du Peuple,* 114–16. That Vallès's paper appealed to many young bourgeois was the view of one pro-Communard writer suspicious of "les jeunes gens qui font métier de révolutionnaire dans la boutique du *Cri.*" They were from the respectable *quartiers* and were not signing up to fight in a regiment against the Versaillais. *Le Prolétaire,* May 24, 1871.

40. Bellet, 394. "Le drapeau rouge" ("The Red Flag"), *Le Cri du Peuple,* 81.

41. *L'insurgé,* 154, 143–44, 156, 123–28, 290.

42. In a letter of 1872, Vallès said that the Commune represented "the realized dream of my life, in a besieged city a hundred thousand individuals, men and women, were buying my piece of paper. I was paid back for all my sufferings." Vallès, *Correspondance avec Hector Malot,* ed. Marie-Claire Bancquart (1968), 38ff., cited by Bellet, 400 n. Bellet's interpretation of Vallès's relation to the Commune is quite different from mine at this point, however.

43. Vallès, preface to Benoît Malon, *Le nouveau parti (The New Party)* (1881). For his comment on the preface, see his letter printed in *L'Intransigeant,* May 14, 1881, a clipping of which is in PPo B^{a}879. The letter appeared in other papers as well. On the years in London, see Gérard Delfau, *Jules Vallès, l'exil a Londres, 1871–80* (1971).

44. The two articles from *Le Réveil,* October 23 and 31, 1881, are reprinted in Vallès, *Oeuvres complètes* (Livre Club Diderot, 1969), III, 179–88.

45. Vallès, *La Commune de Paris,* preface and notes by Marie-Claire Bancquart and Lucien Scheler (1970). A remarkably similar portrait of another literary Communard, Félix Pyat, appears in Gaston da Costa, *La Commune vécue,* 3 vols. (1903–05), II, 200ff. Da Costa regarded Pyat as motivated by literary jealousies and personal resentments, and insisted that the revolutionary movement owed very little to the fantasies dear to the generations of 1830 and 1848. Da Costa, a Blanquist, was a close friend of Raoul Rigault. He did not refer to Pyat as a Bohemian, and certainly did not know that it was Pyat who had first referred to artistic hangers-on as "the Bohemians of today" way back in 1834.

CHAPTER 8

1. Émile Goudeau, *Dix ans de Bohème (Ten Years of Bohemia)* (1888); *La vache enragée* (1885).

2. *La vache enragée,* 112.

3. *Ibid.,* 136–37, and *passim.*

4. On Cros, see E. Raymond, *La Bohème sous le second Empire: Charles Cros et Nina* (1930); and Goudeau, *Dix ans de Bohème,* Chap. 6.

5. *La vache enragée,* 303ff., 330ff.

6. *Dix ans de Bohème,* 95ff. Also Lisa Appignanesi, *The Cabaret* (New York, 1976), Chap. 2; Mariel Oberthur's *Cafés and Cabarets of Montmartre* (New York, 1984) appeared too late for me to make use of it.

7. *Dix ans de Bohème,* 102–3, 206.

8. Léon Maillard, "Un cénacle littéraire: Les Hirsutes," *La Plume,* May 15, 1889, 23–27; see also the account in *L'Hydropathe,* January 22, 1879, said to be taken from an article of Francisque Sarcey. I have not been able to trace the article, and *Le Chat Noir* later published articles it pretended were by Sarcey: attaching his name to this one may have been a joke. But the account of the gatherings as being open to a wide audience certainly represented the group's goal at the time. See also Raymond de Castras, *Avant Le Chat Noir: Les Hydropathes* (1954).

9. The paper changed its name to *Tout-Paris* in May 1880, before ceasing to appear.

10. *Le Chat Noir* continued to appear until Salis's death in 1897.

11. There is some interesting information in Appignanesi, *The Cabaret*, as well as in Goudeau's memoirs and in the newspaper itself.

12. On the rebuilding of Paris, see David H. Pinkney, *Napoleon III and the Rebuilding of Paris* (Princeton, 1958); Howard Saalman, *Haussmann: Paris Transformed* (New York, 1971); Jeanne Gaillard, *Paris, la ville, 1852–70* (1977).

13. On the department stores, see Michael B. Miller, *The Bon Marché: Bourgeois Culture and the Department Store* (Princeton, 1981); Gaillard, *Paris, la ville*; the quote comes from the forthcoming study by Philip Nord, *The Politics of Resentment* (Princeton, 1985). See also Rosalind H. Williams, *Dream Worlds: Mass Consumption in Late-Nineteenth-Century France* (Berkeley and Los Angeles, 1982).

14. *Le Chat Noir*, January 14, 1882 (see the travelogue of Paris by "À. Kempis").

15. On authors' contracts, see the letter of Zola quoted by John and Muriel Lough, *An Introduction to Nineteenth-Century France* (London, 1978), 253, where there is also a good deal more evidence on the transformation discussed here; also Eugenio di Rienzo, *Intellettuali e società in Francia dall' Ancien Régime al Secondo Impero* (Rome, 1983), Chaps. 5 and 6. Something more will be said about the Impressionists below.

16. Daniel Halévy, *The End of the Notables*, trans. Alain Silvera and June Guicharnaud (Middletown, Connecticut, 1974).

17. *Dix ans de Bohème*, 94, 131. On Gambetta, cf. Theodore Zeldin, *France, 1848–1945* (Oxford, 1973), I, 612–13.

18. On Boulangism and publicity, see Adrien Dansette, *Le Boulangisme* (1946).

19. The building later housed other newspapers. For some photographs of the interior, see "Le crépuscule de L'Aurore," *L'Express*, January 28–February 1, 1980. See also Jules Bertaud, *L'opinion et les moeurs* (1932), Chap. 6, on Xau and *Le Journal*.

20. *Mercure de France* XVI (December 1895), 409–10. See also Rachilde's preface to F.-A. Cazals, *Le jardin des ronces, 1889–99* (1902).

21. On poster art, see Max Gallo, *L'affiche* (1973); Hermann Schardt, ed., *Paris 1900: Masterpieces of French Poster Art* (New York, 1970); Hayward and Blanche Cirker, *The Golden Age of the Poster* (New York, 1971); Victor Arwas, *Belle Époque Posters and Graphics* (New York, 1978). On Toulouse-Lautrec, Ph. Huisman and M. G.

Dartu, *Lautrec by Lautrec*, trans. and ed. Corinne Bellow (Secaucus, New Jersey, 1964).

22. *Le Chat Noir*, January 14, 1882.

23. *Dix ans de Bohème*, 263–64.

24. Félicien Champsaur, *Dinah Samuel*. Champsaur's books were often touted in *Le Chat Noir*.

25. H. [enri] R. [ivière], in *Le Chat Noir*, October 14, 1882.

26. See Bloy's autobiographical novel, *Le désespéré*, in *Oeuvres de Léon Bloy*, ed. Joseph Bolery and Jacques Petit, III (1964). For his view of Rollinat, see Bloy, "Maurice Rollinat," *Le Chat Noir*, September 2, 1882. See also the description quoted in Guy Michaud, *Message poétique du symbolisme* (1947), II, 243. On Barbey and Rollinat, see Émile Vinchon, *La vie de Maurice Rollinat* (Issodun, n.d.).

27. Goudeau, *Dix ans de Bohème*, 156ff. *Le Chat Noir*, February 4, 1882; October 28, 1883; and *passim*.

28. On Bruant, see A. Zervaes, *Artistide Bruant* (1943); France Vernillot and Jacques Carpentreau, *Dictionnaire de la chanson française* (1968); Pierre Brochon, *La chanson sociale de Béranger à Brassens* (1961).

29. Aristide Bruant, *Dans la rue* (1889–95); *Sur la route* (1897); *L'argot au XXe siècle* (2d ed., 1905).

30. Oscar Méténier, *Le chansonnier populaire, Aristide Bruant*, with drawings by Steinlen (1893).

31. See Zervaes, *Aristide Bruant*.

32. *Sur la route* (1897).

33. Roland Dorgelès, *Bouquet de Bohème* (1947), 20–21.

34. See W. C. Morrow and Édouard Cucuel, *Bohemian Paris of Today* (London, 1899), the chapter "A Night in Montmartre."

35. The writer was a friend of Paul Verlaine, Edmond Lepelletier. See *L'Écho de Paris*, June 26, 1895.

CHAPTER 9

1. Max Nordau, *Aus dem wahren Milliardenlande: Pariser Studien und Bilder* (Leipzig, 1878), 225–36.

2. On Verlaine's life, see A. E. Carter, *Verlaine: A Study in Parallels* (Toronto, 1969). For the obituaries, see the collection "Nécrologies de Paul Verlaine," Paris, Bibliothèque Nationale. The papers cited are *Le Libre Parisien, Le Petit Journal,* and *Le Radical.* See also Carter,

208, on the police order. Ironically, Nordau later applied the notion of degeneration to Verlaine.

3. See Carter, *Verlaine*. There is a great deal of information in the apologetic biography by Verlaine's old friend Edmond Lepelletier, *Paul Verlaine, sa vie et son oeuvre* (4th ed., 1907). I have also used the helpful chronology by Claude Cuenot in Verlaine, *Mes prisons* (Le livre de poche, 1973).

4. Rimbaud to Verlaine, July 5, 1873, in Rimbaud, *Complete Works, Selected Letters*, trans. and ed. by Wallace Fowlie (Chicago and London, 1966), 321. On Verlaine's approaching conversion, Rimbaud, *A Season in Hell, The Illuminations*, trans. Enid Rhodes Peschel (London and New York, 1973), 67ff. See also Carter, 100.

5. Gianni Mombello, "Il 'Dossier Verlaine' delle Archives du Dept. de la Seine et de la Ville de Paris," *Atti dell' Accademia delle Scienze di Torino* 96 (1961–62).

6. Carter, 194–96.

7. On Verlaine's last years, see Carter, 197ff., and F.-A. Cazals and Gustave Le Rouge, *Les derniers jours de Paul Verlaine* (*The Last Days of Paul Verlaine*) (1911; 2d ed., 1923).

8. Verlaine, *Oeuvres poétiques complètes*, ed. Yves Le Dantec (Pleiade, 1954), 206.

9. Verlaine, *Oeuvres en prose complètes*, ed. Jacques Borel (Gallimard, 1972), 977, 946–48. Cazals and Le Rouge, *Les derniers jours de Paul Verlaine*, 147–49.

10. Verlaine, *Oeuvres en prose*, 73–74, 127–29 (and notes); Verlaine cited the early poem in "Confessions," printed in *Mes prisons*, 64.

11. *Ouevres poétiques*, 377–80. The line about limits abolished was a reference to Ponsard, who wrote: "Quand la borne est franchie, il n'est plus de limite."

12. Barrès, "Paul Verlaine," *Le Figaro*, January 10, 1896.

13. Lucien Aressy, *La dernière Bohème, Verlaine et son milieu* (1923). Cazals and Le Rouge, cited above.

14. Cazals and Le Rouge, Chap. 5; esp. 138 and 154.

15. *Ibid.*, 192–95.

16. Huysmans quoted in Carter, 193. On the subject of Verlaine's growing reputation, see Guy Michaud, *Message poétique du symbolisme* (1947), Vol. II. On decadence see A. E. Carter, *The Idea of Decadence in French Literature, 1830–1930* (Toronto, 1958), and Jean Pierrot, *The Decadent Imagination, 1880–1900*, trans. Derek Coltman (Chicago and London, 1981).

17. Verlaine, *Oeuvres en prose*, 810; Carter, 191.

18. *La Plume*, September 15, 1890, 168–69.

19. On Retté, see the article by Henri Degron in *La Plume*, December 15, 1895; and Michel Décaudin, *La crise des valeurs symbolistes . . . 1885–1914* (1960); Retté, *Le symbolisme, anecdotes et souvenirs* (1903), 161ff.; Georges Bonnamour, "Émile Goudeau," *La Plume*, April 15, 1889. On the *soirées* organized by *La Plume*, see Léon Maillard, *La lutte idéale* (1892).

20. Cazals and Le Rouge, *Les derniers jours*, 163; Verlaine, *Mes prisons*, 307; *Oeuvres en prose*, 978–79.

21. Carter, 238. Cazals and Le Rouge, 190–92.

22. For Mathilde's view, see [Mathilde Mauté] Ex–Madame Paul Verlaine, *Mémoires de ma vie* (1935; but written in 1907). The other information is in Édith Thomas, *Louise Michel, ou la Velléda de l'anarchie* (1971), 108.

23. Lepelletier, *Paul Verlaine* (1907), 7; cf. also 19–22; *L'Écho de Paris*, June 26, 1895.

24. Yves Bonnefoy, *Rimbaud*, trans. Paul Schmidt (New York, 1973), 39. The best account in English is Enid Starkie, *Arthur Rimbaud* (1938). Much interesting information about Rimbaud can be found in the Pleiade *Album Rimbaud*, ed. Henri Matarasso and Pierre Petitfils (1967); the most complete biography is Pierre Petitfils, *Rimbaud* (1981). See also Michaud, *Message poétique du symbolisme*, I, 127–58.

25. Verlaine, *Oeuvres en prose*, 977; *La Plume*, May 15, 1890, where Dargens is cited.

26. For these events, see Carter, 73ff., and *Album Rimbaud*, 106–25.

27. The best translation (printed together with the original) is by Enid Rhodes Peschel, cited above.

28. Rimbaud, *Complete Works, Selected Letters*, 346, 352, 354. Robert Klein, *Form and Meaning*, trans. Madeline Jay and Leon Wieseltier (Princeton, 1979), 203.

29. See the letters in Rimbaud, *Complete Works, Selected Letters*, 302–10.

30. Bonnefoy, 43. *A Season in Hell*, 70, 80, 86.

CHAPTER 10

1. Georges Jeanneret, *Un cénacle Neuchâtelois au Quartier Latin, ou Bohème artistique et littéraire* (1879), see 144 for the quote. Jean-

neret also published an account of *Paris pendant la commune révolu-tionnaire de '71* (Neuchâtel, 1871).

2. See Saul Friedlander, *History and Psychoanalysis,* trans. Susan Suleiman (New York and London, 1978), 103ff.

3. Goudeau, *Dix ans de Bohème,* 52ff. In *La vache enragée,* Gou-deau's portraits of the pair may have been colored by other characters as well, and the two were given the explicitly Jewish pseudonyms of Virgile Lopez and Jacques Seiglefort. See 130, 171, and *passim.*

4. Michel Mansuy, *Un Moderne, Paul Bourget,* Annales Littéraires de L'Université de Besançon (1960), xxxix, 179–80.

5. Paul Bourget, *Edel, poème* (1878), 67. Goudeau quoted the same passage in *Dix ans de Bohème,* 56–57.

6. Mansuy, *Bourget,* 238.

7. *Ibid.,* 239–40, 274–76.

8. On Richepin, see Howard Sutton, *The Life and Works of Jean Richepin* (Geneva, 1961).

9. Jean Richepin, *Les étapes d'un réfractaire: Jules Vallès (The Stages of a Réfractaire)* (1872).

10. *Ibid.,* 28, 54, 77ff.

11. Jean Richepin, *Le chemineau* (1897).

12. Sutton, 91, 107; on Barrès, see Note 18.

13. Sutton, 55; Adolphe Brisson, *La comédie littéraire* (1895), 87–92. On this theme, see also E. Raymond, *La Bohème sous le Second Empire: Charles Cros et Nina* (1930).

14. Carl E. Schorske, *Fin-de-Siècle Vienna: Politics and Culture* (New York, 1980), Chap. 3.

15. The best account of Barrès in politics is by Zeev Sternhell, *Maurice Barrès et le nationalisme français* (1972); also Robert Soucy, *Fascism in France: The Case of Maurice Barrès* (Berkeley, 1972). For a general view of Barrès, see Pierre de Boisdeffre, *Barrès parmi nous* (1952, 1969).

16. Charles Maurras, *Maîtres et témoins de ma vie d'esprit* (1954), 23.

17. Maurice Barrès, *Le Quartier Latin: Ces messieurs—ces dames* (1888), 11, 13.

18. Barrès, *Réponse au discours de Jean Richepin* (1909); *Le Figaro,* January 10, 1896.

19. Barrès, "Le caractère de Baudelaire," *Le Voltaire,* June 7, 1887. Cf. Pierre-George Castex, "Barrès, collaborateur du *Voltaire* (1881–88)," in *Maurice Barrès: Actes du colloque . . . de l'Université*

de Nancy, 22–25 Octobre 1962 (1963). Maurice Davanture, *La jeunesse de Maurice Barrès (1862–1888)* (1975), II, 677, for the last quote, in a review of Félicien Champsaur's ballet, *Les bohémiens.*

20. Maurice Barrès, *Sous l'oeil des barbares* (I use the 1922 ed.). Anatole France, "La littérature du 'moi'—Maurice Barrès," *La Plume,* April 1, 1891.

21. *Un homme libre,* Book IV, Chap. 12. See Anthony A. Greaves, *Maurice Barrès* (Boston, 1978), 38ff.

22. *Un homme libre,* Book IV, Chap. 12. *Sous l'oeil des barbares* ("Examen"), 12.

23. Barrès, "Le secret merveilleux" (1892) in *Du sang, de la volupté et de la mort* (1894), 73, 75.

24. *Le jardin de Bérénice (Berenice's Garden)* (1891; 1912 ed.), 181.

25. Cf. *Le jardin de Bérénice,* 155, 225, 232.

26. *Ibid.,* 212.

27. *Réponse au discours de Jean Richepin* (1909). *Le jardin de Bérénice,* 108.

28. François Coppée, "Pour un buste," *Le Journal,* June 6, 1895. Georges Rodenbach, "Murger et la Bohème," *Le Figaro,* June 16, 1895. See also Catulle Mendès, "Puisque François Coppée a parlé de Murger," *Le Journal,* June 11. Also *Le Gil Blas,* June 19 and 21, and E. Lepelletier in *L'Écho de Paris,* June 26.

29. *Le Journal,* June 27 and 29, 1895. *La Presse,* June 26.

30. "Tybalt" [Laurent Tailhade], "Chronique," in *L'Écho de Paris,* June 27, 1895. On the riot, see *La Presse,* June 28; *Le Journal,* June 28; *La Libre Parole,* June 27. For the later banquets, Paris, Arch. PPo Bᵃ23, documents dated June 26, 1896, and July 3, 1899.

CHAPTER 11

1. On Impressionism as an avant-garde movement, see Renato Poggioli, *The Theory of the Avant-Garde,* trans. Gerald Fitzgerald (Cambridge, Massachusetts, 1968), 132. The best general account of Impressionism remains that of John Rewald, *The History of Impressionism* (rev. ed., New York, 1961).

2. See Rewald, Chaps. 6 and 11. One important source for these meetings is George Moore, *Confessions of a Young Man,* ed. Susan Dick (Montreal, 1972); also *Memoirs of My Dead Life* (London, 1906). On

Degas and the Goncourts, see Theodore Reff, *Degas: The Artist's Mind* (New York, 1976), 170.

3. Clément-Janin, *La curieuse vie de Marcellin Desboutin* (1922), 85–86, for the letter (of October 8, 1874) quoted in the text; on the Café Guerbois and the Nouvelles Athènes, 89ff.

4. On Manet and Desboutin, see Rewald, 366–67, 405; on Degas and Desboutin, Rewald, 376, 526. Also Joan Sutherland Boggs, *Portraits by Degas* (Berkeley and Los Angeles, 1962), 116; and Theodore Reff, *Degas*, 271. On Degas's dislike of all personal dramatization, see George Moore, "Degas," in Moore, *Impressions and Opinions* (London, 1891).

5. See Zola's articles in *Mon salon, Manet, écrits sur l'art*, ed. Antoinette Ehrard (1970), 93ff., also in *Manet raconté par lui-même et par ses amis* (1945), 77ff.

6. *Manet raconté*, 69–70.

7. In addition to Rewald, see the writings of Antonin Proust and Théodore Duret in *Manet raconté par lui-même*; and Henri Perruchot, *La vie de Manet* (1959), 71 and 79–80 on Manet's milieu and associations. See also Anne Coffin Hanson, *Manet and the Modern Tradition* (New Haven, 1977), 157–58, on Manet and Couture.

8. Zola, in *Manet raconté par lui-même*, 106. The catalogue entry is quoted by Duret, in the same volume, 140.

9. For Zola's evolution, see F. W. J. Hemmings, *The Life and Times of Émile Zola* (New York, 1977). For his relationship with Manet and Cézanne, Robert J. Niess, *Zola, Cézanne and Manet* (Ann Arbor, 1968).

10. Zola, *The Masterpiece*, trans. Thomas Walton (Ann Arbor, 1968), 361ff. Cf. also 246, 248.

11. *The Masterpiece*, 240 and 366. For Zola's general views of the Impressionists by the 1880s, see his article, "Le naturalisme au Salon," in Lionello Venturi, *Les archives de l'impressionisme* (1939), II, 277–80.

12. Castagnary's article appeared in *Le Siècle*, April 19, 1874. Quoted in Jacques Lethève, *Impressionistes et symbolistes devant la presse* (1959), 68.

13. *The Masterpiece*, 251. A similar view of the relationship between Impressionism and the possibility of mental unbalance was suggested in 1883 by J.-K. Huysmans, *L'art moderne* (*Oeuvres complètes de Huysmans*, VI, 1929), 105–6.

14. Zola, *Mon salon*, 67. On Durand-Ruel, see Harrison C. White

and Cynthia A. White, *Canvases and Careers: Institutional Change in the French Painting World* (New York, 1965); and Raymonde Moulin, *Le marché de la peinture en France* (1967), 29ff.

15. Rewald, 310, 416, 301–2; Moulin, 345.

16. For the notion of "overcomprehension," see Moulin, 36. Gautier in *Le Moniteur Universel*, May 11, 1868, quoted by F. W. J. Hemmings, *Culture and Society in France, 1848–1898* (New York, 1971), 177; and by Francis Haskell, "Enemies of Modern Art," *The New York Review of Books*, June 30, 1983, 19.

17. Laforgue's article is published in translation in Barbara Ehrlich White, ed., *Impressionism in Perspective* (Englewood Cliffs, New Jersey, 1978), 34. See also Émile Blémont's comments in *Le Rappel*, April 9, 1876, who said that the Impressionists sought to render the relations of things through their own perceptions of them, "and since there are not two men on earth who perceive exactly the same relations in the same object, the painters see no necessity to modify their personal and direct sensation to follow some convention or other." In Venturi, *Les archives de l'impressionisme*, II, 298.

18. Leo Steinberg, "Contemporary Art and the Plight of Its Public," in *Other Criteria: Confrontations with Twentieth-Century Art* (New York, 1972), 3–16.

19. On Jarry, the best and most convenient account in English is in Roger Shattuck, *The Banquet Years* (New York, 1955), 187–251. An extensive and careful biography in French is Noël Arnaud, *Alfred Jarry, d'Ubu roi au Docteur Faustroll* (1974). See also Maurice Marc LaBelle, *Alfred Jarry: Nihilism and the Theatre of the Absurd* (New York, 1980). Breton's comment in André Breton, "Alfred Jarry," *Anthologie de l'humour noir* (1939; 1950 ed.), 218.

20. Eugenia Herbert, *The Artist and Social Reform: France and Belgium, 1885–98* (New Haven, 1961), for the whole topic, and p. 129 for the quote from Pierre Quillard. For the quote from Remy de Gourmont, see Jacques Monferier, "Symbolisme et anarchie," *Revue d'Histoire Littéraire de la France* LXV (1965), 237.

21. Cf. Shattuck, 189.

22. See Shattuck, and Arnaud, 256ff., who provides more information on Hébert.

23. Jarry, *Exploits and Opinions of Doctor Faustroll, 'Pataphysician*, in *Selected Works of Alfred Jarry*, ed. Roger Shattuck and Simon Watson Taylor (New York, 1965), 192–93; Quillard in *Mercure de France*, September 6, 1892, 47–49.

24. Jarry's opening-night speech in Alfred Jarry, *Oeuvres complètes,* ed. Michel Arrivé (Pleiade, 1972), 399.

25. All this is excellently developed by Roger Shattuck.

26. See, for instance, Rachilde, *Alfred Jarry ou le surmâle de lettres* (1928).

27. The two comments in Jarry, *Oeuvres complètes,* 1059, and Arnaud, 252–53.

28. On Jarry and Fargue, Arnaud, 96–97; see the text in *Oeuvres complètes,* 214–29.

29. *Exploits and Opinions,* in *Selected Works,* 240.

30. *Selected Works,* 112.

31. Rachilde, 28–29; Arnaud, 127. The quote from *Days and Nights* is in *Selected Works,* 145. Shattuck, 195ff. and 212ff., on Jarry's dwellings.

32. The stories about Jarry are collected in Fernand Lot, *Alfred Jarry, son oeuvre* (1934).

33. Arnaud, 430–31; Rachilde, 35.

34. Jarry, *La chandelle verte,* ed. Maurice Saillet (1969), 483; on Donzé, see Arnaud, 93.

35. Rachilde, 28–29.

36. *Selected Works,* 142.

37. *Ibid.*

38. On removing oppositions, *César-Antichrist,* in *Oeuvres complètes,* 281; Rachilde, 37. Letter in Lot, 23–25.

39. Again the best introduction is Shattuck, *The Banquet Years,* 113–85. See also Anne Rey, *Satie* (1974); Rollo H. Myers, *Erik Satie* (New York, 1961); Pierre-Daniel Templier, *Erik Satie,* trans. Elena L. French and David S. French (Cambridge, Massachusetts, 1969).

40. Erik Satie, *Écrits,* ed. Ornella Volta (1977), 216–17, 45.

41. Rollo Myers, *Erik Satie,* 82.

42. Contamine de Latour quoted in Rey, 44.

43. *Écrits,* 19, 22–23.

44. Rey, 47. Shattuck, 126.

45. *Écrits,* 111, 113.

46. *Ibid.,* 47 (and note, 334); 201–15.

47. *Ibid.,* 187–89.

48. *Ibid.,* 307, 190 (and the editor's notes).

49. Shattuck, 130. The letter to his brother is quoted by Templier, *Satie,* 32.

50. Shattuck, 149–51; Templier, 84 n; Myers, 80–81.

CHAPTER 12

1. Jean-Paul Crespelle, *La vie quotidienne à Montmartre au temps de Picasso, 1900–1910* (1978).

2. André Warnod, *Le vieux Montmartre* (1911), Chap. 3.

3. Warnod, *Le vieux Montmartre*; see also *Bals, cafés et cabarets* (1913).

4. Crespelle, 150–71. There are accounts of the Lapin Agile also in Warnod, and in Roland Dorgelès, *Bouquet de Bohème* (1947), 16ff.

5. Francis Carco, *De Montmartre au Quartier Latin*, in *Mémoires d'une autre vie* (Geneva, 1942), 210–11.

6. The best summary of Depaquit's antics and activities is in Crespelle, 54–57.

7. Warnod, *Les berceaux de la jeune peinture: Montmartre, Montparnasse* (1925).

8. Francis Carco, preface to G. Apollinaire, G. Bannerot, et al., *Les veillées du "Lapin Agile"* (1919), v–vi, xvi; Carco, *Bohème d'artiste* (1940), 52–53, 158–59, 89–93, 164. There is a collection of Carco's letters in the Bibliothèque Nationale, NAF 17167.

9. *Bohème d'artiste*, 243.

10. *Ibid.*, 195–213.

11. *Ibid.*, 157–58; cf. Crespelle, 24ff. *Du Montmartre au Quartier Latin*, 233ff.

12. Jean Crespelle, *Utrillo, la Bohème et l'ivresse à Montmartre* (1970).

13. *Bohème d'artiste*, 234, 239ff.

14. *Ibid.*, 241–42, also 15–16.

15. Dorgelès, *Bouquet de Bohème*, Chap. 11; Carco, *De Montmartre au Quartier Latin*, 214–15.

16. On Apollinaire, see first of all Shattuck, *The Banquet Years*, 253–322. On his poetry and its relationship to Symbolism, Michel Décaudin, *La crise des valeurs symbolistes*. For his biography, Marcel Adéma, *Apollinaire*, trans. Denise Rolliot (New York, 1955); and Francis Steegmuller, *Apollinaire: Poet among the Painters* (New York, 1963). A convenient selection of his writings is *Selected Writings of Guillaume Apollinaire*, trans. and ed. Roger Shattuck (New York, 1949).

17. I rely on Adéma for the biography.

18. Adéma, 11, 72.

19. Claude Bonnefoy, *Apollinaire* (1969), 29ff.; cf. 78ff. See also

P. A. Jannini, *Le vanguardie letterarie nell'idea critica di Guillaume Apollinaire* (Rome, 1971), 12–13.

20. Adéma, 148.

21. Bonnefoy, 15ff.

22. *Les Lettres Modernes,* cited in Michel Décaudin, *La crise des valeurs symbolistes,* 259. The only surviving copy of this periodical I have been able to discover is in the Bibliothèque Jacques Doucet, Paris.

23. Many details about Apollinaire are found in the recollections of his friend André Billy. See *Apollinaire vivant* (1923), and *Avec Apollinaire* (1966). Shattuck's account in *The Banquet Years* is rich in detail, and Claude Bonnefoy's book cited above is good on these aspects of the poet's character.

24. For accounts of the Rousseau banquet, see Adéma, 106–11; Shattuck, 66–71; Carco, *Bohème d'artiste,* 76ff. Crespelle, 243ff.

25. The texts are translated in *Apollinaire on Art: Essays and Reviews, 1902–18,* trans. Susan Suleiman, ed. Leroy C. Breunig (New York, 1972), 49, 50–52, 66, cf. also 98–99; and on Picasso, *Selected Writings,* ed. Shattuck, 48.

26. Marcel Raymond, *From Baudelaire to Surrealism* (London, 1957), 227.

27. Adéma, 80. Mary Matthews Gedo, *Picasso: Art as Autobiography* (Chicago and London, 1980). For a different view, see Rosalind E. Krauss, "In the Name of Picasso," in *The Originality of the Avant-Garde and Other Modernist Myths* (Cambridge, Massachusetts, and London, 1985), 23–40.

28. Quoted in Adéma, 83.

29. The essay is translated in *Selected Writings,* 227–37.

30. On the first performance, see Richard Buckle, *Diaghilev* (London, 1970), 331–32; Shattuck, 151–58.

31. Buckle, 253–55.

32. Cocteau's definition in Shattuck, 155. The scenario in Jean Cocteau, *Oeuvres complètes,* 11 vols. (1946–51), VIII, 303.

33. The preface to *Les mariées de la Tour Eiffel,* in Neal Oxenhandler, *Scandal and Parade: The Theater of Jean Cocteau* (New Brunswick, New Jersey, 1957), 182. Cocteau, *Le rappel à l'ordre,* (1948), 36.

34. Cocteau, "Le secret professionel," in *Le rappel à l'ordre,* 183, 187, 199.

35. *Ibid.,* 88–89, 190.

36. *Ibid.,* 27, 55.

37. Bettina Liebowitz, *Jean Cocteau* (New York, 1970). André Fraigneau, *Cocteau par lui-même* (1957). *Le rappel à l'ordre*, 44–45. Oxenhandler, 3.

38. *Le rappel à l'ordre*, 56ff., 187–88, 199.

39. On *Parade*'s role in popularizing the avant-garde, see Raymonde Moulin, *Le marché de la peinture en France*, 36.

CHAPTER 13

1. Lucien Descaves, "La conversion de Murger," *L'Intransigeant*, March 26, 1922. Other articles include Francillon, "Trente ans de Bohème," *Le Gaulois*, July 1, 1922; Gustave Simon, "Henry Murger: Lettres inédites à Victor Hugo," *Le Temps*, April 18, 1922; Pierre Dufay, "Des buveurs d'eau à la 'vie de Boheme,' " *Mercure de France*, April 1, 1922; Georges Montorgueil, "À la maison de Murger," *Le Temps*, March 10, 1922.

2. Matthew Josephson, *Life among the Surrealists* (New York, 1962); Peggy Guggenheim, *Out of This Century* (1946); also John Glasco, *Memoirs of Montparnasse* (New York, 1970).

3. "Je vais recommencer chaque jour": André Breton, "La confession dédaigneuse," in *Les pas perdus* (1924), quoted by Mary Ann Caws, *André Breton* (New York, 1971), 32. For the general history of the Surrealist movement, see Maurice Nadeau, *The History of Surrealism*, trans. Richard Howard (1968; Pelican ed., 1973); Philippe Audoin, *Les surréalistes* (1973); Marcel Jean, ed., *The Autobiography of Surrealism* (New York, 1980); Patrick Waldberg, *Surrealism* (New York and Toronto, 1965). The view of Surrealism presented here agrees in many regards with Peter Bürger, *Der französische Surrealismus* (Frankfurt/Main, 1971). But see below, Note 37.

4. Marguerite Bonnet, *André Breton: Naissance de l'aventure surréaliste* (1975), 36, 51. On Breton, see also Anna Balakian, *André Breton: Magus of Surrealism* (New York, 1971), and Clifford Browder, *André Breton: Arbiter of Surrealism* (Geneva, 1967).

5. Bonnet, 70ff.

6. On Vaché, see Bonnet, 86ff., and Breton's Preface to Jacques Vaché, *Lettres de guerre* (1970), 17–18, for the quote.

7. Breton in Vaché, *Lettres de guerre*, 17–18; also Vaché's letter of August 18, 1913, *ibid.*, 57–58; and to Breton, September 5, 1918, 60. On his death, Bonnet, 95ff.

8. Aragon, *Anicet*, quoted in Bonnet, 93; Bonnet, 95. For *Littéra-*

ture, see *The Autobiography of Surrealism*, 55ff., as well as Bonnet and the general histories of Surrealism.

9. Bonnet, 153–54.

10. In addition to the general works on Surrealism, see above all Michel Sanouillet, *Dada à Paris* (1965); Hans Richter, *Dada: Art and Anti-Art*, trans. David Britt (London, 1965). Also William S. Rubin, *Dada and Surrealist Art* (New York, 1968); Robert B. Motherwell, *The Dada Painters and Poets* (New York, 1951); Georges Ribemont-Dessaignes, *Déjà jadis* (1958), on Dada and Surrealism in Paris, by a participant. For the quote in the text, see Bonnet, 211.

11. The position taken in the text is that of Bonnet rather than the one developed by Michel Sanouillet. See also Robert Short, "Paris Dada and Surrealism," *Journal of European Studies* IX (1979), 75–98.

12. Bonnet, Chap. 6.

13. Breton, "Pour Dada," *Nouvelle Revue Française* XV (1920), 212. André Breton, *Manifestes du surréalisme* (Gallimard, 1977), 37.

14. *Manifestes du surréalisme*, 21–22.

15. André Breton and Philippe Soupault, *Les champs magnétiques* (1920). For this period in Breton's life, see Bonnet, Chap. 5.

16. *Manifestes du surréalisme*, 50–51.

17. *Manifestes*, 26, 23. Louis Aragon, *Le paysan de Paris (Paris Peasant)* (Gallimard, 1953), 145.

18. *Le paysan de Paris*, 109, 111.

19. *Ibid.*, 113. Breton, *Mont de piété* (1919). Aragon, *Le paysan de Paris*, 50.

20. On Dada in this regard, see Richter, *Dada: Art and Anti-Art*. *Manifestes*, 64. Breton, *Picasso dans son élément*, quoted in Caws, *Breton*, 46ff. Nadeau, 118ff.

21. Josephson, *Life among the Surrealists*, 134–35; Nadeau, 122ff. *Manifestes*, 78.

22. *Manifestes*, 18, 139.

23. Michel Sanouillet, Introduction to Marcel Duchamp, *Salt Seller: The Writing of Marchand du Sel*, ed. Sanouillet and Elmer Petersen (New York, 1973), 6. Jacques Rivière, "*Les aventures de Télémaque*, par Louis Aragon," in *Nouvelles études* (new ed., 1947), 214.

24. Breton's letter to Simone Kahn, Bonnet, 235; Josephson, 120, 141; on the rejection of suicide, *Manifestes*, 92–93. Raymonde Moulin, *Le marché de la peinture en France*, 36, for the group's acceptance.

25. Nadeau, *The History of Surrealism*, 121; Bonnet, 203.

26. On Picabia, Bonnet, 206. On Soupault, *ibid.*, 165. For Barbey, see above, Chapter 4, note 23.

27. On Breton and Barrès, see Breton's letter of 1913, quoted in Bonnet, 29. *Manifestes*, 11–12.

28. On the crisis of the object, see Robert Klein, "The Eclipse of the Work of Art," in *Form and Meaning* (New York, 1979; Princeton, 1981), 176–83.

29. For the quote from Vallès, see Chap. 7.

30. Nadeau, Part III. Roger Garaudy, *L'itinéraire d'Aragon* (1961). Robert S. Short, "The Politics of Surrealism," in *The Left Wing Intellectuals Between the Wars, 1919–39*, ed. Walter Laqueur and George L. Mosse (first published in *Journal of Contemporary History* II, 1966), 3–26.

31. *Manifestes*, 92, 86–87.

32. *Ibid.*, 27, 48–49.

33. André Chastel, "Le jeu et le sacré dans l'art moderne," *Critique*, May–June 1955, cited by Raymonde Moulin, *Le marché de la peinture en France*, 55.

34. Renato Poggioli, *The Theory of the Avant-Garde*, trans. Gerald Fitzgerald (Cambridge, Massachusetts, 1968). Poggioli's view seems to me to assimilate the whole of the avant-garde too much to the Futurists, and not to recognize the limits many figures set up against the qualities of "nihilism, agonism, futurism and decadence" he invokes to characterize it. But readers who know his book will recognize many similarities between its perspective and the one employed here. It still seems to me a more adequate account than the ones referred to below.

35. Daniel Bell, *The Cultural Contradictions of Capitalism* (New York, 1976), 14, 15, 49–50. For a similar view, see Suzi Gablik, *Has Modernism Failed?* (New York, 1984).

36. Jürgen Habermas, "Modernity vs. Postmodernity," *New German Critique* 22 (1981), 7.

37. For the classic statements of the Frankfurt School point of view, see Theodor W. Adorno, "On the Fetish Character in Music and the Regression of Listening," in *The Essential Frankfurt School Reader*, ed. Andrew Arato and Eike Gebhardt (New York, 1982), 270–99; Herbert Marcuse, "The Affirmative Character of Culture," in *Negations: Essays in Critical Theory* (Boston, 1968); also the collective volume *Aesthetics and Politics*, ed. Ronald Taylor, with an afterword by Fredric Jameson (London, 1977). The debates about modern culture within critical the-

ory are discussed very well in Eugene Lunn, *Marxism and Modernism* (Berkeley and Los Angeles, 1982). For a recent attempt to reformulate the perspective, Peter Bürger, *Theorie der Avantgarde* (Frankfurt/Main, 1974), translated by Michael Shaw as *Theory of the Avant-Garde* (Minneapolis, 1984). Bürger's views about the avant-garde agree with those presented here in making the fusion of art and life a central theme. But whereas he believes this project implied a dissolution of the forms of artistic practice characteristic of bourgeois society, the history of Bohemianism suggests that it flowed smoothly out of a reconstruction of artistic identity that had been proceeding since 1830. Bürger's views have been criticized from quite a different viewpoint by some of the contributors to *"Theorie der Avantgarde": Antworten auf Peter Bürgers Bestimmung von Kunst und bürgerlicher Gesellschaft*, ed. W. Martin Lüdke (Frankfurt/Main, 1976). Current art historians who continue this tradition in English include T. J. Clark, in his various writings, explicitly in "Clement Greenberg's Theory of Art," *Critical Inquiry* IX (1982), 139–56; and Thomas Crow, "Modernism and Mass Culture in the Visual Arts," in *Modernism and Modernity*, ed. Benjamin H. D. Buchloh et al. (The Vancouver Conference Papers, Halifax, Nova Scotia, 1983). For a different sort of objection to these views, see Michael Fried's reply to T. J. Clark in the same issue of *Critical Inquiry*. There are some similar comments on Right and Left accounts of the avant-garde to those made here in Poggioli, 168ff.

38. The statement is in the preface to *A Contribution to the Critique of Political Economy*: see Karl Marx and Frederick Engels, *Selected Works in One Volume* (New York, 1968), 183.

39. François Furet, "The French Revolution Is Over," in *Interpreting the French Revolution*, trans. Elborg Foster (Cambridge, England, and Paris, 1981), 1–79.

INDEX

944.
S

ver County Public
New   Library
      Main Library

http://www.nhclibrary.org

- Checkout Receipt -

tron Barcode:

Number of items: 1

Barcode: 34200000062709